State Formation in Chin

This is an ambitious comparative study of regime consolidation in the "revolutionary" People's Republic of China and the "conservative" Republic of China (Taiwan) in the years following the communist victory against the nationalists on the Chinese mainland in 1949. Julia C. Strauss argues that accounting for these two variants of the Chinese state solely in terms of their divergent ideology and institutions fails to recognize their similarities and their relative successes. Both, after all, emerged from a common background of Leninist party organization amid civil war and foreign invasion. However, by the mid-1950s they were on clearly different trajectories of state building and development. Focusing on Sunan and Taiwan, Strauss considers state personnel, the use of terror, and land reform to explore the evolution of these revolutionary and conservative regimes between 1949 and 1954. In so doing, she sheds important new light on twentieth-century political change in East Asia, deepening our understanding of state formation.

Julia C. Strauss is Professor of Chinese Politics at SOAS, University of London, where she served as editor of *The China Quarterly* from 2002 to 2011. She works on the twentieth-century Chinese state in China and Taiwan, the performative dimensions of politics, and China's "Going Out" to the developing world, particularly towards Africa, and has published widely on these topics.

State Formation in China and Taiwan

Bureaucracy, Campaign, and Performance

Julia C. Strauss

SOAS, University of London

CAMBRIDGE
UNIVERSITY PRESS

CAMBRIDGE
UNIVERSITY PRESS

University Printing House, Cambridge CB2 8BS, United Kingdom

One Liberty Plaza, 20th Floor, New York, NY 10006, USA

477 Williamstown Road, Port Melbourne, VIC 3207, Australia

314–321, 3rd Floor, Plot 3, Splendor Forum, Jasola District Centre,
New Delhi – 110025, India

79 Anson Road, #06–04/06, Singapore 079906

Cambridge University Press is part of the University of Cambridge.

It furthers the University's mission by disseminating knowledge in the pursuit of
education, learning, and research at the highest international levels of excellence.

www.cambridge.org
Information on this title: www.cambridge.org/9781108476867
DOI: 10.1017/9781108569163

First published 2020

Printed in the United Kingdom by TJ International Ltd. Padstow Cornwall

A catalogue record for this publication is available from the British Library.

ISBN 978-1-108-47686-7 Hardback
ISBN 978-1-108-70165-5 Paperback

Dedicated to the memory of Charles M. Strauss

Contents

Figures

Acknowledgments

The completion of a fifteen-year project necessarily incurs a host of intellectual, personal, and emotional debts. As a semi-itinerant academic with a position in the United Kingdom, family in the United States, sites for intensive research in the People's Republic of China and Taiwan, and, in the initial years of collecting materials, a toddler in tow, my debts run exceptionally wide as well as deep. My first order of intellectual thanks goes to William Kirby and Liu Shi-yung. In the winter of 1997–1998, I happened to be in the Shanghai Municipal Archives, collecting for another project. After a casual conversation in which Bill mentioned the Campaign to Suppress Counterrevolutionaries as a possible topic for interesting research, I took the liberty of checking the then very primitive computer catalog for open records on the campaign. As the hard drive whirred, just as I was thinking to myself that there was no *way* that anything this sensitive could possibly have been declassified, the machine coughed slightly as some twelve records popped up. After constraining my impulse to squeal, I duly filled out the form to request these documents, and to my utter astonishment twelve fat files were in due course delivered to my desk. These materials were ideal in that they comprised just enough to go through and hand copy in the subsequent several years of snatched weeks here and there that I could get to Shanghai. Although I had no way of knowing it at the time, research that would occupy the next nearly twenty years had commenced. This first set of very rich documents provided the basis for "Paternalist Terror: The Campaign to Suppress Counterrevolutionaries and Regime Consolidation in the People's Republic of China, 1950–1952," *Comparative Studies in Society and History* 44:1, January 2002, pp. 80–105. Follow-up came in Taibei in the winter of 2000, when Shi-yung told about the slow, but impending declassification of large numbers of records from the February 28 Incident in Taiwan. With this information, a project on regime consolidation on the two sides of the Taiwan Straits was conceived.

The second order of thanks goes to SOAS, which has provided a safe haven, amazing students, and supportive colleagues for the last quarter century. SOAS has been unfailingly generous in permitting the leave to take the multiple fellowships and sabbaticals necessary for collecting on three different topics in two such different locations, and colleagues have been more than wonderful in covering my short and not so short absences from teaching and administration. SOAS has also been a very congenial place in which to present the different incarnations of this project. Teaching "State and Society in Asia and Africa" with Donal Cruise O'Brien that then led to workshops and the edited volume *Staging Politics: Power and Performance in Asia and Africa* (I.B. Tauris, 2007) sharpened my thinking on the performative dimensions of politics. Other colleagues, particularly Laleh Khalili, Stephen Chan, and Salwa Ismail, have also given generously of their time in responding to early drafts of chapters.

I am also grateful for the generous support of three separate fellowships. The Fulbright Foundation and the Chiang Ching-kuo Foundation supported the collection-intensive phase of the project in 2005–2006. And the Center for Historical Research's two-year project on the Histories and Cultures of Statehood at the Ohio State University under the directorship of John L. Brooke and Greg Anderson provided a stimulating environment for getting to grips with masses of data on the White Terror and questions of culture and state formation in 2013–2014. In retrospect, I was incredibly fortunate to be collecting when archives and libraries across China were at their most relaxed and open. It goes without saying that without the extraordinary patience and kindness of archivists and librarians in China and Taiwan, multiple research trips even in this period would have come to nothing. In China the staff at the Shanghai Municipal Archives, the Suzhou Municipal Archives, and the Minhang District Archives consistently went that extra mile, as did Yu-feng Chiou at the ROC National Archives Administration, the staff at Taiwan Historica (Guoshiguan Taiwan Wenxian Weiyuanhui), Academia Historica, and the Gaoxiong County Archives in Taiwan, whose hospitality even extended to wild rides on motorscooters across Gaoxiong. Librarians in the Shanghai Municipal Library and the National Central Library (Taiwan Branch) in Taiwan were also unfailingly helpful. Affiliations – on multiple occasions – at the Shanghai Academy of Social Sciences and at Academia Sinica, where I was hosted at the Institute of Modern History, the Institute of Taiwan History, and the Institute of Political Science smoothed the way for research and have since become working homes away from home. Jin Caihong, then at the SASS Office of International Cooperation became a dear friend, and Lin Xiujuan always makes my return to IMH a joy.

In much the same way that it takes a village to raise a child, it takes a worldwide community of scholars to produce a data-rich monograph. Over the years, I have been lucky to have been able to present different pieces of this project at venues across three continents. Audiences at East China Normal University, the Chinese University of Hong Kong, Academia Sinica's Institute of Modern History, its Institute of Taiwan History, Sun Yat-sen University (Gaoxiong), the Taiwan Foundation for Democracy, and Academia Historica all made important interventions, suggestions about sources, and ever-important introductions to those who knew more. Hsü Hsüeh-chi (Xu Xueji), who was at that time the Director of the Institute of Taiwan History, is deserving of particular thanks, as it was she who suggested that I look into a previously unexplored link between land reform and terror, opening up an important and utterly unanticipated line of inquiry. Seminars at the Institute of Development Studies (Sussex), the University of Vienna, and Göttingen University aided critical thinking. In North America, colleagues at the University of Chicago, the University of California Riverside, and the University of Michigan all provided critical feedback that forestalled many an error in logical reasoning. Participation in the Princeton Network on State Building in the Developing World offered a welcome opportunity to engage with scholars in the world beyond China.

Although none of the chapters here has been published elsewhere as a recognizable whole or part, some of the ideas, data, references, and text have made early appearances elsewhere. Part of the section on the labeling of civil administrators in Chapter 1 was published in the Indiana Working Paper series on keywords as "*Wenguan* (lettered official), *Gongwuyuan* (public servant), and *Ganbu* (cadre): The Politics of Labelling State Administrators in Republican China," Indiana East Asian Working Paper Series on Language and Politics in Modern China, No. 6, Summer, 1995, available at https://scholarworks.iu.edu/dspace/handle/2022/22839. Bits of Chapters 2 and 3 were first published in "Paternalist Terror: The Campaign to Suppress Counterrevolutionaries in the People's Republic of China, 1950–1953." Some of the ideas and examples in Chapters 4 and 5 appear in "Campaigns of Redistribution: Land Reform and State Building in China and Taiwan," in the edited volume by Miguel Centeno, Atul Kohli, and Deborah Yashar, *State Building in the Developing World* (Cambridge University Press, 2017), pp. 339–362, and "Regimes and Repertoires of Statebuilding: The Two Chinas and Regime Consolidation in the Early 1950s," in John L. Brooke, Julia C. Strauss, and Greg Anderson, *State Formations: Global Histories and Cultures of Statehood* (Cambridge University Press, 2018), pp. 244–257. A very early version of my thinking on performance through public accusation meetings as public trials was published as "Bureaucracy, Theatre, and the Accusation of Counterrevolutionaries in the Revolutionary People's Republic of China, 1950–1957," in Julia C. Strauss and Donal B. Cruise O'Brien, eds., *Staging Politics: Power and Performance in Asia and Africa* (London: I.B. Tauris, 2007). And the calculations of the numbers of those repressed in Sunan and Taiwan in Chapter 2 were first made in the chapter on "Traitors, Terror and Regime Consolidation on the Two Sides of the Taiwan Straits: 'Revolutionaries' and 'Reactionaries' from 1949 to 1956," in Sharika Thiranagama and Tobias Kelly, eds., *Suspicion, Intimacy and the Ethics of State Building* (University of Pennsylvania Press, 2009), pp. 89–109. The permission of the Indiana Working Paper Series, University of Pennsylvania Press, I.B. Tauris, and Cambridge University Press to include this content is gratefully acknowledged. Figures 3.4, 3.5, and 3.6 are in the poster holdings of the International Institute of Social History (IISH) Chinese posters website at https://chineseposters.net.

In addition to the formal venues of seminars and presentations, friends and colleagues beyond SOAS have been a huge support over the different incarnations of the manuscript. Susanne Weigelin-Schwiedrzik, Melanie Manion, Stephen A. Smith, Jacob Eyferth, Yang Kuisong, Zhang Jishun, Mick Moore, Dan Slater, Patrick T. Jackson, Stephan Feuchtwang, Yu Mingling, Chu Wanwen, Joseph White, and Lisa Raphals painstakingly went through all or part of the text, sometimes in multiple incarnations. Thanks are also due to Andrew Devine, editor *extraordinaire*, whose expert eye has saved me from countless small errors and language infelicities.

Fellowship and sanity flowed in my direction no matter where I was collecting or writing. In Taiwan, I got through one of the rainiest winters on record with a newly mobile little one through the friendship of John Kieschnick and Regina Llamas, Rebecca Karl, Yu Min-ling, and Chang Jui-te. In Ohio, Tina Sessa and Chris Otter invited us over for meals and loaned us furniture, Diane King provided wise counsel, Darlene Rosado repeatedly stepped in with offers of play dates at critical junctures, and Zhang Ying engaged me in conversation about periods of Chinese history very far from my own. No parent brave enough, or foolhardy enough, to haul a toddler and then preschooler across continents solo on a regular basis can possibly survive without wonderful child carers. I was impossibly fortunate to find Mrs. You in Nangang, Xu Meili in Shanghai, Melina Acosta in Greenwich, and Jeannie's Day Care in West Los Angeles. In London, Charlotte and Matt Hall, and Celia McKiernan and Mark Turner have for a decade and a half provided friendship, wine, and playdates, and in West Los Angles, Diane Cyr has done much the same. These wonderful humans made it possible to shuttle back and forth between Taibei, Shanghai, London, and Los

Angeles without missing a beat during the critical early years of collecting materials.

My parents, Charles and Patricia Strauss, have both been thrilled to have their first grandchild visit while their daughter raced off to chase a reference, give a talk, or accept a conference invitation that otherwise would have been impossible, while wonderful cousins Tony Hill and Sheila Hill Cain have stepped into very much the same role on the West Coast. Chris Chinni and Jennifer Ozeir have been my stalwart supporters for upwards of two decades: always ready to share triumphs, offer advice, or commiserate as the situation has demanded. In the virtual world, KPTI has offered daily companionship and reasons to laugh. In the real world, the unexpectedly long duration of the project has meant that an elder generation of cats was there at the beginning while another is seeing out the end, but in all cases purrs and occasional demands for a wild game of "chase the cat dancer" have provided welcome companionship and diversion. Finally, the greatest thanks go to my nearest and dearest. R. Bin Wong has long been my biggest cheerleader, most stringent critic, and greatest support: going through the entire manuscript (more than twice), providing excellent advice, and rushing to my aid across half a continent when the washing machine flooded my documents. Our daughter Phoebe had just begun to walk when I first started to seriously engage this comparative project. Now an active and academically engaged mid-teen, she reminds me every day of how quickly time passes and how compelling the nexus of family and intellectual life can be.

Introduction
Modalities of State Building and Institution Building: Bureaucracies, Campaigns, and Performance

What makes for states that are well consolidated, with high levels of capacity for engaging in the kinds of actions essential for governing and legitimacy? Is there a general formula, or at least a common set of patterns, that distinguishes states that are relatively successful in these ways, and conversely, is there a comparable core of problems and institutions that are widely shared by states that are not well consolidated with high levels of capacity? To what extent, if any, do subjective "soft" factors like norms, ideology, and the prior existence of traditions of governance render it easier or more difficult for those involved in state making to create, stabilize, or transform state institutions? Does the way in which chosen policies are implemented matter for the institutionalization of the state organizations that are doing the implementing?

While these seemingly simple questions about what the state is, how it forms, how it behaves, and how it becomes more (or less) effective has been debated from the time of the great nineteenth-century sociologists to the present, there is little resolution to these questions. Those who write on the state are deeply divided over what the state is, how real it is as an entity, and whether it can be considered separate from either the society over which it ostensibly presides or the government that directs it. Max Weber and the multiple generations of his intellectual descendants in sociology and political science from Reinhard Bendix to contemporary comparative historical institutionalists see the state and the institutions that constitute it to be a self-evident and obvious entity that is distinguishable from both the government that sits atop the institutions of the state at any given moment in time and the societies over which the state rules. Others subscribe to different variants within a broadly Marxist tradition. Some, like Marx himself, tend to reduce the state to class interests (that "the state is nothing more than the executive committee of the ruling bourgeoisie"),[1] while Gramsci and a long line of his intellectual heirs from Poulantzas and Foucault to Jessop, Mitchell and beyond stress the "realm

---

[1] Karl Marx and Frederick Engels, *The Communist Manifesto*, p. 11

of ideology and cultural practices and the ways in which states and citizens are mutually constitutive."[2]

Although this is now changing, many (but by no means all) of the cases taken up by sociologists and political scientists working in comparative historical analysis focus on state institutions in Europe and the Americas. These scholars have, reasonably enough given their subject matter, tilted to the "big questions" of advanced industrial or rapidly industrializing economies, variation within Latin America, the state's role in development, or some combination of these three. There is a substantial literature on institutional variation in social democracy, welfare regimes, and industrial policy for Europe, the United States, and Japan, an intersecting clutch of works on variation in state capacity (often but not exclusively measured by willingness and ability to tax populations) for Latin America, and a third that broadly engages the question of how developmental states arise and function.[3] In the last decade, these approaches have been supplemented by major historical institutional works that engage variation within both South Asia and Southeast Asia.[4] There is also an exciting new wave of comparative historical-institutional work on arenas of long-overlooked state action: counterrevolution, state coercion, and violence.[5] And we are now beginning to see historical/institutional

---

[2] I am enormously indebted to John L. Brooke, who did the lion's share of the heavy lifting in constructing the bibliography and the preliminary analysis on the different lineages of thinking about the state. For a fuller discussion and bibliography see John L. Brooke and Julia C. Strauss, "Introduction: Approaches to State Formation," in Brooke, Strauss and Anderson, eds., *State Formations, Global Histories and Cultures of Statehood*, pp. 1–12.

[3] An only very partial list of the some of the most significant books would include: Thomas Ertman, *Birth of the Leviathan*; Theda Skocpol, *Protecting Soldiers and Mothers: The Political Origins of Social Policy in the United States*; Sven Steinmo, *The Evolution of Modern States: Sweden, Japan, and the United States*; and Stephen Skowronek, *Building a New American State: The Expansion of National Administrative Capacities*. An entire sub-field of comparative industrial policy for Northeast Asia was kick-started by Chalmers Johnson's classic work *MITI and the Japanese Miracle: The Growth of Industrial Policy, 1925–75*. Important works on Latin America include: Deborah Yashar, *Contesting Citizenship in Latin America: The Rise of Indigenous Movements and the Postliberal Challenge*; Tulia Falleti, *Decentralization and Subnational Politics in Latin America*; Marcus Kurtz, *Latin American State Building in Comparative Perspective: Social Foundations of Institutional Order*, and Hillel David Soifer, *State Building in Latin America*. For Africa see Jeffrey Herbst, *States and Power in Africa: Comparative Lessons in Authority and Control*, (Princeton, 2002/2014, 2nd ed.). See also Erik Kuhonta, *The Institutional Imperative: The Politics of Equitable Development in Southeast Asia* (Stanford: Stanford University Press, 2012) and Tuong Vu, *Paths to Development in Asia: South Korea, Vietnam, China, and Indonesia* (Cambridge University Press, 2010).

[4] For Southeast Asia see Dan Slater, *Ordering Power: Contentious Politics and Authoritarian Leviathans in Southeast Asia* (Cambridge, 2010); for South Asia see Maya Tudor, *The Promise of Power: The Origins of Democracy in India and Autocracy in Pakistan* (Cambridge, 2013).

[5] Sheena Chestnut Greitens offers a satisfying and sophisticated analysis of the ways in which the institutional origins of coercion and state violence vary in Taiwan, the

work that explicitly engages comparative cases in very different world regions, notably Brazil and South Africa, and Africa and Southeast Asia, albeit to explain some of the "harder" elements of state institutions, namely taxation and the longevity of single-party systems.[6]

There is much of value in each of these sub-groupings within the comparative historical-institutional approach. These are works that are historically well grounded, give due attention to such important factors as temporal sequencing and critical junctures (when political actors have much more in the way of openness to make decisions about institutional design, mission, or the coalitions formed in support), and build in room for both contingency (e.g. exogenous shocks) and the agency of state actors. Much of this analysis either implicitly or explicitly employs notions of path dependence, whereby decisions made early in a particular political process of building state institutions may well foreclose other possibilities further down the line, leading to "lock in."[7] These works are also excellent on the ways in which states interact with core elites, especially if those core elites are relatively well organized, forming "protection pacts" or "provision pacts" (Slater), developing state administrations that are either patrimonial or bureaucratic depending on the relative strength of corporate bodies and the timing of the state building effort (Ertman), or opting for "deployed rule" versus "delegated rule" (Soifer). While this scholarship is superb on sketching out broad comparative trends, it reveals relatively little about process, implementation, and the intelligibility of the state's core projects at the time they were undertaken, for example, *how* protection or provision pacts were formed and justified (to both participatory elites and larger publics), or *how* aspiring state makers attempted to move from patrimonial to bureaucratic forms of state administration (and with what kinds of tactics, legitimating arguments, and responses) in early modern Europe. In Latin America, did state makers adopt either deployed or delegated rule simply because it had long been that way and no other options were conceivable? When state makers attempted to move from delegated to deployed rule, what sorts of normative appeals did they make, and what kinds of coalitions (if any) did they attempt to create? Did successful policy implementation in one arena have an impact on policy implementation in other spheres of state activity? In short, in their focus on the outcomes and

---

Philippines, and South Korea in *Dictatorships and Their Secret Police: Coercive Institutions and State Violence.*

[6] Evan Lieberman, *Race and Regionalism in the Politics of Taxation in Brazil and South Africa*; Dan Slater and Nicholas Rush Smith, "The Power of Counterrevolution: Elitist Origins of Political Order in Asia and Africa."

[7] Paul Pierson, "Power and Path Dependence"; Giovanni Capoccia, "Critical Junctures and Institutional Change."

broad trends within state making, these comparative institutional accounts rarely explain the often messy and complex processes by which institutions came into being, how they garnered or failed to garner the loyalty of their administrative staff, how they generated sufficient capacity to make it possible to implement core (or new) projects, or how they went about explaining, justifying, and communicating the wisdom and validity of their state projects to wider audiences in order to establish legitimacy – the very warp and weft of what states *do* above and beyond system maintenance.

While in no way disregarding the excellence of these works and indeed drawing substantial inspiration from them, this monograph has a slightly different focus. It goes "one level down" from outcomes and structures to consider many of the substantive details – the "hows" that are either assumed or elided in most comparative historical analysis: what are the state's core agendas, how its political and administrative elites frame questions of strategy, how new capacity is generated, and how state-building programs and policies are implemented in practice. John Brooke and I have suggested elsewhere that while scholarly writing on the state has tended to fall into "broadly two competing lineages informed by Max Weber and Antonio Gramsci, focusing respectively on a macro approach to institutions and capacities and a micro approach to cultures and practices," Weberian/institutional and Gramscian/cultural approaches might well be complementary, rather than in opposition to one another.[8] This book is, at heart, an effort to integrate the macro Weberian concern with institutions and capacities with the Gramscian sensitivity to the impact of cultures and practices by asking the following question: *how* do signature state policies and the way in which they are implemented have an impact on the development of state capacity and instruct citizens in the norms and ethos of the state? In this way I hope to suggest ways in which cultures and practices inform the creation and expansion of institutions and capacities in times of critical (dis)juncture, when a new government is engaged in a wider process of regime consolidation, establishing new institutions of control and social order, setting out new rules of political engagement, and in the ideal generating new legitimacy among the citizenry.

I take as axiomatic the Weberian notion of the state as a set of institutions that embody some form of centrality, claim ultimate political authority over a given territory, and are backed up by set of administrative and indeed coercive organizations.[9] But I go beyond a Weberian focus on

---

[8] Brooke and Strauss, pp. 1, 20–21.
[9] Michael Mann, "The Autonomous Power of the State: Its Origins, Mechanisms and Results."

institutions to stress how the state's administrative organizations make themselves visible and intelligible through different kinds of performances that signal what the state aspires to be and what it expects of its citizens. States are comprised of formal organizations, which are in turn formed, staffed, and deployed by human agents to implement particular activities and programs – often in the teeth of indifference or resistance from other human agents in society. Thus state making necessarily involves (often multiple and contending) imperatives in first thinking through what ought to be done, developing policies and programs to pursue core state agendas, and overcoming often substantial inertia or resistance. It is here, in the realm of state agendas and activities, that a broadly post-Gramscian set of questions become pertinent: how state activities are framed, circumscribed, embedded in (or removed from) society, acted out, and made visible in ways that are intelligible and legitimate (or alien and illegitimate) within particular cultural and social contexts.

In exploring more fully the ways in which the micro (specific norms, preferences, and cultures) have an impact on the macro (state building as the creation and expansion in the capacity of state institutions), this book delves deep into the histories and practices of two highly competitive states in a particular time, cultural context, and place. The time was the immediate aftermath of 1949, which was by any standard a "critical juncture"[10] – a time of relative openness when, politically, a great deal was up in the air, amid the rapid hardening of Cold War boundaries and globally shared concern about the possibility of an outbreak of world war fought with nuclear weapons. The cultural context was China, a culture and civilization of great antiquity, a strong indigenous tradition of statecraft and imperial state organization that had been subject to nearly unceasing internal warfare, external invasion, bottom-up revolution, and a succession of weak central governments for an extended generation after the fall of the imperial dynasty in 1911–1912. The place was also China – a now reintegrating political entity that aspired to state-ness, greatness and "modernity." By accident rather than by design, in 1949–1950 political China possessed two unequal rival regimes in the early stages of regime consolidation – the explicitly revolutionary People's Republic of China, concentrating on its wealthy economic core in Sunan, in and around Shanghai, and the other equally explicitly conservative

---

[10] For further elaboration of the concept of critical junctures and their importance for institutional formation, see Capoccia, 2015, Giovanni Capoccia and Daniel Kemelen, "The Study of Critical Junctures: Theory, Narrative and Counterfactuals in Historical Institutionalism," and Hillel David Soifer, "The Causal Logic of Critical Junctures."

Republic of China, now immensely shrunken and relegated to a shaky existence on the island outpost of Taiwan.

The question I ask regarding these two cases is deceptively simple: how did two such ideologically diametrically opposed regimes manage to impose themselves over territories to which they came as armies of occupation with little natural base in society, build state institutions in their preferred images, and emerge with such well-consolidated states only a few short years thereafter? Regime consolidation is, of course, an ambiguous term; like "democratic consolidation" there may well be reasonable disagreement about when the process is complete, if ever. But if gauged by such markers as: (1) the establishment of internal security and social order over its territory; (2) the extension of state power to very local levels of society; (3) the development of sufficient capacity to implement core state policies; and (4) the ability to elicit the behavioral acquiescence if not the active support of key sectors of society, then both the PRC in Sunan and the ROC in Taiwan were by any standard rapid and thorough in their consolidations in the early 1950s. One might question the wisdom of their preferences and choices, and certainly from a human rights perspective both engaged routinely in actions that were nothing short of appalling, but no one can doubt that on their own terms they were both unusually successful in circumstances in which they might reasonably have been expected to falter, if not to fail altogether.

Twenty years ago, when I was preparing my first monograph for publication, I asked a related set of questions: why was it that the National Government of China in the late 1920s and 1930s – a weak and ineffective state that never managed to fully consolidate – managed to establish several core state institutions that were also unusually efficient and effective? The analytical framework that ensued from eighteen months of archival work in *Strong Institutions in Weak Polities: State Building in Republican China, 1927–1940* focused on four of the most critical state-building organizations for which information was available: the Examination Yuan, which attempted to implement a systemwide civil service system, two tax collecting agencies (the Salt Inspectorate and the Direct Tax Division within the Ministry of Finance), and the Ministry of Foreign Affairs.[11] While the Examination Yuan's activities were more symbolic than consequential, the three remaining cases did exhibit clear

---

[11] External defense and internal security were, of course, spheres even more fundamental to state building than tax and foreign affairs in 1930s China; but I was interested in civilian, rather than the military dimensions of state-building, and in any case the data for military and internal security organizations were at that time either unavailable and/or too fragmentary to be useful.

evidence of unusual efficiency and effectiveness. I argued that these successes were the outcome of twinned strategies of internal bureaucratic insulation and external goal achievement; core administrative elites in tax and foreign affairs were permitted to buffer their organizations from a hostile and politicized environment by retaining control over personnel appointments and promotions, entry and promotion by strict civil service examination, and separate (and higher) salary scales. The price paid for this relative autonomy was demonstrable success in goal achievement in arenas of action without which the state could not survive. Tax organizations found goal achievement to be a particularly straightforward business, as their effectiveness or lack thereof (more tax receipts flowing to the central state) and efficiency (continued reduction of administrative costs as a percentage of tax intake) were at least easily measurable if not always easily achievable. These broad strategies of internal bureaucratization and insulation "bought" with externally visible high levels of goal achievement were, in principle, universal.[12]

These case studies were undoubtedly important – even necessary – components of state building and regime consolidation. Tax administration in particular has long been recognized to be so crucial that it is often used as a proxy for effectiveness in state building: particularly in a European context, the effectiveness of the state in extracting tax in order to field armies for war making was one of the key indicators of state strength and success.[13] With the important exceptions of rentier states (e.g. Kuwait) or city-state entrepôts (Hong Kong, Singapore), whose size and economic position make it relatively easy for the state to rely on indirect taxes, state-building efforts are often, even typically, correlated to the state's ability to extract resources from society in taxes of one sort or another.[14] What I had not quite realized twenty years ago is that in comparison to other arenas of state action such as welfare administration, education, public health, or indeed any activity that involves either resource redistribution or significantly changed behavior on the part of citizens, tax administration and foreign affairs are typically

---

[12] Julia C. Strauss, *Strong Institutions in Weak Polities*. Roughly a decade after the publication of this book, a literature in development administration emerged on ARAs (Semi-Autonomous Revenue Authorities) that almost perfectly replicated the strategies of the Sino-Foreign Salt Inspectorate; see Robert R. Taliercio, "Administrative Reform as Credible Commitment: the Impact of Autonomy on Revenue Authority Performance in Latin America," *World Development* 32:2, pp. 213–32. Odd-Helge Fjeldstad, "Fighting Fiscal Corruption: Lessons from the Tanzania Revenue Authority", *Public Administration and Development* 23:2, pp. 165–175 and Odd-Helge Fjeldstad "Revenue authorities and public authority in sub-Saharan Africa", *Journal of Modern African Studies* 47:1, pp. 1–18.

[13] Charles Tilly, "Reflections on the History of European State Making," Introduction in *The Formation of States in Western Europe*.

[14] Marcus J. Kurtz, *Latin American State Building in Comparative Perspective*.

relatively straightforward arenas of state activity. Neither attempts to alter the routine behavior of citizens, beyond compliance with tax payment. Both are comparatively easy to insulate from social pressures and claims, possess clear and consistent mandates from political leaders about what ought to be done, and, in the case of tax, engage in activity that is quantifiable. The government's orders to its tax agencies in the 1930s were straightforward and consistent: collect more in revenue and consume less in administrative costs. Insofar as they produced the goods, tax organizations were normally trusted and allowed to get on with the job. Highly educated diplomats possessed expertise that most political and party leaders did not: they spoke foreign languages, were able to mix socially with other diplomats and world leaders, and were well versed in the language and principles of international law. With this unique and crucial skill set, they were entrusted to plead China's case to international courts and special committees for the new League of Nations, negotiate for the removal of unequal treaties and to settle disputed borders, and raise international sympathy for China in its effort to isolate Japan. Like the imperative to raise increasing amounts of revenue for the central government, these core foreign policy goals of the 1930s were so consistent that they could be, in broad brush strokes, simply assumed. Hence there was little need to analyse the ideology, preferences, or norm building that predated policy choices, or to delve into how policies were implemented, as both were highly bureaucratic in the ways in which they approached their core tasks: they both justified and executed policy through strict application of impersonal rules. Tax administrators assessed tax according to bureaucratic rules about rates and penalties to those who did not comply, and responded to political masters by continued efficiencies in terms of administrative costs and effectiveness in returning ever larger amounts to the central government. Ministry of Foreign Affairs diplomats also upheld bureaucratic strategies of policy implementation. They utilized bureaucratic, precedent oriented and rule-bound arguments, as they relentlessly applied international law (i.e. rules) to work in favor of the Chinese state. They tirelessly applied the minutiae of international law and international legal precedent to a variety of situations: negotiating with Western powers to (among other things) voluntarily give up extraterritoriality, adjudicate unclear borders, and censure the Japanese, and were, given China's weak international position in the 1930s, surprisingly successful at using these tactics to represent China and invoke international rules to China's advantage. However, for all their importance and effectiveness in providing core services necessary to the state, these cases suggested little about many other arenas of state activity: redressing severe inequality, promoting rural development, providing social welfare, or altering the everyday behavior of citizens, where the Guomindang's efforts, as exemplified in the roundly mocked New Life Movement of 1934, were patchy to outright embarrassing.[15]

Temporally, empirically, and analytically, this work expands on *Strong Institutions in Weak Polities*. It picks up nearly a decade after *Strong Institutions* ends with the government's rapidly accelerating de-institutionalization under the stresses of the war against Japan. It focuses on a period of radical (dis)juncture in state building: the formative period of regime consolidation between 1949 and 1954, when the rump Nationalist government (Guomindang) under Chiang Kai-shek had retreated to the island of Taiwan and the nascent People's Republic of China was confronted with the staggering problem of how to rapidly build a credible party and state structure on a vast continent, much of which it had little to no recent experience of governing. It expands on the subject matter of *Strong Institutions* by engaging a direct comparison between two variants of the Chinese state: the People's Republic of China in China's wealthiest region – the lower Yangzi valley (Sunan) and the Republic of China in Taiwan. It also widens the case study selection. It carries over questions of state personnel recruitment from *Strong Institutions in Weak Polities*, but focuses on two other, quite different core projects undertaken by both Chinese states: (1) the suppression of domestic "subversion"; and (2) land reform. And analytically it considers not only what the state-making agendas and policy practices of these two rival regimes happened to be, but the actual rhetoric, dynamics and performative strategies by which these core policies were understood, justified, and implemented.

Thinking Comparatively about China and Taiwan at Mid-century: Cases of Success in Interesting Times

A comparison between the large, politically Communist People's Republic of China and the small, politically conservative Republic of China now confined to the island of Taiwan might seem to be at best misguided. With very few exceptions, notably Bruce Dickson's early work *Democratization in China and Taiwan: The Adaptability of Leninist Parties* (1997), and the somewhat more recent *Political Change in China: Comparisons with Taiwan* volume edited by Bruce Gilley and Larry Diamond (2008), there is little scholarly work that explicitly engages China-Taiwan (or PRC/ROC) comparisons. There are two solid and interrelated reasons for this reluctance: geographical scale, and the

---

[15] Arif Dirklik, "The Ideological Foundations of the New Life Movement"; Wennan Liu, "Redefining the Legal and Moral Roles of the State in Everyday Life."

impact of Cold War politics. First, the political units encompassed by the People's Republic of China and the ROC after 1949 are vastly different in scale. Give or take some outlying border areas, the young People's Republic of China inherited a vast area whose borders were largely coterminous with those of the multi-ethnic Qing empire, while the ROC central government retreated to a small island that had undergone a twentieth-century history separate from the rest of China as a direct colony of Japan. Second, since the GMD regime so tied its post-1949 claims to legitimacy to its successes and good management in Taiwan, many have been reluctant to work on the 1950s and 1960s at all. For different reasons, work on the 1950s continues to remain sensitive in China and Taiwan. The People's Republic of China still draws legitimacy from what it considers to be its foundational Golden Age between 1949 and 1956; within Taiwan sensitivities about the martial law era's most violent phase in the early 1950s are still sharp, and those who portray the early 1950s in anything other than a starkly negative light are often marked as apologists for a brutal regime.[16] The dominant Cold War rhetorical stances of both have long insisted that these regimes were fundamentally different in kind, and the post Cold War combination of democratization and growing identification with Taiwan-ness within Taiwan also reinforces a contemporary sensibility of utter difference.

Despite these difficulties, comparisons between the PRC and ROC/ Taiwan have the potential to be very fruitful, because these regimes had significantly more in common than either their Cold War rhetoric or their obvious differences in scale would otherwise suggest. In 1949, both shared a common Leninist single party-state structure that went back to the mid-1920s, when the CCP was a party fraction within a Guomindang reorganized by Soviet advisors. Both were deeply marked by China's political weakness in the face of imperialist pressure and by a previous half century of accelerating militarization, invasion, and civil war. Both assumed that their developmentalist goals were to be realized politically by *yidang zhiguo* (以黨治國 – "utilizing the Party to rule the country"). And, albeit in different ways, both continued to be deeply influenced by the institutional and normative legacies of late imperial governance.

---

[16] In Taiwan Guomindang conduct in the 1950s and 1960s continues to be a pertinent line of political fracture, with pan-Greens (the DPP and associated parties) deeply critical of the enormous human rights abuses committed by the Guomindang during this period, and pan-Blues on the whole choosing to avoid the topic entirely. In the process of organizing a workshop on Taiwan history during the martial law Chiang Kai-shek years with sessions in both Taibei and London in August and September 2009, it proved to be extremely difficult to get Taiwanese scholars to contribute. When one of the few who agreed presented her work, the tension in the room was palpable.

In order to pursue the comparison between regime consolidation in the PRC's very large territory and the ROC's now quite small one, I shrink the focus to a particular region within the PRC: Sunan ("South Jiangsu"), including the metropolis of Shanghai, its outlying districts (*jiaoqu* – 郊區), and the counties in what is now the province of Jiangsu that are south of the Yangzi River. Before it was amalgamated with Subei ("North Jiangsu") in 1954, Sunan possessed its own provincial-level government that was in turn directly administered by the East China Military Region. In principle, other regions of China taken over by the PLA – Minnan (south coastal Fujian), Sichuan, or the Pearl River Delta could have been equally good choices, but there are two especially compelling reasons for the choice of Sunan. First, the importance of the greater Shanghai/Sunan region for "New China" is hard to overstate. Because the region had long been China's wealthiest, and was in 1949 the center of China's industrial and modern economy, the otherwise impoverished young People's Republic required its political compliance and its economic flows: without the resources of Sunan and Shanghai, it was hard to see how state as a whole could be put on a solid footing. Second, the combination of unusually liberal archival and library access for foreign scholars in the late 1990s and the 2000s in Sunan and Greater Shanghai, and a wealth of secondary literature in both English and Chinese for the early 1950s has meant that the range of available sources is especially rich.

There are, of course, questions that could be raised about the validity of a comparison between a sub-national/provincial unit of government such as Sunan and a central government that was to all intents and purposes coterminous with an island-province. Indeed the ROC on Taiwan experienced no small degree of awkwardness from the anomalous presence of a "central" government cheek by jowl with the still existing Taiwan provincial government.[17] But two factors mitigate these differences. *Yidang zhiguo* in the People's Republic was implemented through a fractally organized state, wherein self-contained local units of the party-state replicated the form and organization of the party-state units above them. Occasionally, higher-level authorities would send down inspectors or work teams to see how policy was or was not being implemented, and under extreme conditions could censure or dismiss local cadres. But for the most part, territorial units of the party-state at more local levels mirrored higher levels, and

---

[17] Indeed the anomaly was so deeply felt that in the early 1960s, the Taiwan provincial government was relocated to a distant, but central, site in rural Taiwan as a new model community signifying progress and modernity. See Bi-yu Chang, "The Rise and Fall of Sanminzhuyi Utopia," in *Place, Identity and National Imagination in Post-War Taiwan*, (Routledge, 2015) pp. 112–154.

responded to signals from above in party line, propaganda, and directives. There were occasions when the signals from above became stronger, and were presented as direct "suggestions." Sub-national government units were expected to *replicate* the form and implement the broad directives from above, but to do so in the light of their own circumstances, personnel, and resources. In the end implementation was down to the local governments, and local governments in Sunan/Shanghai were so important to the central party-state that they were seldom, if ever, directly interfered with.

Perhaps the most important similarities between these bitterly opposed regimes in Sunan and Taiwan lay in the things that they needed to accomplish under highly challenging, and similar, circumstances. These undifferentiated party-states came to Sunan and Taiwan as external occupiers, with but weak and shallow social roots in the territories over which they exercised coercive control. Initially, neither had particularly promising materials with which to work. Years of invasion and warfare had done their worst: devastated economies, hyperinflation, armies, and populations in need of resettling were just some of the most pressingly immediate problems. Both needed to establish state hegemony over the societies over which they presided when the societies in question were at best passive and nervous and at worst smoldering with hostility. In so doing, they needed to exercise control and mobilize the state's use of material, social, and ideational resources, and moreover they needed to do it quickly, as in the early Cold War environment of the 1950s, nothing less than survival was felt to be at stake. And both were, by any reasonable measure incredibly *successful* in grasping these nettles. They managed to establish internal security, close off exit options and harden borders, extend state power to very local levels of society, implement core policies, fundamentally remake the countryside, and garner at least acquiescence if not active support from core constituencies of their populations. Indeed, the Communist, revolutionary, mobilizational People's Republic in Sunan, and the Nationalist, conservative, developmentalist Republic of China on Taiwan stood out as virtual prototypes for these different forms of state reintegration and development in the 1950s and 1960s. Yet there was nothing foreordained about these successes. In 1949 an incredibly daunting policy environment of weak domestic institutions, lack of popular support, and very sharp regional security tensions all pointed to precisely the opposite outcomes.

Critical Contingencies: From Cold to Hot War and Back Again, 1949–1954

In the early stages of the Cold War, the coercive core at the heart of the state lay close to the surface in a way that is difficult to recapture two full generations later. This was particularly so for the divided states of Germany, Korea, and China. The war-torn 1940s made for great fluidity: decisions had to be made in circumstances under which much was still uncertain. Many who had supported the losing side in the civil war had only a brief window to act on their ideological and political commitments, and they had to do so in a situation in which there were a great many unknowns. Remaining in China, leaving the country, starting over abroad, or following the GMD to Taiwan were all possibilities, and each of these possibilities carried risks: how likely the GMD was to survive on Taiwan, and how punitive the incoming Communists would likely be to GMD supporters were very open questions. Either by conviction or chance, individuals made different decisions or had different opportunities and constraints; families often split.[18] For several months after October 1949, the situation in militarily insecure southwest China was uncertain enough that it was not clear where new borders would be settled. Over the course of 1949 and 1950, the Chinese state was increasingly sharply divided between two ideologically supercharged, mutually antagonistic regimes, each claiming legitimacy over the whole. Each allied with a different nuclear superpower in an increasingly bipolar world. Sharp ideological and moral differentiation from the evil "Other" was imperative, as was the hardening of previously porous borders. And both deployed relentlessly harsh propaganda and didactic indoctrination of their populations in order to stiffen a sense of identification and differentiate the purity of the self from the craven Other across the Taiwan Strait.

Although the term "Cold War" very shortly thereafter came to be used widely to describe the tense bipolar world order that was then gelling, for neither of the two Chinas was the Cold War an abstraction, a metaphor, something far away, or even particularly "Cold." The regional heat (and its accompanying blasts of deeply felt insecurity) generated by the outbreak of the Korean War in June 1950 had a lasting – and unintended – impact on these two Chinese states. It artificially preserved the ROC regime in Taiwan. The rump of the GMD regime had retreated, battered and in shock, to Taiwan, and was in no position militarily to resist a PLA amphibious landing. The US Secretary of State Dean Acheson had publicly refrained from including either Taiwan or South Korea in the US "defensive

---

[18] What is often overlooked is that the majority of those who ended up following the GMD to Taiwan had no choice in the matter, as they were young, typically peasant males who formed the GMD troops that were recalled to Taiwan between 1949 and 1952.

perimeter" in the Pacific in January 1950.[19] Other sources, particularly the "China White Paper" (*United States Relations with China: With Special Reference to the Period 1944–49, based on the Files of the Department of State*) published in August 1949, ascribed the outcome of China's civil war in the CCP's favor to purely internal domestic causes, and made it clear that enough billions had been poured into supporting ineffective Nationalist armies.[20] With these signals from the ROC's hitherto chief patron, almost no one anticipated that the co-existence of two different Chinese regimes would last beyond the summer of 1950.

The widely expected PLA invasion of Taiwan in the summer of 1950 never came. An unexpected exogenous shock – the outbreak of war in Korea on June 25, 1950, dramatically redefined US foreign policy towards Asia. Overnight, the US defensive "security perimeter" was redrawn to include both Korea south of the 38th parallel and the island of Taiwan. Within three days, the US Seventh Fleet was dispatched to "neutralize" the Taiwan Straits and prevent either of the belligerents in the Chinese civil war from launching amphibious actions against the other. Since the ROC/Taiwan government was in no position to do any such thing, the US naval intervention in the Taiwan Straits could only prevent the PRC from concluding the Chinese civil war. Were it not for two contingent events, Kim Il-song's miscalculation in believing he could forcibly oust the Syngman Rhee regime south of the 38th parallel and the United States' unexpectedly strong intervention on the side of South Korea, in all likelihood there would have been no ROC/Taiwan regime to consolidate its rule in Taiwan after 1950. A more perfect instance of a critical juncture with outsized downstream effects is difficult to imagine.

The protagonists in the Chinese civil war were simultaneously shapers *of* and fundamentally shaped *by* the emerging Cold War. The very existence of rival regimes on opposite sides of the Cold War deepened rifts in the global Cold War, while the Cold War hegemons – the Soviet Union and the United States – wielded extraordinary influence over the statebuilding efforts of the two Chinas in direct and indirect ways. The

---

[19] Dean Acheson, "Speech on the Far East" (at the National Press Club), January 12, 1950. http://teachingamericanhistory.org/library/document/speech-on-the-far-east/ accessed November 8, 2016.

[20] Robert Beisner, *Dean Acheson, A Life in the Cold War*, pp. 185–189. Lyman Van Slyke, ed. *The China White Paper,* https://archive.org/details/VanSlykeLymanTheChinaWhitePaper1949. See especially Li Tsung-ren (Li Zongren, Acting President of the Republic of China in the spring of 1949) to President Truman in a letter dated May 5, 1949: "It is regrettable that, owing to the failure of our then Government to make use of this aid and to bring about appropriate political, economic, and military reforms, your assistance has not had the desired effect. To this failure is attributable the present predicament in which our country finds itself." Page 409, accessed November 8, 2016.

overwhelming influence of the United States on the ROC/Taiwan is undeniable: it served as military guarantor, funder, trainer, source of technology transfer and the eventual unprecedentedly open market so crucial for the later economic "miracle" of the 1960s and 1970s. At the same time, the ROC/Taiwan was by no means the puppet of the United States: the GMD government proved to be extremely adept in accepting the aid and technical advice that it wished to adopt while deflecting the more liberal political advice that it wished to ignore, by playing on US fears of a regional Communist threat and presenting itself as a stable and secure ally.

Although the degree of the Soviet Union's influence on the People's Republic of China was certainly less direct than was the US impact on the ROC/Taiwan, it was still considerable. Here it suffices to point out two salient features: (1) Mao took the young PRC's relationship with the Soviet Union so seriously that his one foreign trip was to Moscow, in the winter of 1949–1950, to conclude the Treaty of Friendship, Alliance, and Mutual Assistance; (2) the political economy of "New China" was set up along explicitly Stalinist lines in ways that fostered close to total state economic and political control, and the material aid given by the Soviet Union in the 1950s in combination with a favorable set of terms by which China participated in a "socialist world economy" was important for establishing the core of China's heavy industry. Thus, even though the Soviet Union's direct aid to the People's Republic of China was less than that provided by the United States to the much smaller ROC/Taiwan, the Soviet Union's ideational legacy was essential to the key political institutions and core agendas of the revolutionary state. Without the lessons learned from international socialism in general and the Stalinist form of the planned economy in particular, one cannot make sense of the PRC's subsequent choices in terms of squeezing out markets, rapid building of state channels for the production and distribution of goods, the establishment of the *tonggou tongxiao* (unified purchase and sale of grain), the establishment of the *danwei* (work unit), and eventually the unbelievably rapid nationalization of industry and collectivization of agriculture in 1955.[21]

International alignment on opposite sides of the Cold War did not mean that decision makers in the Chinese regimes on the opposite sides of the Taiwan Straits lacked agency. Within these broad international and regional alignments, each had a set of basic state building goals, a set of demographic, social, and economic conditions as background givens, and a range of preferred repertoires through which decisions were made to

[21] William Kirby, "The Internationalization of China."

work with the givens in realizing those goals. "New China" and the ROC on Taiwan had remarkably overlapping core agendas at the outset of regime consolidation in 1949. Both had to simultaneously secure the state's territory against external incursions, rid the country of internal security threats, and ensure, if not active support then at least the passive acquiescence of core sectors of society to the new regime. These basic commonalities in turn led to remarkably similar programs: to bring down hyperinflation to stabilize the economy and ensure the subsistence of cities unable to feed themselves, register populations, establish internal security and mutual surveillance at the grass roots, and implement land reform. Effective pursuit of these tasks required much-expanded institutions of the state, which in turn meant the ability to mobilize individuals working in state institutions to implement these core programs, and wherever possible, to lessen the cost of social resistance to new state programs. But clarity over the desirability of agreed state-building agendas is one thing: translating those goals into practice is quite another. Agents staffing state organizations might blunt the application of central policy: key groups in society could resist or subvert government initiatives.[22]

In order to keep their own state agents on board and their populations at least quiescent, if not actively enthusiastic, the PRC in Sunan and the ROC in Taiwan drew on a shared set of repertoires within two overlapping modalities of state building and policy implementation: (1) the bureaucratic; and (2) the campaign. Both modalities reached back into the "deep history" of the late-imperial Chinese state, now revived and adapted by the particular combination of party, state, and military fusion that had characterized the CCP and the GMD since the mid-1920s. State-making elites in Sunan and Taiwan were clear in their understanding that campaign and bureaucratic modalities of state making were mutually supporting: campaigns could be, and were, applied to establishing and strengthening the bureaucratic institutions of the state itself by mobilizing the commitments of cadres and civil servants and overcoming social resistance. In the early 1950s, this presumption of mutual reinforcement between campaign and bureaucracy was largely accurate. But campaign and the bureaucratic modalities of state making and policy implementation, in turn, comprised fundamentally different logics and principles that were in tension with each other, overlapped and interacted

---

[22] Harry Truman's comments about Dwight D. Eisenhower winning the Presidential election of 1952 are particularly apt: "He'll sit here, and he'll say, 'Do this! Do that!' And nothing will happen. Poor Ike – it won't be a bit like the Army. He'll find it very frustrating." Cited in Richard E. Neustadt, *Presidential Power, the Politics of Leadership* (Wiley, 1960), p. 9.

with each other in unpredictable ways, and were only partially reconcil-able. Over the long run, state makers could only fully deploy one while rowing back on the other.

Modalities of State Building (I): Radical Simplification through Creating and Expanding Bureaucratic Institutions

The state's administrative organizations are obviously important for state building and policy implementation, but there is surprisingly little in poli-tical sociology that conceptualizes how state administration works or fal-ters. Those who study China have long acknowledged its state's longevity, its history of civil service by open competitive examination, its struggle-laden transformation to the "modern" in the twentieth century, the nomenklatura system of appointment it adopted from the Soviet model in the People's Republic of China, and the way it did or did not work in different sectors or at different spatial scales.[23] Some point explicitly to Mao Zedong's deep mistrust of "bureaucracy" as a key factor in the launching of the enormously disruptive campaigns of his later years.[24] Ironically, the more radical the revolutionary state became in wanting to purge itself of suspected counterrevolutionaries, counterrevolutionary backsliding, and "bureaucracy," the more coercion, state power, and state personnel to exhaustively comb through the background files of suspects was necessary was necessary to ensure the purity of the revolution.[25] But despite the frequency with which the state is invoked as integral to most subjects on post-1949 China, after Franz Schurmann's seminal work *Ideology and Organization in Communist China* (1966, 1969), very few have systematically explored the concept of bureaucratic state organizations, and what this has meant, both normatively and practically, in a mid-twentieth century Chinese context.

Part of the problem is that the terms "bureaucracy" and "bureaucratic" *guanliao* ("bureaucratic" – 官僚) and "bureaucratism" (*guanliaozhuyi* –官

---

[23] The literature here is vast; but a very preliminary bibliography would include: Benjamin A. Elman, *Civil Examinations and Meritocracy in Late Imperial China*; John Burns, *The Chinese Communist Party's Nomenklatura System*; Vivienne Shue, *The Reach of the State*; and Frederick Teiwes, *Politics and Purges in China*. Kimberley Ens Manning and Felix Wemheuer's edited volume, *Eating Bitterness New Perspectives on China's Great Leap Forward and Famine* also illustrates beautifully how central policies played out very differently in different locations.

[24] Maurice Meisner, *Mao's China and After: A History of the People's Republic*, 3rd ed., pp. 156–157, 251–259; Roderick MacFarquhar, *The Origins of the Cultural Revolution*: (Vol. 1) *Contradictions Among the People 1956–57*, p. 59; Frederick Teiwes, ibid., pp. 7–8, 192–193, and 198–199.

[25] I am indebted to Michael Schoenhals for this insight.

僚主義), carry even more noxious connotations in Chinese than they do in English, conveying official arrogance, remoteness, paper pushing, and utter lack of responsiveness or accountability. Mao railed against "bureaucracy," despised the "bureaucratic work style," and went to great lengths to maintain a Yan'an-era revolutionary technique of the "mass line" that maintained "close links with the people." This distaste notwithstanding, whether called "bureaucracy," "administration," "state organs," "bureaus," or "the government," formal, hierarchical administrative organizations are an essential component of any state that claims centrality over a given territory. Administrative organizations provide the skeletal structure of the state: at a minimum they extract resources, maintain centrality, establish internal order, and provide for external defence. Beyond these minimums, they either implement or promote a wide range of other activities, depending on the state's core projects. These might include such tasks as providing for famine relief and road maintenance, establishing the guidelines by which young people will be socialized in school, regulating businesses, administering justice, and/or a host of more "revolutionary" measures (radically redistributing wealth, fundamentally reshaping gender and family relations, nationalizing industries, and so on). Revolutionary regimes are particularly prone to require substantial state administrations, for the simple reason that administrations that make the projection of state power possible are necessary to implement revolutionary programs of transformation.

But what are the essential properties of these state administrative organizations, how do they function, and how do they come into existence when they were previously either non-existent or weak? It is precisely this set of questions that is addressed by what I call "bureaucratic modalities of state building." Following Weber, I define the "bureaucratic" as the stuff of which "state institutions" are made: formal organizations, hierarchical lines of authority that garner the compliance of lower levels in the hierarchy, and behavior that relies on impersonal rulemaking and rule implementation.[26] By definition, a bureaucratic organization is one that is organized hierarchically. Decisions reached at higher levels must be incumbent and binding on lower levels in the hierarchy to ensure internal coherence. Bureaucratic decisions function by rulemaking over relevant classes of things, situations, or circumstances.[27]

---

[26] For the classic statement of Weber's conception of bureaucracy, see H. H. Gerth and C. H. Mills, *From Max Weber*, pp. 196–203.

[27] This is known in public administration circles as the "politics/administration dichotomy," but is often elided as "the policy/administration dichotomy." It has a lengthy lineage dating back from Woodrow Wilson's seminal article "The Study of Administration," *Political Science Quarterly* 2:2 (1887), pp. 197–222.

James Scott suggests that the core activity of the state is in "making legible" the societies and economies within which the state works.[28] The kinds of legibility to which Scott refers are realized through a fundamental bureaucratic logic: to radically *simplify* complex realities through *depersonalization*: disaggregating wholes in order to classify, record, and monitor data broken down into standardized categories of constituent units (people, incomes, housing, miles of railroad track or tarmac, grade of land, hectares of forest cut, trees from those cuttings assessed by specific grades), so that units can be measured, information can be passed up through the organizational hierarchy and then policy decisions about implementation passed back down. In principle each standard classification will merit the application of the same rule for as long as the rules are not changed.

The kinds of standardized classification, monitoring, and record keeping so integral to the bureaucratic modality and so necessary for the state to be able to implement preferred policies presuppose the existence of a coherent and responsive state organization with a fair amount of capacity. As this trifecta of desirable attributes – coherence, responsiveness, and capacity – was in uncertain evidence in the years immediately after 1949, both the PRC and the ROC were deeply committed to strengthening their states in order to establish coherence, augment responsiveness, and expand capacity, and they instinctively turned to bureaucratic logics in so doing. While the term *guanliao* (bureaucratic) is never encountered in Chinese as anything other than a pejorative, the young People's Republic of China in Shanghai issued a constant stream of exhortations to "strengthen organization" and "strengthen [state] organs (*jiaqiang zuzhi* – 加强組織, *jiaqiang jiguan* – 加强機關). In practice, "strengthening organization" meant expanding the capacity of state organizations to collect and record information according to standardized units of measure, recording this information in a timely way, and implementing and reporting on policies decided by higher levels of the organization. Personnel sufficiently trained in the meat and potatoes of the bureaucratic modality – statistics and accounting to standardize, simplify, and exert a modicum of control through counting, recording, and checking on local implementation – were in perennially short supply, and the need to "strengthen statistical and accounting work" (*jiaqiang tongji/kuaiji gongzuo* – 加强統計會計工作) continued to be acute well into the 1950s.

The ROC/Taiwan discourse on state administration betrayed little worry over the state's capacity for standardized counting and record keeping, but it was, if anything, even more concerned than was the PRC

---

[28] James C. Scott., *Seeing Like a State.*

about compliance with standardized rulemaking. It insisted with some vigor on the morally charged norm of "legality" in its state organizations that operated "according to law." The law in question was martial law and/or administrative law, but the principles of precedent and uniform application were, in essence, identical to those of bureaucracy. The young PRC and the ROC/Taiwan alike required bureaucratically organized administrative organizations to establish control over society, exhibit internal coherence, keep records, transmit information up the hierarchy, and begin to implement the kinds of signature policies by which society would be fundamentally remade in the preferred vision of the dominant party-state. Whether called "strengthening state organs," "strengthening organization," or "implementing policy according to law," the institutionalized hierarchy, inequality, standardization, rulemaking, rule implementation, and record keeping that are so characteristic of the Weberian conception of bureaucracy were an inescapable part of regime consolidation and state building in the immediate aftermath of 1949 on both sides of the Taiwan Straits.

Modalities of State Building (II): Radical Simplification through Campaigns and Narratives

Yundong (運動) is typically translated into English as "campaign" a word with multi-vocal connotations and denotations. Originally French (*campagne*), "campaign" can mean quite different things in English. It makes its first appearance at roughly the time of the English civil wars of the mid-seventeenth century in an explicitly military context of relatively short, often seasonally defined periods of army field operations. Roughly a century later, "campaign" also came to refer to actions *analogous* to military campaigns, either "having a distinct period of activity, in being of the nature of a struggle, or of an organized attempt aiming at a definite result." By the early nineteenth century, the term encompassed both collective action (e.g. rent-reduction campaigns in Ireland) and elections, although the term for organized collective action eventually became separate as "movement," a word with a similarly wide range of different uses and connotations.[29]

Originally, the Chinese term *yundong* also had a restricted set of meanings in the realms of physics and medicine: denoting the movement of objects or the quickening of blood flow through the intestines to signify greater energy and vigor. By the end of the second decade of the twentieth

---

[29] See entry for "campaign," *Compact Edition of the Oxford English Dictionary* (Oxford, 1991), p. 324.

century, *yundong* came to refer to the broadly based social movements emblematic of Republican China that protested the weak and corrupt Republican-era governments so ineffective in dealing with foreign imperialism (whether of the Western or Japanese variety).[30] From 1925 onward, such social movements were often entangled with leftist organization and agitation. While Mao's polemic, "Report on the Peasant Movement in Hunan" was immortalized in 1927, it took until the CCP was pushed into the countryside for it to begin a long process of experimentation by which *yundong* would come to be as much directed, planned, and staged processes from above by the vanguard party as they were social movements from below. Throughout the 1930s and 1940s, the CCP launched large numbers of *yundong* in such different arenas as directed mass mobilization in rent reduction and radical land reform in the Jiangxi Soviet, public hygiene, the harsh internal campaigns of party rectification in early 1940s Yan'an, and the strictly military "Hundred Regiments" campaign against the Japanese in 1941–1942.[31]

The GMD also used *yundong* in nearly identical ways: in the military "Encirclement campaigns" to wipe out the Communist Jiangxi base area, in the ongoing legitimacy it continued to draw from the May 4 Movement of 1919, in public hygiene, and, by the mid-1930s, in a clumsy effort to impose a party directed *yundong* to state building ends through the much mocked "New Life" movement (*Xin shenghuo yundong* – 新生活運動), which attempted to change the personal habits, attire, and cleanliness of the urban population from above, albeit without either popular mobilization or input.[32] By the late 1940s, when the GMD was locked in mortal battle with the CCP, there was substantial mimesis between the two rivals. The "Liquidate Traitors Campaign" (*xiaojian yundong* – 消奸運動) in the National Industry Defense Corps almost perfectly foreshadowed the CCP's own Campaign to Suppress Counterrevolutionaries only a few years later, and its "Oppose American Support for Japan Campaign" (*fanmei furi yundong* – 反美孚日 運動) for the 1948 May Day celebrations – strongly paralleled the CCP's first mass mobilization after 1949, the "Resist America, Support Korea" campaign (*fanmei yuanchao* – 反美援朝).

---

[30] *Cihai*, 3rd ed. (Shanghai: Shanghai Lexicographical Publishing House, 1979), p. 96.
[31] Stephen C. Averill, *Revolution in the Highlands: China's Jingganshan Base Area*, pp. 199–221, 239–252.
[32] Arif Dirlik, "The Ideological Foundations of the New Life Movement: A Study in Counterrevolution"; Federica Ferlanti, "The New Life Movement in Jiangxi Province, 1934–1938"; Chieko Nakajima, "Health and Hygiene in Mass Mobilization: Hygiene Campaigns in Shanghai, 1920–1945."

In the generation prior to 1949, *yundong* had come to refer to overlapping, yet different, phenomena: exercise to remake the body, military campaigns, social movements of protest from below, and attempts by the Leninist single party – be it Communist or Nationalist – to mobilize populations under its control towards party-directed goals in such different spheres as rooting out traitors and public hygiene. As such, its expansion closely paralleled the rise of the party-state, in both its GMD and CCP variants, moving from physical activity and sports, to social movements, to something fairly close to the notion of campaign that is most commonly used in Chinese now: the state's extraordinary mobilization of people and resources to implement a specific program to accomplish particular goals in a defined period of time.

Much of the writing on the CCP, both in terms of its pre-1949 antecedents and its first revolutionary decades in power tends to plot the politics and history of the CCP against its nearly annual *yundong*. The conventional political history of the People's Republic of China, punctuates time and its successes by the great mass mobilizational campaigns from the Aid Korea/Resist America patriotic campaign of the autumn of 1950, to the campaigns of the early 1950s (the Campaign to Suppress Counterrevolutionaries and land reform campaigns (1951), the "Three Antis" (1951–1952), the "Five Antis" (1952–1953), and Thought Reform (1953)). These were followed by campaigns for mutual aid teams, collectivization, nationalization of private enterprises, another "clearing out of counterrevolutionaries" (*sufan*) campaign, and the anti-Hu Feng campaign of the autumn of 1955. These were but a precursor to some of the most destructive campaigns of all: the Hundred Flowers and Anti-Rightist campaign of 1957, the Great Leap Forward and its various sub-campaigns (1958 and passim), the Socialist Education Campaign (1963), and eventually the Cultural Revolution and its myriad sub-campaigns (1966–1976). Indeed, the broad-brush outline of successive national campaigns after 1949 serves as a kind of shorthand for revolutionary China itself during these years, which was above all characterized by frontal attacks in service of whatever line the CCP was then promoting: intense pushes of government focus on a given set of goals with state directed social mobilization.[33]

Important as these mass campaigns obviously were for the Chinese Communist Party and its approach to rule after 1949, there is much that is lost in equating state campaigns exclusively with those of the ever-more radical Mao-era People's Republic of China. A broader view suggests that there is a range of practices that can all be called "campaign," even when

---

[33] Merle Goldman, "The Party and Intellectuals."

they were devoid of the kind of public mass mobilization so typical of those launched by the young PRC in the 1950s and 1960s. If campaigns are instead defined as *extraordinary* and *temporary* mobilizations of human and material resources for the rapid accomplishment of a specific goal, it is clear that the Chinese state resorted to campaigns as a method of policy implementation both before and after the revolutionary Maoism of the People's Republic of China. For example, the eighteenth-century Qing state launched campaigns in such different policy arenas as water conservancy, internal security, and distribution of relief from state granaries to ameliorate local famines. But unlike its counterparts in Europe, the Qing state did not seek to regularize campaigns into permanent expanded state organizations of greater infrastructural power.[34] The Guomindang as well as the Chinese Communist Party attempted to launch campaigns to build social support, engage in military training and battle, and (ultimately in Taiwan with much greater success) push through a major party rectification, and major policy initiatives.

Although the Mao-era mass mobilizational campaigns are best remembered, both before and after 1976, there were many other types of campaigns with very different goals and often substantially less (if any) popular involvement. Rather than defining the campaign as a unique feature of the revolutionary People's Republic of China that was renounced when the CCP leaders convened at the 3rd Plenum of the Central Committee in December 1978 shortly after Mao's passing, it is perhaps more accurate to conceive of a broad range of campaigns with only one variant – the mass mobilizational campaign – abandoned in the post-Mao reform era. In the post-1978 era People's Republic, such different policy arenas as "Spiritual Pollution," crime, corruption, and the enforcement of birth control quotas have all involved extraordinary concentrations of political will and bureaucratic mobilization to realize a given goal without a concomitant level of mass mobilization.[35]

---

[34] I am indebted to R. Bin Wong for his helpful formulation of this definition of a campaign. See also R. Bin Wong, "Formal and Informal Mechanisms of Rule and Economic Development: The Qing Empire in Comparative Perspective," *Journal of Early Modern History* 5:4, pp. 387–408.

[35] While the importance of mobilizational campaigns in revolutionary China is acknowledged in nearly all works on the subject of Chinese politics in the Mao years, surprisingly few have attempted to develop a comprehensive analysis of campaigns. For two relatively early works see Charles Cell, *Revolution at Work: Mobilizational Campaigns in China* (Michigan: Academic Press, 1977) and Gordon Bennett, *Yundong: Mass Campaigns in Chinese Communist Leadership* (Berkeley: Institute of East Asia Press, 1976). More recent research makes clear how important campaign dynamics continued to be in the reform period. See Melanie Manion, *Corruption by Design: Building Clean Government in Mainland China and Hong Kong* (Harvard University Press, 2004), see especially Chapter 5. M. Scot Tanner, *Strike Hard: Anti-crime Campaigns and Chinese Criminal*

State-led campaigns in pre-and-post 1949 China had different policy objectives, were directed to different sectors of the population, and encompassed differing levels of social participation and mass mobilization. Some campaigns began and ended within the state's own bureaucracy, as it geared up and mobilized to implement a particular policy or program. Others drew in and mobilized the general population to tackle fixed and relatively short-term goals (draining a swamp, building a bridge, wiping out schisomatosis), or were aimed at a specific industry or sector (e.g. steel production drives or the rapid collectivization of agriculture). Some attempted to change the chronic behavior of defined groups (e.g. the anti-prostitution and anti-opium campaigns launched by the local governments in Chinese cities in 1949 and 1950), or the public more generally (anti-spitting campaigns), and still others involved the full-scale mass mobilization that publicly targeted internal or external enemies of the state (the three "Great Campaigns" of the early People's Republic).[36]

I suggest that irrespective of goals, type, or time period, a campaign modality of policy implementation is characterized by the following three attributes: (1) the mobilization of state administrative organizations ("the bureaucracy") for the intensification of focus around implementing a particular program; (2) fixed and typically short duration; and (3) a big and well publicized push to accomplish clearly defined targets and goals. Like the bureaucratic modality of policy implementation, the campaign modality *radically simplifies* complex realities. But it does so in an utterly different way. Rather than break down complex and interconnected phenomena into constituent and standardizable parts amenable to rules, the campaign simplifies by fusion, compression, and frontal attack, merging the complex and multifaceted into an organic whole, condensing the time allotted for implementation, and engaging the emotional commitments of those it draws in with explicit appeals to normative goods.

State campaigns invariably require as a first step the extraordinary intensification of focus and mobilization of resources within the regularly constituted administrative organizations of the state, and it is here that the campaign intersects with the Chinese state's other key modality of bureaucratic implementation. The campaign focuses on readily graspable objectives, justifies its policies towards the objectives in straightforward morally

Justice, 1979–85 (Ithaca: Cornell University Press, 1999). Ralph A. Thaxton, Jr., *Force and Contention in Contemporary China: Memory and Resistance in the Long Shadow of the Catastrophic Past* (Cambridge: 2016).

[36] See Julia C. Strauss, "Morality, Coercion and State Building by Campaign in the Early People's Republic of China: Regime Consolidation and After, 1949–1956," in Strauss, ed., *The History of the People's Republic of China* (Cambridge University Press, 2007).

based stories, and claims that a rapid push to achieve the objectives will solve a larger outstanding social, political, or economic problem. But in contrast to bureaucracy, which is organized around the regular, the standardizable, and the predictable in its rule-based implementation, a campaign is *by definition* extraordinary, often sidestepping or overriding the procedural and rule bound in its efforts to realize quick results. For this reason, the campaign exists in ambiguous tension with bureaucracy. It needs the organizational capacity and coherence that bureaucratic hierarchies provide, but its modality – extraordinary mobilization, sharp focus, compressed time scale, and sidestepping rules – is the opposite of the bureaucratic, which stresses rules, precedent, and defined temporal sequencing. Campaigns cannot completely undercut the formal institutions of the state, whose normal workings reify hierarchy and impersonally determined rules, but without strict limits, their defining modality of implementation runs the risk of so doing.

Performance in Policy Implementation: The How Is as Important as the What

Questions of performance permeate both bureaucratic and campaign modalities of state building. "Performance," like "campaign," is a highly charged term with many different meanings and uses. It can refer to an evaluation of the effectiveness of something ("a non-performing loan"), an evaluation of how well or appropriately something is done as in an individual's work ("annual performance review"), or a matter of public policy ("the performance of USAID in the mosquito net program in Malawi"). It can refer to the world of theater, film and music ("the performing arts"), or a particular instance of "performance" on a stage. Perhaps its most confusing use is in academia, as the term takes on distinct but overlapping meanings when used by different disciplines and interdisciplinary networks. In the realm of philosophy and semiotics, following the lead of J. L. Austin, "performance" is often understood in terms of a "speech act," best exemplified by the minister's classic utterance "I now pronounce you man and wife."[37] In theater studies it overlaps with notions of "theatricality."[38] In sociology and anthropology an important literature ties questions of performance to rituals, and rituals to the state.[39] A different interdisciplinary network of

---

[37] John L. Austin, *How to Do Things with Words*, 2nd ed.

[38] Richard Schechner, *The Future of Ritual: Writings on Culture and Performance*; Schechner, *Performance Studies: An Introduction* (3rd ed.).

[39] The list of key writings in sociology and anthropology on the intersection of performance, meaning making, and ritual is enormous. Key texts include: Erving Goffman, *Interaction Ritual: Essays on Face-to-Face Behavior* (New York: Anchor Books, 1967); Randall Collins,

sociologists, historians, and political scientists focuses on contentious politics and social movements, and applies theatrical metaphors of repertoire and analysis of performances by claim makers.[40] And Jeffrey Alexander makes a cogent case for the importance of performance, complete with background symbols, scripts, actors, audiences, and staging, to create "the emotional connection of audience with actor and text and thereby to create the conditions for projecting cultural meaning from performance to audience" as a way that society is "re-fused with meaning."[41] While the disciplines and levels of social theory engaged by all of these literatures differ, there is broad agreement that the content of political performance is made through culturally coded symbols, and commonly understood narratives and practices communicated through the content and the delivery of speech, dress, and manner of performance.

Important political speeches over the course of an electoral campaign (e.g. Presidential debates[42]), public trials and hearings (e.g. Gandhi's trial and the hearings of Truth and Reconciliation Commission in South Africa[43]), electoral campaigns (in the United States and elsewhere[44]), and demonstrations/social movements (e.g. the civil

---

Interaction Ritual Chains (Princeton: Princeton University Press 2004); Victor Turner's many works, the most important of which are perhaps *The Ritual Process: Structure and Anti-Structure* (Ithaca: Cornell University Press, 1969), and "Social Dramas and Stories about Them," *Critical Inquiry* 7:1 (Autumn 1980), pp. 141–168. Still useful is the collaboration between Victor Turner and Richard Schechner in Richard Schechner, *Between Theatre and Anthropology* (Philadelphia: University of Pennsylvania Press, 1985), for which Turner wrote a forward. Schechner has also made a sequence of video recordings entitled "Performance Studies: An Introduction," that were uploaded to youtube in December 2012. Of these, Schechner's own explanation of Victor Turner's notions of social drama is particularly relevant. See weblink, www.youtube.com/watch?v=Pnsw5xF uXHE accessed November 19, 2016. Clifford Geertz's *Negara: The Theatre State in 19th Century Bali* (Princeton: Princeton University Press, 1980) stands out as the anthropological work that is the most directly relevant to concerns of state building, with his assertion that "the expressive power [of the Balinese state] was toward spectacle, toward ceremony, toward the public dramatization of the ruling obsessions of Balinese culture: social inequality and status pride ... the stupendous cremations, tooth filings, temple dedications, pilgrimages and blood sacrifices, mobilizing hundreds and even thousands of people and great quantities of wealth, *were not means to political ends; they were the ends themselves: they were what the state was for*"(emphasis added), p. 13.

[40] Charles Tilly, *Contentious Performances; Regimes and Repertoires*, pp. 34–35.
[41] Jeffrey C. Alexander, *Performance and Power*, p. 53 and passim.
[42] David Zarefsky, "What 'went wrong' with the first Obama-Romney debate."
[43] Sudipta Kaviraj, "Gandhi's Trial Read as Theatre," in Julia C. Strauss and Donal D. B. Cruise O'Brien, *Staging Politics* (London: I.B. Tauris 2007), Tanya Goodman, Ron Eyerman, and Jeffrey C. Alexander, *Staging Solidarity*, and Catherine M. Cole, *Performing South Africa's Truth and Reconciliation Commission.*
[44] Alexander, *Staging Solidarity*; see also Dafydd Fell, "Putting on a Show and Electoral Fortunes in Taiwan's Multi-party Elections," and Vincent Foucher, "'Blue Marches': Public Performance and Political Turnover in Senegal," in Strauss and Cruise O'Brien, ibid., pp. 173–194, and pp. 111–132.

rights movement,[45] the "color" revolutions of Eastern Europe in 1989 and after, the symbolic confrontations between protesters and the government in the "Beijing Spring" of 1989),[46] and the pageantry of mass fascism[47] are all suitable phenomena to study the dramaturgy and performance of power from both above and below. The combination of limited duration, playing out in public space, and the media attention they attract makes for good theater, commanding narratives, and condensation into readily understood morality plays. However, with few exceptions, most of the work on performance in politics takes as its subject matter a defined performance or cluster of performances, rather than the wider political processes of which the performance is a part.[48] There is little reason to doubt that performance in politics is as important in regions of the world presented in scripts encoded with cultural references and moral resonances unfamiliar to the Western journalists who disseminate news more widely.

Regional insecurity, the need to build effective state institutions quickly, and the indifference, wariness and outright hostility of local populations led the Chinese Communist Party in Sunan and the Guomindang in Taiwan to establish order and implement signature policies, and to do so in particular performative registers that communicated regime identity and expectations of the population. In short, *how* policy was communicated and performed was as important as *what* policies were decided on and implemented. Campaigns played out in public space were obviously theatrical, seeking to engage the emotions (support, righteous indignation, a sense of opportunity), while they displayed regime norms to the population. But so too could key elements of a bureaucratic modality also be performative: was the state official a remote presence who feasted behind closed doors, only venturing out to demand requisitions for the state? Was the state official invariably male

---

[45] Alexander, "Performance and Counter-Power: The Civil Rights Movement and the Civil Sphere," in Alexander *Staging Solidarity*, pp. 147–158; Alexander, *The Performance of Politics: Obama's Victory and The Democratic Struggle For Power*, Tilly, *Contentious Performances*.

[46] Joseph Esherick and Jeffrey Wasserstrom, "Acting Out Democracy: Political Theatre in Modern China," *Journal of Asian Studies* 49:4 (November 1990), pp. 835–865: Rudolf Wagner, "Political Institutions, Discourse and Imagination in China at Tiananmen," in James Manor, ed., *Rethinking Third World Politics*, originally published by Longman Press, 1991, republished (London: Routledge 2013), pp. 121–144.

[47] Mabel Berezin, "The Festival State: Celebration and Commemoration in Fascist Italy." *The Journal of Modern European History*, 3(1): pp. 60–74.

[48] Lisa Wedeen's two monographs, *Peripheral Visions: Publics, Power and Performance in Yemen* (Chicago and London: University of Chicago Press, 2008) and *Ambiguities of Domination: Politics, Rhetoric and Symbols in Contemporary Syria* (Chicago and London: University of Chicago Press, 1999) are the outstanding exceptions to this tendency.

and in his fifties or sixties, or female and/or in his/her twenties or thirties? Was s/he dressed in foreign clothes and speaking a substantively different language by using a dialect so different that direct communication was impossible, or through scientific and technocratic jargon)? Were new rules (orders, directives, regulations) communicated by loudspeaker blaring in a singsong official voice, newsprint that reproduced the state's legalese or code words, or through trusted (or not so trusted) locals who spoke the same language as other locals? Did the state's official representative get to field sites by black Mercedes with smoked windows, or by bicycle, or foot? All these actions so inherent in the everyday rule orientation of state administration were equally part of the dramaturgy of state power – the Gramscian micro practices linked to the establishment and institutionalization of key state institutions of Weberian bureaucratic hierarchy and authority.

Outline of the Book

In order to explore the ways in which performance, bureaucratic and campaign modalities of statebuilding were deployed in the regime consolidation of the young People's Republic of China in Sunan and the traumatic rebuilding of the ROC in Taiwan in the early to mid-1950s, I turn to three paired case studies: (1) state personnel; (2) the terror unleashed by the state against its presumptive domestic enemies; and (3) land reform.

Chapter 1 on virtue and talent in the making of the two Chinas returns to a theme first articulated in *Strong Institutions in Weak Polities*: the importance of state administrators as implementing agents *for* the state without whom state-making programs could not be implemented and ideal reflections *of* the state, walking and talking embodiments of how the state wished to represent itself vis-à-vis society. Identifying, recruiting, and deploying individuals who were simultaneously: (a) sufficiently loyal and disciplined; (b) adequately competent to implement the tasks required by political masters at higher levels in the state; and (c) presenting a reasonable facsimile of the image that the state wished to project of itself and its core values, was, however, a tricky business. By delving into what state administrators were called, how they were recruited, and the terms by which they were evaluated, this chapter shows that while the PRC selected for heroic, generalist cadres as individuals and the ROC privileged formal civil service systems of recruitment and evaluation, both were deeply influenced by a late-imperial set of norms that presumed that moral virtue and technical ability were mutually reinforcing, and that the state had to select for individuals with a full quotient of both. Through traditional rhetorics of *de jian cai* (德兼才 – virtue and talent) and "select-ing for talent," each of these regimes sought to harness the individual state administrator's self-cultivation, responsiveness, and ability to do more with less. In this early stage of regime consolidation in the People's Republic of China, the Maoist tension between "Red" and "Expert" that would emerge in the late 1950s was quite unthinkable. The discourse on cadres and personnel systems assumed that an individual's virtue and talent were indispensably two sides of the same coin. State cadres in the young People's Republic of China were charged not only with imple-menting correct policy, but also with implementing it in the correct way. In a Maoist context, the "correct way" meant in accordance with the principles of the mass line: advanced consciousness, close links to the people, patient explanation of both what was being done and why it was being done. For its part, the formal civil service system of the ROC/Taiwan incorporated into its annual evaluations a surprisingly heavy component of "virtue," which was similarly defined by *how* work was done: in a diligent and timely manner; in a morally upright way; and with the ability and willingness to endure hardship. In Sunan and Taiwan, systems of formal state administration reflected the different goals to which each regime aspired: individual heroism reflecting the best of the Chinese Communist Party versus well-functioning systems that selected for the best to serve the party-state. The People's Republic of China in Sunan and the Republic of China in Taiwan faced similar dilemmas: how to recruit, socialize, and keep on board sufficiently loyal and capable state administrators to implement core state programs in a locale in which the regime was externally imposed. Despite their political differences, their assumptions about what state administrators should do, how they should behave, and what kind of face they should present to society overlapped substantially.

Chapters 2 and 3 turn to the first and perhaps most important activity of a state: the establishment and maintenance of internal security and social order by defining internal enemies, and then rigorously separating such threats from supporters or those with the potential to be won over. Because a generation of mutual interpenetration by spies amid accelerat-ing regional insecurity with the outbreak of war in Korea meant that it was far from straightforward to determine who was friendly, neutral, hostile, or outright subversive, it was incumbent on authorities in Sunan and in Taiwan to launch campaigns against presumptive domestic enemies. The People's Republic of China did so in Sunan by organizing and imple-menting a vicious campaign against a range of undesirables whom it labeled counterrevolutionaries in the Campaign to Suppress Counterrevolutionaries; the ROC/Taiwan declared martial law and launched a series of police-cum-military actions against Communists and their fellow travelers, inaugurating the period that is now known in Taiwan as the "White Terror."

Chapter 2 focuses on questions of how such undesirables were categorized and identified, how wide ranging the terror was, and the ways in which the drive to root out enemies of the state was deliberately linked to wider questions of state building in Sunan and Taiwan. It lays out how both regimes instrumentally deployed what might well have been reasonable worries over internal security to target a broad range of presumptive domestic enemies in order to clear the ground of potential resistance in the future. In Sunan a wide range of political (ex-Guomindang) and social (secret societies, local bullies, leaders of heterodox religious sects) enemies were targeted. In Taiwan far more individuals were rounded up, imprisoned, and either executed or sent to prison camps on Green Island than there were Communists on the island. Although the scale of the terror in absolute numbers and as percentage of the population was significantly greater in Sunan than Taiwan, the campaign in Sunan was restricted to those who held high positions in the Guomindang's Party, military, security, and youth corps and others who were comprehensible as socially undesirable (local toughs, gangsters, the leaders of religious sects, and traitors). The majority of the urban population, and cadres in the CCP had little cause to worry about becoming targets of the campaign. In Taiwan, however, there was no sector of society that was safe from uneven and sporadically vicious police action campaigns under martial law, which overlapped with a stringent Guomindang Party rectification. Card-carrying Communists, rural Taiwanese who happened to know those now identified as Communists, party members and military officers who fell afoul of Chiang Kai-shek, and teachers and journalists caught with reading material recently banned as "Communist" were all fair game for suppression.

Chapter 3, "Performing Terror: Lenience, Legality, and the Dramaturgy of the Consolidating State" details the ways in which the state in Sunan and Taiwan implemented campaigns of terror in the early 1950s and communicated about its processes of implementation with wider (non-accused) publics. Each claimed that vigorous action against enemies of the state was essential for regime survival and social order, deployed theatrical forms to punish wrongdoers and disseminated regime norms to the population at large. What the content and staging of these shows communicated about the state to citizens was very different. The party-state in Sunan convened mass public accusation meetings, while the GMD insisted on (faux) legality through a formal process of closed military courts. The show in Sunan was put on to mobilize the public and to garner its complicity in extreme violence against defined enemies of the state; the show in Taiwan was put on by the state itself for itself to provide a reassuring wrapper of legality and correct procedure around its extreme violence against defined enemies of the state.

Chapters 4 and 5 turn to the question of land reform, a signature policy for both the People's Republic of China and the ROC/Taiwan in the early 1950s. Chapter 4 considers why both the PRC and the ROC/Taiwan staked so much of their legitimacy on the successful implementation of land reform in the countryside. It explores the ways in which a consensus grew throughout the 1930s and 1940s, when the Chinese Communist Party, its foreign and domestic sympathizers, New Deal progressives, technocratic agronomists, and the Guomindang all converged on a set of core assumptions about rural China: (1) there was a crisis of rural immiseration and exploitation; (2) substantial land reform was necessary to restore a modicum of rural social justice; (3) land reform was therefore popular and demanded from below by the peasantry; and (4) as an agricultural country, China required the agricultural surplus that land reform could provide as the basis for further economic development. In 1949, it was obvious to all who reflected on the matter that the Guomindang had been so badly beaten because, in contrast to the Chinese Communists who had built a reservoir of support among the rural population at least in part because of its attention to land reform, the GMD had either ignored rural China or done too little too late.

What was manifestly self-evident to this consensus in 1949 was, however, not born out in the actual conditions of rural Sunan or Taiwan. The chapter then illustrates how in both landlordism was in decline, landlords were weak and/or not commonly hated by those in the rural population who remained in the countryside, and indeed in many places locals thought that their landlords were not such bad sorts at all. In Sunan, a vigorous market in small landholding meant that many of modest means like shopkeepers and petty traders owned and rented out small parcels of land, while in Taiwan the vast majority of landlords owned relatively small amounts of land, and those that held more on paper often only appeared to hold more because in many places brothers or cousins with adjoining fields had one family member register the entirety in his name. Mobility out of full-time farming was commonplace, as the young often migrated in search of factory work, only returning to the land at peak planting and harvesting times. Yet in both Sunan and Taiwan, land reform initiatives were implemented from above according to principles and rules determined by outsiders, who in turn imposed a ready-made solution and set of categories quite irrespective of local rural realities.

Chapter 5 engages the ways in which land reform campaign implementation in Sunan and Taiwan exhibited surprising commonalities and significant divergences. The early to middle stages of land reform campaigns illustrate how these two regimes drew on similar campaign repertoires: the mobilization of the bureaucratic institutions of the state, the dissemination of intensive propaganda, and the substantial expansion of the state through the extraordinary recruitment of temporary staff, often patriotic and young, to go down to the countryside to aid regular officials in conducting land reform. The forms of public propaganda that accompanied campaigns to educate the rural population about such basic issues as why land reform was necessary, what measures it would involve, and the righteousness by which it would be implemented were strikingly similar. Both utilized similar forms for propaganda such as posters, newsreels, songs, and plays. Propaganda content to educate the rural population was also markedly similar, stressing the ways in which concentrated land holdings resulted in both social injustice and stagnant development in the countryside. Public performances were deployed to educate, persuade, and garner the participation of rural populations in land reform, but the form and content of these performances were markedly different. In Sunan, the state put on highly stage-managed public accusation sessions on makeshift stages in public space. Local cadres, who were responsible for these public shows, were given detailed instructions about how accusation sessions were to proceed: with sympathetic (and heavily coached) accusers to mount the stage at key moments, to confront the accused with their past evils and wrongdoings through dramatic "face to face" accusation in front of a large crowd whipped up into a frenzy of righteous anger. In Taiwan the state put on a very different kind of show: the limited public theater of local elections to the Farm Tenancy Committee, which, once the elections were held went on to adjudicate land disputes according to the laws and regulations handed down by the state behind the closed doors of the local Land Division Office.

The different ways in which these competitive regimes implemented violence against putative enemies and land reform initiatives reveal a great deal about how each understood itself, represented itself to society, and signaled what it expected from society in terms of political behavior. The dramaturgies of power that each of these consolidating states employed was not simply symbolic fluff that concealed the "harder" realities of state repression or land redistribution; they were an integral part of these more coercive components of state building. But carrying out any state policy first required a large number of committed state officials to do the state's bidding, and it is to the ways in which these states imagined and created their agents and implementers that this book now turns.

1   Virtue and Talent in Making Chinese States
Heroes and Technocrats in Sunan and Taiwan,
1949–1954

All states face a basic conundrum: how to attract and retain a cadre of
state agents that will be loyal *and* competent, willing *and* able to implement state directives and programs. This need is particularly acute in
revolutionary and radically reformist environments in which the societies
on the receiving end of directives and programs are mystified, uncon-
vinced, or hostile. Except for conquest states, colonies ruled directly from
the metropole, or states small and rich enough to contract out state
services to foreign professionals, the state's agents normally come from
the society they administer. Society in turn may be fragmented along
ethnic, religious, or economic lines; key social or economic elites may
only pay lip service to the state's goals, or be in active opposition to them.
Often those very same elites come from social groups that make, and
indeed are expected to make, clientelistic claims on any of their number
who become state administrators.

The perennial problem of ensuring that state agents be both loyal and
competent is one of two main reasons why Max Weber imagined legal-
rational, "modern" bureaucracy to be "the most perfect form of administration" in the early twentieth century. (The other was, of course, the
presumptive superiority of the expertise that legal-rational officials were
supposed to possess.) In the late nineteenth and early twentieth centuries
in central Europe, a depersonalized, expert "legal-rational" bureaucracy
appeared to offer both efficiency and effectiveness, particularly when
juxtaposed against its immediately preceding ideal type of patrimonial
(household) bureaucracy.[1] Specifically, legal-rational bureaucracy was
characterized by hierarchical state structures in which the individuals
who staffed them were: (1) separable from their positions; (2) functional
experts in their arena of knowledge; and (3) obedient to political masters.
In principle, legal-rational bureaucracy's impersonal and technical basis
solved the problem of ensuring both competence (because competence
was presumed to be technical) and loyalty (because lack of obedience to

---

[1] Hence Weber's own statement that "bureaucracy was the most perfect form of administration the world has yet known," see Gerth and Mills, *From Max Weber*, pp. 196–198.

political masters was unthinkable). Such depersonalized, hierarchical, and technocratic organizations even held out the promise of simplifying state administration to a set of "scientific" principles of public management, a notion at least as attractive to Leninist revolutionaries as it was to the newly developing field of public administration.[2]

China at mid-century faced a problem common to many developing countries. It was far from clear how to acquire sufficient numbers of "good men" – administrators who were (technically) competent, (politically) loyal, and (ideologically) committed to implementing the state's programs.[3] This chapter lays out the ways in which state makers in the young PRC and the rejuvenating ROC/Taiwan framed this conundrum and developed a range of policies to guarantee the loyalty, effectiveness, and moral commitments of their (typically male) state agents. Both adhered to the form of a unitary party-state in which members of the dominant party concurrently held almost all the important decision-making positions within state organizations. Both were also influenced by centuries-old Mencian notions of the natural sociability, malleability, and perfectability of individuals given the right kinds of education and models, and stressed the importance of individual self-cultivation to meet government-mandated forms of behavior.[4] Liu Shaoqi's seminal text,

---

[2] See Sochor, "Soviet Taylorism," for how enamored V. I. Lenin was with Taylorist principles of scientific management.

[3] While women were present in the state administrations in the PRC and the ROC/Taiwan and could be important politically, especially if married to high-status male leaders, even in the revolutionary PRC they were shunted into ceremonial positions, gendered "women's work," and/or low-status clerical support. For example, the Jiangsu provincial-level Women's Federation had 1,481 *ganbu* in 1956, all but six of whom were female. The statistics on the number of female cadres serving in all provincial-level units in Jiangsu put the total percentage of female cadres at 14.55 percent (38,470 of 264,455), with 13.08 percent (1,287 of 9,837) of cadres at the level of section chief and above. This is a surprisingly high percentage of female cadres: it was far ahead of most other states at the time. However, even in progressive Jiangsu, the absolute numbers and percentages of female *ganbu* dropped dramatically in more rural areas: particularly for positions of leadership. Of 5,556 village party secretaries only 67 (1.21 percent) were female; and in large villages, there were no female party secretaries at all; here most female cadres (142 of 179) were in the Women's Federation; of those remaining a total of only two (2,099) ranked as assistant party secretary or village head. See JPA, "Funü Lianhehui, 41/2" "Quansheng 1956 nian funü ganbu dizi biao," and "Daxiang ganbu tongji biao," both dated December 31, 1956. Much more research needs to be done to ascertain the degree to which these large numbers of female cadres at the provincial level in Jiangsu were in genuine positions of leadership, or whether they were quietly confined to gendered positions. In the Taiwan Province Grain Bureau there were 196 staff in post at the end of 1950. Of these, 23 were female. These individuals were concentrated in the research department (5), as clerks and assistant clerks (*banshiyuan/gubanshiyuan*) (7), and general workers (*guyuan*) (11). None had even a regular *weiren* (basic section-level) status TPA. Taiwan sheng Liangshi Ju, 39/67/497. "Benju zhiyuan lü" (Personnel Records 1950).

[4] Munro, *The Concept of Man in Contemporary China*, pp. 15–25.

How to Be a Good Communist, first given as a set of lectures in July 1939 in Yan'an, but then reprinted and reproduced widely from 1949 on, made explicit the linkages between Mencian "steeling and self-cultivation that a great man must undergo" and the contemporary importance of Communist Party members shouldering the "unprecedentedly 'great office' of changing the world ... through such steeling and self-cultivation."[5] During the Sino-Japanese War, the Guomindang equally favored *dangzheng xunlian* (黨政 訓練 – party-government training) based on the twin pillars of military discipline and self-cultivation of the individual.[6] Each was also influenced by its own perception of what had and had not been successful during the highly militarized late 1930s and 1940s. For the CCP, the lessons of the immediate past were straightforward in principle, if not always so in practice: to scale up and extend to the rest of the country the techniques of mobilization and party discipline that had been such an integral part of the CCP and its successes in the civil war, undergirded by a notion of the state administrator as a supercharged hero able to overcome all odds if armed with the right kinds of thoughts through political study, self-examination, criticism/self-criticism, and maintaining close links with the masses. The GMD drew the exact opposite "lessons" from recent history: to rectify the severe weaknesses of both the civil service and GMD party systems deemed to be integral to its loss of China.

Over the course of the 1930s, the Nationalist party-state's guiding principles towards constructing its national state administration had tacked from notions of process and technocratically driven civil service to the increasing militarization and partification of the 1940s. This legacy of militarization and partification undertaken by the GMD in the late 1930s and 1940s was amplified under the much stronger PRC government of the early 1950s. In contrast, the explicitly restorationist rhetoric of the GMD in Taiwan after 1949 led to a revival of the formal civil service and examination system that was first and only partially instituted in the 1930s. Although this revival was in practice undercut by immediate political imperatives for the regime to provide employment for the exceptionally loyal GMD devotees who had chosen to follow Chiang Kai-shek to Taiwan, publicly articulated notions of good governance and civil service downplayed the kinds of militarization and cronyism that had been so prominent in the 1940s. While the post-1949 PRC and GMD party-states trumpeted different rhetorics, organized what appeared to be fundamentally different systems for state personnel, and were predicated

[5] Liu Shao-ch'i (Liu Shaoqi), "How to Be a Good Communist," 9.
[6] Strauss, "Strategies of Guomindang Institution Building," pp. 195–221.

on the PRC's unexpectedly rapid triumph versus the ROC's unexpectedly rapid collapse, the young PRC and the now shrunken ROC/Taiwan drew on similar repertoires in their overlapping assumptions about what was necessary and desirable in terms of the types of individual the state needed to recruit. They both took as given that observable behavior and demeanor reflected inner morality, and that properly deployed commitments generated by campaign-style mobilization would enable state administrators to do more with less. They also held that there was no contradiction between expert knowledge, political loyalty, and individual morality: indeed these characteristics were equally essential and mutually reinforcing. What differed were the ways in which each went about recruiting, evaluating, and establishing norms of appropriate behavior. These differences in turn revealed a great deal about how each state understood itself and projected its image in microcosm – through the figure of the state administrator.

What's in a Name: The Ambivalence of Labeling State Administrators[7]

What things are called, and how they are valenced either positively or negatively, is as much political as it is descriptive. During the Republican period and the early 1950s, what state administrators were called was highly variable. Some of the terms used were quite old, while others were of relatively recent vintage. At present, the terms *gongwuyuan* (公務員 – "public servant" or more literally, "public matters person") for the ROC/Taiwan and *ganbu* (幹部 – cadre) for the revolutionary PRC have become so naturalized that it is difficult to imagine a world in which *gongwuyuan* and *ganbu* were not the standard designations for state administrators. But in the quarter century before 1949, other terms jostled and overlapped with *gongwuyuan* and *ganbu*, and they continued to do so into the early 1950s. *Gongwuyuan* came into use in the early 1930s, after the establishment of the National Government's Examination Yuan and Ministry of Personnel. These government bodies were ideationally and normatively supported by a loose coalition of reformist politicians, state administrators, academics, and journalists whom I elsewhere call the Administrative Efficiency School, after the journal *Xingzheng Xiaolü* (Administrative Efficiency – 行政效率), which was published in the mid-1930s in

---

[7] Parts of this section draw from Julia C. Strauss, "*Wenguan* (lettered official), *Gongwuyuan* (public servant), and *Ganbu* (cadre): The Politics of Labelling State Administrators in Republican China," Indiana East Asian Working Paper Series on Language and Politics in Modern China, No. 6, Summer, 1995. Available at https://scholarworks.iu.edu/dspace/handle/2022/22839.

simultaneous English and Chinese editions. This pocket of administrative reformers in state rather than GMD party organizations was animated by the then prevailing tenets of US public administration, particularly by a key textbook by Leonard White entitled *Introduction to the Study of Public Administration* (1927, with a further six editions, the last of which was published in 1955). White and others in the growing field of American public administration endorsed the principles of technocratic and "scientific" administration, just as the reach of the US federal state was expanding under the New Deal. In this view, the way to achieve "scientific" administration was to establish a strict separation between the political and the administrative. The impartiality and obedience of a strictly neutral bureaucracy was to be protected from patronage and political interference through, among other things, entry by open examination.[8] These features would, in principle, lead to high degrees of efficiency, effectiveness, and loyalty – all strong desiderata for a weak central government such as Guomindang China in the 1930s.

Throughout the Republican period, *gongwuyuan* was, however, a category that was more aspirational than it was based in reality. Even in the Nanjing Decade (1927–1937), the lack of resources, political infighting, ongoing militarization and civil war, and de facto incorporation of warlords and local elites under a thin veneer of national unity made for a government with weak projective power that devolved much of its formal authority to provincial and local elites. Even at the very center of power, there was strife between different factions within the GMD party-state. In the regime's critical early years, central government positions were parceled out on the basis of political considerations to rivals, to protégés, or given to experienced "Old Beiyang" bureaucrats from the warlord government era of the 1910s and 1920s.

There was also a great deal of confusion within the Guomindang as to how the Sun Yat-sen unitary principle of *yidang zhiguo* (以黨治國) – to use the (GMD) Party to rule the country – should be squared with his chosen form of "Five Power Government," which suggested division of power for central authority. The Examination Yuan and Ministry of Personnel were established in the early 1930s as part of Five Power Government, and convened prestigious (and murderously competitive) civil service examinations from 1931 onwards, but these exams only ever provided the route into state service for a tiny minority. *Gongwuyuan* were

---

[8] Taylor, *Principles of Scientific Management*, p. 29. The notion of a strict separation between "policy" and "administration" in the "science" of public administration went back more than a generation to Woodrow Wilson's foundational piece, "The Study of Administration," in 1888. But it found new life and a range of new applications under the expanding American state of the New Deal.

"created" through the Ministry of Personnel (Quanxu Bu), which established and enforced a central system of appointment classification called the *jian jian wei* (簡薦委 – "selected, recommended and appointed") that standardized pay scales and grades of service, and limited the number of upward promotions. Some wings of the National Government – notably in organizations like the Maritime Customs, the Salt Inspectorate, and the National Postal Service – already possessed strict civil service systems modeled on either the Indian Colonial Service or French civil service and were permitted to retain those separate systems of recruitment and advancement until well into the 1930s. The Ministry of Foreign Affairs had always recruited through its own very difficult entrance examinations. Still, over the course of the 1930s, state ministries increasingly came to request that the Examination Yuan put on specialized civil service entry examinations tailored to their needs.[9]

These incremental steps towards depoliticization and a technocratically based civil service ended with the outbreak of war in 1937. During the Sino-Japanese war (1937–1945), the GMD lost quality control over its own civil bureaucracy, which swelled by a factor of four or more. Associated as it was with strict norms and rules of impersonal civil service and recruitment by examination that were undercut by the stresses of wartime, it is little wonder that the new Ministry of Personnel's own preferred term of *gongwuyuan* never achieved universal currency. Instead, hybrid terms to denote state administrators proliferated: *zhengwuguan* (政務官 – political affairs official) *shiwuguan* (事務官 – practical matters official), and *zhiyuan* (one in an office/position – 職員). Variations on *renyuan* (人員 – personnel) also proliferated: *xingzheng renyuan* (行政人員 – administrative personnel), and *caizheng renyuan* (財政人員 – finance personnel) were also common. In popular discourse, the term *guanyuan* (官員 – one who is an official) also continued to be used, typically as invective.

Relatively little is known about recruitment, promotion, and the workings of personnel in the CCP in the pre-1949 periods in which it administered territory and thus behaved in state-like ways. The term that would later come to dominate the CCP's discourse on party, state, and military administrators – *ganbu* (幹部 – cadre) was not in common use for civil administrators until the early 1950s. *Ganbu* itself was a foreign import. Sources agree that the term was originally *cadre* in French, but diverge on whether *ganbu* came into Chinese as a loanword from Japanese in the 1920s or via Russian in the late 1930s.[10] What is clear is that *ganbu* was seldom used in the 1920s,

---

[9] See Strauss, *Strong Institutions in Weak Polities*, pp. 29–57 for a fuller discussion of these trends in the 1930s.

[10] Yang Youwu and Wang Zhenchua, *Zhongguo gongwuyuan baike cidian*, p. 191; Gong Jianhua, *Xiandai Ganbu Xue*, p. 11.

and only with a fair amount of ambivalence and confusion for two decades thereafter. In the 1920s and 1930s, both the CCP and the GMD preferred the term *dangyuan* (黨員 – party member). Insofar as it was necessary to refer to administrators with distinctly civilian rather than military or party roles, the CCP tended to go by *renyuan* and *zhiyuan* (personnel/person in office). Even Mao preferred to use *gongzuo renyuan* (工作人員 – work personnel) and *zhengfu gongzuo renyuan* （政府工作人員 – government work personnel).

Originally, *ganbu* was reserved for special "backbone" (*gugan* – 骨干) individuals who were core activists. It was not until the Jiangxi Soviet period of the early 1930s, when the CCP held a significant territory that needed to be administered, that *ganbu* began to circulate more widely. Even then, there was so much confusion about who was and was not a *ganbu* (as well as so little separation of civilian and military roles) that training manuals had to lay this out by explicitly equating *ganbu* with relevant military rank: a middle-ranking *ganbu* was the equivalent of a platoon to assistant company commander, and upper-ranking *ganbu* corresponded to commanders from the company to the assistant regiment.[11] It wasn't until the outbreak of the Sino-Japanese War in 1937 that Mao significantly expanded the notion of *ganbu* to encompass *all* revolutionary heroes:

> To guide a great revolution, there must be a great party and many excellent cadres ... these cadres must understand Marxism-Leninism, they must have political insight and the ability to work, they must be full of the spirit of self sacrifice, capable of solving problems independently ... they must be the *selfless heroes of the nation and the class* [emphasis added] ... our revolution depends on the cadres, just as Stalin has said.[12]

Uncertainty about what to call those in administrative positions within the party-state lingered for quite some time. As late as December 1951, internal documents of the Shanghai Bureau of Personnel were still citing a Rao Shushi speech from August 1951 entitled "How to Be a Good People's Public Servant" (*zenyang zuo yige haode renmin gongwuyuan* – 怎樣做一個好的人民公務員), as a key text for the work of the Shanghai cadre training school.[13] It took until the completion of the *sanfan* and

---

[11] CC, Reel 8, Document 31, "Ganbu zhengzhi jiaoyu jihua" (A draft plan for cadre political education). N.d.

[12] *MZX* "Strive to Win Over Millions," Vol. 1, pp. 267–268.

[13] SMA B23/1/24. "Shanghai shi renmin zhengfu ganbu xuexiao di'yi qi jiaoyu jihua an" (Draft plan for the Shanghai people's government first cadre training and education session) (p. 1 of internal document), n.d. 1951. Rao Shushi gave the original report "Zenyang zuo yige hao de renmin gongwuyuan" on October 30, 1951 to the East China Military Region Committee's Summing up Meeting on Study in Government Organs. This report was reproduced for widespread dissemination within officialdom in *Huadong Zhengbao* No. 21 (December 20, 1951), pp. 1–12.

wufan campaigns in 1952–1953 for *ganbu* (civil administrators as generalist heroes of the nation and the class) to fully drive out the use of *zhiyuan* (someone holding an office or position). It wasn't until the mid-1950s that *ganbu* expanded to "all those who are working personnel in party, state or military units with a definite culture, a level of specialization and ... exclusive of soldiers, handymen, and workers of that sort."[14] In marked contrast to its military organization, which sorted out standard hierarchical ranks early and seemingly without much cognitive dissonance, the CCP settled on and standardized the meaning of *ganbu* for civil administrators only with great reluctance over a period of many years, suggesting that it wasn't until the revolution was tied to state building that all working state personnel had to become heroes alongside party and army personnel who already *were* heroes.

Wartime conditions also led the GMD to *ganbu,* as the party increasingly subjected previously distinct party, military, and state administration to very similar kinds of military-cum-party indoctrination. Given the GMD's severe dearth of resources once it lost its economic and political base in the lower Yangzi delta after the Japanese invasion of 1937, it turned to short-term intensive training courses (*xunlian ban/xunliantuan* – 訓練班/訓練團) as an inexpensive way to shore up loyalty and socialize large numbers of young, unproven recruits into the GMD's norms and aims. Some of these training courses, particularly the more functionally specialized ones set up by central ministries in such fields in finance, tax collection, communications, accounting, and hygiene, continued to refer to their trainees by the more neutral term *renyuan* (人員 – personnel). But training courses for GMD Party members, for those with high-ranking state offices, and for generalist civilian administrators working in county and municipal government organizations all openly used the term *ganbu.*

Open civil service examinations continued to be held during this time of militarization and deinstitutionalization. But the GMD's shift towards emphasis on loyalty and military-style discipline resulted in partification and militarization that had a direct impact on the Examination Yuan's norms of merit and politically neutral civil service. In 1939, the rules of the civil service examinations changed dramatically, when the Examination Yuan was forced to approve a new system called the *chushi zaishi* (preliminary examination/re-examination – 初試再試). This required those who passed the civil service examination to then spend another six months of political training at the Central Political University (Zhengzhi Daxue) prior to a secondary examination on GMD Party principles and ideology before assignment to a post. In short, wartime

---

[14] Yang Youwu and Wang Zhenchuan, op cit.

pressures *ganbu*-ified state administrators who only a few years previously would have been understood to be *gongwuyuan*. In 1939, the leader of the Guomindang's central *xunlian* apparatus, Wang Dongyuan, could proclaim:

Why do we need cadres (*ganbu*)? Upon whom, then, will our mission of reviving the race and building a new country then depend, [if not for cadres]? . . . cadres are the leaders of the revolution . . . and although we currently lack cadres, we must look for cadres from party, state, and army . . . to lead and organize the broad masses of people.[15]

Such sentiments, and even the supporting vocabulary, were virtually indistinguishable from those of Mao at this time. Given the difficult circumstances of the late 1930s and 1940s – militarization, invasion by a much stronger foe, weak institutions, and aroused nationalism – both the CCP and GMD converged on the notion that *ganbu* were more than government functionaries; they were the heroic, generalist leaders of the revolutionary party and the state who would lead China, despite its weaknesses in conventional terms, to victory through the triumph of human organization and will. Wartime intensified a latent fracture within the GMD in how it imagined its state and the agents who represented it. The GMD's founding formula of *yidang zhiguo* (using the party to rule the state – 以黨治國), in combination with Chiang Kai-shek's own prefer-ences for military models and metaphors, presumed the dominance of the single, now heavily militarized party to lead the country into modernity. In contrast, the entire apparatus of the Examination Yuan and Ministry of Personnel (as well as the larger structure of Sunist Five Power Government) presumed sober technocracy, efficiency, and obedience to political masters. Under the stress of the militarization of the 1940s, the GMD's take-up of *ganbu* suggested patterns of thinking not unlike the concurrent CCP's: a state administration of militarized, partified heroes able to accomplish the extraordinary. Under wartime conditions of scar-city and isolation, the hero-*ganbu*'s ability to make do with less to create more, his self-reliance, and his intensive inculcation into party-state norms would result in an individual who could make correct decisions under any situation.

Ganbu were thus the very opposite of sober *gongwuyuan* technocrats, with their procedural rule orientation, mechanical application of policy, and constant need for more resources to function. Nor did *ganbu* dis-appear entirely from the GMD lexicon once it had retreated to Taiwan. Although *ganbu* seldom surfaced in open publications and proclamations

---

[15] Wang Dongyuan, *Ganbu Xunlian Wenti*, pp. 4–5.

about central state administrators or the civil service, and very rarely appeared in any of the English-language materials disseminated by the ROC/Taiwan, *ganbu* continued in party-state discourse long after 1949. As late as 1970, the Taiwan provincial GMD was still publishing handbooks for sub-provincial "cadres to preserve talent" or "cadres in Taiwan's local self-government."[16] In Taiwan, open "cadre speak" after 1949 appears to have been confined largely to party, military, and quasi-military organizations like the police, and in training for local government personnel. Formally, state organization labels and procedures were organized along the lines of *gongwuyuan* civil service. In parallel with its rival across the Taiwan Strait, the GMD party completely controlled the civil bureaucracy and indeed strengthened its grip on state organizations after 1949. Most of those in positions of responsibility also belonged to the GMD. Important policies were announced in state organizations only after the relevant GMD Party session or committee meeting to decide on what policy should be. In the Taiwan of the 1950s and after, the same individuals were *ganbu* for GMD Party meetings and training institutes, but *gongwuyuan* once they walked back into their offices in state organizations. Under these circumstances it is little wonder that there was slippage in terminological use, not the least for those who held simultaneous GMD Party and ROC government positions.

As these two competitive regimes claiming legitimacy over all of China established themselves in their respective territories in the years immediately after 1949, each needed to set up a credible system for recruiting, assessing, and promoting civil administrators who could: (a) serve as the embodiment of the new state; and (b) implement state directives in a competent manner. In so doing, each drew quite different lessons from the successes (for the CCP) and failures (for the GMD) of the recent past, which made those in charge of state personnel unusually receptive to different models propagated by their respective international patrons (the Soviet Union and the United States) about what "good systems" ought to look like. At the same time each drew from a common framework of assumptions about how a "good administrator" was supposed to behave when in post as a servant of the party-state and its revolution.

---

[16] See *Sheng yixia gejii lingdao ganbu baoju rencai shouce* (Handbook to preserve talent for leading sub-provincial cadres), and Pan Zhenqiu, *Gongtong wei fazhan difang jiaoyu er nuli: xiang geming shishi yanjiuyuan 57 nian taiwan difang zizhi ganbu jiangxi huiyi* (Together develop local education industriousness: implement the revolution institute's 1968 Taiwan self-government cadre conference). On police cadre training, see Cai Huiyu (Huiyu Caroline Tsai), *Guangfu Taiwan yu Zhanhou Jingzheng: Taiwan Jingcha Ganbu Xunlian Ban Koushu Fantan Jilü.*

Becoming Ganbu: Lessons from the North Applied in Sunan

The young PRC was no less influenced by its recent history than was the shrunken and attenuated ROC/Taiwan, and was no less determined to implement its experiences in regions far removed from their original context. For the CCP, these were quite the opposite of the negative lessons drawn by the GMD as it assessed its catastrophic failures of the 1940s. For the CCP, the years of civil war and class struggle culminated in a much quicker outright military victory than anyone had predicted. This startling success led to disproportionate influence for Mao Zedong, and validated his favored tactics: mass mobilization, close links with the people, criticism and self-criticism, and voluntarist utopianism. If the CCP had managed to win the civil war so quickly against such long odds on the basis of Mao's preferred strategies, who was to say what sorts of victories in consolidating the revolution and transforming state and society could not be as rapidly achieved now that the CCP had taken power and established the People's Republic of China? A natural affinity existed between the revolutionary goals of a Leninist party that meta-phorically conceived of itself as a heroic combat party and the actions of its revolutionary army that *was* undeniably heroic in overcoming a larger, better-equipped foe during the civil war.[17] And who better to serve as the foot soldiers of the heroic combat party than a collectivity of individual heroes? Mao was already on record as hating the institutionalized inequal-ity and hierarchy of regular state institutions in bureaucracies:

We must not be bureaucratic in our method of work in mobilizing the masses . . . this great evil, bureaucratism (*guanliao zhuyi* – 官僚主义) must be thrown into the cesspool, because no comrade likes it . . . one of the manifest actions of bureau-cracy is slackness in work due to indifference or perfunctoriness: another mani-festation is authoritarianism . . . what is needed is energetic agitation to convince the masses[to] do all kind of work for economic mobilization.[18]

How, exactly, state administrators were to be both revolutionary heroes and functional administrators was unstated, as were the finer details of how "energetic agitation" was to result in the kind of mobilization that would translate into national economic development. Any plan for crash economic development would necessarily involve record keeping, target setting, regular evaluation, and most importantly, regular channels of information flow between higher and lower levels in a government

---

[17] See Jowitt, *Revolutionary Breakthroughs and National Development*, p. 7 for the definition of revolutionary breakthrough.
[18] Mao Zedong, "Bixuzhuyi jingji gongzuo," *MZX* Vol. 1, pp. 118–119. In English transla-tion, "We must attend to economic work," *SWM*, pp. 135–136.

hierarchy which presumed the most basic rule of all for both party and state: that decisions made at higher levels were incumbent and binding on lower levels. Even if this was not all spelt out, the clear intention of Mao and others in the top echelon of the CCP in the early 1950s was to recruit individuals capable of heroic and practical action able to, on demand, switch into a bureaucratic modality with all the rules, forms, bureaucratic box ticking, and report filing that came along with the first ordering principle of bureaucracy: obedience and submission to formal hierarchical organization. This was, needless to say, a combination of attributes that very few possessed.

How organizations that were not inherently military and heroic could be created given such a back history of insistence on mobilization, agitation, and application of concentrated human will to overcome objective obstacles was unclear. Nor were there many hints as to how bona fide revolutionary heroes would be expected to adapt to and function within a set of everyday demands that were routine, sedentary, hierarchical, and paperwork oriented. In Sunan, the young People's Republic of China required a large number of committed civilian administrators to set up the basic institutions of the state, stabilize the economy, resettle refugees, ensure that taxes were collected and urban populations fed, and get people back to work. This would have been a tall order for any government coming to power in 1949. But the CCP expected more than just loyalty and a modicum of competence. It also demanded highly committed individuals ready to utterly transform society. In addition to their technical competence, the state's agents had to be activist heroes whose "close links to the masses" would make possible the implementation of heroic revolutionary programs.

The sheer demands of economic reconstruction in 1949, in combination with the PRC's plans to establish a planned economy, meant that from the outset the new revolutionary government had to rapidly build state capacity by quickly recruiting newcomers and adequately managing those already in post. Of necessity, there was a multiplicity of paths to becoming *ganbu* in Sunan immediately after 1949. Holdover government officials, revolutionary cadres from already liberated areas, newly educated students, and specially targeted individuals from respectably proletarian backgrounds all found places in the service of the new regime. The logic for the inclusion of each group differed, as did the potential upsides and shortcomings that each of these groups was presumed to possess.

Personnel retained from the Nationalist government were assumed to have high degrees of knowledge and technical competence, but to be from reactionary political backgrounds and of highly suspect political reliability. In Sunan they were initially retained in large numbers because the young state did not have nearly enough technically competent personnel to staff critical state organizations. Cadres from "Old liberated areas" and high-ranking demobilized soldiers (there was no significant distinction between these two categories until 1953) had impeccable revolutionary credentials with high political reliability, but their lack of education and technical competence was a perennial headache for the regime's planners. Recently graduated students from universities and technical schools, particularly if they came from non-elite backgrounds, as well as literate youth from good class backgrounds, were the least problematic, as the CCP assumed that young minds were amenable to correct political ideas, with the added benefit of soaking up new technical skills relatively quickly.

The takeover of Shanghai illustrates in microcosm how these processes worked on the ground. In the spring and early summer of 1949, the CCP came into the big cities along the Yangzi (and Shanghai in particular) in a relatively smooth way due to good troop discipline and the CCP's own announced policies of moderation and inclusion. With a fairly small incoming group of 3,000 cadres and 895 special police, many of whom continued south with the army after a short period of time, the new government had to take over and set up party branches from scratch in nine Shanghai municipal bureaus (*ju* – 局) ten offices (*chu* – 处), the police, municipal district administrations, and the major state factories under the outgoing National Government. The official moderate policy of "unity, education and reform" (*tuanjie, jiaoyu, gaizao* – 團結, 教育, 改造) was born out in the actions of the new government in its first year in power. The first and most common path to eventual cadre-dom in 1949 was one of inertial motion: to have been a Nationalist government civilian administrator with *yewu* (業務 – functional) skills who was already in service. According to one internal report, of the 45,280 holdovers from the National Government Shanghai municipal administration, nearly 85 percent (38,331) were eventually reassigned to official positions in their spheres of competence. At this early stage, it was only those with high ranks in Guomindang Party, military, or intelligence organizations who were considered irreconcilable counterrevolutionaries who could not be worked with.[19]

---

[19] SMA B1/1/1000. "Renshi chu gongzuo zongjie, 1949 xiabannian" (Summary of Office of Personnel Work, second half of 1949). It is not clear how these numbers were calculated: but it is likely that they included central municipal organizations, district municipal organizations, and, at this early date, quite possibly included areas that would in short order become the separate category of *jiaoqu* (outer districts – 郊区). Only two and a half years later, internal statistics put the total numbers in the Shanghai central municipal administration at 10,377. SMA B23/1/85. Shanghai Renshi Ju. "Sanfan qianhou ganbu qingkuang tongji, 1–2" 1952 (Statistics on ganbu before and after the sanfan movement).

While we do not know exactly how many revolutionaries active in military units before 1949 were assigned to permanent positions in Shanghai, it is clear that under the system of regional military rule (1949–1953), the most important positions in Shanghai and Sunan went to old cadres of high military rank with co-appointments in the East China Military Region. Most of the 3,000 *ganbu* active in the take-over in Shanghai in mid-1949 also hailed from the military. Some remained in Shanghai (and other big cities along the Yangzi) while others joined the military drive south after Shanghai was taken.[20] But there was a vast gap between CCP leaders at the very top of the East China Military Region and rank and file old *ganbu*. One report from the Shanghai Bureau of Personnel made plain that the latter were more than a little disgruntled by the higher salaries of the more numerous (and better educated) hold-over officials. They "hated getting too close to holdover officials" whom they considered to be ideologically suspect and prone to "poor work styles."[21] They chafed at repeatedly being passed over for promotion by a tsunami of young upstarts with educational qualifications and/or practical technical skills recruited into state service in the early 1950s, and they griped that these youngsters had only a superficial knowledge of Marxism-Leninism and sometimes weren't even party members.[22] Personnel regulations actively encouraged the recruitment of those with "clean histories, good health, progressive thought, and assured education levels" (*lishi qing, shenti jiankang, sixiang xianjin, jiaoyu jianding* – 歷史清, 身體健康, 思想先進, 教育堅定), which meant that old cadres, while granted some positions, were in practice shunted aside in favor of the young and more technically qualified.[23]

Recent graduates of technical schools, universities, and upper senior schools (*gaozhong* – 高中) were much in demand and actively recruited, particularly when they came with the benefit of clear calligraphic hands and clean class backgrounds.[24] The young PRC's preference for the

[20] We do not know how many, because the archives of the East China Military Region are closed, as are the personnel files (*geren dang'an* – 個人檔案) of individuals, kept by the CCP's organization department rather than by Bureaus of Personnel.

[21] SMA B23/1/32/ "Shifu xunlianban diyinian lai gongzuo zongjie" (Summary work report on the first municipal training course), n.d. 1950/1951.

[22] SMA B23/1/34. Shanghai Renshi Ju, "1952 xia bannian shishi daliang tiba ganbu fangzhen de gongzuo baogao" (Work report on the implementation of the guiding principle to promote large numbers of cadres, second half of 1952). See also Neil Diamant, *Embattled Glory* (Rowman & Littlefield, 2009), on how reluctant most *danwei* were to accept veterans for permanent posts.

[23] NMA 5010/3/158. Nanjing Renshi Ju." Guanyu xishou renyuan" (on recruiting personnel)," 1955.

[24] Wang Wenqing (王文清), interview. In this lengthy interview nearly half a century after his initial recruitment into the precursor to the Jiangsu Provincial government, he

young, the easily molded, and the at least minimally technically competent is borne out in the partial statistics that are currently available. By one count at the end of 1956, the total in the Shanghai Municipal Tax Bureau *bianzhi* (including district and branch offices) stood at 6,329. Of this number, 4,726 (74.67 percent) had joined the organization after 1949. Some 3,339 (52.75 percent) were under the age of 30; and 2,997 (47.35 percent) had either an advanced senior or upper middle school education. While at the end of 1949 holdover officials had been the majority, by 1956, GMD holdover officials and old cadres *together* comprised only 1,603 (25.32 percent), and those above the age of 35 had smaller numbers still at 1,409 (22.26 percent).[25] The early to mid-1950s were indeed a good time to come of age if one possessed technical skills, a modicum of formal education, and a class background that wasn't obviously landlord or reactionary.

Ensuring Virtue and Talent: Paths to State Administration in the Early 1950s

Despite their claims to be utterly different from each other, the young PRC and ROC/Taiwan organized their party-states and conceptualized the role of their state administrators in similar ways. Both established a formalized, hierarchical *bianzhi* structure with ostensibly strict limits on how many could be appointed, at what rank, and with what salaries. While both formally distinguished between party and state, in practice there was so much overlap that even those who spent their entire careers in state administrative organizations were hard put to point clearly to where and how party and state were differentiated. This was no less true for the GMD than it was for the CCP. In the words of one administrator with a long career in the Ministry of Personnel (who was himself most unusual as a non-GMD Party member in the Ministry of Personnel), "well, they never hung a sign outside indicating this is a GMD work unit (*danwei*) but of course everyone knew that it was! Nothing ever happened in the office until after the Party meetings were held."[26] *Yidang zhiguo* – be it Communist or Nationalist – meant that the dominant party did not merely pass legislation to then be implemented by state organizations. Since most state agents were themselves members of the ruling party, and

cheerfully chanted the recruiting slogan of the time: *sixiang jinbu, shenti jiankang, shehui guanxi qingbai* (advanced thought, healthy physique, and clean social relations).

[25] SMA B97/1/238. Shanghai Shuiwu Ju. "Shi shuiwu ju 1956 nian quanguo ganbu dingqi tongji baogao" (Shanghai Tax Bureau Statistical Report on Set Numbers of Cadres for 1956).

[26] Zhao Qiwen, interview, July 4, 1995.

nearly all with substantial decision-making authority held comparable rank in party organization, the CCP and GMD were shadow organizations that operated within the formal structure of the state. Policy was not established and communicated from outside formal state organizations through orders and directives relayed by a political appointee at the top; rather it was carried into the organization by party members on the basis of party meetings and Leninist discipline by individuals who were already there, often meeting as party committees in the same offices and rooms that were used for state activities.

In addition to these similar structures, the PRC and ROC/Taiwan worked within overlapping ideational frames regarding their state personnel: what kind of faces their state administrators were supposed to present to society, how they should look and behave, and (in a covert affirmation of much older Confucian notions of self-cultivation), how they as individuals should improve themselves through study, demeanor and proper training. Both held that mechanical implementation of orders from above was insufficient: the state needed *committed* men, preferably committed *young* men, with the right kinds of attitudes, the right emphasis on self-mastery, and the right kinds of acceptance of discipline and hierarchy. For these reasons, the pre-1949 war years led both to focus on training (*xunlian/peixun*) as an inexpensive way to generate the right kinds of political commitments and the right kinds of skills.

For neither the young PRC in Sunan, nor the now shrunken ROC in Taiwan was there any contradiction at all between the desire to inculcate the right kind of values (including but going far beyond loyalty) and the necessity for technical/applied expertise. Although we now know that, in the late 1950s, Mao's own worries about revisionism and party institutionalization would prompt a series of campaigns in which "Redness" (*hong* – 紅) and "Expertise" (*zhuan* – 專) were rhetorically invoked in such a way that the former crowded out the latter, in the early 1950s this intractable tension was in an unimagineable future. Instead, documents produced by personnel offices in Sunan repeatedly referred to the need to inculcate both "virtue (*de* 德) and talent (*cai* 才)." The notion of virtuous and talented state officials had a lengthy pedigree that went back to the late imperial period. Quite unlike the later uneasy juxtaposition of "Redness" and "Expertise," the early- to mid-1950s pairing of virtue and talent presumed that these two elements were mutually reinforcing: an excess of virtue would properly inform the deployment of talent.

In Sunan, the young PRC was clear in its desire to select for *ganbu* who possessed simultaneous virtue-and-talent (*de jian cai* – 德兼才). By late

1952, the Shanghai Bureau of Personnel defined how to recognize the presence of *de jian cai* through the individual's: (1) visible activism in political campaigns; (2) being of good political background; (3) having begun practical work in the previous few years; (4) having gained a degree from an advanced special school on an applied subject (*zhuanke*); and, whenever possible, (5) possessing either CCP or Communist Youth League membership.[27] The order of these desirable attributes suggests that virtue (as demonstrated by action in involvement in campaigns and as an inherited attribute of good class background) was the most important factor. At the same time, the indicators of virtue and talent encompassed potential and already demonstrated action. Good political background predisposed one to virtue, activism in political campaigns demonstrated that virtue, and either China Youth League or CCP membership reinforced both, a degree in a functionally useful subject indicated dedication to study, and several years of work experience confirmed the practical application of that dedication.

At the outset of regime consolidation in 1949 and 1950, candidates who fulfilled all the desiderata for *de jian cai* were in regrettably short supply. Most of those available possessed a modicum of either *de* or *cai* but not both, or not enough of both. Holdover officials had *cai* (talent in technical expertise and higher education) to spare, but were typically lacking in the types of revolutionary virtue that the CCP wished for its state administrators: loyalty, enthusiasm, and close links to the people.[28] "Old (military) cadres" by definition had a surfeit of heroic virtue, but they seldom had any *cai* to speak of as many were functionally illiterate, and were utterly ill equipped with the knowledge base to administer urban areas and make a planned economy work. The young had the virtue of little attachment to the old ways of doing things and tended to absorb both technical knowledge and revolutionary values more quickly than the middle aged. But they were still unformed, with much to learn in terms of how to manifest both *de* and *cai*. Recognizing these problems, the revolutionary state made it its business to fill in those gaps by intensifying the kinds of techniques that had served the CCP so well during the civil war years: intensive small group settings to train the individual in what he lacked in either virtue or talent.

---

[27] SMA B23/1/34. Shanghai Renshi Ju, "Guanyu 1952 xiabannian shishi daliang tiba ganbu fangzhen de gongzuo zongjie baogao" (Summary work report on the principles of realizing large-scale promotion of ganbu in the second half of 1952).

[28] SMA B23/1/32. Shanghai Renshi Ju. "Sifu xunlianban diyinian lai gongzuo zongjie" (Shanghai Bureau of Personnel, "Work Summary of the Municipal Government's First Year of Training Groups"), 1950.

"The Master Leads the Apprentice: system for reserve *ganbu*": Irregular and Intensive Training for "Virtue and Talent"

In response to these gaps, the young PRC established a range of intensive short-term training sessions at all levels for both technical and generalist personnel, so that the individual *ganbu* would be forever equipped to inculcate himself in proper norms of virtue while also being practically and functionally competent. In Sunan, this started almost immediately upon takeover. By late August 1949, the CCP in Shanghai had set up training institutes or specialist schools for cadres in such different areas as youth work, general reconstruction, personnel and appointment, Shanghai's outer districts, the Women's Federation, arts and culture, primary and secondary education, CCP party affairs, the police, and the East China Military Region news outlet. Large numbers attended. The smallest group was the Women's Federation at 60, and the largest two were in education (704) and the police (683). These early training courses were, for the most part, short-term informational sessions of between one and ten days that concentrated on current government policy and how it was distinguished from the outgoing Guomindang.[29]

Holdover officials were a special headache. In 1949–1950, the Shanghai government was reliant on the many holdovers who had very high educational qualifications, were industrious, and were a veritable fount of technical knowledge about how their domains worked and how to get things done, thus scoring very well on "talent." But these holdovers typically had "complicated personal histories" (*lishi fuza* – 歷史複雜), displayed an intolerable superiority complex over workers and peasants, and went through only the most superficial of motions with respect to political study. Worse, they were also cynical about politics, carped over many of the CCP's policies, and even openly doubted the ability of the CCP to reconstruct Shanghai. Highly placed division chiefs (*sizhang* – 司 長) in their fifties and sixties were the most recalcitrant. In the late autumn of 1949, these senior municipal administrators were brought to a special training center to learn the new regime's policies, norms, new ways of speaking, new official vocabularies, concepts, and use of titles. Evidently, the Shanghai Bureau of Personnel had its work cut out: in late 1950 it admitted that "even after nearly a year of training activities, there was not much success in altering the outlook of these oldsters." It noted trenchantly that these senior holdovers were intelligent enough "to recognize

---

[29] SMA A94/1/33. "Zhonggong Shanghai shiwei zuzhibu guanyu benshi xunlianban gaikuang biao" (CCP Shanghai Municipal party committee organization department general situation on Shanghai training courses table) August 20, 1949.

their dependence [on the CCP's new regime] but by the same token remaining deeply mistrustful, passive, and conservative in their thinking ... as the targets were so complicated and so used to operating in a backward political environment."[30] Although the new government's results in training holdover officials were disappointing, the Bureau of Personnel's persistence in continuing to train this group for nearly a year suggests that the CCP cared a great deal about infusing holdover personnel with proper revolutionary virtues as they implemented new policy dictates. The external forms of grudging compliance were recognized for what they were and were repeatedly deemed to be unacceptable. New China wanted state administrators who not only obeyed, but who also internalized its values as their own. Holdover personnel with "a subjectivist and functionalist stand, believing that without them nothing would happen; only interested in their on-the-job competence despite their non-existent grasp of politics ..." were not to be tolerated for long, and were either eased out or diluted with an influx of new recruits as quickly as the new government could manage.[31]

Old cadres (*lao ganbu* – 老幹部) who came south with the army but remained in Sunan suffered from a different set of shortcomings. They possessed a surplus of revolutionary *de* but were also almost totally lacking in *cai* due to their "low cultural level" (*wenhua shuiping di* – 文化水平低 i.e. lack of formal education). Like holdover officials, they needed *xunlian*. But this was to be a very different sort of training in order to ensure a bare minimum of *cai*, now assessed on the basis of elementary literacy. Municipalities and counties throughout Sunan set up large numbers of cadre training institutes and schools to teach basic reading and writing. Provincial and municipal-level schools for administrative cadres (*Xingzheng Ganbu Xuexiao*) that put on other training courses also offered supplementary education for old cadres to raise their educational qualifications to "at least" the equivalent of upper primary school (*gaoxiao* – 高小), in medium-length training sessions that lasted anywhere between several and six months. In theory, all *ganbu* without the equivalent of an upper primary school education had to report for this kind of supplementary training, and in at least Shanghai and Nanjing, there was a steady stream of less well-educated old cadres who attended.[32]

[30] Ibid.
[31] SMA B1/1/38. Shanghai Shi Zhengfu, "Guanyu diaocha shuiwuju ganbu shiyong qingkuang de baogao" (Shanghai Municipal Government Report on Investigating the Tax Bureau's Use of Ganbu), May 18, 1951.
[32] SMA B1/2/1817. Shanghai Shi Zhengfu, "Zhonggong shanghai shi renmin weiyuanhui xingzheng ganbu xuexiao weiyuanhui guanyu fengming banlie xuexiao jiesu shiyi de qingshi baogao" (CCP Shanghai municipal government people's committee and administrative cadre school committee eleventh requested report on school completion),

The requirements of construction and a planned economy made it necessary for the face of the revolutionary cadre to be transformed from a charismatic (if often illiterate) military hero to a practical and applied one with basic literacy and functional knowledge. In reality, the assignment of revolutionary old cadres to new government work units was fraught with tensions. Offices were reluctant to accept revolutionary veterans, technocrats already in office resented their potential for stroppiness, and their lack of formal education and technical expertise tended to limit them to the lowest rungs of the salary scale.[33] The contempt many old cadres held for holdover officials was, evidently, more than repaid by the arrogance of college educated and technically skilled holdovers, who openly called them country bumpkins (*tu baozi* – 土包子) who understood little, reckoning that "even if [their] simple and forthright ways stirred admiration, [their] lack of education, work ability, and social knowledge fell far short [of what was required]."[34]

Peixun (培訓 – cultivation and training) through officially recognized units was an integral part of both "getting good men" and therefore "strengthening organization" (*jiaqiang zuzhi* – 加強組織).[35] As almost all prospective *ganbu* had weaknesses of some kind that required extra inculcation into state norms of knowledge and behavior, Sunan and Shanghai institutionalized training for increasingly large numbers of *ganbu*. The Shanghai Bureau of Personnel wrote a lengthy report in April 1950 on the necessity of training *all ganbu*. According to this plan, cadres would be mixed together (from different units), with methods of study to include receiving reports from senior officials, listening to lectures, question and answer evening meetings, individual study, and informal discussions.[36] In 1951, the Sunan District General Office submitted a training plan for cadres from worker, peasant, and intellectual backgrounds that included party members, Youth Corps members, and the "masses." By 1951, Sunan had the infrastructure in place for training a projected 6,733 individuals. It had already established a party training school that covered political study, a Worker and Peasant Functional

August 31, 1956, and JPA 1/1/3 "Jiangsu sheng xingzheng ganbu ganbu xuexiao, 'Diyi qi gexiang gongzuo zongjie' (General work report on the first session [of the Jiangsu administrative ganbu school]), March 31, 1954.

[33] Diamant, pp. 155–177.

[34] SMA B23/1/10, "Guanyu sanda wenxian xuexi yu kaoqin zhidu shishi qingkuang de zongjie baogao" (Summary report on the implementation of the three great contributions for study and system for checking on work attendance) April 15, 1950.

[35] JPA Caizheng ting, 3/135. "1953 nian shuiwu ganbu peixun jihua caogao" (1953 Draft plan for [Jiangsu Bureau of Finance] Cultivation and Training of Tax Cadres), February 1953.

[36] SMA B23/1/10, "Guanyu sanda wenxian xuexi yu kaoqin zhidu shishi qingkuang de zongjie baogao," op cit.

Training Middle School for supplementary training, and specialized training institutes for public security and law, investigation and accounting, and infrastructure and water management.[37] Additional specialized training institutes were established in 1952. A training school for generalist municipal *ganbu* was set up by the Shanghai municipal government in late 1952. Sunan finance cadres were accommodated in Nanjing by a training institute for finance and tax personnel that had its first intake in October 1952, and other organizations within the Shanghai municipal administration (notably in the Hygiene Bureau and the Shanghai division of the People's Bank) were ordered to set up their own in-house training centers at roughly the same time.[38]

In early 1953, just after the *sanfan* (Three Antis) movement, when a tranche of holdover officials was expelled and the bureaucratic institutions of the state began a long period of expansion, there was a particularly pressing need for well-qualified cadres to step into roles in a rapidly growing state apparatus. In 1953, the Shanghai government's official *bianzhi* cadre totals were increased from 25,915 to 30,863. Of these new recruits, roughly 2,500 needed to be higher than the section level, but "the Shanghai government was short by over 80 backbone cadres at the section level and above."[39] The government was more than a little dissatisfied with many of those who had joined it in the early days after Liberation, as "the standard of their political work was low, and work was disconnected from their words and actions." In 1952, 9,161 cadres were still not up to a middle school standard (初中以上), although the majority of these (7,667) were in district rather than central municipal units. This presented huge problems, as "in auditing and accounting units there were cadres who didn't understand arithmetic, and those responsible for accounts in cooperatives had no idea how to review accounts." Between 1,500 and 2,000 holdover and newly appointed cadres also needed supplementary political training. Finally, organizations with large numbers of staff such as hygiene and the People's Bank were exhorted to step up their in-house "general social" training. When police, hygiene workers, and bank staff were included, the total number of those trained in house and at

---

[37] JPA. Sunan Gongshu (Sunan Government Bureau) 1/3070/192, "Ganbu xunlian jihua" (Cadre training plan) (n.d. but in a folder of documents from 1951).

[38] SMA B2/3/1/35. "Shanghai 1953 nian ganbu peixun zongjihua gaiyao" (Outline of Shanghai comprehensive ganbu cultivation and training plan for 1953).

[39] SMA B1/2/3179. "Shanghai shi renmin zhengfu xitong 1953 nian ganbu peiyang xunlian jihua gaiyao" (Shanghai Municipal People's Government system 1953 plan for cadre cultivation and training), January 1953. JPA Caizheng ting, 3/1. "Jiangsu shuiwu ganbu peixun ban diyi shiqi jiaoxue hezuo zongjie" (Jiangsu Bureau of Finance Summary Report on the first cooperative training and education session for tax cadres), October 1952.

specialist training institutes was expected to be 11,975, or slightly more than a third of the entire projected size of the Shanghai civil bureaucracy.[40] The Shanghai Bureau of Personnel estimated that there would be a need for an additional three-month intensive course focused on "integrating political study, cultivating backbone cadres, and thought reform" for between 3,100 and 3,600 cadres for the Shanghai government in 1953 alone. In the same year, the Jiangsu Bureau of Finance set forth its actual education and study plan to encompass "thorough political and functional education and training" in order to meet the different requirements of "using thought and consciousness as the base, alongside specialized functional training."[41]

But the young PRC's priorities in how it imagined its state agents can be best seen in the way the party-state marked those for leadership. Under the twin slogans of "The Master Leads the Apprentice" and "[establishing] the Reserve Cadre system", the Shanghai Bureau of Personnel stated its need for some 600 prospective "backbone" cadres to be targeted for an immediate reserve list to in turn become eligible for swift promotion. An intensive three-month training course was an integral component of drawing up this reserve list. New potential leaders were to be chosen after an internal process by which the unit leader would draw up a personnel plan that stated new open positions, and then targeted potential individuals according to their political consciousness and "excellence." After candidates were identified, they were then "lined up" (i.e. had the materials in their individual dossiers assembled and investigated-*paidui* – 排队) for scrutiny.

The intensive training process by which new cadres were to be groomed for quick promotion is instructive in its insistence on *de* and *cai*. While the Shanghai Bureau of Personnel acknowledged the subjective element of assessing virtue, it suggested several criteria by which virtue could be gauged. As *de* was manifested in an individual's ability to "establish a revolutionary position," a constant awareness and willingness to work on one's own shortcomings, an openness to "revealing oneself" (*biaoxian ziji* – 表現自己), and the ability to "bring one's accomplishments and good work back to the organization" (*gongzuo youdian he chengji yinggai guigong yu zuzhi* – 工作優點和成績應該歸功于組織) all pointed to *de*. Behaviorally, *de* also meant obedience to superiors and inculcating values of obedience and correct values in others: "grasping the thought of others, reporting to superiors and

[40] Ibid.
[41] JPA. Caizheng ting, 3/135. "1953 nian shuiwu ganbu peiyang xunlian jihua caogao," February 1953.

criticizing those who complain and are scattered in their work, support-ing the revolution with education, and continuing with one's own political study." In this context, virtue was not something that one did or did not possess, it was an inner quality that was made visible through an ongoing process that required constant vigilance, active practice, cultivation, and further study or training. Those with proper *de* were *also* able to discern its manifestation (or lack thereof) in co-workers. Perhaps because the criteria for *cai* were more objectively knowable and measurable, little specific instruction was given on how to evaluate it. For entry or promotion, *cai* was often equated with a formal educational qualification, typically in a technical or applied subject. But on the job itself, *cai* was understood to be as functional competence in actual work (*yewu*). When "talent" was assessed as behavior one manifested rather than a qualification one possessed, the criteria were relentlessly pragmatic: demonstrated by the individual who provided what the organization required rather than the functional competence that the individual already possessed, with a high premium placed on the degree to which the individual solved work problems independently.[42]

The young PRC insisted on state agents, preferably state agents who were young and of good class backgrounds, who manifested both virtue and talent. Virtue was made visible through the expression of the right kinds of thoughts, demeanor, ways of implementing the state's directives, and endless study and self cultivation. Talent was more prosaically man-ifested through technical qualification and applied functional expertise. If in reality individuals were more deficient in one or another, the party-state insisted that its state agents possess (or acquire) a minimum degree of both. The CCP aimed to achieve this through short-term intensive train-ing courses, which came in many different forms. Some, such as those set up for hygiene workers and the Shanghai branch of the People's Bank, were conducted in house by a newly established training division. Others, like the intensive three-month training given for cadres to make up a reserve list of cadres, were run by residential generalist training insti-tutes or party schools. Still others, as was the case in Jiangsu for cadres in tax and finance administration, attended specialist training institutes. Some concentrated on basic literacy, others on political study, and still others on functional skills and knowledge about policy. Whatever their specific emphasis, all required inculcation into both *de* and *cai*. The very

---

[42] SMA B1/2/3179, "Guanyu 1953 nian disi jidu jiaoyu gongzuo yewu huiyi de tongbao" (Circular from the [Bureau of Personnel] fourth quarter meeting on education work), December, 1953.

concepts of virtue and talent presumed that self-cultivation was never complete. While training courses and institutes could launch the process, there was always more that the individual could do to cultivate and manifest these qualities. There would always be more consciousness that could be raised, more rapidity of responsiveness to superiors that could be augmented, more creativity in solving problems that could be demonstrated, or more close links with the masses that could be forged. Insofar as there were systems for inculcating *de* and *cai*, they were as varied in organization and type as there were state administrators who needed to either reinvigorate their virtue or cultivate their talent. But in all cases they existed to kick-start a process that the individual would then continue on his own, unmediated by organizations through his direct commitment to the revolution.

The GMD Party-State after 1949: Formal Systems for Virtue and Talent

In contrast to the CCP in Sunan, the GMD was predisposed to privilege formal organizations, regular procedures and "law" (which in this context meant regularity and uniformity of administrative law) both before and after 1949. GMD legitimacy was explicitly grounded in a proclaimed continuity with the past. This presented immediate problems, because "the past" meant the GMD's ideational inheritance from Sun Yat-sen, and its formal position as the legitimately recognized government of China from 1928 onward. Unfortunately, the National Government's dismal record of governing during the 1940s suggested that too much emphasis on continuity could also be the kiss of death. The way around this was to claim that the formal institutions and regular procedures of the recent past had been correct in design, but had suffered from poor implementation and insufficient political commitment; with appropriately vigorous implementation and committed leadership, the structures and plans of the recent past could now be properly realized in Taiwan.

The GMD had a much easier time setting up a formal system for civilian state administrators in Taiwan than did the CCP in Sunan. It already *had* central government structures as well as a full complement of procedures that could be relocated to Taiwan (as well as an unpopular, but established, provincial government already in existence in Taiwan). It had a much smaller territory to control. It had nothing like the difficulties that the CCP did with having to depend, at least in the short term, on holdover officials from the old regime who were reluctant to accept new regime norms. The trauma of defeat and the long retreat to Taiwan for what was at best an unpromising future in 1949 and the first half of 1950 had weeded out most who were not highly committed, and the GMD Party rectification unleashed in 1950–1953 further pressured those in high positions who were engaging in now proscribed kinds of factional (or otherwise undesirable) activity.

Because it had at least nominally ruled China for the previous twenty-three years, the GMD also already possessed a formal structure based on Sun Yat-sen's notions of "Five Power Government," with top executive organizations of state being the Executive, Legislative, Judicial, Examination and Control Yuans, under which there were a variety of ministries and commissions. If before 1949 the actual activities of the government were highly concentrated in the Executive Yuan and in the military organizations closely associated with Chiang Kai-shek, the less powerful Examination Yuan and the Control Yuan were still part of the Nationalist central government that relocated to Taiwan, where the fluid circumstances after 1949 offered the political space for old institutions to be revived. The catastrophic loss of the mainland emboldened reformers within the GMD to conduct a root-and-branch review, the upshot of which allowed some policy space for the reestablishment of norms of impersonal civil service. The Central Reform Commission (*Zhongyang gaizao weiyuanhui* – 中央改造委員會) was established in August 1950 with an explicit mandate to do everything necessary to figure out what had gone wrong on the mainland and revive the GMD party-state in the here and now. Under the leadership of Chiang Ching-kuo, the CRC insisted on: (1) quashing subversion; (2) ridding the party-state of factionalism; (3) bringing the military under strict central control; (4) thorough party rectification; (5) land reform; and (6) re-establishing the norm of "the career open to talent."[43]

Like the young PRC in Sunan, the ROC/Taiwan was alert to the importance of attracting and retaining virtue and talent. The way in which it went about doing so was, however, quite different. For the GMD "talent" was, at least in principle, to be defined and ensured through formal examination and civil service systems. This emphasis on systems had multiple advantages. First, public servants who came to state service through open competitive examination acquired their positions in a way that was widely acknowledged to be fair while setting a high bar in terms of the objective measurement of "talent." Second, formal civil service systems provided for steady progression and reward through a system of "fair" annual evaluations. And third, the notion of civil service and its enduring trope (and partial myth) of the "career open to talent"

[43] Jay Taylor, *The Generalissimo's Son*, pp. 202–03; Bruce Dickson, "The Lessons of Defeat: The Reorganization of the Kuomintang on Taiwan, 1950–52."

had strong political and symbolic valence. The ideal of civil service had been bound up with notions of Chinese statecraft and the legitimacy of the late imperial state for centuries, but it was also uniquely resonant in the contemporary world of the "advanced" developed states of the West as well as China's chief competitor and nemesis, Japan.[44] An impartial civil service and a meritocracy validated by open civil service exams was that most useful of institutions – one that simultaneously validated China's deep past and was associated with contemporary progress and power. This was particularly so when the immediate political environment was characterized by exactly the kinds of favoritism and nepotism that open civil service exams were supposed to contain.

At first blush, the circumstances in which the Examination Yuan and Ministry of Personnel found itself after 1949 did not appear to be any more promising than those of the 1930s and 1940s. If anything, they seemed to be worse. The Examination Yuan had survived – if only just – the government's retreat from Nanjing and its eventual relocation to Taibei, where it was initially located in the old Confucius temple just north of downtown. The Examination Yuan was a relatively low priority for the retreating National Government, which concentrated on more pressing matters, like removing its core assets to Taiwan: the air force, the gold reserves, and the art treasures of the Forbidden City.[45] It was only the truly committed who left Nanjing in the spring of 1949 to commence what all knew to be a retreat with a highly uncertain outcome. Of these, it was only the most fortunate who managed to reach Taiwan. The experience of the Ministry of Personnel serves as an example of what so many had to go through to get to Taiwan at all. In the late 1940s, the Ministry of Personnel had 501 regular staff. Slightly more than half (264 of 501) set out from Nanjing with 350-odd boxes of archives in advance of the PLA in the spring of 1949. (The other half of the Ministry of Personnel remained in Nanjing, "passing the days idly and waiting for the end" until the PLA took over the city in April 1949.)[46]

The retreat from Nanjing was protracted and searing: from Nanjing to Wuzhou, Wuzhou to Chongqing, Chongqing to Chengdu, and then from Chengdu to Taiwan. At each stage the Ministry of Personnel lost people and boxes of archives. By August 1949, when the Ministry of Personnel retreated to Chongqing, their numbers were down to 166 individuals and

[44] Tsai, pp. 52–60.
[45] For the removal of the gold and silver reserves to Taiwan, see Lin, p. 83; on the removal of the art of the Palace Museum and Central Museum to Taiwan, see National Palace Museum, "Chronology of Events," www.npm.gov.tw/en/Article.aspx?sNo=03002803, accessed September 20, 2016.
[46] Interview, Zhou Weixun.

40-odd boxes of archives. Only 57 managed to follow the November 1949 order to leave Chongqing and regroup in Chengdu as quickly as possible. Hazardous transport by horse and three-wheeled cart made it impossible to salvage most of the remaining boxes of documents, which were abandoned in Chongqing. After a difficult ten days of travel, forty-seven arrived in Chengdu in early December. A lucky few managed to get on airplanes straight to Taiwan, but most had to make their way from Chengdu to the airport in Kunming, or somehow get to Hainan, from which air and sea links to Taiwan were still in operation.

When Ministry of Personnel staff regrouped in Taiwan in January of 1950, their numbers comprised less than 10 percent of the original organization (47 of 501).[47] This remnant arrived in Taiwan in a state of shock. A year of retreat resulted in trauma and economic ruin. Most had left major assets behind (and the money that was in circulation was in any case increasingly worthless due to hyperinflation). In Taiwan, there was nothing: no housing, salaries, and few organizational records. Worse, there was every reason to believe that the PLA would launch a successful amphibious invasion in the summer of 1950. Morale was extremely low. Those who made the journey to Taiwan had good reason to remember the early months and years on Taiwan to be the most difficult time of their lives.[48] But almost immediately after the GMD government on Taiwan was saved by the unexpected outbreak of the Korean War, these Examination Yuan refugees swung into action.

With the existence of the Guomindang regime no longer hanging by a thread, the Examination Yuan deemed it essential to convene a special sitting of its most prestigious examination, the *gaokao* (高考 – upper civil service examination) at the earliest possible moment. In a decision that was remarkably reminiscent of late-imperial county magistrates who held special sittings of the imperial civil service examinations as soon as possible after a restive area had been "pacified," the head of the Examination Yuan, Niu Yongjian, pulled out all the stops to hold a first "national" upper civil service examination in September 1950. Examination Yuan personnel were at this time so thinly stretched that they had to go to Hong Kong to personally cajole some ten former members from the Ministry of Examinations to relocate to Taiwan to administer this first *gaokao*.[49] (Later, Niu Yongjian, privately considered having pulled off a sitting of the *gaokao* so soon after the government's removal to Taiwan

---

[47] XKCJT, pp. 25–26.   [48] Luo Wanlei, interview.

[49] Li Feipeng, "Zhongguo kaozheng xuehui zhi tezhi yu wushi zhounian zhi huiyi" (Recollections for the fifty-year commemoration and study conference on the special nature of China's examination and government), in Kong Dejie, ed. *Zhongguo Kaozheng Xuehui Wushi Zhounian Jinian Tekan* (Taibei: Kaoshi Yuan, 1985), p. 8.

to be one of his most important career successes.)[50] This first *gaokao* in Taiwan was important mostly for its symbolism in demonstrating the regime's stability and its commitment to positively charged norm of the career open to talent even though the 1950 sitting of the examination credentialed 186 of 693 examinees, which was a much higher pass rate of 37.2 percent than had ever been the case on the mainland, which tended to have pass rates of roughly 10 percent.[51]

The Central Reform Commission, which first convened in early August 1950 to critically assess the failings of the past in order to reinvigorate the GMD party-state, also afforded the Examination Yuan the space to reconsolidate. In 1951, the Examination Yuan and the Ministry of Personnel moved from its makeshift offices in the old Confucius temple in Taibei to the then distant, semi-rural suburb of Muzha on the southeastern edge of the city.[52] From Muzha the Examination Yuan convened a set of special meetings, conferences, and discussions that served as a postmortem on GMD rule on the mainland and set forward a path to the future.[53]

The first of these gatherings was a small conference in May 1951 to discuss general matters of civil service and state administration. The surviving record details remarkably frank analysis of the GMD's failures on the mainland. The "chaos" of war, frequent military interference in government, the evils of factionalism, "rule by man" rather than "rule by law," and a lack of coordination within the National Government were repeatedly cited as the key factors that prevented the effective functioning of a neutral and competent civil service system. Even relatively junior participants in the meeting got up and spoke their minds freely – an unthinkable breach of convention and manners under normal circumstances.[54] The Examination Yuan proposed that once these ills were remedied, it could get on with its part in turning Taiwan into a model province through its promotion of civil service expertise, technocracy, depersonalization, and establishing a regular path for a career open to talent.

As was the case with the examinations in the 1930s and 1940s, those who came into the state's civil service by competitive open civil service examination in Taiwan in the early 1950s were but a tiny percentage of those appointed. While there are no figures that give aggregate numbers of the number of officials appointed, it is certain that the majority of those who came into state service in the early to mid-1950s were "black

---

[50] Wang Hua-chung, interview.   [51] XKCJT, p. 19.

[52] Before the Taibei MRT system expanded to cover distant suburbs in the 2000s, the ride down to Muzha from central Taibei on the bus took a good three-quarters of an hour.

[53] The records for these meetings are available in KJY.   [54] Niu Yongjian, RXC.

officials" who did not go through the examination process, and were rewarded with official posts on the basis of their party loyalty and commitment to the GMD in following the Chiang Kai-shek government to Taiwan.[55] Despite this unsavory gap between theory and practice, the principles of impersonal civil service and entry by examination continued to command significant moral authority. In mid-1951, Niu Yongjian quietly slid in a bid for the Examination Yuan to exercise independent influence over the state bureaucracy, arguing that "all viable governments have [effective] personnel systems … and the establishment of an independent civil service system will quickly lead to effectiveness."[56] It was in this context that despite its weak institutional position, the Examination Yuan was able to re-establish itself amid the massive uncertainties of the early 1950s. Reformers in the Examination Yuan could reasonably argue that, given the association between the regime's very *lack* of a properly functioning civil service systems between 1937 and 1949 and its catastrophic failure on the mainland during this period, a strong Examination Yuan presence and solid civil service systems were required for the overall reinvigoration of the ROC on Taiwan.

From unpromising beginnings that were depressingly similar to the conditions under which it was first created in 1930–1931, the Examination Yuan did succeed in enlarging its policy space in a modest and incremental manner. Over time it did become the main channel by which civil servants were recruited. Examinations were convened annually for the *gaokao* and the *pukao* (general civil service exam) after 1950. Until 1958, special examinations reserved for positions in local government offices were also held specifically for Taiwanese. Gradually, Ministries and Commissions began to request that the Examination Yuan hold *tekao* (special examinations – 特考) to fill upcoming vacancies. Over the course of the 1950s and 1960s the Examination Yuan began to set up small sub-offices "attached" to the personnel offices within the major ministries and commissions of the National Government. These small detached units, on loan to functional organizations, eased questions of coordination and getting those organizations to agree to accept those credentialed by the Examination Yuan. In 1969, a new organization called the Administrative Personnel Committee (the Xingzheng Renshi Weiyuanhui – 行政人事委員會) was established. This committee was

---

[55] There is no precise data on how many people were appointed by what means during the years of strenuous regime consolidation and reinvigoration (1950–1953). Since the personnel records that were kept (and are presently available) make no mention of how individuals were recruited, only that they were recruited at a certain level and pay grade, it is likely that we will never know the exact figures.

[56] Niu Yongjian, Welcoming Speech in RXC, n.p.

composed of high-level Examination Yuan and Executive Yuan officials to manage and fully coordinate processes of examination with those of appointment.

The chequered history of the Examination Yuan neatly captures the ambivalences inherent in the Nationalist variant of the Chinese party-state. The presumptive division of power structured through Five Power Government (of which the Examination Yuan was one of the top five "Powers") never aligned well with the party-state's other core principle of *yidang zhiguo* (the party ordering the nation). The Examination Yuan's raison d'être – ensuring a meritocratic career open to talent in state service – collided head on with the party-state norm of rule by committed and loyal revolutionary cadres. Originally a weak organization in charge of matters it was in no position to implement in 1930–1931, it managed to modestly enlarge its remit in the mid-1930s until it was weakened by wartime hyper-expansion and militarization. Once in Taiwan it had to, as it were, start over with a state that was much smaller, but where again its proper functions were once again overridden by the immediate political imperatives to reward the loyal who had accompanied the Guomindang to Taiwan. In other ways, the experience of the Examination Yuan exemplified the GMD's strategy of state building by gradualist, incremental evolution: it took nearly *forty years* after the Examination Yuan was first established for it to function in accordance with its claims to be the guarantor of civil service systems. Even on the reduced spatial scale of Taiwan, it took a full *two decades* after 1949 for the Examination Yuan's qualification exam (*zige kaoshi* – 資格考試) to become a functional appointment exam (*renyong kaoshi* – 任用考試).

Virtue and Talent Assessed: Informal and Formal Systems in Sunan and Taiwan

With their similar Leninist structures, developmental goals, experiences of scarce material resources during protracted war, and longstanding late imperial norms of the official as the embodiment of morality and self-cultivation, the CCP and GMD overlapped substantially in their notions about state personnel. They both believed that effective implementation of their state projects required committed individuals who possessed moral virtue and practical talent, and that such individuals would, given the right kind of training, overcome a variety of objective difficulties. But the strategies by which the CCP in Sunan and the GMD in Taiwan went about ensuring a steady supply of individuals with sufficient virtue and talent were very different. And these differences revealed in microcosm the ways in which each regime imagined itself.

Although state administrators were clearly necessary for the tasks the young People's Republic of China set itself, the ruling CCP seems to have been uncomfortable with the notion of establishing anything like an institutionalized and regular path to recruitment and promotion in Sunan. In 1949–1950, the retention of holdover officials and old cadres was necessary because of the technical knowledge of the former and the loyalty and heroism of the latter. New China went out of its way to identify other likely individuals with good class backgrounds and a modicum of education (particularly in technical subjects) to serve the state. Sometimes individuals themselves came forward to register with authorities as intellectuals in the hope of being assigned a good office job.[57] Others were identified by chance or through personal networks. Upper middle school and university students were often targeted for supplementary training to help with campaigns, and often these campaigns were the point of entry for becoming *ganbu*.

In Sunan formal systems of recruitment, assessment, and promotion within state organizations remained attenuated when they existed at all. The Soviet Union's administrative practices of "one man management," themselves influenced by Taylorist notions of scientific administration, were in turn adopted by the young PRC when it set up its state administration in the early 1950s.[58] As a result, the CCP's personnel practices in early regime consolidation also allowed some room for the use of material incentives as a way of increasing functional productivity. Material incentives relied on relatively objective ways to measure performance and make decisions about promotion. This approach to managing state personnel was attractive to some, because from a very early stage, there were those in government who recognized that its egalitarianism might well result in mediocre performance. In December 1949, a *ganbu* by the name of Tao Xijin publicly raised these concerns in a Tianjin government periodical that circulated widely enough in official personnel circles to appear as a clipping in the files of the Nanjing Municipal Office of Personnel, where it presumably served as a cautionary signal that local officials ought to be aware of. Tao worried about lazy comrades with hyper-egalitarian streaks and criticized what he viewed as the common attitude of "done or not, we still get our two and a half *jin* [ration]" (*ganbugan erjinban* – 敢不敢，二斤半). In order to counter such negative outcomes, Tao proposed a system of regular checking on work attendance (*kaoqin* – 考勤) and regular work

<hr />

[57] Eddy U, "The Making of Chinese Intellectuals: Representations and Organization in the Thought Reform Campaign." Once the *danwei* system took hold in the mid-1950s, educated urbanites were simply assigned to their jobs.

[58] Schurmann, *Ideology and Organization*, pp. 253–262, 267–272.

evaluations (*kaoji* – 考績).[59] In this spirit of encouraging efficiency and scientific forms of management with positive material incentives, in Shanghai there was some discussion of internal labor competitions" (勞動競賽 – *laodong jingsai*) in the early 1950s. The Shanghai Bureau of Tax went as far as to hold one such competition in the late autumn of 1952, which was graded on numerical criteria of productivity such as the number of cases solved and the amount of tax collected in a defined period of time. Those who came out on top of the competition were awarded recognition and a modest one-off monetary bonus.[60] This move towards regular evaluation of productivity combined with material reward appears not to have lasted for long: in Shanghai the internal records of neither municipal tax nor personnel organizations reveal any evidence of any further internal labor competitions of this sort after 1952.

Nor did personnel offices in Sunan seem to have made any effort to promote wider regular evaluation and promotion in other work units. Occasionally, a state organization would nod in this direction. For example, the Shanghai Bureau of Tax floated a tentative plan to regularize an annual performance review with *kaoji* (考績 – evaluations) and criteria for promotion (*tiba* – 提拔) in early 1953.[61] This trial balloon was not followed up, perhaps because personnel offices at this juncture became much more preoccupied with managing a flush of departures and new recruitment after the *sanfan* (三反 – Three Antis) campaign. Thereafter appetites for creating new systems to conduct routine evaluation appear to have been lost in the wake of other, more pressing campaign initiatives. Even though these tentative steps in the direction of regularization and institutionalization of evaluation were undertaken during the course of the *sanfan* campaign, they were quite contrary to campaigns, which came at frequent but irregular intervals. A regular system of evaluation required procedures, forms, and unit leaders who in principle applied the same criteria to all. Campaigns, on the other hand, stressed mass mobilization, reliance on activists, "high tides" to overcome recalcitrance, and quick, decisive results. Regular evaluations delinked from campaigns appear to have been abandoned in Sunan after early 1953. Evaluation and

[59] NMA, 5010/2/136. File Shifu jiguan ganbu kaoqin zhanxing banfa jiqi cailiao deng, "Zenyang jianli jiguan renyuan kaoji zhidu" report by Tao Xijin, reproduced in a clipping from *Tianjin Shizheng* No. 63, October 7, 1950.

[60] SMA B1/2/5185. "Shuiwu ju renshi chu 1953 nian chunji gongzuo jihua" (1953 spring work plan for the Shanghai Tax Bureau Office of Personnel), January 10, 1953.

[61] It is also within the realms of possibility that there may have been numerical *kaoji* (annual evaluation) within *Party* organizations via the Organization Department that have simply not been made available in the archives. Even if such evaluations were undertaken, however, their results were never made known to the individuals being evaluated because the contents of individual dossiers were confidential.

promotion remained informal, occurring in an ad hoc manner, often part of post-campaign consolidation and record keeping. In some years there was an annual report on the individual's political thought and/or practical work, but it was never clear to those being evaluated whether the assessment was generated by the unit's personnel office or the party's organization department. Informally, people in government offices came to realize that for both evaluation and promotion the most important factor was to obey one's work unit leader and to get on well with him, because he wrote the eventual work reports and had the power of veto over any recommendation for promotion from "the masses."[62]

The hesitation and reluctance to formalize and regularize either formal rules for recruitment or internal processes of evaluation that so characterized personnel policy in the young PRC in Sunan could not have been more different in the ROC/Taiwan, which made much of its "scientific" approach to annual appraisal and review. Unlike the PRC in Sunan the ROC/Taiwan actively publicized its formal and centralized systems for annual appraisal as a sign of the state's fairness, sound public management, and modernity. Those who worked in state organizations in the ROC – at central, provincial, and local levels were evaluated annually by a formal system (*kaoji* – 考績) that was first developed by the Ministry of Personnel in the mid-1930s. The ROC/Taiwan government's regular annual *kaoji* had several strengths. First, its very existence provided institutional continuity with the National Government in the immediately preceding Republican period on the mainland, with a lineage of nearly twenty years. *Kaoji* was also one of the relatively few nationwide personnel initiatives to have become so well institutionalized in bureaucratic operations in the 1930s that it continued during the war-torn 1940s. *Kaoji* also generated useful information for higher ups about their subordinates, and it also provided a logical rationale by which to dampen down pressure for promotion and raises. *Kaoji* required the chief in every government organizational section to conduct an annual numerically based evaluation of each and every person working in his department. In December, every individual working in a regular government position was ranked by his immediate boss on a scale of zero to 100. The general format was that "work accomplished" (*gongzuo* – 工作) counted for 50 percent, "work conduct" (*caoxing* – 操行) for 25 percent, and "work knowledge (*xueshi*– 學識) for the remaining 25 percent.

In principle, annual evaluation was also linked to material reward. Those whose totals came in above 90 were eligible for a monetary bonus. Those between 80 and 89 were deemed "very good," those between 70 and 79 as

---

[62] Wang Wenqing, interview.

varying degrees of average, and anyone whose score was below a 70 could be issued with a demerit (although these cases appear to have been rare in practice). Individuals were then given an overall assessment of "superior," "middling" or "deficient."[63] Although there are not many personnel records available from the ROC/Taiwan archives, there is one tranche of forms from the *kaoji* of 25 *weiren* (委任 – "delegated" or fully commissioned) staff at the end of the work year of 1949 from the Tainan District station of the Taiwan Province Grain Bureau (臺灣省糧食局). This brief glimpse of how the *kaoji* system worked in practice suggests that in this organization at least, annual *kaoji* was not used to actively reward or discipline staff. All in the sample were scored between 70.5 (the lowest) and 84 (the highest), with roughly one-third (8) in the range of 80–84, and the remaining 17 at various points in the 70s. No one in the sample gained a high enough mark (above 90) to qualify for a bonus, or low enough (below 70) to get a demerit.

These categories of work assessment are, however, very revealing of how the ROC/Taiwan imagined its state agents to be when they were at their best. Even for technically based organizations like the Taiwan Province Grain Bureau, these broad categories of "work accomplished," "work conduct," and "work knowledge" were further broken down in ways that suggested that the individual's temperament and manner of working were almost as important as the work done. The most heavily weighted category of "work accomplished" (at 50 percent) was further sub-divided into ten (with each sub category worth 10 points for a total of 100 within the category): (1) work done in accordance with regulations; (2) work done in a thorough and reliable way; (3) ability to cooperate with others; (4) smarts and perseverance (*shifou jimin, shifou hengxin* – 是否機敏 是否恆心); (5) asking for leave within regulation allotted days off; (6) scrupulousness in keeping to work hours; (7) prompt return of vehicles used for work purposes; (8) work speed; (9) work volume; and (10) ability to endure hardship (*nailao ku* – 耐勞苦). Even putatively objective practical work standards included such moral and human dimensions as getting along with others, perseverance, and willingness to "endure hardship." The category of "work conduct" put even more weight on how the civil servant behaved as an exemplar of the state. It was broken down into five subcategories of: (1) being law abiding; (2) being upright; (3) being clean and non-corrupt; (4) showing respect to others; and (5) sincere acceptance of leadership (*chengken jieshou zhidao* – 誠懇接受指導). In this evaluation

---

[63] TPA. Taiwan Liangshi Ju (Taiwan Province Grain Bureau). Tainan Shiwusuo (Tainan District Station). 38 nian (1949), 021.2. "Taisheng Liangshi Ju Tainan Shiwusuo weiren reyuan 1938 nian du kaoji qingce" (1949 end of Year Appointed Personnel Annual Evaluation Listing).

rubric, even the seemingly most neutral and objective category of "work knowledge" edged back into notions of individual self-cultivation and morality, with four (somewhat redundant) sub-components of practical or book knowledge, thorough knowledge of the job, general knowledge, knowledge of how to do things, and a final sub-category of "spirit of learning" (*jinxiu jingshen* – 進修精神). For the ROC/Taiwan, even in technically based organizations like the Grain Bureau, eight of the twenty specific categories by which civil servants were evaluated directly reflected the state's interest in officials who manifested inner morality of some sort, made visible not only by *what* work was done (and objectively measurable), but also by *how* the work was done.

Like the young PRC across the Taiwan Straits, the post-1949 National Government expected its agents to manifest their virtue through practical work. Virtue was also made visible through the individual's attitude and moral character. Unlike the PRC in Sunan, where processes of evaluation remained informal and at the discretion of the organization in question, for the ROC/Taiwan attitude and moral character were both quantified and regularized in a centralized, formal system of assessment and reporting. The central government's Ministry of Personnel (rather than specific organizations or local governments) was clearly the driver behind this annual system of assessment: the very uniformity of *kaoji* (down to the categories assessed and the layout of the forms) suggests that the Ministry of Personnel set standards that were complied with. In contrast, the young PRC was quite ambivalent about the prospect of instituting a norm of regular *kaoji* assessment in state organizations. There was no evidence at all of regular *kaoji* in the East China military region: neither the Shanghai, nor the Nanjing Personnel bureaus ever mentioned it. Insight into how cadre assessment worked in practice will likely have to await the opening of personnel archives and individual dossiers that are at present unavailable, but we can venture to guess that these were matters decided by the CCP's organization department. In practice, the relative importance of *de* and *cai* in evaluation likely varied between different sectors and over time. But it is clear that when it occurred assessment was ad hoc rather than routine, was not monitored by higher levels of state organizations, and that no formula for judging different categories of work performance was ever formalized, as was the case for the GMD in Taiwan.

State Administrators as Objects and Implementers of Campaigns: *Sanfan*

Cadres occupied an ambiguous, Janus-faced space between state and society in the young People's Republic of China. As the foot soldiers of the state, they were the agents who administered and implemented state directives and policies. Many of these state directives were routine, precedent driven, and in practice rule bound through hierarchy and regulations – the "bureaucratic modality" of policy implementation. Others were by design *extra*ordinary; involving extreme mobilization, telescoping policy into hyper-drive, and quick results through achievement of a "high tide" – via the "campaign modality." As exemplars and agents of the state, cadres were required to internalize both the campaign and the bureaucratic, and to tack between one and the other on demand. If cadres were (as Stalin and Mao had it) "everything," then they were simultaneously campaign *subjects* and campaign *implementers*. Cadres were the first to receive political propaganda about a campaign, engage in intensive political study of its policies and objectives, and become deeply committed to successful implementation. But occasionally, government cadres (and their behavior) were themselves the primary targets of a campaign.[64] And nowhere is this tension between cadre as target and cadre as implementer more visible than in the *sanfan* ("Three Antis") campaign of 1951–1953.

Like many campaigns, *sanfan* emerged from a set of concerns in one part of the country that were then implemented nationally by different regional and local administrations. The party secretary of the Northeast Military Region, Gao Gang, was the first to raise the problem of cadre corruption at a meeting of the party leadership of the Northeast military region at the end of August, 1951 – only weeks after the peak of the Campaign to Suppress Counterrevolutionaries and the land reform campaigns in Sunan.[65] Over the next several months, Gao's initial attack on corruption merged with other concerns about endemic waste and the need to economize in state organizations. The *sanfan* campaign was launched nationally on the first of December 1951, with a sharply written "Decision" from the central government enjoining cadres to "perfect the military, simplify government, intensify frugality, and open up the struggle against corruption, waste, and bureaucratism" (*jingbin jianzheng zengchan jieyue fandui tanwu, fandui langfei fandui guanliao zhuyi jianzheng*), and to do so in party, government, and military systems.[66] In Sunan, the "Decision" was dutifully followed up with an important regional meeting

---

[64] Party cadres had, of course, for years been subjected to rectification campaigns by the early 1950s.

[65] Yang Kuisong, *Zhonghua Renmin Gongheguo Jianguo shi yanjiu* p. 263.

[66] *Yidu* (read one), "Fandui tanwu, fandui langfei, fandui guanliao zhuyi de douzheng" (The struggle against corruption, waste, and bureaucratism), *Shouji Renmin wang*, https://read01 .com/x0xnxK.html, accessed August 5, 2016. JZWX, Vol. 2, "Zhonggong zhongyang shixing jingbin jianzheng, zengchan jieyue, fandui tanwu fandui langfei, he fandui guanliao zhiyi de jueding" (CCP Central Decision on implementing order to perfect the military,

of first-level organization cadres from the East China Military Region in mid-December. A directive on thorough implementation of the campaign was duly issued on December 25. Some weeks later, Bo Yibo, in his capacity as chair of the PRC's Committee on Supervising Economizing, gave a lengthy speech which was disseminated and studied intensively throughout January 1952.[67]

The *sanfan* campaign began for reasons that were not dissimilar from party rectification campaigns prior to 1949: the upper leadership's fear of cadre complacency, arrogance, and distance from the masses. Exactly the kinds of "bureaucratic" forms of behavior that Mao loved to hate were singled out for particular opprobrium: (1) misappropriation of state funds (embezzlement); (2) waste; and (3) "bureaucratism," which was a residual, but potentially very large category for any kind of behavior not intrinsically measurable but deemed normatively undesirable in a cadre. In practice, this meant anything from being remote and unapproachable, to ordering people around in an imperious manner, to engaging in extramarital affairs or consorting with prostitutes.

In the fourteen months prior to the *sanfan*, state cadres had already spent a good portion of their time learning how to conduct campaigns with increasingly wide targets and aims. The Aid Korea/Resist America campaign (autumn 1950) required mass mobilization but only against a generalized, external bogeyman. The Campaign to Suppress Counterrevolutionaries required both mass urban mobilization and "striking hard" against individual targets and their property, but the campaign was not accompanied by the classification of the entire urban population. Land reform in the countryside also featured mass mobilization of the rural population against identified targets, and also required the classification of the entire rural population, as well as investigation and reapportionment of all of China's rural land. In

---

simplify government, intensify frugality, and oppose corruption, waste and bureaucratism), December 1, 1951, pp. 471–485.

[67] Bo Yibo, "Wei shenru de pubian de kaizhan fan tanwu, fan langfei, fan guanliao zhuyi yundong er douzheng" (How to deeply enter the general opening campaign and struggle against corruption, waste and bureaucratism), and Huadong Junzheng Weiyuanhui, "Guanyu renmin zhengfu gongzuo renyuan fandui tanwu fandui langfei, he fandui guanliao zhuyi de jilü" (East China Military Region Committee "Rules for personnel working in People's Government on opposing corruption, opposing waste, and opposing bureaucratism"), December 25, Rao Shushi, "Wei kaizhan zhengchan jieyue, fandui tanwu fandui langfei, fandui guanliaozhuyi" (How to open up the struggle for increasing economizing, oppose corruption, oppose waste, and oppose bureaucratism), report given at the East China Military Region First Level Organization Cadre Meeting, to "fandui langfei he fandui guanliaozhuyi douzheng de zhishi" (East China Military Region Committee decision on thoroughly increasing economizing, and opening the struggle to oppose corruption, oppose waste, and oppose bureaucratism), December 25, 1951. 1951 *HDZB* January 9, 1952, pp. 4–17.

short, the wave of mass campaigns in the early 1950s required that *ganbu* learn how to respond to signals from above and utilize the specific repertoires deemed necessary by the CCP for campaigns: propaganda and intensive small group study, propaganda dissemination, and eventual orchestration of public mass mobilization and accusation sessions.

The *sanfan* campaign was the first time that state cadres found themselves on the *receiving* end of such repertoires. Unlike earlier party rectification campaigns which were run by party organizations and aimed exclusively at party members, *sanfan* was implemented by state organizations (regular government offices as well as state factories) whose targets included large numbers who were not party members. *Sanfan* was also the first (but not the last) occasion when cadres themselves were simultaneously implementers as well as the targets of the campaign. This necessarily required that some (e.g. in the organization department, the party committee, and those designated by them to be on an investigating working committee) to be beyond reproach as they carried out the necessary internal investigations of corruption, waste, and untoward behavior. *Sanfan* also relied on repertoires learned over the previous sixteen months in the context of other campaigns (investigation, political study, small group discussion, isolation of the wrongdoer followed by his self-criticism and an eventual public accusation session). By 1952 these campaign repertoires would have been quite familiar to those in government offices, but only as practices that cadres deployed against undesirables in society. On this occasion the campaign directed these repertoires inward within government offices against coworkers.

Although earlier generations of scholars have typically understood *sanfan* as a campaign to replace politically unreliable holdover officials, records from Shanghai suggest that this is only partially correct.[68] *Sanfan* was not only to purge the party-state of "bureaucratism" and corruption by holdover officials, but was also in principle to provide the "base" for implementing a party rectification, suggesting that the malfeasance of party members caught by the campaign would be treated harshly by party organizations.[69] The Shanghai government's own inconsistency in the way it counted its own personnel makes it impossible to assess the exact scope of *sanfan*, but it is clear that the campaign went very deep

---

[68] Meisner, 86–87, and Schurmann, p. 376.
[69] SMA A47-1-392. "Shiwei zhishu jiguan dangwei guanyu zai sanfan yundong de jichu shangxing zhengdang jiaoyu de jihua" (Party committees of organs under the Shanghai Party Committee plan on the three antis movement as the base for implementing party rectification education). October 16, 1952.

indeed.[70] In one accounting, more individuals were investigated than there were officially appointed cadres. By mid-1952, 95,683 individuals had been investigated, and of these an astonishingly high percentage of 38.5 percent had been found to have engaged in some degree of corruption.[71] This unusually large number in turn hints that the *sanfan* crackdown on "corruption" was aimed at both the "big tigers" of corruption, and the rank and file, whose "corruption" was in all likelihood so naturalized that many considered it to be normal working practice.[72]

Uncovering cases of malfeasance and corruption required that investigators invest a great deal of time combing through the accounts of all in government offices or state factories who had access to cash, raw materials that could be sold at market prices, or permits. A draft plan sent out to all Shanghai's state-owned industries and factories specified in excruciating detail exactly what had to be audited for evidence of backhanded corruption, waste, or "bureaucratism": accounts for primary materials or transport (the former could be sold at higher market prices and permits for the latter entitled the holder of the permit to free shipment of goods), administrative fees charged by the factory, union fees, salary payments, repair orders, and receipts of all sorts.[73] Even if the bulk of the investigation was geared to objective indicators like amount of money skimmed, diverted or received rather than the more amorphous category of "bureaucratism," the sheer number of hours spent on going through accounts, comparing receipts, and listening to charges of malfeasance must have been daunting and tedious. And with such a large proportion of staff eventually deemed to have engaged in some degree of corrupt

---

[70] There is enormous inconsistency in the internal statistics on as basic a question as the size of the Shanghai municipal government. Some records counted only the central municipal government organizations; others include police, banking, and hygiene workers; still others include outer district administrations. Some included support staff, while others do not. And none included "off system" staff who were not formally part of the *bianzhi* quotas, so all formal counts are an underestimate to some degree. These differences in which kind of categories were included resulted in numbers as low as 10, 949 and as high as 83,993 for late 1951. SMA B23/1/85, "Sanfan hou shifu suoshu ge danwei quanshu renyuan" (Post-sanfan total personnel statistical form of all units under the Shanghai Municipal government," "Sanfan qian yu sanfan hou ganbu qingkuang tongji" (1) and (2) and (3) (Statistics on ganbu before and after sanfan).

[71] Ibid. If this second set of statistics had included the police, for example, the totals would come to thousands higher.

[72] Although Lieberthal's classic work on Tianjin this period details the *wufan* [Five Antis] in Tianjin against "corrupt businessmen" rather than the *sanfan* focus on "corrupt bureaucrats," the campaigns had a great deal in common, were conducted at the same time, and overlapped in practice. See Lieberthal, pp. 130–142, 149–152.

[73] SMA A38/1/144. "Shanghai ge guoying, guoying gongchang kaizhan fan tanwu fan langfei, fan guanliao zhuiyi yundong jihua [cao'an]" (Draft Plan for Shanghai national enterprises and factories campaign against corruption, waste, and bureaucratism), January 15, 1952.

activity, almost everyone who was not part of the investigating team must have felt that they had reason to worry.

In the end, the *sanfan* campaign did fall more heavily on holdover officials than on other categories of cadres. According to one set of figures, holdovers accounted for only slightly more than a third of the total cadres in the Shanghai central administration (3,991 of 10,949 or 36.45 percent), while comprising close to two-thirds of those dismissed (348 of 572, or 60.84 percent).[74] Considerable numbers of cadres with less politically suspect backgrounds were also netted. Another table compiled after the conclusion of the campaign counted the corrupt as follows: holdover officials at 58 percent, the newly appointed (since 1949) at 28 percent, members of the Chinese Communist Youth Corps at 10 percent, and party members at 4 percent. In the short term, the vast majority of the guilty (83 percent) got off fairly lightly. They were not sanctioned other than having a "hat" put on (i.e. a black mark entry was made in the individual's permanent dossier, but the full impact of the "hat" would only become visible with the much more stringent leftist campaigns of the late 1950s and 1960s). A further 13 percent received an administrative sanction; 239 (0.8 percent) were placed under administrative arrest/ supervision by their work units; 236 (0.7 percent) were sent for labor reform; and only miniscule numbers (139) received a prison sentence. In a sharp break with the Campaign to Suppress Counterrevolutionaries and Land Reform Campaign of the previous year, in Shanghai only three individuals (of an investigated 95,683) were given the death sentence.[75] While this small number might seem to indicate a relatively mild campaign, the thoroughness and the process of the *sanfan* campaign suggest something quite different. The *sanfan* extended the campaign modality to those who manned the party-state itself as targets rather than implementers. It made clear that old forms of behavior – from petty graft and overclaiming on expenses to consorting with prostitutes in off hours – would no longer be tolerated. Being investigated and on the receiving end of campaign repertoires must have come as a shock and a searing experience. And, although no one could have known it at the time, those unfortunate enough to have been slapped with a "black hat" that was formally entered in one's individual dossier now possessed a damaging and permanent political status. "Black hats" would thereafter be very vulnerable: always the first to be trotted out and vilified in later campaigns.

[74] SMA B23/1/85. "Sanfan qian yu sanfan hou ganbu qingkuang (1)" (The cadre situation before and after the sanfan campaign), 1952.
[75] SMA B23/1/85. "Sanfan ding'an, tuizei, chuli qingkuang zongbiao" (Comprehensive table for sanfan settling cases, restitution, and decisions), June 12, 1952.

Conclusion

The "new regimes" of the PRC in Sunan and ROC in Taiwan both faced significant challenges in the immediate aftermath of 1949. While they heartily despised each other and represented themselves as being completely "other" than the rival across the Taiwan Strait, they had much more in common than either was willing or able to admit. They drew on an analogous pre-1949 tradition of *yidang zhiguo*. The lengthy partification and militarization of the preceding decades meant that there was no one standard term to label civil administrators. Unclear boundaries between party and state continued to foster terminological ambivalence and confusion even after 1949. Each was wedded to the notion that civil administrators could not, and should not, be mere technicians. Civil administrators were required to cultivate themselves and externally manifest inner virtue. They were expected not only to implement the directives and policies of the state as formulated by their superiors; but also to do so in a manner that visibly represented the state's own correctness, morality, and core ethics.

The differences between the PRC in Sunan and the ROC on Taiwan were equally important. The *ways* in which each regime went about creating civil administrators diverged sharply. The CCP demanded committed revolutionary heroes as much as it required functionally competent technocrats, and across the board it insisted on training programs to inculcate not only obedience but also requisite amounts of both virtue and talent. The actual management of state personnel in post was, however, devolved to the unit in question. In contrast, the GMD aimed to create "scientific" systems of management. In principle if not in practice, it signaled its commitment to fostering talent via open civil service examinations held by a central government organization from the earliest possible moment in 1950. Regular, centrally mandated systems of annual *kaoji* for all state personnel in national, provincial, and local government bodies ensured that virtue remained a core component of what individual public servants were expected to demonstrate on an annual basis. The CCP wanted both good systems and good heroes, and it insisted that it was possible to have both manifested in individuals who combined mutually reinforcing virtue and talent. Later in the 1950s, this understanding of virtue and talent was undermined by pressure from Mao to resist institutionalization and require *ganbu* to become ever more generalist and heroic – in a pattern that would become even more strained from the leftist campaigns of the Great Leap Forward onward. The ROC/Taiwan also assumed that virtue and talent in its state administrators was equally important, but opted for a very different set of strategies to select for these traits. The GMD on Taiwan assumed that the proxies for determining virtue and talent (hard work, obedience, commitment, demeanor, continuing to strive under difficult circumstances) would be best ensured by regular systems. In contrast to the CCP's deep ambivalence about the institutionalized inequality inherent to hierarchical state organizations, the leaders of the ROC/Taiwan were enamoured of regularity, rules, and institutions – be they legal, executive, or personnel. The Examination Yuan argued for a vision to establish and institutionalize the kinds of proper systems that had not worked well on the mainland in order to turn Taiwan into a model province to demonstrate the virtue of its government to the rest of China. Even when there were gaps in implementation, *how* each regime implemented its personnel policy for state administrators suggested a great deal about its core values, and the directions in which it wished to go for the future. What began in the early 1950s as reluctance to formalize systems of personnel management in PRC Sunan would eventually, under pressure from Mao, ultimately weigh revolutionary virtue more heavily than talent, while the ROC-Taiwan benchmarked its success against a norm of creating and institutionalizing "good systems." Next we turn to further explore how these similarities and differences played out in campaigns against domestic subversion: the Campaign to Suppress Counterrevolutionaries and the "White Terror."

2 Comparative Terror in Regime Consolidation
Sunan and Taiwan, 1949–1954

What Is This Thing Called Terror? Campaigns of Coercion as Integral to Regime Consolidation

Political violence has been recorded as a means of extirpating enemies, heretics, and "others" for as long as written history itself, but the state's resort to terror as a deliberately applied strategy of revolutionary regime consolidation emerged with the French Revolution. The first practitioner explicitly to link revolution and terror, Robespierre, proclaimed that "Terror is nothing else than justice, prompt, severe, inflexible; an emanation of virtue."[1] This intertwining of physical coercion, virtue, and the notion of purification through bloodshed has continued to animate much of the justification for revolutionary terror and its reactive twin, counterrevolutionary terror, ever since. Nevertheless, the contours of "terror" are much contested. If it is relatively straightforward to label a sequence of highly coercive actions "terror" when the perpetrators proudly publicize those actions as such (as was the case for campaigns of terror in Robespierre's France, Stalin's Soviet Union, or Mao's China), labeling becomes much more difficult when leaders are reticent. The label "terror" can become either a warning that enemies of the state are now on notice, or a political charge against state-sponsored terror by the regime's domestic or external political opponents. Thus, how to distinguish full-fledged terror from everyday political coercion, revolutionary from counterrevolutionary terror, or any of the above from prerevolutionary forms of state-initiated political violence is at best unclear.

Terror is experienced subjectively: what might be widely recognized as extraordinarily coercive and terrifying for one individual, group, sector, or region might be either a distant news item or a source of popular entertainment for others. Even such seemingly "objective" facts as the numbers of victims of terror are often contested. Given the frequency with which state terror accompanies regime consolidation, invasion, the

---

[1] Robespierre. "Speech to the Convention," February 5, 1794, www.worldfuturefund.org/wf fmaster/Reading/Communism/ROBESPIERRE'S%20SPEECH.htm, accessed September 24, 2012.

aftermath of messy civil wars, or the pursuit of revolutionary state projects, determining how these numbers ought to be assessed is necessarily subjective. Should the millions who lost their lives in civil wars, deportations, or forced labor in precarious physical circumstances be counted as victims of terror? What about those who suffered or perished due to the inept implementation of radical revolutionary programs? Or should the field be narrowed to focus only on those victims of state violence who were deliberately targeted and dispatched as counterrevolutionaries, "bad elements," subversives, "Reds," or enemies of the state? If the latter, how should those who were families or close associates of targeted victims be counted? If the state tacitly encouraged, or merely did nothing to prevent, communal violence against ethnic or religious minorities, do these incidents fall under the rubric of terror, or are they classified as communal/sectarian violence? What of the wider publics that may have been terrified, or entertained, or simply instructed by the display of the state's terror against those proclaimed enemies? How do we conceptualize situations in which "the people" are mobilized by either right-wing or left-wing regimes to turn on their neighbors and commit massacres, as was the case in Indonesia in 1965–1966, or in Rwanda in 1994? Thus, deeply political claims about the incidence of terror, the difficulty of establishing intentionality and scope, and the messily intertwined nature of revolution and counterrevolution are likely to continue to cloud conceptual clarity about how to understand "terror" more generally.

Many of these difficulties are also experienced by the implementers of terror themselves. Historically, perpetrators of domestic terror have often been unclear about how to demarcate the loyal from the disloyal, the friend from the enemy, the supporter from one with something to hide, the externally quiescent from the secret doubter, and the secret doubter from the actively disloyal. This is particularly problematic when domestic and regional security is uncertain, enemies are invisible because they live among us and look just like us, the organizations in charge of domestic security are nascent and unclear about their basic remit, and information about credible threats is imperfect and/or distorted.[2] Irrespective of political system, overreach and excess are, almost by definition, built into the vigorous prosecution of presumptive state enemies. While sustained extreme coercion against large numbers of citizens is normally thought of as an inefficient (as well as an immoral and illegitimate) way to hold on to power, more states than one might think – including liberal democracies – resort to terror, which is implicated in colonization, decolonization, regime consolidation, (counter)

---

[2] Greitens, *Dictators and Their Secret Police*, pp. 43–51, and passim.

revolutionary programs, issues of internal political security, and/or ridding the polity of unsavory political competitors.[3]

In the next two chapters on the dynamics of terror and regime consolidation in the Sunan region of the People's Republic of China and the island of Taiwan for the Republic of China between 1949 and 1954, I claim that both regimes instrumentally mobilized the instruments of state in campaigns of terror in the name of ensuring internal regime security. Through highly concentrated, extraordinarily coercive actions against proclaimed internal enemies, these two consolidating states simultaneously pursued three other interrelated goals: (1) dramatically expanding the state's coercive presence throughout society, down to very local levels; (2) ridding the state of any source of political, social, or economic competition; and (3) using different kinds of performance to instruct society into core regime norms. While invariably justified as necessary for basic security and social order, state instigated terror also served to build the coercive apparatus of the state, reduce social resistance to a wide tranche of state action, foster cultures and practices of paranoia and informing, and begin a process of deep penetration into the grass roots of workplaces, schools, and social organizations. Less obviously, but no less importantly, campaigns of terror were also heuristic devices that conveyed broad regime norms to the population at large about which people and what kinds of behavior were, or were not, acceptable. At the same time, the exact lines of demarcation between the good and pure "inner" and the bad and irredeemable "outer" were made vague enough that large numbers of individuals were kept on edge.[4] The ways in which these campaigns of repression were performed also revealed a great deal about how political leaders imagined the state and its relationship with its citizens, through the PRC's passionate and public participatory theater in Sunan and the closed procedural displays of quasi-judicial state power in the ROC/Taiwan. Campaigns of coercive terror also amplified plausible concerns about internal security and social order to buttress the new regime and to lower social resistance to its coercion and control, formed new institutions of coercion, transformed older ones, and wove into the fabric of daily life new practices of informing, accusation, and social isolation of the accused and their families.

---

[3] The controversy over the opening of the first tranche of the UK colonial-era archives in the early 2010s illustrates this in regions as far flung as British Guiana, Kenya, and Malaysia. See www.theguardian.com/uk/blog/2012/apr/18/national-archives-release-colonial-papers-live-blog, accessed November 2, 2013.

[4] I am indebted to Dan Slater for helping me to clarify this point.

Repertoires of Combating Subversion: Historical Experiences and Ongoing Insecurity

As is true for all newly consolidating regimes born of civil war, establishing internal security, and solidifying the acquiescence of the local population was of paramount importance for both the young PRC in Sunan and the newly shrunken ROC on Taiwan. Each resorted to a complex of repertoires to promote these objectives. Some, like the PRC's insistence that security work be led by generalist party secretaries rather than an extra-Party organization like Stalin's NKVD, resulted from what key decision makers took to be the negative lessons of the Soviet Union and the CCP's own history, when a secret extra-Party organization terrorized the CCP and was used to resolve factional differences in the 1930s.[5] Others, like the CCP's insistence on the "mass line," "the mountains of information generated by highly public criticism and self-criticism sessions,"[6] and the recurrent campaigns of excess against "counterrevolutionary" cadres and citizens developed over the course of Mao's rise to power. Similarly, the Guomindang categorically, if disingenuously, insisted on the legitimacy of its rule due to its careful implementation of (martial) law, employing techniques and norms that the GMD had developed over the course of the earlier Republican period. Still other components of these repertoires, notably the promises extended by both to go lightly on those who turned themselves in and show greater severity for those who did not, hearkened back to judicial practices of late imperial China.

The deployment of these repertoires in the early 1950s cannot, however, be understood apart from two immediate factors: (1) the entangled immediate history of mutual betrayal and bloodletting between the CCP and GMD from the mid-1920s until 1949; and (2) the domestic and regional insecurity perceived by each at the outset of regime consolidation in 1949–1950. The quarter-century before 1949 was marked by a nearly incessant and toxic combination of mutual betrayal, regional insecurity, foreign invasion, and civil war, all of which served to justify no small amount of paranoia. Throughout these years, both the GMD and the CCP learned at tremendous cost that it was as difficult as it was necessary to distinguish friend from foe. The very first preoccupation of Mao Zedong, as evidenced in his *Selected Works,* was to distinguish friend from enemy.[7]

---

[5] M. Scot Tanner, "Who Wields the Knife?," unpublished manuscript, pp. 4–5, and passim; Xuezhi Guo, *China's Security State*, pp. 34–46, 56–57.

[6] Yung-fa Chen, "Suspect History and the Mass Line," p. 244.

[7] Michael Schoenhals, *Spying for the People*, p. 83; Michael Dutton, *Policing Chinese Politics*, pp. 3, 67.

After the GMD coup against the Left in 1927, the subsequent two decades would be rife with cases of mutual infiltration, sometimes at very high levels. At one point in the early 1930s, two positions at the heart of the GMD's security apparatus – the confidential secretary to the chief of the central intelligence forerunner to the Central Bureau of Investigation and Statistics (Zhongtong – 中统), in Shanghai intelligence, and at a major listening post in Tianjin – were manned by Communist moles.[8] These two individuals, Qian Zhuangfei and Xie Fusheng, were "reportedly [able] to obtain much of the GMD order of battle before each of the five 'encirclement campaigns'."[9]

The case of Gu Shunzhang illustrates in microcosm the frequently shifting loyalties and the difficulty of distinguishing trusted supporter from nefarious betrayer. As Wakeman relates the tale, GMD counterintelligence captured Gu Shunzhang in 1931. Gu was, along with Zhou Enlai and then Secretary Xiang Zhongfa, one of the top three most important figures in the CCP in special security work, and head of the "Red Brigade," its operational wing in Shanghai. When politely given the choice to come over to the GMD or be shot, Gu decided that collaboration was the better part of valor. He promptly gave GMD counterintelligence name after name and network after network, starting with none other than the aforementioned Qian Zhuangfei, who was his interrogator's own right-hand man. (Fortuitously for the CCP, Qian was able to intercept the telegram relating Gu's arrest, escape himself, and warn Zhou Enlai and others to flee Shanghai.) In reprisal, the Red Brigade wreaked vengeance on Gu's entire family along with other "waverers," killing and burying them under concrete at multiple locations throughout Shanghai.[10]

The story did not end there. Gu eventually became frustrated at the fact that his knowledge was not being used by the Zhongtong. After being blocked from switching to the Zhongtong's rival spy agency, the Juntong (军统 – Military Bureau of Investigation and Statistics) in 1936, he eventually attempted to re-contact the CCP, with the express goal of assassinating the head of the Zhongtong, Chen Lifu. This venture was foiled by GMD counterintelligence, and the luckless Gu was executed in secret shortly afterwards.[11] Wakeman notes in passing that, at the time of Gu's final exposure, there were some "fifty to sixty" ex-Communists in the Zhongtong.[12] This large number suggests, at least implicitly, that many party-based loyalties were conditional, uncertain, and/or subject

[8] Frederic Wakeman, *Policing Shanghai, 1927–1937*, p. 141.
[9] Tanner, "Who Wields the Knife?," pp. 27–28. This information is from fn. 31.
[10] Wakeman, *Policing Shanghai, 1927–1937*, pp. 151–155.   [11] Ibid., pp. 253–254.
[12] Ibid., p. 253.

to personal persuasion. And yet, once "turned," on what basis and according to which criteria would these "turnees" be trusted by the "turners"?

The Republican-era world of internal security was a grey one of unclear borders, uncertain loyalties, and those who either switched sides or attempted to do so, some more than once. It was also a world subject to vicious factionalism and excesses even among those who were ostensibly on the same side. Pre-1949 Communist experience in security work was littered with anti-counterrevolutionary campaigns of excess and false accusations, a normative culture in which superiors punished "right" errors far more seriously than "left" errors, and in which anti-counterrevolutionary campaigns were hijacked by local power holders to settle factional differences or personal vendettas.[13] For its part, the GMD was equally riven by other sorts of problems, including severe internal competition between three separate intelligence agencies: the Zhongtong, controlled by the factional network associated with the Chen brothers Lifu and Guofu; the Juntong, headed by the shadowy and much-feared Dai Li; and the Neizheng Bu Diaocha Tongji Ju (Ministry of Interior Bureau of Investigation and Statistics). All were bitter rivals and would not share intelligence with each other. Worse, as the government's efficacy declined in the late 1940s, it became ever quicker to tar any criticism of the government as "Communist," and to use its intelligence organizations in increasingly heavy-handed and ultimately alienating ways.[14]

The PRC in Sunan and the ROC in Taiwan also had to contend with an identical problem in 1949–1950: how to distinguish who in the local population was actively plotting against the occupying regime from who was simply acquiescent, grudgingly or otherwise. The chaos left in the wake of the GMD's hasty retreat from the greater Shanghai area made for a security nightmare, where holdover *tewu* – those who had worked for GMD intelligence services – were a pressing problem. By one reckoning, Shanghai was swarming with leftover GMD agents in 1949; by another, the CCP's public security system literally *bought* the services of "more than 3,300 *tewu*, renegades and counterrevolutionary elements" to become "anti-espionage backbones."[15] The Shanghai Public Security

---

[13] Stephen Averill, "The Origins of the Futian Incident," pp. 100–108. Guo, *China's Security State*, pp. 27–55, especially pp. 28–30.

[14] Suzanne Pepper, *The Civil War in China*, p. 43 and passim.

[15] Schoenhals, *Spying for the People*, p. 93, fn. 24. Original citation in fn. 24 is *Chedi Liu Deng Peng Luo zai Shanghai gongan bumen de liudu* ([Thoroughly eradicate the poison that Liu, Deng, Peng, and Luo spread throughout the public security organs of Shanghai]: (Shanghai: Shanghai shi gongan ju lianhe doupingai xiaozu, 1967), p. 1. Frederic Wakeman, "Cleanup: The New Order in Shanghai," p. 52.

Bureau's own estimate of the numbers of active *tewu* from the outgoing regime ran to "over 5,000," but the possible number of *tewu* in the greater Shanghai area might have been even higher – if intelligence agents were good at what they did, they might have gone undetected.

Internal security in Taiwan was equally problematic. Like the CCP in the greater Shanghai area, it had to quickly and rigorously separate "them" from "us," and it had to do so under local circumstances that were even less favorable. If the CCP had to win over a Shanghainese population that was nervously watchful in the late spring of 1949, the GMD had to contend with a population that roundly despised the government as a murderous and incompetent regime. Taiwanese memories of the GMD's violent suppression of the February 28, 1947, uprising were still raw. Most of the non-mainlander population was implicated in some degree of collaboration with the Japanese and those least tainted who had escaped the February 28 repression were also the most politically suspect. The most anti-Japanese tended also to be most committed to democracy and self-determination for Taiwan.

In addition, the GMD was profoundly paranoid about its own internal cohesion and purity. This was felt to be such a pressing issue that the GMD mobilized for what Bruce Dickson has characterized as the Guomindang's "first, last, and only effective Party rectification," between August 1950 and 1952.[16] There were indeed reasons to launch this kind of stringent GMD Party rectification; not only had the GMD been ineffective, weak, and faction riven, it had even been subjected to very recent penetration by Communist moles. In 1949, Chiang Kai-shek's personal stenographer, Anna Shen, was revealed to have been a deep undercover Communist agent, with access to the most sensitive of information over a decade of service at the very highest level in the Central Executive Committee of the Guomindang Party.[17]

In the ideologically charged circumstances of scarce concrete information, unclear loyalties, regional insecurity, and ongoing civil war, in 1949–1951, neither regime possessed an excess of delicacy in standards of proof, or in the rights of the accused when each could plausibly claim that the state's survival was at stake. In the young People's Republic, the number of unaccounted-for *tewu* in Sunan, how active they were, what their continued links with the Guomindang might be, and how to

---

[16] Bruce Dickson, *Democratization in China and Taiwan*, pp. 56–84.

[17] After a remarkable career of service at the highest levels in the GMD Central Party Committee, Anna Shen simply avoided retreating south with the rest of the Guomindang, returned quietly to Shanghai to await the PLA, and eventually passed away in Beijing at the age of ninety-five. See Schoenhals, *Spying for the People*, p. 102, fn. 60.

distinguish them from the majority who had simply gone along with the outgoing GMD, provided a set of conditions for legitimate concern that could then be ratcheted up or down as needs shifted. In the weeks after takeover, a number of cases were broken that involved *tewu*, small caches of arms, and telegraphs (ostensibly for communication with either the GMD and/or the CIA). Since families frequently split in their alignments on opposite sides of the civil war, those who were on the losing side were sometimes shielded by family members.[18] If most of the GMD "big fish" had fled to either Hong Kong or Taiwan, there was likely a substantial reservoir of lower level sympathizers still in Sunan, at least some of whom might well be in contact with the GMD.

It is also beyond question that, in 1949, the CCP was laying the groundwork for the eventual takeover of Taiwan. After the Japanese colonial government had thoroughly extirpated Communist networks on Taiwan in the late 1920s, Communist Party organization on the island was entirely directed by the Chinese Communist Party from the East China Military Region. In February 1946, the CCP sent two Taiwanese cadres, Cai Xiaoqian （蔡孝乾) and Zhang Zhizhong (張志忠), to Shanghai for training. It was in Shanghai that the Taiwan subsidiary of the Chinese Communist Party was formally established as the "Taiwan Provincial Work Committee" (Taiwan Sheng Gongzuo Weiyuanhui/ Taigonghui – 臺灣省工作委員台共會/ 臺共會). Its brief was identical in language and tone to CCP directives elsewhere: to build party organizations, to unite with workers, peasants, and revolutionary intellectuals, and to engage in multiple activities – to collect intelligence on the GMD military, economy, and the local people's mood, establish Communist militias, and prepare for a local uprising to welcome the eventual military liberation of Taiwan.[19] And certainly, the growth of the Communist underground in Taiwan from almost zero in early 1946 to "more than 70" at the time of the February 28 Incident in 1947, 400 in June 1948, and "over 900" by August 1950 must have given cause for alarm.[20]

---

[18] For example, in the Republican period, Deng Tuo was frequently bailed out by his GMD official brother. Timothy Cheek, *Propaganda and Culture in Mao's China*, pp. 8, 44, 52. The problem of cadres who quietly shielded counterrevolutionary family members is also referred to indirectly in scattered official accounts. See also SMA A22/2/50, "Shifu jiguan ganbu buchong tianbiaozhong de xuanchuan jiaoyu gongzuo zhongjie" (Summary report on the dissemination and education work on municipal government cadre supplementary forms). Unfortunately, there is no way to ascertain how frequent this sort of quiet shielding was.

[19] This listing is drawn from "Fei taisheng gongzuo weiyuanhui panluan an" (Case on the bandit Taiwan provincial work committee's rebellion), taken from the archive of the National Security Bureau, NZASH Vol. 1, pp. 55–61.

[20] Ibid., p. 60.

Selection bias and/or overclaiming make it very difficult to tell whether either of these consolidating regimes was seriously compromised in the early 1950s. By the time a case was sanitized for entry in a gazeteer or a legal ruling was generated, the accused was assumed to be guilty. Given the prevalence of forced confessions, guilt by association, the presumption of guilt, and the wider hysteria of the time, it is virtually impossible to assess the veracity of these claims from the currently available official record.[21] However, the balance of evidence that we have at present suggests that in Sunan and Taiwan, for every major network that was broken, there were many more that were populated by relatively minor and often not terribly bright characters. For example, in the early days after the Communist takeover of Nanjing, police apprehended a Guomindang *tewu* agent, who led them to where his co-conspirators lived. When the police arrived, they noted a large sign on the door which proclaimed: "only democrats living here: entry forbidden to those from new government or military organizations."[22] These conspirators might as well have sent an engraved invitation to the new public security bureau to come and take them away. In another case, an attempted establishment of a Guomindang spy station for the greater Shanghai area in late May 1949 was broken within weeks. The other networks about which we have information possessed "hardware" amounting to a few rifles and/ or handguns, some rounds of ammunition, and a portable telegraph or two. This degree of organized subversion was hardly going to be enough to bring down, or even seriously hamper, the new regime.

Based on fragmentary available evidence, the case of Feng Qizeng (風企曽) was among the most serious in the early months after the PLA's takeover of Sunan. Feng had held a variety of positions in the Guomindang military, security, and civilian administrations, and had been active in counterintelligence. He spent the summer of 1949 holed up at Xiaoyangshan on the Zhoushan archipelago, which continued to be held by the GMD military until July 19, 1950. In September 1949 he made a trip to Taiwan, where he met with Mao Renfeng (毛人風 – head of the GMD Security Bureau). Mao duly appointed Feng head of a newly created Jiangsu-Zhejiang special intelligence station. With additional and secret support from the CIA, in January 1950 Feng was dispatched to

---

[21] For an excellent example of revisionist scholarship on this period for the People's Republic of China, see Kuisong Yang, "Reconsidering the Campaign to Suppress Counterrevolutionaries," pp. 102–121, and Jeremy Brown, "From Resisting Communists to Resisting America." For Taiwan, see Feuchtwang, *After the Event*, which uses oral histories to outline the GMD suppression of a putative base area in Luku, just to the east of Taibei, in 1952–1953, pp. 116–119.
[22] *NGZ*, p. 187.

Sunan via Zhoushan with "7 telegraphs, 500 short-barrelled pistols, and a monthly fund of 2,700 silver dollars," and promptly began to establish small networks in coastal locations that included Songjiang, Nanhui, Taicang, and Pinghu. But once the GMD military abandoned the Zhoushan archipelago in mid-July 1950, Feng's base of operations was no longer secure. He was detained in Shanghai on July 28, along with forty-three other uniformed *tewu*, one telegraph, two recording devices, and six handguns. What happened to the other 6 telegraphs and 494 pistols is not stated.[23]

We now know that, apart from the still unsecured and distant southwest of China where the civil war still raged, neither of these regimes faced a significant insurgency. While there were secret agents and informers who infiltrated both sides, in the long run each of these governments would not only survive, but also become well consolidated and very successful. Realistically, what were the chances of Feng and his forty-three recruits, or Cai Xiaoqian and an almost non-existent party underground, making much of a dent in the territories in which the state's coercive and military power was so thoroughly established? Hindsight suggests that they were very low. At the time, though, the leaders of both regimes were keenly aware of their outsider status and lack of deep support from the population.

There were also regional and international security factors to consider. In 1949, the Occupation in Japan turned in an increasingly conservative direction and Douglas MacArthur, the chief of SCAP, had a well-deserved reputation as a notorious anti-Communist with a penchant for exceeding his brief. A *de facto* civil war between Communists and non-Communists was already in motion on the Korean peninsula. The official position of the United States was in flux: the Department of State was indicating unwillingness to become further involved in the Chinese civil war while conservative Republicans in Congress and the press were apoplectic over the rise of the Communists in China. But historic US support for the Chiang Kai-shek regime provided good reason for the CCP to be suspicious. When ROC bombers, using American planes, succeeded in carrying out a raid on Shanghai's two main electrical power plants on February 1, 1950,[24] the alarmist view that the Americans were likely to re-arm Chiang Kai-shek to return to China suddenly became much more plausible.

---

[23] *SGZ*, p. 100.

[24] Office of Shanghai Chronicles (in English), see www.shtong.gov.cn/node2/node82288/node82292/node82294/userobject1ai111197.html, accessed January 21, 2014.

The Guomindang on Taiwan had even more reason to be concerned about external security. It was confronted by a much larger foe only a short distance away, the official American position had decisively washed its hands of the Chinese civil war, and the regime had ample grounds to expect that the PLA would launch a successful amphibious invasion of Taiwan in the summer of 1950. It was only the unexpected outbreak of the war in Korea in June 1950 that prompted the United States to redefine its strategy of containment explicitly to include South Korea and Taiwan in its "defensive perimeter."[25] The almost immediate dispatch of the US Seventh Fleet to "neutralize" the Taiwan Straits after the outbreak of hostilities in Korea preserved the GMD regime in Taiwan, artificially freezing the status quo. By the early autumn of 1950, the PRC faced a security nightmare: a well-equipped, US-dominated military campaign headed towards its border. Worse still, this army was commanded by MacArthur, who was prone to make alarming statements about widening the war, bombing along the Yalu River, and rolling back the Communists in China. Both the PRC and the ROC had good reason to be paranoid about continued existential threats amid a Cold War turned hot.

The PRC and the ROC sought to manage external security through formal and informal alliances with militarily stronger partners. That Mao was on his way to the Soviet Union so soon after the formal establishment of the People's Republic, and that the Sino-Soviet alliance was concluded barely three and a half months after October 1949 likely reflects some of this urgency for the PRC. A formal treaty between the United States and the ROC/Taiwan was not concluded until December 1954. But a *de facto* alliance came into existence immediately after the outbreak of the Korean War, and staggering amounts of military and economic aid began to flow into Taiwan from mid-1950.[26] Securing the state through alliances protected each from external attack. But ensuring internal security was a domestic business, pursued by drawing of increasingly sharp lines of demarcation between the inner (good) and the outer (depraved), and by strengthening the domestic organizations of the state to combat real and imagined subversion.

Measures to ensure domestic security were implemented through a mix of campaign and bureaucratic modalities. The formal, bureaucratic, and procedural included the establishment of the East China Military Region's Public Security work group and the Taiwan Garrison Command (TGC). These organizations established policy and required

---

[25] Nancy B. Tucker, *Taiwan, Hong Kong, and the United States, 1945–1992,* pp. 28–32.
[26] Gerald Chan, "Taiwan as an Emerging Foreign Aid Donor: Developments, Problems, and Prospects," cites the figure of $1.5 billion in economic aid and $2.5 billion in military aid given between 1950 and 1965.

more local organizations in the government apparatus to implement such measures as universal registration (to fix and monitor the population), augmenting everyday state coercion by expanding formal institutions (the police, security services), and increasingly routinizing measures such as opening domestic mail and recruiting informers. Other parts of the effort to ensure domestic security involved campaign modalities that intensified policy focus, stressed quick results, and suspended regular rules and procedures. These included crackdowns on crime, rapid sweeps to identify and prosecute political subversion, and, in the case of the PRC, popular mobilization that concluded with public accusation meetings against the accused. In both Sunan and Taiwan these campaigns – sharp, vigorous intensifications of policy focus – merged with other ongoing campaigns. In Sunan, active implementation of the Campaign to Suppress Counterrevolutionaries so overlapped with land reform campaigns that in the exurbs around Shanghai and other large cities in Sunan it was often impossible to tell which "targets" properly belonged to which campaign. In Taiwan, a series of highly coercive police-cum-military actions now known as the "White Terror" similarly overlapped with a stringent party rectification campaign between 1950 and 1952, a series of purges in the military, and land reform.[27]

Combating Subversion: Defined Beginnings Versus Rolling Starts

At first glance, the ways in which concerns about internal security and subversion were voiced and acted upon in the PRC and ROC/Taiwan appeared to diverge quite sharply. Was the campaign openly labeled and trumpeted as a sharp break from the past, or was it concealed and represented as simply a more effective intensified continuation of earlier practices? The CCP openly recognized its campaigns of the early 1950s, and it valorized them as demonstrations of its popularity and righteousness in winning over the masses. What has since become recognized as the "Maoist" approach to politics, comprising a blend of techniques including reliance on the poor peasantry, the "mass line," and widespread social mobilization directed by the Chinese Communist Party to pursue goals is so intimately wrapped up with campaigns that it is virtually impossible to speak of Maoism without the mass line and mass campaigns. Campaigns were widely understood to be a – if not *the* – critical cluster of practices

---

[27] Dickson, 1997, pp. 55–56; Dickson 1993, pp. 56–84; Ramon H. Myers and Ting-lin Hsiao, "Breaking with the Past: The Kuomintang Central Reform Committee on Taiwan, 1950–1952."

that allowed the CCP to mobilize such popular support and win the civil war against all odds. Under these circumstances, it is little wonder that mobilizational campaigns became the signature means by which policies were implemented and "the masses" in theory drawn in once victory in the civil war had been won.[28]

The era of mass movements in the young PRC commenced a scant year after the CCP came to power, with the "Three Great Campaigns" (*sange da yundong* – 三個大運動) that began in the autumn of 1950 with the Aid Korea-Resist America campaign, rapidly followed by the Campaign to Suppress Counterrevolutionaries, and the Land Reform Campaign (for the regions of the country that had not already undergone land reform, including Sunan). The Campaign to Suppress Counterrevolutionaries marked a critical departure for the regime. It was the first to be directed at internal enemies, the first to draw in large numbers of regular citizens to shout their approval of the state's violence, the first to disseminate categories drawn from Marxist-Leninist theory to mobilize urban populations, and the first to resort to quotas of "targets." Many of these characteristic features had, of course, been in evidence during the Jiangxi Soviet (1930–1934), in the crucible of Yan'an in the early to mid-1940s, and in the rural campaigns of the late 1940s in the parts of the north China countryside under the control of the CCP.[29] But 1950–1951 was the first occasion that such techniques were deployed on a national scale, in regions with significant urban concentrations and economies far removed from impoverished rural base areas. Within China, the Campaign to Suppress Counterrevolutionaries' core repertoires: intensive propaganda and small group study, mobilizing the masses, defining and hitting hard against undesirables as enemies of the state, and ridding society of evil as defined by the vanguard party were propagated and commemorated in official histories and narratives as correct, hugely successful, and essential components in the establishment of New China.

The abrupt harshness of the Campaign to Suppress Counterrevolutionaries was an enormous contrast to the "New Democracy" policies designed to reassure and include as many patriotic Chinese as possible during the government's first year in power. Nowhere had this accommodating tone

---

[28] Dutton, p. 16, pp. 143, 162, and passim.

[29] The literature on the core practices of the Maoist variant of the Chinese revolution is vast. Some of the more important works include Mark Selden, *China in Revolution: The Yen'an Way Revisited*; Pauline Keating, *Two Revolutions, Village Reconstruction and the Cooperative Movement in Northern Shaanxi 1934–1945*, Odoric Wou, *Mobilizing the Masses: Building Revolution in Henan*, and David E. Apter and Tony Saich, *Revolutionary Discourse in Mao's Republic*.

been more in evidence than in Sunan, which the government needed for its industrial production and enormous wealth. Initially, the young PRC stressed patient education and integration of nearly all social classes apart from those that were *tewu* who had worked for the GMD's Zhongtong and Juntong. In late 1949 and early 1950, the CCP explicitly reassured capitalists that they would not be expropriated at any time in the foreseeable future, encouraged factories to re-open, and revived local markets. Although some in the highest reaches of the CCP were beginning to think about a major campaign against counterrevolutionaries as early as March 1950, the actual preparation for the campaign occurred as regional tensions over Korea were rising in the summer of 1950. The public face of the campaign was launched with maximum patriotic fervor to coincide with the Republican era's national holiday on October 10, 1950, and, not entirely coincidentally, the run-up to China's dispatch of "volunteers" to fight on behalf of the Kim Il-sung regime in Korea.[30] Thus, the shift to the vigorous prosecution of domestic counterrevolutionaries was framed by intense worry over regional (in)security, and was unimaginable apart from the surrounding backdrop of war in Korea.

The Campaign to Suppress Counterrevolutionaries was inaugurated with no little fanfare through the dissemination of the "Double 10" Directive on the symbolically important date of National Day, October 10, 1950.[31] This foundational document publicly called upon the entire country to abandon its previous "excessive lenience" (*kuanda wubian* – 寬大無邊) in favor of "harsh and quick suppression" (*yanli jisi de zhenya* – 嚴厲緝私的鎮壓) of counterrevolutionaries. Although the word "terror" (*kongbu* – 恐怖) was not used directly, campaign documents and speeches were replete with language that made no apology for directly terrorizing counterrevolutionary enemies: cadres were enjoined to "hit hard" against lurking counterrevolutionaries, and "not to fear executing people, only to fear wrongly executing people."[32] When the campaign accelerated in the late winter of 1951, Peng Zhen, then mayor of Beijing, characterized the Campaign as necessarily comprising a full complement of "shaking

---

[30] Dutton, *Policing Chinese Politics*, pp 169–170.

[31] "Zhonggong zhongyang guanyu zhenya faneming huodong de zhishi" (Party and center directive on the suppression of counterrevolutionary activities), October 10, 1950. JZWX, Vol. 1, pp. 421–422.

[32] Luo Ruiqing," Zhonggong zhongyang pizhuan zhongyang gong'an bu 'guanyu quanguo gong'anhuiyi de baogao'" (Party and center approval and circulation of the central government Ministry of Public Security "Report on National Police Conference"), December 28, 1950. JZWX, Vol. 1, p. 443.

and stirring" (*zhendong konghuang* – 震動恐慌).[33] Like Robespierre before them, the authorities in charge of the revolutionary PRC were more than willing to acknowledge, and even celebrate, the violence and excesses of the Campaign to Suppress Counterrevolutionaries as a necessary and just part of revolutionary regime consolidation.

Just how plausible these concerns about domestic insecurity were remains unclear. In the eighteen months between the CCP's takeover Shanghai and the end of 1950, public security cracked 652 cases of *tewu* spies, and arrested 5,675 – suggesting that the young PRC's security and intelligence organizations were neither idle, nor ineffective.[34] Other sources document a relatively small figure of 274 of those executed for counterrevolutionary activity between December 29, 1949, and January 11, 1951, all of whom were *tewu* intelligence agents.[35]

The central government was, however, deeply dissatisfied with the *way* many regions in the country had been unreasonably mild in their treatment of counterrevolutionaries. The Sunan region was particularly singled out for criticism for its "gentility" in smashing counterrevolutionaries, for the painfully slow way that it processed cases through the regular courts, and its dearth of sharp and clear results. When Luo Ruiqing, Minister of Security, toured the cities of central and south China in February of 1951 to check on the progress of the campaign, he was shocked by the local authorities' cautious attitude, reluctance to forge links with the masses, and insufficiently strong implementation.[36] While central authorities conceded that Nanjing, the recent Guomindang capital, had smashed a satisfying number of counterrevolutionary networks, they opined that Nanjing's regular judicial procedures were far too slow and its sentencing inappropriately lenient, with only two counterrevolutionaries given a death sentence for the entirety of 1949–1950. On these grounds Nanjing was publicly held up as a particularly egregious example of "excessive lenience" (*kuanda wubian* – 寬大無邊) that needed rectification.[37]

---

[33] Peng Zhen, "Guanyu zhenya fangeming he chengzhi fangeming tiaolie wenti de baogao," February 20, 1951 (Report given at the Eleventh Conference of the Central Government Committee). JZWX, Vol. 2, p. 51.

[34] *SGZ*, p. 99.

[35] SMA B1/2/1339. "Fangeming zuifan chuxign fenlei tongjibiao" (Classification and statistical form for counterrevolutionary criminals), January 1951.

[36] Luo Ruiqing, "Guanyu Wuhan, Shanghai deng chengshi zhenfan gongzuo de kaocha baogao" (Investigation report on the suppression of counterrevolutionaries in Wuhan, Shanghai and other cities), March 20, 1951. LRGZ, pp.55–58.

[37] "Zhongyang gong'an bu guanyu quanguo gong'an huiyi de baogao," (Central Ministry of Public Security report on all-country meeting on public security) October 26, 1950, JZWX, Vol. 1, p. 442; *NGZ*, p. 190.

Evidence from Shanghai further suggests that the municipal party committee had a great deal of work to do to overcome the moral scruples of its local cadres. Government work unit leaders "generally held a 'merciful view' (*renci guannian* – 仁慈 觀念), which supposed that 'education could solve all problems.'" Others insisted that their own offices did not harbor any counterrevolutionaries, or even grumbled that a major Campaign to Suppress Counterrevolutionaries was "like cracking a nut with a sledgehammer" (*xiaoti dazuo* – 小題大作).[38] If Nanjing and Shanghai are typical of Sunan, then the problem was not that the police, internal security forces, and judiciary were not doing their jobs, and doing them well. Rather the complaint was that the *way* Sunan local cadres prosecuted counterrevolutionaries was insufficiently campaign-like. Until February 1951, local authorities in Sunan conducted the campaign through a "normal" bureaucratic modality: adhering to regular judicial procedure, which involved a lengthy process of evidence gathering, arrest, questioning, presentation of evidence to a court, and eventual sentencing. These processes were in turn heavily rule oriented in terms of regular procedures, standards about evidence, documentation, and hearsay. They also required authorization from superiors before the imposition of the death penalty. Judicial procedures by their very nature (rule, precedent, procedurally oriented, and lengthy delays for confirmation of death sentencing) blunted the kinds of quick results, popular participation, and publicly performed justice demanded by the campaign modality. This was exactly what was at stake when Luo Ruiqing so severely criticized party authorities in the big cities in the Yangzi Valley in February 1951: Luo was in effect ordering that a campaign modality of policy implementation overrule the "regular" bureaucratic and procedural one.[39] The Campaign to Suppress Counterrevolutionaries in Sunan was not only a means to apprehend and rid the country of enemies of the state. It was also an effort to galvanize the commitments of its regional and local state agents into setting aside their own bureaucratic modality of policy implementation by rule, procedure, and process, and to at least temporarily replace it with a campaign modality of mass mobilization and extraordinarily quick, visible, public results.

In contrast to the PRC, which blared the inauguration of its campaigns to all and sundry while demanding immediate and visible large-scale

[38] SMA A22/2/50, "Shifu jiguan ganbu buchong tianbiaozhong de xuanchuan jiaoyu gong-zuo zongjie" (General report on the dissemination and education work on the municipal government cadre's supplementary forms), July 31, 1951.

[39] Luo Ruiqing, "Guanyu Wuhan, Shanghai deng chengshi zhenfan gongzuo de kaocha baogao" (Investigation report on the suppression of counterrevolutionaries in Wuhan, Shanghai and other cities), in LRGZ, pp. 55–58.

bureaucratic and social mobilization, the ROC/Taiwan moved into its campaign to suppress subversion in a manner that was restricted to the nascent security organizations of the truncated ROC state. Unlike the PRC, which publicly and sharply reversed the explicit moderation and inclusiveness in its first year in power, the ROC/Taiwan's anti-subversive actions were not dramatically and clearly delineated from what had come immediately before. The intensification of coercion in Taiwan in the early 1950s that is now called the "White Terror" began with much more of a "rolling start" than was the case in the PRC.[40]

Guomindang authorities on Taiwan seldom, if ever, referred publicly to their activities to ensure internal security as "campaigns" (*yundong* – 運動), and they only rarely used the term in internal documents.[41] Still less did they identify their actions either publicly or privately as a "Terror" (*kongbu* – 恐怖) – of White, Blue (the color of the Guomindang), or any other hue, preferring instead to deflect embarrassing questions about internal security measures in the 1950s and the decades thereafter. When it was impossible to evade such questions from concerned US advisors, the government represented itself and its actions as the morally necessary outcome of *law* that guaranteed social and political order in the face of Communist subversion.[42] For the ROC/Taiwan, openly visible campaigns involving mass mobilization were markers that distinguished the [illegitimate and chaotic] Communist "them" from the pure and orderly Nationalist "us."

If, however, campaigns are characterized as extraordinary periods of sharp and delimited intensifications of policy implementation that mobilized manpower and resources to quickly achieve particular objectives, then the ROC/Taiwan's rapid acceleration of arrests and prosecution for political crimes in the early 1950s were campaigns, albeit without the

---

[40] I am indebted to Michael Schoenhals for his suggestive application of the notion to the beginnings of campaigns in the People's Republic of China. The metaphor was applied originally to the US-led "War on Terror." See the BBC News article, "Analysis: America's 'Rolling Start Attack," Monday, January 13, 2003, http://news.bbc.co.uk/2/hi/americas/2652559.stm. Accessed on February 2, 2014.

[41] One rare exception can be found in an internal statistical form filled out as part of the Taiwan Garrison Command's Work Report of 1951, "Jiansu feidie yundong jingban zishou anjian fenban tongji biao" (Statistics on managing the cases of surrender [due to] the Clearing Out Communist Traitors' Movement). NZASH, Vol. 1, p. 47.

[42] DS LM075, Reel 6, 794. "Formosa Peace Preservations HQ Functions," Chiang Kai-shek comments to Allen Whiting, Ford Foundation Grantee, Dispatch No. 262, November 30, 1954; see also Greitens, *Dictators and Their Secret Police*, which suggests that in 1950, the otherwise liberal pro-American K. C. Wu and General Tang Zong were both unapologetic about the vigor of the crackdown, which the US State Department in Taibei estimated at around "around 15,000 victims" in 1949. As of mid-August, the estimate ran to an additional 23,000, amounting to a stunning one in every 200 who was arrested on political grounds over a 17-month period, p. 191, and fn. 36.

openly proclaimed and mass mobilizational aspects that were such prominent features of the PRC variant. The ROC/Taiwan suppression of subversion was conducted almost in its entirety in the shadows. Nameless security organizations operated and reported to their superiors in the party-state in secrecy. Walls of silence were erected everywhere. The government declined even to name its activities, cloaking itself in the rhetoric of maintaining security and expunging spies.

Unlike Sunan, where the new regime explicitly offered an initial year-long period of moderation and inclusion towards all but the most diehard supporters of the GMD, in Taiwan there was no first year of reconciliation and moderation. Instead the GMD defaulted to replicating and intensifying the kinds of heavy-handed tactics of repression that it had used to so little effect to quell the "sedition" of student movements in the Anti-Hunger, Anti-Civil War student movements of 1947 and 1948, when GMD authorities in large cities in China had responded harshly and ineffectively to student movements, declaring that they were the product of Communist agitation.

In Taiwan even overlapping and chaotic security organizations were able to quell a nascent student movement in the spring protest season of 1949, just as its fortunes were entering their lowest ebb with the military loss of the big cities in the Yangzi river valley in China. What, then, was so different about Taiwan in 1949 compared to the mainland, where these tactics had been so singularly ineffective? There are four possible factors at play in explaining this significant difference in outcome: (1) Crude as it was, GMD coercive capacity in the Taiwan of 1949 was sufficiently concentrated to quell the "disturbances" at hand. Even in its weakened and fragmented state, GMD security systems in Taiwan were much more powerful relative to the size of the population than had been the case when it had to cope with student unrest in China's main cities in the previous two years.[43] (2) Because the security response to the first hints of public protest was instantaneous and harsh, it was able to shut things down in very short order. (3) University students in Taiwan lacked the dense networks and recent histories of cross-institution and trans-urban organization, communication, and repertoires of protest that had been so prominent in Republican era Shanghai and Beijing. In 1949, Taiwan's only two universities – National Taiwan University and Taiwan Normal Institute (today's Taiwan Normal University) – were geographically nearly contiguous and within walking distance of the government seat in Taibei. There were no other comparable institutions or cities to which the protests could easily spread. (Several Chinese universities, along with

---

[43] Greitens, *Dictators and Their Secret Police*, pp. 83–86.

Academia Sinica, would eventually be reconstituted in Taiwan in the early 1950s, but in 1949 this had not yet occurred.) And finally, (4) unlike the situation in Beijing or Shanghai in the late 1940s, bystanders did not appear to get involved in the student protests, perhaps because of the collective memory of the GMD's brutal suppression of the islandwide uprising only two years previously.

The links between the regime's handling of restive students on the mainland and in 1949 in Taiwan are clear: they built on and intensified earlier repertoires in the more geographically more circumscribed location of Taibei.[44] In the springtime protest seasons of 1947 and 1948, waves of student demonstrations had broken out in the large cities of Nanjing, Shanghai, Beijing, and Tianjin. Students protested over a range of issues – the appallingly low salaries for academics and declining stipends for students due to hyperinflation, the prosecution of a deeply unpopular civil war, and the regime's own harsh responses to the protests in the "Provisional Measures for Maintaining Public Order" that criminalized protest, met protest with violence, and justified mass arrests on highly dubious legal grounds.[45] When protests continued, the authorities' reactions drove underground the nascent all-China Federation of Students organization, blacklisted student protesters, and invoked provisions of martial law.[46]

Only in retrospect do these government responses appear to be a harbinger of the GMD's successful intensification of repression in Taiwan. The event that straddles the weak and ineffective repressiveness of the GMD on the mainland and the infinitely stronger, more effective, and still repressive GMD on Taiwan broke out under circumstances that would have been painfully familiar to the GMD from its unhappy experiences with student strikes in 1947 and 1948. In early April 1949, student grain ration stipends in Taiwan were suddenly cut from the market rate of 12Y for 30 Taiwanese *jin* (roughly 500 grams) to an unspecified less than market rate for only 25 Taiwanese *jin*. With this sudden reduction of basic caloric entitlement, two students at Taiwan Normal Institute called a meeting at the main campus auditorium at 8:25 a.m. on April 6. Three recommendations emerged: (1) to push for change; (2) to engage in obstructive measures; and (3) to call for student strikes. The division heads for the Taiwan Normal Institute's Training, Student Life, and Military Education sectors were called immediately to the scene, but

[44] "Effectiveness" in this respect only means effectiveness from the point of view of the government, which wished to close down displays of public protest.

[45] For a full consideration of the Anti-Hunger, Anti-Civil War protests of 1947 and 1948, see Pepper, *Civil War in China*, pp. 42–94.

[46] Ibid, pp. 66–67.

were unable to satisfy student grievances. (This was not surprising, as educational division heads had no authority to alter the terms of the grain rationing system.) At 9:30 a.m., students from the Taiwan Normal Institute walked to the Taiwan Provincial Executive Office (Taiwan Changguanshu– 臺灣長官署) where they shouted "disruptive" slogans from 11:00 a.m. to 5:00 p.m. When a reporter from a small daily news outlet in Jilong happened on the scene, a student surnamed Zeng began to openly castigate the government, cursing that the Three Principles of the People (*sanmin zhuyi* – 三民主義) weren't nearly as good as Japanese military rule had been, and provocatively "began to slander outsiders who have come to Taiwan . . . and disturb social order."[47]

When a meeting of the Taiwan Provincial Advisory Council was convened to review the incident some two months later, it asked tough questions. How had a state of such popular dissatisfaction with the government gotten so out of hand so quickly? Why was resentment so deep? What could be done to prevent a further occurrence? The official responses to these questions were bland to the point of meaninglessness. But when the official judgments on the April 6 protests were revealed, their severity was stark. One protestor, an ex-student by the name of Ou Zhenlong, was retroactively found to have been an active leader in the proscribed Taiwan Democratic Self-Governing Alliance (Taiwan Minzhu Zizhi Tongmeng – 民主自治同盟), and was sentenced to death. Two other protesters, Wu Shixiong and Hong Jinsheng, were given fifteen-year sentences, three others were given ten years, and another unnamed protester got off fairly lightly with only a five-year sentence. Of Zeng there is no further mention.[48]

The GMD's invocation of the death penalty and such lengthy periods of incarceration were unprecedentedly harsh punishments for students, who were normally treated more leniently than protesters from other sectors. In the previous two protest seasons in China, the government had not been able to make any of its claims stick: in the end all arrested students were released amid waves of popular anger.[49] Such was not the case in Taiwan for those who demonstrated in April 1949, when draconian sentences were passed on student protesters who, ironically enough, were conspicuous in their relative *lack* of demonstrable ties to the Communist underground in Taiwan. After the capture and "turning" of almost the entirety of the senior Communist Party leadership a year later, interrogations revealed that only one of the sentenced individuals was linked to the Communist underground in Taiwan in any way. Rather, the

[47] TSSA, pp. 11–12.   [48] TSSA, pp. 174–181.   [49] Pepper, pp. 77, 82–83.

students who marched and dared to openly criticize the government in the spring of 1949 were outraged by exactly the kinds of issues that animated students in China's other cities: the abrupt and high-handed reduction of subsistence in combination with official inability or willingness to respond to student concerns. In addition, Taiwanese protesters were still resentful of the GMD's brutality in the February 28 Incident of 1947, and contemptuous of the government's ineffectiveness and corruption.[50] The reasons for student protests and the government's justification for the crackdown were identical in late 1940s China and Taiwan in the spring of 1949. What differed was the effectiveness of the government's response in Taiwan, when the multiple security organizations of the ROC/Taiwan began to radically intensify scrutiny and issue harsh responses to individuals and groups who could in any be imagined as forces for social disorder.

Despite the profound uncertainty about the survival of the regime in the unsettled period between April 1949 and the outbreak of the Korean War, security organizations in the ROC/Taiwan used this time to intensify the harsh tactics it had displayed in crushing the student demonstration of April 6. The government declared a state of martial law for the island some six weeks later, on May 20, 1949, immediately followed by new regulations that proscribed a range of activities (many of them previously entirely legal, such as reading left-wing newspapers). Surveillance, undercover work, and the "smashing" of major cases accelerated in September 1949, when the key institution for the apprehension and sentencing of subversives, the Taiwan Garrison Command, began to keep official records.[51] By the early autumn of 1949 an entire extra-civilian system of military courts had been set up to process the intensified detection and prosecution of

---

[50] XGWA, pp. 21–23. Unusually, this documentary collection also contains the transcripts of interrogations of the accused. The editor helpfully creates a table which lays out the self reported reasons each individual had for participating in the Communist party. Of these twenty-nine individuals, eight explicitly mention the February 28 Incident, seven refer to dissatisfaction with the government and/or its corruption, five to the plight of the proletariat, eight mention that they thought that there would be personal material gain (a job, free tuition) with a Communist government, and only one had participated in the April 6 Incident.

[51] Between late 1945 and August 1949 the Jingbei Siling Bu (臺灣省警備司令部), or Taiwan Provincial Garrison, was the key instrument of domestic security in Taiwan. In mid-August 1949, it was renamed the Taiwan Provincial Security Command or Taiwan Sheng Bao'an Siling Bu (臺灣省保安司令部). In 1958, it merged with the Taiwan Provincial Defence Command (臺灣省防偽總司領部) and the Taiwan Provincial Civil Defence Command (臺灣省民防 司令部) when it became known as the Taiwan Garrison Command (臺灣警備總司令部). For the sake of simplicity, in the text I refer to these three organizations, perhaps a touch anachronistically, as the Taiwan Garrison Command (TGC). In footnote translations, I use the original proper names.

the increasing numbers who fell afoul of newly invoked martial law. Clumsy and chaotic though it may have been, the engine of repression was already in high gear before the outbreak of war in Korea guaranteed the survival of the regime.[52]

While the CCP needed to bypass the regular judicial organizations of the state and overcome the natural rule orientation of its subordinate government organizations to signal that the period of lenience and inclusion was to be replaced with a mass campaign, the GMD on Taiwan equally deliberately set about doing just the opposite: establishing a legal framework and rule-oriented set of organizations for processing the results of its campaign of intensification against undesirables.

"Counterrevolutionaries" and "Bandits" in Theory and Practice

It has long been understood that one of the most important activities of the CCP after 1949 was to create and disseminate a new revolutionary language, with new categories of class analysis and new narratives to make a sharp rhetorical and linguistic break with the past. In so doing, the CCP scaled up a process that was well underway in the Yan'an period (1937–1945) to the entirety of the country.[53] Conversely, the Guomindang was faced with exactly the opposite problem, namely how to establish continuity – linguistic as well as institutional – with the pre-1949 past, despite the very different and "scaled down" circumstances in which it found itself in Taiwan. Both regimes needed terms that

---

[52] Dating the onset of the White Terror is deeply contentious. Some take the promulgation of martial law on May 20, 1949, as the beginning, JTZRK, p. iv. Others begin with the slightly earlier "April 6" (1949) student demonstrations. Still others see the White Terror as a simple continuation of the February 28 suppression of 1947. While absolute numbers remain contested, there is general agreement that the worst years for "White Terror" were the early 1950s, after which the number of political cases fell dramatically. See Greitens, Figures 6.1 and 6.2, p. 181, for an analysis of the numbers of individuals sentenced and executed over the course of martial law in Taiwan. See also Hsiao-ting Lin, *Accidental State: Chiang Kai-shek, the United States, and the Making of Taiwan* pp. 180–183. While a case can certainly be made for any of these points of origin as the repression was characterized by a "rolling start," I prefer dating that is consistent with the government's own record keeping and methods of suppression. The key institutions of suppression in Taiwan only began to keep systematic records, logs, and statistics on cases of subversion at the end of September, 1949, and this suggests that repression, while it certainly existed prior to the autumn of 1949 began to intensify as a systematic and widespread campaign at this time. See NZASH Vol. 1, "Taiwan Jingbeizongbu gongzuo baogao (38 nian) (Taiwan Garrison Command Work Report, 1949), pp. 12–13.

[53] Apter and Saich, pp. 35–36; Chang-tai Hung, *Mao's New World: Political Culture in the Early People's Republic*, (Ithaca and London: Cornell University Press, 2011) pp. 1–2.

simultaneously conveyed what was in principle impermissible and impure, while labeling individuals and groups that were themselves engaged in actions that were proscribed. It was imperative for each clearly to demarcate itself from the impure and evil Other, and nowhere were the rhetorical signals more important than in the ways each used language to demarcate the pure majority from the depraved minority. The most common words to denote internal enemies: *fangeming* (反革命 –counterrevolutionary) for the PRC and *panluanzhe* (叛乱者 – rebel – one engaging in armed rebellion or covert "sedition") for the ROC/Taiwan, do invoke quite different norms. The very term "counterrevolutionary" in the PRC made it clear that "revolution" (however the state defined it) was both desirable and the key criterion for loyalty and patriotism. In Taiwan the category of "rebel" equally presumed the legitimacy of government authority and social order being rebelled against.

At the same time, there was substantial overlap in the ways in which the PRC and ROC/Taiwan used rhetorics of cleansing the body politic. Both characterized their efforts to ensure internal security with the transitive verb *su* (肅), which conveyed connotations of washing out, removing stains, whiteness, and purity. *Su* was also almost perfectly congruent with the Russian term *chiitski*, which similarly evoked cleansing and purity as it was used to describe what were in reality bloody purges, thus implicitly linking the redness of blood with the whiteness of purification. For both, the object of the cleansing and purification was the noun *fei* (匪) or "bandit," a term with a lengthy lineage from the late-imperial period that referred to any who countered regularly constituted state authority with arms. In the year between the establishment of the People's Republic of China and the launch of the Campaign to Suppress Counterrevolutionaries, official efforts to clean out leftover enemies were normally labeled *sufei* （肅匪 – literally "cleaning out bandits"）. In the new People's Republic of China, those who most required "cleansing" were *tewu* intelligence agents. But in the early years of the PRC, there was significant slippage between the contemporary category of heinous *tewu* and a much older notion of the "bandit" *fei* (匪). As late as January 1951, well after the Campaign to Suppress Counterrevolutionaries had been launched nationwide, internal records in Shanghai still labeled those already "cleansed" (i.e. captured and executed) in advance of the campaign's springtime "high tide" in Shanghai as variants of *tefei* （特匪） – "[GMD] intelligence organization bandits," thus bringing a double-barreled linguistic opprobrium on the most irredeemable of internal enemies: GMD intelligence agents now tarred with the much older epithet of illegitimate "banditry." The enemy that could not be "cleansed" because he was across the Taiwan Strait and beyond reach was also resoundingly referenced as the *Jiang Feibang* （蔣匪幫 – Chiang Kai-shek Bandit Gang).[54]

In Taiwan, the "bandit" Other was a modifier that was invariably attached to any noun that referenced the Communists: *feidie* – (匪碟 – "bandit spy"), *feifan* (匪反 – "bandit criminal"), *feidang* (匪黨 – "bandit party"), and what was to become the most common of all epithets to refer to the PRC until well into the 1970s – *gongfei* (共匪 – "Communist bandit").[55] In addition, both regimes fell back on two very common mid-century wartime terms to denote illegitimacy in the context of foreign invasion by Japan – *wei* (偽) for puppet or collaborator, as well as *jian* (奸) or traitor. In the People's Republic, traitors (*hanjian* – 漢奸) and "puppets" (偽) were folded into the category of counterrevolutiony as specific sub-types.[56] For the ROC/Taiwan, *all* subversives and those prosecuted under the White Terror were by definition *jian* (奸 – traitors). The records of the Taiwan Garrison Command indicate clearly that its primary mission was to "clean out traitors" (*sujian* – 蕭奸), where the conflation between "traitors," "puppets," "banditry," and "sedition/rebellion" was nearly complete.[57]

Despite their marked ideological differences, the CCP and GMD shared surprising overlaps in the terms they used for domestic enemies in the early 1950s: Leninist revolutionary vocabularies of cleansing/purification; mid-century labels that stigmatized traitorous and collaborationist behavior; and a much older Chinese set of terms denoting politically illegitimate armed rebellion. Given the protracted nature of

---

[54] SMA B1/2/1339, "Fangeming zuixing chufenlei tongjibiao" (Statistics and classification of counterrevolutionary criminals' punishment) n.d., but file from mid-January 1951. SMA S64/4/134, "Shanghai shi zaoqi gongye tongye gonghui. 'Benhui huiyuan xuexi zhenya fangeming shishi zhengce de xuexi jihua jhe zongjie baogao'" (Shanghai Municipal Association of Lacquer Makers "study plan and general report for accurate policies on study for the Campaign to Suppress Counterrevolutionaries"), May 11, 1951–July 20, 1952.

[55] For good but by no means unique examples of the way in which the GMD in the early 1950s attached the adjective *fei* to other nouns to denote the Communist or Communist allied, see NZASH, Vol. 1, "Guojun Dang'an, Taiwan Jingbei Zongbu gongzuo baogao" (41 nian) (National Military Archive, Taiwan Garrison 1942 Work Report); "Taiwan Sheng Bao'an Siling Bu 41 niandu yuan zhi 12 yuefen jingban panluan anjian tongjibiao" (Taiwan Provincial Security Command statistics on the processing of armed rebellion cases), January–December 1952, p. 57.

[56] SMA C21/2/179, "Shanghai shiwei guanyu fandong tewu dangtuan dengji gongzuo zhishi" (Shanghai Party Committee directive on registration of reactionary security party and corps), December 10, 1950.

[57] NZASH, Vol. 1. In "Taiwan Jingbei Zongbu gongzuo baogao [39 nian]" (Taiwan general police work report), the part of the report that presents the draft work plan for the next year clearly indicates its core work as "*sujian fangdie*," clearing out traitors and guarding against spies, p. 11. See also, p. 6 for a reference to the CCP as "bandit puppets" in the same report.

the intelligence wars between Communist, Japanese collaborationist, and Nationalist regimes between the mid-1930s and 1949, it was extremely difficult to clearly delineate friends from enemies, supporters from traitors, and those who were simply getting along in difficult circumstances from those deliberately engaged in activity that was traitorous and collaborationist.[58] Applying these labels was a deeply political process. This was particularly so in Sunan, which had for so long been the Guomindang's base of economic and political support, and Taiwan, where fifty years of Japanese colonialism had rendered all but the most politically dissident and independence-minded potential collaborators.

Assessing Impacts (I): Counting Victims and Gauging Scales

If the outbreak of war in Korea made it appear much more reasonable for the PRC and ROC to launch or intensify vicious campaigns against presumptive domestic subversives, getting to grips with the impact of these actions on those who lived through this time is much trickier. Although access to archival materials within China has increased and an extraordinary amount of material on these years has been released in Taiwan, how to comparatively assess the effects of these repressions for local society continues to be fraught. Individuals experience state violence subjectively, and the materials that record these experiences – memoirs, oral histories, diaries – necessarily reflect that subjectivity. Less frequently recorded, and at least as important is the way in which state violence against political enemies rippled out beyond the accused to encompass the victim's family, friends, wider circle of acquaintances, and co-workers. When we move towards what is countable in archives or published statistics, the ground is only somewhat firmer because there are at least three different metrics by which terror might be gauged: (1) the number of victims (as either absolute numbers or a percentage of the population); (2) the likelihood of being given a death sentence once arrested and convicted; and (3) the degree of unpredictability in terms of who was arrested and on what grounds.

In principle, the most objective method of assessing the impact of terror is straightforward and numerical: the numbers of people arrested, convicted, and executed as either absolute numbers or as percentage of the population. But even this is less straightforward than might be imagined because gaps in data make direct comparison difficult, and the statistics

---

[58] Frederic Wakeman, "*Hanjian* (traitor)!: Collaboration and Retribution in Wartime Shanghai," pp. 322–333.

that have been published, referred to in publicly available speeches, or available in archives in Sunan and Taiwan are a combination of inconsistent, incomplete, contested, or falsified. At different points in the 1950s, the central leadership of the PRC suggested that the Campaign to Suppress Counterrevolutionaries executed anywhere between 700,000 and two million out of a population of 574,800,000 or between 0.122 percent and 0.347 percent of the total population.[59] This does not tell us much about the individuals arrested, tried, and given lesser sentences, but those numbers must have been considerably higher. And in many areas the record keeping and reporting on the numbers apprehended and executed either overlapped with concurrent "bandit extermination" campaigns in the southwest, with land reform in central and south China, or, particularly in south central and southwest China, were concealed by local cadres.[60]

Rates of execution frequently exceeded Mao's suggested ratio of "around 0.05 to 0.1 percent of the population," in many areas easily surpassing 0.15 percent.[61] Sunan was a region in which cadres were initially reluctant to impose draconian waves of arrest and execution. Whether because there were so many ex-GMD personnel and sympathizers in Sunan, or because local cadres so took to heart the CCP's explicit mildness and inclusiveness that stressed "patient education" in its first year in power, cadres were slow to catch on to what was expected of them in implementing a mass campaign that targeted internal enemies. The "sharp strikes" of April and May 1951 must have been shocking to Sunan cadre sensibilities and to the population at large.

Even so, the top party leadership had good reasons for not wanting too much in the way of excess in Sunan cities. The "suggested" quotas were at the far low end of the announced spectrum of 0.05 to 0.1 percent of the population. In February 1951 Mao Zedong "suggested" to the Shanghai party committee that appropriate execution targets for the upcoming campaign for 1951 would be "at least 3,000 ... of a population of 6 million," or 0.05 percent, and that Nanjing ought to execute "more than 200 ... of a population of half a million [or 0.048 percent]."[62]

---

[59] The figure of 2,000,000 was mentioned in a work report of 1952; the figure of 800,000 was released at the Eighth Party Congress in September,1956. Cited in Domes, *The Internal Politics of China*, p. 52. Domes, "conservatively" estimates the total numbers executed to be upwards of 3,000,000, or 0.535 percent of the total population.

[60] Yang, "Reconsidering the Campaign to Suppress Counterrevolutionaries"; Brown, pp. 107, 122–125, 128–129.

[61] Yang, ibid., pp. 102–121.

[62] Mao Zedong, "Directive on the work of suppressing counterrevolutionaries in Shanghai and Nanjing, 12 February 1951" (original in the Central Archives). Cited in Yang, 2008, fn. 24, p. 109.

Statistics from the Shanghai Municipal archives confirm Shanghai's compliance with these "suggestions." The total numbers for 1951 stood at 14,391 counterrevolutionaries sentenced, or 0.24 percent of a population of 6,000,000.[63] Of these, 2,916, or roughly one-fifth of the total at 0.048 percent of the urban population, were sentenced to death. Unlike the situation in south-central and southwest China, which underwent additional waves of arrests and executions throughout 1952, in Shanghai the Campaign to Suppress Counterrevolutionaries comprised one series of "sharp strikes" in the spring and summer of 1951, after which almost all state's activity on the campaign involved the final resolution, recording and tallying of cases.[64]

When we turn to the contemporaneous Terror across the Taiwan Strait, the publicly accessible statistics on the scale of the White Terror in the 1950s are even more contested. In contrast to the CCP, the Guomindang party-state was unwilling publicly to acknowledge the scale of the terror and avoided public statements confirming its severity. Such was the decades-long lacuna about the terror that official silence itself became an object of political mobilization and claims by the Taiwan opposition. After martial law eased, in the 1990s it became possible to publicly debate the scale and impact of the White Terror, but the numbers bandied about by the opposition were frequently imprecise and articulated for maximum political effect.

One frequently reported (and anonymously referenced) statistic claims that between 1949 and 1955 some 90,000 were arrested, of whom half were executed, but these numbers were based on unattributed allegations and are highly exaggerated.[65] Other estimates are plagued by a lack of information, inconsistent use of categories, and sampling bias. To give a sense of some of these difficulties, consider the initial forays of the Foundation for Compensation for Improper Verdicts during the Martial Law Era (財團法人戒烟時期不當叛亂‘匪諜審判案件補償基金會 or FCIV). The FCIV was established in 1998 to compensate those victims of the White Terror who could come forward with documentation

---

[63] Mao Zedong's figures for the population of Shanghai were loose and approximate, and indeed the total population of Shanghai between 1949 and 1953, can only be estimated. We do know that in 1949, the population was roughly 4,500,000. By the time of the PRC's first census in 1953, the total had risen to 6,204,000. Since I use figures for 1952 (the year after the height of the Campaign to Suppress Counterrevolutionaries) elsewhere for purposes of comparison, "around 6,000,000" is a good rough estimate. See Jos Gamble, *Shanghai: in Transition: Changing Perspectives and Social Contours of a Chinese Metropolis*, p. 71.

[64] SMA B1/2/1339. "Fangeming zuifan zhixing fenlei tongjibiao" (Implementation of classification for counterrevolutionary crimes statistical form), 1951.

[65] Mendel, p. 120; Zhang Yanxian, "Daoyan: Baise kongbu yu zhuanxing zhengyi," pp. 2–3.

to prove their mistreatment. An early FCIV effort to present an overview of the White Terror produced a sample of 2,555 cases, but since "cases" could refer to anything between one and scores of accused individuals, this first rough cut was not particularly helpful in establishing the scale of the repression.[66] Around 2005, the FCIV estimated the total number of victims over the course of the White Terror period to be 6,022, with over three-quarters of these victims (4,601) charged and punished between 1949 and 1960. Twelve years later, the FCIV again revised its rough estimate upwards to "something more than 8,000," and as of June 30, 2009, had processed 8,786 individual claims.[67] Other reports have suggested that much larger numbers were investigated, arrested, and sentenced in the early 1950s. An official DPP investigation into the martial law period estimated that there were 10,000 trials and between 2,000 and 3,000 executions. Another initially calculated the victims of the White Terror to be 27,350, which was later revised downward to 16,132 (likely because many cases ended up being recorded in different organizations' internal reports).[68]

My own estimates on the scale of the White Terror between September 1949 and mid-1954 rely on internal reports from the Taiwan Garrison Command (TGC), but even these documents represent an undercount.[69] They do not include cases of repression before mid-September 1949, or most of those that involved the military, and only

---

[66] "Cases" (*anjian* – 案件) could range in size from an accusation against one individual to an entire network of thirty or more. Therefore, the numbers cited regarding individuals were always higher, sometimes much higher than the numbers cited for cases. ZAFLT, p. 255.

[67] The first number is taken from Wu Naite who researched this article some time before its publication date of July 2005, when claims were still coming in. When I met with the FCIV in August 2008, the deputy director told me that the FCIV's best estimate of the total number of claims was "something more than 8,000," but cautioned that this figure was still likely to be an undercount, as the peak of the violence was in the early 1950s, and many victims had either long since passed away, or had lost their documentation. The figure of 8,767 comes from Zhang Yanxian, p. 3. See also Greitens, *Dictators and their Secret Police*, pp. 180–183.

[68] Greitens, *Dictators and Their Secret Police*, p. 183, and fn. 10. At present there is an enormous initiative underway by the DPP-led government in Taiwan to establish the scale of the Terror. The Transitional Justice Commission, which is under the Executive Yuan, organized a special working group in 2017 to create a database on all victimized by the Terror. This in turn has required that large numbers of military organizations and government bodies that had not already turned over their personnel archives to do so, creating a mountainous backlog for a small and underfunded body to process in a limited period of time. As of February 2019, the Commission working group had received 20,000 documents from the government's Investigation Bureau and was awaiting another 30,000 from police departments. (Personal communication from a researcher at the working group, February 8, 2019.) See www.tjc.gov.tw/, accessed February 1, 2019.

[69] NZASH, collection in five volumes.

seldom include statistics on those who were accused and questioned but then let go before sentencing for lack of evidence. They also do not count the hundreds of individuals who turned themselves in prior to trial in order to apply for an official pardon (*zishou* – 自首), and they only occasionally record individuals whose cases resulted in suspended sentences of "administrative supervision" *guanzhi/ganhua* (管制/感化) – an intermediary punishment that was less than a proper stint in prison, and could mean anything from house arrest to *de facto* incarceration in political reform training institutes.[70]

To compound the confusion, in 1949 there were multiple, overlapping security organizations in operation in Taiwan involved with apprehending and processing suspected subversives. The TGC itself included three different divisions (martial law, internal security, and police affairs) and was in principle responsible for handling cases of "sedition," compiling year-end reports, and keeping statistical information. But there were four other security organizations that also actively apprehended and processed suspected subversives. The Ministry of Defense Internal Security Office (Guofang Baomi Ju – 國防部保密局), the Ministry of the Interior Investigative Bureau (Neizheng Bu Diaocha Ju – 内政部調查局), the Taiwan Provincial Police Affairs division (Taiwan sheng Jingwu Ju – 臺灣省警務居), and a stand-alone Military Police Headquarters (Xianbing Silingbu – 憲兵司令部). Until the end of 1953, these different security organizations were in competition with each other to capture the largest number of potential subversives, and were not in the habit of sharing information.[71]

The TGC's own figures on the numbers arrested and prosecuted between the last quarter of 1949 through the first half of 1954 are inconsistent, with one count of 5,856, and another of 6,565.[72] Even the larger of these figures is certainly too low, because in all years other than 1952,

---

[70] It is likely that the database now being compiled by the Transitional Justice Commission will eventually shed light on the numbers of these kinds of cases.

[71] See Greitens, *Dictators and Their Secret Police*, p. 84 for a discussion of the fragmented security apparatus in the late 1940s and early 1950s, and pp. 94–967 for Chiang Ching-kuo's reforms, that began to centralize security operations in the National Defense Council, ultimately culminating in the National Security Bureau (Guojia Anquan Bu 國家安全部), in 1955.

[72] For example, one set of statistics compiled by the TGC gives the totals of sentenced "rebels" as 1,151 cases and 3,942 individuals for the period between September 1949 and the end of 1952. Unfortunately, these "final numbers" do not add up when juxtaposed with the numbers cited in the TGC's own annual reports. The total of seditious (*panluan* – 叛亂) individuals reported by the TGC totaled 633 in the last quarter of 1949, 1,506 in 1950, 1,895 according to one table and 1,180 according to another for 1951, and either 1,283 or 1,925 in 1952. The numbers only began to tail off significantly in 1953 to 607. Ibid., pp. 12, 35, 43–45, 57–59.

the compiled totals do not include the numbers apprehended and processed through the Ministry of Defence, the Ministry of the Interior, or
the Military Police Headquarters. If we assume that the figures from
the year 1952 are comparable to earlier and later years then the likely
number of political cases processed to result in formal incarceration
(including the death penalty) is around 11,672 for this four-year period.[73]

Even this estimate of 11,672 is a likely undercount. None of the tables
generated by the TGC includes credible numbers on the numbers of
accused "subversives" in active military units. Given the GMD's stringent implementation of a political commissar system in the military in the
early 1950s, the effort to weed out Communists and their sympathizers in
both army and party under the aegis of the Central Reform Commission,
and to simply purge potential military rivals to Chiang Kai-shek, they
must have been considerable.[74] We know that there were sweeping witch
hunts for Communists in the central organization of the Navy, among
relatively young officers who had attended the Naval Academy during the
1940s, and in a putative network of over twenty military officers from
Fujian. There were likely many more about which information has not
come to light.[75] If we accept the provisional number of 11,672, the
percentage of the population who were *direct* victims of terror in Taiwan

[73] NZASH, Vol. 1. The Division of Internal Security within the Taiwan Garrison
Command produced the official statistics for the number of individuals sentenced for
political crimes in the early 1950s, and the first volume of the NZASH reproduces 144
pages of archival material that includes annual reports and statistics on internal security
work from September 1949 until December 1954. Unfortunately, neither the categories
nor the organizations included in the final tally are consistent from year to year. Only in
1952 did the statistics include the numbers from all the security organizations involved in
arresting and charging individuals for political crimes. If one assumes that the breakdown
in 1952 was typical for the proportions of cases handled by the Internal Security
Headquarters (798 of 1,925, or 41 percent), then the given totals for 1950, 1951, and
1953 have to be increased by roughly 116 percent, for a crude final estimate of 11,672 for
a total over this four-year period. See "Taiwan sheng baoan silingbu 39 nian, 9 yue zhi
sishiernian shenli zongjie anjian chuli qingxing tongjibiao" (Taiwan Garrison Command
review and summary reports statistics on case management, September 1950 to
December 1953) pp. 80–81, "Taiwan sheng bao'an silingbu junfachu 39 nian 9 yue zhi
12 yue jiaocha anjian tongji biao" (Taiwan Provincial Security Command Martial Law
Division recheck of cases between September 1949 until December 1949), p. 12, Taiwan
sheng bao'an siling bu junfa chu 39 niandu shenjie panluan anjian beigaosuoshi feifa
zuzhi mingcheng ji chuli qingxing tongji biao" (Taiwan Provincial Security Command
Martial Law Division 1950 yearly statistics: the names of seditious cases and how they
were handled), p. 35, and "Taiwan sheng bao'an silingbu 40 niandu yuan zhi 12 yuefen
jingjin panluan anfan tongji biao" (Statistical table of Taiwan Provincial Security
Command cases of economic sedition from January–December 1951), p. 45.
[74] Dickson, *Democratization in China and Taiwan: The Adaptability of Leninist Parties*, p. 56.
[75] NZASH, Vol. 5, "Jia Huachang Koushu Fangwen" (Oral History interview with Jia
Huachang), August 24, 1996, pp. 75–77; see also "Yuanqi" (Origin [of sedition in the
military]), pp. 9–23.

over the four-year period from September 1949 until mid-1953, was 0.14 percent (11,672 of 8,053,569). In contrast, the total population of Shanghai in 1952 was roughly 6,000,000, and Shanghai sentenced 14,391 counterrevolutionaries or 0.24 percent in the preceding year alone. If the percentages sentenced in Shanghai were representative of the wider region, then by the first metric of assessing comparative terror – numbers of the repressed as either absolute numbers or a percentage of the population, the terror was roughly two times greater in Sunan than it was in Taiwan.

When one turns to the second indicator of regime terror: the severity of sentencing for those arrested and charged, the statistics available at present are also inconclusive. In the greater Shanghai area, the death penalty handed to accused counterrevolutionaries in 1951 was an almost even 20 percent, in turn reflecting the target quotas handed down from above. This consistent percentage suggests little about how arbitrarily or non-arbitrarily these quotas were imposed on individuals. For Taiwan sources diverge widely in their estimates of how frequently the death penalty was meted out to accused subversives, and here the statistics generated by the TGC in the early 1950s are again inconsistent. One set of figures that covers the period between September 1949 until the end of 1952, states a death penalty rate as 456 of 3,335 (or 13.6 percent), but other year-end tables for 1952 and 1953 have significantly higher proportions of 20 percent (186 of 888) for 1952, and 19 percent (121 of 607) for 1953.[76] Even this higher percentage masks the unpredictability of sentencing for individual cases. Timing, spatial distance from Taibei, and closeness to the central government all seem to have been factors in the relative severity of sentencing. For example, in August of 1949, when security organizations broke up a Communist network in Jilong, 18 percent (7 of 38) were sentenced to death, but when a very similar group was suppressed in Gaoxiong only a month later, most of the accused received only a standard five-year jail term, and none were condemned to death.[77] On the other hand, the January 1950 suppression of the "Taibei Working Committee" of the Communist Party in Taiwan resulted in 29 percent (15 of 51) executed.[78] The suppression of a supposed Communist network in national level Ministry of Social Affairs in May 1950 received the most severe penalties of all, with a staggering death penalty rate of

[76] ZAFLT, p. 261; 50 NZASH, Vol. 1, p. 129, p. 80, p. 88, and p. 122.
[77] NZASH (Vol. 2)."Jilong Shi Gongzuo Weiyuanhui Zhong Jiedong dengren an" (Jilong Municipal Work Committee Case of Zhong Jiedong et al.," pp. 8–11.; "Gaoxiong Shi Gongzuo Weiyuanhui dengren an" (Gaoxiong Municipal Work Committee Case), pp. 23–24.
[78] Ibid., "Taibei shi Gongzuo Weiyuanhui Guo Xiuzong dengren an" (Taibei Work Committee case of Guo Xiuzong et al.), pp. 69–73.

57 percent (19 of 33). And even allowing for the greater security of the regime a few years later, when the putatively "Communist" Luku base area just to the east of Taibei was crushed in 1952–1953, 35 of 165 (21 percent) accused subversives were given the death penalty).[79] When it so chose, the Guomindang party-state could be at least as repressive as its opposite number across the Strait. By this metric of unpredictability in severity of punishment towards the accused, the ROC/Taiwan's results were in the end nearly as terrifying as the PRC's mass campaigns in Sunan despite the former's emphasis on law and procedure.

Assessing Impacts (II): Unclear Targets and Concentric Circles of Intimidation

When we turn to other metrics, political terror in the early 1950s in Taiwan might have been equal to, if not worse than it was in Sunan. Both evidenced slippage in lenience or viciousness of sentencing, and abruptly altered what was and was not politically acceptable by government fiat. But in the early 1950s the range of potential targets was significantly larger in Taiwan than it was in Sunan. In Sunan an individual had to have belonged to a designated counterrevolutionary organization or be engaging in ongoing behavior that the regime designated as counterrevolutionary. In contrast, in Taiwan one had to have actually *done* very little to be fair game for suppression in the early 1950s.

Both party-states cast broad nets in their definitions of subversion, and struggled with how to define targets for arrest and repression with enough precision to ensure domestic security while leaving local authorities flexibility in actual implementation. The background of Cold War hysteria made for a political environment in which emergency rules made for significantly lower standards of evidence and proof than would have been the case under normal judicial proceedings.[80] This left unresolved problems. The state needed to be able to recognize, arrest, and process those whose political crimes merited violent response, but it also had to be

---

[79] Ibid., "Zhongyang Shehui Bu qiantai jiandie Su Yilin dengrenan" (Central Department of Social Affairs case of spy Su Yilin et al.), pp. 328–329.

[80] In principle, military rule was dominant in both the young PRC and in the ROC/Taiwan: it was explicitly invoked in the latter, and the country was broken into military regions until 1954 in the former. But military rule was exercised in very different ways. In the PRC there is no evidence that the regular local cadres were ever swept aside in favor of military courts in the Campaign to Suppress Counterrevolutionaries, and indeed there is a good deal of evidence that the prosecution of counterrevolutionaries in an explicit campaign modality of policy implementation was entrusted to local cadres. In Taiwan, while many different security organizations were involved in apprehending "rebels," all were processed through a highly centralized system of military courts.

able to distinguish these individuals from those who were merely politically or socially "backward." Since these lines of demarcation were at best soft, differentiating the counterrevolutionary or subversive from the "backward" or insufficiently committed was necessary but difficult.

In the People's Republic of China, identifying some counterrevolutionaries was crisply straightforward, while determining others was murkily difficult. Counterrevolutionaries came in one of three types: (1) the bureaucratically definable; (2) the criminal; and (3) the socially undesirable. The first of these categories was the easiest to determine. Guidelines included a list of GMD organizations and ranks now deemed to be counterrevolutionary: those who had been employed by Guomindang domestic intelligence organizations (*tewu* – 特務), held high positions in the vanquished Guomindang military, or served as leaders of either district branches of the Guomindang Party, or the Sanmin Zhuyi Youth Corps. Although trawling through old records to determine exactly who had done what for which organization was tedious, identifying and classifying these individuals simply meant time digging through old files. Since the GMD kept large archives, paper trails of evidence were normally not difficult to track.[81]

The Campaign to Suppress Counterrevolutionaries also targeted individuals engaged in behavior now deemed counterrevolutionary, rather than neatly definable through formal position in the outgoing regime. Those who were the second (criminal) or third (socially undesirable) type of "counterrevolutionaries" in 1950–1953 were much more difficult to ascertain because the categories themselves were unclear. Determining bullies (*e'ba* – 惡霸), hardened bandits (*guaifei* – 拐匪), leaders of counterrevolutionary sects (*fandong huimen tou* – 反動會悶頭), or traitors (*hanjian* 漢奸) was much more subjective. In practice, the campaign mentality of intensification made it almost impossible for local cadres to consistently distinguish "local bullies" from the merely disliked, "hardened bandits" from garden-variety robbers, the leaders of counterrevolutionary religious organizations from followers, "hoodlums" (*liumang* – 流氓) from local bullies, and any of the these categories of counterrevolutionary individuals from each other, because in practice the behavioral markers of each putatively separate category frequently overlapped. In addition, what to do with "historical offenders" (*lishi zuixing* – 歷史罪行) – who had previously engaged in acts now deemed counterrevolutionary, or held a status now determined to be counterrevolutionary – was uncertain. Regulations

---

[81] SMA C21/2/179. "Shanghai shiwei guanyu fandong tewu dangtuan dengji gongzuo zhishi" (Shanghai Party Committee work directive on the grading of counterrevolutionary special affairs, party and corps), December 10, 1950.

stipulated that those who had historical problems (*lishi wenti* – 歷史問題) were not to be prosecuted as counterrevolutionaries, but the finer points of how to distinguish a "historical offender" from one with "historical problems" were not clearly laid out in the guiding documents for the campaign. After *tewu* (4,395 of 9,614, or 45.79 percent of the total), "historical offenders" were in fact the second largest category of counterrevolutionaries prosecuted in Shanghai in 1951 (1,738 of 9614 or 18 percent of the total). "Historical offenders" – a category that did not exist in central campaign documents – were even slightly more numerous than "evil bullies" (*e'ba*), a category that was repeatedly stressed as a target entirely deserving of suppression due to the masses' hatred.[82] As the levels of the campaign were respectively ratcheted up and dampened down from above, those entrusted with implementing the campaign often found themselves in real quandaries; one month admonished for being too soft, and then next for not being sufficiently precise in distinguishing between regular crime and counterrevolutionary crime when the standards for making these determinations were vague and subject to change.[83] It was up to local officials to interpret signals from above, and implement them – irrespective of vague directives and shifting de facto quotas – in the light of local circumstances.

Even though the ROC/Taiwan refrained from openly labeling its actions a campaign, and claimed in the light of considerable evidence to the contrary that its actions were necessary, legal, and procedurally sound under martial law, crime in Taiwan in the early 1950s – whether political, violent, or everyday, was also subject to the strictures of martial law. Like the authorities in Sunan, the ROC/Taiwan used the background atmosphere of insecurity and terror to stamp out the sorts of behavior that in more normal times would be considered either criminal, socially undesirable, or merely careless. Smuggling, counterfeiting, thievery, illicit entry or departure across the state's borders, and damage to state property are all listed in a range of extraordinary regulations under martial law that were prosecutable as instances of sedition. As late as June 1957, well after the initial crises and insecurity of regime consolidation had passed, the government passed a set of regulations on "rectifying thieving bandits"

---

[82] SMA B1/2/1339, "Quanbu 9614 fangeming fenzi zhong tongji wuyuefen zhi jiuyuefen 15 ri" (Total statistics of 9,614 counterrevolutionary elements from May 1 through September 15, 1951). *E'ba* came in at 1,710 of 9,614, or 17.8 percent of the total from this tranche.

[83] SMA C21/1/98. Zhang Ben, "Wusiri shicheng qing nianqing ganbu jinian wusi qingnianjie ji zhongguo xin minzhu zhuyi qingniantuan chengli erzhou nian dahuishang de baogao" (Report on the May Fourth municipal invitation to young cadre commemoration of the May Fourth holiday and the Second Annual Meeting of the establishment of the New Democracy Youth Corps), May 4, 1951.

(*zhengzhi zeifei tiaolie* – 懲治賊匪條例), illustrating the state's continuing tendency to conflate regular – even petty – crime with "banditry" and subversion. The Taiwan Garrison Command's own yearly reports from the early 1950s on the suppression of subversion prominently feature a standard section on suppressing hoodlums (*liumang* – 流氓), a category that was an equally prime target for the Chinese Communists in their suppression of counterrevolutionaries. Thus for both, the party-state redrew the internal boundaries between the pure "us" and the depraved "enemy" to justify a harsh crackdown and the imposition of a particular vision of order and rectitude, and went after not only obvious political enemies, but the soft targets of any law and order campaign: small-time hoodlums, local toughs, urban lumpen hanging around on the street, those outside the regular economy who eked out marginal livings as casual laborers, counterfeiters, smugglers, or others of no fixed abode like the "boat people" (*chuanmin* – 船民) of greater Shanghai. Whether presented through legal formalism or the emotional call to arms of a society wide political mobilization, standards were vague, burdens of proof vaguer, categories were ill-demarcated, and the boundaries between subversion, criminality, and social undesirability were at best blurred.

There was one significant metric by which the White Terror in Taiwan was more sharply felt in the short term than the Campaign to Suppress Counterrevolutionaries. The White Terror cast a much broader social net in terms of who was a potential target of the campaign. The Campaign to Suppress Counterrevolutionaries had as targets a mix of those who were clearly counterrevolutionary because of their positions in the Guomindang government, and the less obviously counterrevolutionary but certainly socially undesirable (local bullies, petty crooks, hoodlums, local toughs, and thieves). Even though the category of "historical offenders" was vague, most white-collar workers, regular workers, students, and intellectuals were relatively immune from being targeted as long as they had not held high rank in proscribed GMD organizations. In addition, Chinese Communist Party cadres, Communist Youth League members, and the military, were entirely untouched by the campaign except insofar as they were expected to implement or cheer for it. Indeed, the efficacy of the campaign in Sunan depended on most of the urban population being able to understand readily that they were part of the "good" majority, and thus mobilize on the state's behalf against the "bad" counterrevolutionary minority.

In contrast, the prospective targets of the White Terror in Taiwan were much wider. *No* group was entirely safe from being spirited off by security forces. The TGC's own statistics, problematic as they are for establishing the real number of victims, do confirm that the Guomindang party-state in Taiwan was an equal opportunity repressor. No sector was immune. Mainlander refugees were targeted at roughly twice the rate of the Taiwanese, but number of Taiwanese victims was still greater due to their larger numbers.[84] Everybody – Taiwanese, *waisheng* ren, professionals, civil servants, workers, farmers, shopkeepers, returnees from abroad, and students were all subject to sudden interrogation and worse. Soldiers and GMD Party members were already subject to extra scrutiny from concurrent GMD Party rectification and purges in the military, and all were prosecuted under the terms of martial law. One set of the TGC's own statistics confirm that in 1952, civil servants (140) accounted for more individuals than professors and students combined (110). Workers (166) and farmers (166) comprised the two largest occupational groups, with shopkeepers and businessmen (114) coming in just after civil servants. Although this form undercounts, soldiers (58) were also put on trial for sedition, coming in right after the unemployed (65).[85] In contrast, in Sunan many of the occupational sectors "hit" by the White Terror in Taiwan in the early 1950s were not folded in with the Campaign to Suppress Counterrevolutionaries. State administrators (*sanfan*), private businesses (*wufan*), rural elites (land reform) intellectuals, and higher education (thought reform) were subjected to intense campaigns between late 1951 and 1953, but with the important exception of rural elites during land reform, they were not labeled counterrevolutionary, imprisoned, or executed.

Finally, in Sunan and Taiwan state terror against subversion reached far beyond those directly charged. Families and close friends of the accused were interrogated and intimidated. Workplaces were raided, and colleagues were disappeared. Wives and children left behind by the suddenly disappeared were socially ostracized at just the time they were left without their primary breadwinners. It was often impossible to get any information from authorities about where the accused was incarcerated or even what specific charges he faced. While we cannot assess with any

---

[84] The 1952 statistics compiled by the TGC's Security Division record that the number of Taiwanese designated "bandit traitors" (870) was slightly more than twice that of mainlander refugee "bandit traitors" (410), at a time when Taiwanese comprised between 80 and 85 percent of the population. NZASH, Vol. 1, "Xiaojian feifan fenlei tongjibiao" (Statistical classification form for extirpating traitors, Communists and criminals), 1952, p. 59. Greitens, *Dictators and Their Secret Police*, also confirms this calculation, p. 183.

[85] NZASH, Vol. 1. "Taiwan sheng bao'an siling bu junfachu, sishiyi niandu shenjie anjian gao shenfen tongjibiao" (Taiwan Provincial Garrison Command, Martial law Division, 1952 review of cases and occupational status statistics), p. 85. These figures, of course, do not include those concurrently being purged from the Guomindang as part of its rectification, nor those purged from the military. Those two campaigns, concurrently run by the organizations in question, would push the figures much higher.

certainty the scale of suffering, internal displacement and fear experienced by those who were not the direct victims of state-sponsored terror against subversion, the numbers in Sunan and Taiwan who were subjected to "jail beyond prison walls"[86] must have been many times greater than those who were formally charged and convicted. In addition to close family members, other relatives, friends, work associates undoubtedly noticed how chillingly the regime demarcated the pure "us" from the worse than profane "them."

Instrumentalities of Terror: Building the State

However plausible the fears about regional (in)security and domestic fifth columns might have been in the early 1950s, it is beyond question that the People's Republic of China and the ROC/Taiwan both deliberately whipped up fear about insecurity for quite another set of reasons: to lower social resistance to their policies, drastically augment the monitoring and coercive capacity of the state, and extend the state's presence to ever smaller social units. These exaggerated responses to domestic security threats do not for a moment suggest that these two consolidating states had *no* reason to worry about subversion from within. There certainly were underground Communists in Taiwan in 1948–1950 who were doing whatever they could to prepare for the expected Communist takeover of Taiwan in the summer of 1950, and we can guess that among the thousands of Guomindang *tewu* and sympathizers left in Sunan there must have been some who were actively spying for the departed regime. At the height of the Communist movement on Taiwan 1949–1950, there were somewhere between 900 and 2,000 active members of the Communist Party, as well as an undetermined but much smaller number of members of the "Taiwan Alliance" (Taiwan Democratic Self-Governing Alliance – *Taiwan Minzhu Zizhi Tongmeng* or *Taimeng* – 台灣民主自治同盟) an organization widely acknowledged to be a Communist Party front organization established to prepare Taiwan for CCP style "New Democracy."[87]

While we cannot know for sure exactly how many underground spies and moles in Sunan and Taiwan were actively working for the opposite

---

[86] This phrase is taken from the oral history compilation *Yuwai zhi qiu: Baise kongbu shou nanzhe nüxing jiashu* (A jail beyond the Prison Walls: Untold stories by female family members of White Terror Victims), Vols. 1–3 (Taibei: Guojia renquan bowuguan choubeishu/Zhongyang Yanjiu Yuan Taiwan Lishi Yanjiusuo), 2015.

[87] Chen Yingtai suggested that the number of Communists was around two thousand. Interview, August 4, 2005. The figure of "upwards of 900" is cited in "Taiwan sheng gongzuo weiyuanhui dengren an" (The Taiwan Provincial Work Committee case et al.), Guojia Anquan Ju (National Security Agency), Original file number 44901/444048/, reproduced in NZASH, Vol. 2, p. 60.

side, it is beyond doubt that both regimes actively repressed *many* more individuals than there were active *tewu* (in Sunan) or Communists (in Taiwan). In the greater Sunan area, the CCP made no apology for "smashing" a broad mix of social undesirables alongside those who were card carrying high-ranking members of the GMD. There is little information about the real numbers of GMD spies among this motley group of former GMD power holders, but given the utter collapse of the GMD and its retreat to Taiwan, there probably were not many. In Taiwan, where there are somewhat better numbers, between three and thirteen times more individuals were repressed than there were Communists at all.[88] These figures suggest that both regimes deliberately exaggerated fear of internal fifth columns and traitorous subversion, now linked to a complex of state-building agendas: to clear the ground of all meaningful social organizations, institutions, and individuals who could blunt the expansion of state power and its reach into city and countryside. This was accomplished by: (1) expanding the state's repressive organizations to reach into the most basic units of urban and rural social and economic organization; and (2) signaling to the population at large what each regime expected in terms of acquiescence.

When we turn to the mechanics of the campaigns of repression in Sunan and Taiwan in the early 1950s, an uneasy mix of bureaucratic and campaign modalities was in evidence. The first impulse was to establish, expand, or recast existing state organizations of coercion. In Sunan, the Campaign to Suppress Counterrevolutionaries was run by municipal and local levels of the state, who were themselves responding to either general signals or direct "suggestions" from the central party-state about how many counterrevolutionaries should be targeted and executed. Since municipal police forces in Sunan were almost completely manned by holdovers from the Guomindang in 1949, campaign implementation was directly linked to the state's "strengthening" of municipal and local police and security organizations. It was a matter of some urgency to get politically suspect holdovers out of the policing business while significantly expanding numbers of police in both quantity (number) and quality (political reliability). Although the

---

[88] If we take the higher estimate of Communists to be 2,000, and the lowest number of the repressed from the TGC's own statistics at 5,856, the GMD suppressed nearly 3 times (2.98x) as many as there were Communists to repress in the early 1950s. If we use my estimate of 11,672 and the higher estimate of 2,000, the total number of the suppressed was nearly 6 times more (5.83) than there were bona fide Communists. And, of course, if we use the lower estimate of 900 Communists with my estimate of 11,672, the numbers balloon to an astonishing figure of nearly 13 times more (12.96) individuals suppressed than there were Communists.

exact scale of this organizational expansion is uncertain, in Shanghai in 1949 there were 14,308 police held over from the Guomindang period. Between 1950 and 1953 several reorganizations of the police took place, along with repeated measures to "strengthen" public security that culminated in the replacement of the police personnel department with a political department in 1953.[89] It is likely that large numbers of police deemed politically unreliable were replaced during these years.

In addition to easing out police holdovers from the Republican era, the East China Military Administrative Region set up a security work committee, which directed cadres at municipal levels in Sunan to establish corresponding work committees to take charge of the campaign. New regulations also required state organizations and state factories to establish internal security committees to report to the relevant municipal internal security authority.[90] Thus, while the East China Military Administrative Region's specially convened Security Work Committee "guided" the campaign, the actual business of implementation was lower down, with specially convened work committees comprised of leading cadres from party and public security organizations. These committees were formed for municipalities, Shanghai's outer districts (*jiaoqu* – 郊區), counties, and in the relatively small number of state factories that had been taken over from the Nationalists.

In the People's Republic of China, which devolved campaign implementation to local levels of government, "strengthening organization" meant that state organizations were required to strengthen themselves. Under non-campaign circumstances, "strengthening organization" revolved around auditing, bookkeeping, reporting, and compliance with directives from above. In the context of a national mobilizational campaign, "strengthening" was accomplished through exhortation from above, through political study and training sessions, or, more rarely, when higher-level cadres were sent down to local units to provide direct instruction in how things should be done. In the spring of 1951, the East China Military Administrative Region dispatched 459 cadres to 255 of Shanghai's larger state factories to guide and oversee the campaign. Activities included propaganda work to engage the masses, teaching factory cadres how to establish conclusive paper trails to root out counter-revolutionaries, and being on hand to keep the necessary internal

---

[89] SG, p. 83. Wakeman, *Policing Shanghai, 1927–1937*, pp. 290–292.
[90] SMA C21/2/179 "Shanghai shiwei guanyu tewu dangtuan dengji gongzuo zhishi" (Shanghai Municipal Party Committee directive on registration work for special affairs party and corps [personnel]), December 10, 1951.

accusation meetings on course.[91] These measures were uniformly and explicitly justified in terms of the necessity of strengthening state organizations (*jiaqiang zuzhi* – 加强組織), by demonstrating to leading cadres in big factories how to run a campaign. The "strengthening" was achieved in three ways: by easing out the disloyal and suspect, establishing new security work organizations within workplaces, and intensifying local cadre training in how to be responsive to the signals coming from higher levels in the CCP that produced the "right" outcomes in the "right" way.

These strategies worked well for big factories already nationalized by the Guomindang. Because of their size, historic association with the state, and importance to the Chinese Communist Party, they were a high priority and relatively easy for the state to penetrate. Their large scale made it more likely that there would be some managers or workers who fell into at least one of the categories of counterrevolutionary. But most enterprises in 1950–1951 were so small and scattered that they could not be effectively visited by cadres from above and here enterprise bosses were utterly on their own. Study materials produced for a meeting of the twenty-one leading members of Shanghai Lacquer Maker's Association on June 5, 1951, reveal just how befuddled many leaders of small factories were by the campaign, even six weeks after the "sharp strikes" of late April.[92] Many, if not the majority, simply had no idea as to how the campaign was relevant to their own workplaces, and had even less understanding of how to conduct it. The June meeting was convened to overcome these crucial gaps. The report from this training meeting makes it clear that higher level cadres running the session were more than a little exasperated by the leaders of the Lacquer Makers' Association, whose shortcomings were of the most elementary sort, notably: (1) their failure to clearly distinguish between counterrevolutionaries and non-counterrevolutionaries; (2) their failure to comprehend the harm caused by *e'ba* (evil bully) crimes; (3) their perception that the campaign was simply a government and party struggle that had nothing to do with them, rather than a mass struggle that involved everyone; and worst of all (4) their view that the CCP's sudden abrogation of "excessive lenience" was a policy error. Given the breadth and vagueness of the Campaign's

---

[91] SMA C1/1/28, "Shanghai gongren canjia zhenya fangeming yundong zongjie baogao" (Summary report on Shanghai worker participation in the Campaign to Suppress Counterrevolutionaries) (July or August, n.d.), 1951.

[92] At this early stage of regime consolidation, the People's Republic of China inherited a small number of large enterprises that had already been state owned under the Nationalists. The local party-state also organized retailers, merchants, and smaller more scattered enterprises into trade associations that could be conveniently gathered to learn about new state policies and to pass reports upward for the sector in question. The Lacquer Makers' Association was one such trade association.

slogans, the leaders of the Lacquer Makers' Association wondered, not unreasonably: (1) how they were to distinguish genuine counterrevolutionaries from "backward elements"; (2) as a matter of practice, why the three main types of counterrevolutionaries were traitors (*hanjian*), GMD intelligence agents (*tewu*), and evil bullies (*e'ba*); and (3) why it was necessary to suppress counterrevolutionaries at all. (Given these queries, one can only assume that the rank and file workers for the enterprises covered by the Lacquer Makers' Association were at first glance not traitorous, or high enough in the preceding Guomindang to have been *tewu*, or currently engaging in the kind of bullying (*e'ba*) behavior that earned mass hatred.) The Lacquer Makers' Association leaders also wondered how, when they operated in such a small sector of under 900 workers, what kind of sabotage they should be on the lookout for, and whether they should expect police to be sent to their workshops to root out counterrevolutionaries for the duration of the campaign.

The official responses fortuitously recorded in the archives to these questions were written up in question and answer format, and dealt in anodyne generalities. Association leaders were assured that the counter-revolutionaries up for suppression were those who were *currently* engaged in subversive activity, rather than those with "historical questions." Problems in distinguishing between counterrevolutionary and non-counterrevolutionary were referred to the same regulations that had so confused the leaders of the Lacquer Makers' Association in the first place. Traitors (*hanjian*), special agents (*tewu*), and evil bullies (*e'ba*) were singled out for sanctions and quashing because these were the individuals who had harmed the people the most, piled up the most blood debts and, significantly, "were the three sorts who did the most to overturn the peoples' democratic power and sabotage the peoples' enterprises." The Lacquer Makers' Association bosses were reassured that "while the police of course took responsibility for the campaign, the [campaign] relied on the enthusiasm and aid of the broad masses to reveal the secret and unlawful activities of counterrevolutionaries," signaling that the police would not be directly sent to small enterprises, but that police work relied on informants within the workplace to bring instances of counterrevolutionaries to their attention.[93] Given the scarcity of workers or managers who obviously fell into any of these categories, the leaders of the Lacquer Makers' Association might have been

---

[93] SMA S64/3/134. Shanghai shi zaoqi gongye tongye hui, "Benhui huiyuan xuexi zhenya fangeming shishi zhengce de xuexi taohua he zongjie baogao" (Shanghai Municipal Lacquer Makers' Association, Association member study discussion and summary report for accurate implementation of the campaign to suppress counterrevolutionaries), June 11, 1951–July 20, 1952.

forgiven from having come away from this day-long meeting none the wiser about whom to single out and turn over.

The way in which the Campaign to Suppress Counterrevolutionaries was implemented in Sunan appears to have varied from sector to sector and from organization to organization. The records of the training meeting organized for the members of the Lacquer Makers' Association suggest that the bosses of small, more scattered enterprises only recently organized into sectoral associations by the CCP struggled to understand the significance of the campaign and were at a loss as to how to implement it. One day of general training and formulaic answers was expected to be sufficient for leaders to return to their workplaces and get on with the campaign. They appeared to be given no pointers from the outside in campaign mechanics, or even whether it was possible to conduct a proper campaign in such small workplaces. In contrast, as we will see in Chapter 3, some of the workers in large state factories were quite amenable to being "stirred up." But the ongoing confusion of Lacquer Makers' Association leaders suggests that that response was less than the CCP hoped for in the small enterprises that made up the majority of Shanghai's workplaces.

At the same time, the Campaign to Suppress Counterrevolutionaries left a residue of practices and institutions in the work units it directly touched and among the urban population at large. It established sub-organizations within the confines of large work units to ensure internal security, monitoring, and latent coercion that remained in place after the conclusion of the campaign. The leaders of smaller enterprises like those in the Lacquer Makers' Association began, if only in a rudimentary way, to learn the essentials of what a campaign entailed. With these precedents established in the workplaces in which the CCP had the strongest presence, permanent security committees and techniques of campaign preparation and mobilization would be extended to all work units over time, and would be drawn on repeatedly in the prosecution of later campaigns.

Absent the mass mobilization and *de facto* decentralization wherein every workplace was expected to conduct its own version of the campaign in microcosm, something very similar occurred in the ROC/Taiwan. Taiwan's smaller scale and the superimposition of the ROC government atop the Taiwan provincial government made it significantly easier to run campaigns in a centralized manner, despite the multiplicity of government organizations involved initially in the suppression of subversion. The precursor to the Taiwan Garrison Command was directly responsible for implementing martial law under the authority of the ROC Presidential Office. Despite the proliferation of competing organizations involved with detecting, and apprehending potential subversives and a burgeoning system of prisons, military courts, and residential centers for political indoctrination (*ganxun* – 感訓) of prisoners given lesser sentences or prior to release back into society, there is little doubt that Chiang Ching-kuo, Chiang Kai-shek's son, was by far the most important figure in the running of counterintelligence and internal security matters. Not only was the son of the Generalissimo unimpeachably loyal, he had all the relevant experience that one could have hoped for: a twelve-year sojourn in the Soviet Union learning about Soviet security arrangements, and he had been the key figure in counter intelligence in Shanghai during the civil war.[94] Chiang *fils* was also the dominant figure in the revitalization of GMD rule in Taiwan after 1949. He chaired the Central Reform Commission, insisted on a stringent system of Soviet-style military commissars for the military, and, as Sheena Greitens so clearly demonstrates, was central to transforming state terror in the ROC/Taiwan from fragmentation and remoteness from Taiwan society to increasing unification and social embeddedness.[95] Ching-kuo's portfolio was diverse and he had many official roles, but his most important post in internal security in the early 1950s appears to have been chairing the Records Section (*ziliao zu* – 資料組) within the Presidential office, which provided overall direction and oversight of the entirety of the military and civilian systems involved in counter subversion.[96]

Like its counterpart across the Strait, the ROC state invoked the stark necessity of security work and the importance of undercutting subversion to extend its domination downward into ever more basic units of society. In early 1950, the TGC expanded with the establishment of sixteen special units to receive intelligence on spies, plus a special security group to monitor intelligence reports in the postal, educational, and overseas Chinese sectors. A combination of regular and military police monitored port traffic and extended surveillance deep into society. Virtually all units of society not directly controlled by the GMD were subject to surveillance and heavy-handed repression. Universities and middle schools, factories, newspapers, and even seemingly innocuous organizations were all heavily monitored. The slightest indications of voiced dissatisfaction and unrest were quickly quelled.[97]

To carry out this kind of pre-emptive monitoring, in an almost exact parallel with practice in the PRC, in early 1952 the ROC government established over fifty in-house security committees with reporting links to

---

[94] Jay Taylor, *The Generalissimo's Son*, p. 49 and passim.
[95] Greitens, *Dictators and Their Secret Police*, pp. 93–99, 107–08.
[96] Chen Cuilian, "Taiwan jieyan shiqi de tewu tongzhi yu baise kongbu fenwei," p. 48.
[97] "Taiwan Jingbei Zongbu gongzuo baogao jielü 39 nian" (Taiwan General Police Department work report notes, 1949), NZASH, Vol. 1, 5–7.

higher levels of the security apparatus in schools, universities, government offices, state-owned factories, and provincial-level enterprises. The educational sector was particularly singled out for scrutiny with the establishment of a county-level Education and Society Security organization.[98] Although details are sketchy, state security organizations also set up networks of secret informants at the most basic levels of society at around this time, and the monitoring of post, telephone, and telegram traffic came to be pervasive and routine. The ROC/Taiwan state also explicitly linked the strengthening of internal security geographically inward and upward to the historically aboriginal highlands. In 1952, thirty "special security small groups" were dispatched to mountainous communities to engage in a combination of "education" and rooting out of suspect subversives who had fled to Taiwan's rugged interior.[99] And by 1953, the TGC and the Taiwan Provincial Police Affairs Department were cooperating well enough to have set up special small group committees in all government organizations to ensure the selection of loyal officials. These small groups also secretly reported on work within government organizations. Over the course of the early to mid-1950s, the ROC government established a fully penetrative police state on Taiwan, with one provincial security work group, 24 county security work groups, and 520 district security work groups, employing a total of 23,126 people.[100] One of the most careful and comprehensive works in the public domain cites a Ministry of Public Security report from 1967 stating that between 1950 and 1967, the Ministry of Public Security held the individual personnel files of around 140,000 people, thus suggesting the creation of an unusually strong surveillance state.[101]

---

[98] "Taiwan sheng Bao'an Silingbu qingbao shouji jihua" (Taiwan Provincial Security Command intelligence collection plan, 1950), NZASH, Vol. 1. p. 17.

[99] "Taiwan Jingbei Zongbu gongzuo baogao 41 nian" (Taiwan General Police Department work report 1952), NZASH Vol. 1, p. 50.

[100] Chen Cuilian, p. 64.

[101] Greitens, *Dictators and Their Secret Police*, p. 183, and fn. 10.

3　Performing Terror
Lenience, Legality, and the Dramaturgy of the Consolidating State

The two consolidating Chinese states both assigned great importance to quelling internal subversion (real and imagined) in the early 1950s. Sharing an insecure regional environment and deeply worried about regime survival, each went to extraordinary lengths to extirpate what it defined as a threat to the state – political subversion, petty criminality, and social undesirability. Each deliberately used the pretext of rooting out subversion to rapidly expand the coercive capacity of the state downward into basic units of society. This was accomplished by strengthening organizations of public security and policing in tandem with the establishing networks of informing and snitching. Each suppressed many times more individuals than there were individuals plotting against the state, thus exterminating and/or marginalizing all sources of potential political and social competition. Each expected that the individual would cultivate himself to reflect values and norms established by the state. Repeated assertions of fundamental ideological differences to the contrary, much about these two consolidating regimes – from their core agendas to their stated rationales to many of their tactics – was in far greater alignment than either was able or willing to acknowledge. Their bitter rivalry and mutually exclusive claims to speak for the entire Chinese nation meant that each had every incentive to trumpet its distinctiveness from the other; for political reasons neither could acknowledge the substantial overlaps in their agendas for ensuring domestic security. Their real, and significant, differences were revealed not so much in *what* was done in the name of internal security. Both arrested and executed putative subversives, conflated social undesirability and petty criminality with counterrevolution/subversion, and promised lenience to those who confessed while abrogating those promises whenever it suited. Rather, the core differences between the Campaign to Suppress Counterrevolutionaries and the White Terror lay in *how* these campaigns were implemented.

120

Bait and Switch Promises of Lenience: Surrender, Remaking the Self, and Conditional Redemption

Like its predecessor imperial state, criminal jurisprudence in the People's Republic of China and the ROC/Taiwan was premised on the assumption of the guilt of the accused. The corollary of this standing assumption was that those who came forward and surrendered were treated with lenience, and those who persisted in denying guilt were considered recalcitrant "hard cases" deserving more severe punishment.[1] Those caught but deemed cooperative in naming names and implicating others fell somewhere in between these two positions. All were expected to admit guilt, recognize mistakes, and ideally be granted the opportunity to "remake" him- (or more rarely, her-) self as a precondition for eventual re-inclusion in society. In Sunan this principle of merciful treatment was widely publicized from the earliest days of CCP rule. In the immediate days and weeks in the late spring of 1949 immediately after Shanghai, Nanjing, and other cities in Sunan were taken over by the People's Liberation Army, a call went out to those who had been *tewu* under the old regime to come forward and register as *tefei* (bandit special affairs – 特匪). Lenience was promised to those who did so.[2] Some responded immediately: the Nanjing Bureau of Public Security registered 412 *tewu* by the end of June 1949. While we do not know how many *tewu* in Shanghai registered in these early days, in December 1950 the Shanghai Bureau of Public Security recorded that 652 cases involving 5,675 *tewu* spies had been cracked in the previous eighteen months, and it is likely that many of these cases were solved because individuals turned themselves in with the expectation of light treatment by the new government.[3]

In the winter of 1950–1951, public security authorities throughout Sunan launched a new, large registration drive for *tewu* counterrevolutionaries that reiterated the promise of lenience for those who came forward, confessed, and registered with their corroborating documents. In retrospect, the enormous publicity given to this registration drive, its extraordinary mobilization of bureaucratic resources, and the sheer scale of the enterprise was itself a pre-campaign sub-campaign to prepare the way for the "sharp strikes" and full-scale social mobilization that occurred later in

---

[1] While there was no concept of innocence until proven guilty in imperial China, concerns about interrogation techniques and false accusations went very far back indeed. Korolkov, "Arguing about Law: Interrogation Procedure under the Qin and Former Han Dynasties," pp. 37–71.

[2] *NGZ*, pp. 187–189. In Nanjing, some 256 *tefei* and a further 160 *tewu* from the Nanjing-Tianjin railroad administration registered with the Bureau of Public Security by the end of June 1949; and the municipal Bureau of Public Security broke up four relatively small subversive networks for an additional 164, but these extra 164 did not count as "coming forward and surrendering."

[3] *SGZ*, p. 99.

the spring of 1951. But as these registration drives were ongoing, what was to come was not obvious at all. Given the kind of lenience offered by the regime from its earliest days in power to those on the losing side of the civil war, this winter registration drive might well have seemed to be nothing more than a straightforward administrative exercise of tidying up.

On January 20, 1951, the Nanjing Military Administration Committee published an edict that required all *tewu* counterrevolutionaries to register with their documentary proofs forthwith while "ordinary" counterrevolutionaries were excused from registering. To manage this workload, Nanjing set up fourteen temporary district registration stations, and all state organizations, schools, and enterprises were all ordered to establish registration stations or registration small groups. Within three days 1,516 registered, and by the end of the fifth day, the number of counterrevolutionaries logged was 4,298. These included such high-level figures as the Vice Chair of the Guomindang Military Affairs Bureau. By the end of March, the city had registered a total of 18,611 *tewu* counterrevolutionaries from GMD Party, Youth Corps, military, and intelligence organizations.[4] When this number was added to the 412 high-level *tewu* who had already registered, there was a substantial reservoir of self-acknowledged counterrevolutionaries who could then be readily drawn upon when the campaign proper was launched two to three months later.[5] In Shanghai there was an identical push to register counterrevolutionaries and *tewu*. Like Nanjing, Shanghai promised "lenience for those *tewu* who sincerely came clean and confessed." To cope with the numbers coming forward to register with the authorities, Shanghai established a general

---

[4] It is not entirely clear how large the population of Nanjing was in 1951, and this makes it difficult to gauge exactly what percentage of the working adult population felt compelled to register as *tewu*. Mao himself estimated the city to have a population of 500,000 at this time. See Yang, "Reconsidering the Campaign to Suppress Counterrevolutionaries," fn. 24. The 1953 census puts the total population of Nanjing at 1,091,600, including men, women, children, and retirees. https://en.wikipedia.org/wiki/First_National_Population_Census_of_the_People%27s_Republic_of_China, accessed June 8, 2017. While Mao was notoriously imprecise in his use of figures, it is also the case that as the capital of the Guomindang, Nanjing must have lost a substantial part of its resident population. Many of those in high enough positions under the Guomindang would likely have fled the city before the arrival of the Communists in 1949. If Mao's very low figure of 500,000 is accurate, counterrevolutionaries who registered accounted for 3.8 percent of the urban population (including women, children, and the retired). If the 1953 census numbers are used, then registered counterrevolutionaries accounted for 1.74 percent of the urban population. If we assume a round figure of 850,000 the percentage is 2.24 percent. The range of 1.74 percent to 3.8 percent of Nanjing's population might seem small until one considers that almost all *tewu* would have been males of working age (thus excluding women, children, and retirees, who would have accounted for at least half of the total population), suggesting that among the relevant category of males of working age, these percentages would have to be at least doubled to between 3.48 percent and 7.6 percent.

[5] *NGZ*, pp. 192–193.

office to register counterrevolutionaries, as well as three branch offices and special registration sections in each police station. It is not clear how many responded to this call in the winter of 1950–1951, but 26,896 "*tewu*, counterrevolutionary party and [Sun Yat-sen Youth] corps back-bones" had registered by the end of July, 1951.[6]

The 1951 winter drive to register counterrevolutionaries in Sunan stressed the education and rehabilitation of those who triumphed over their fear of declaring their status with the new government. As these two juxtaposed cartoons from Shanghai's *Liberation Daily* on January 16, 1951 illustrate in images 3.1 and 3.2, counterrevolutionaries were enjoined to resolutely "become new people" (*zuo xinren* – 做新人) and figuratively unchain themselves from being hauled into a pit of despair by the security authorities to set themselves on a "new road." Equally they were told to "remake themselves early" (*zaori zixin* – 早日 自新). In the first of the cartoons below, the *tewu* who has chosen the right road is racing away from the *tewu* who is still undecided and about to fall into a pit of skulls. The caption reads "don't hesitate – be determined: become a new person," as the *tewu* heads towards the light of Communism and the new regime. The second cartoon headlines "early to register [means] early to remake one-self," and then moves through four panels that depict a clearly anxious counterrevolutionary (denoted as such by his western haircut and clothes) reading the announcement to register, guiltily hesitating in front of the gates of the government office, sitting down with a cadre, and departing the government office with body language that manifests relief.

Image 3.1. "Don't Hesitate: Be Determined and Become a New Person." *Jiefang Ribao*, Shanghai, January 16, 1951

---

[6] *SGZ*, p. 99.

Image 3.2. "Early to Register; Early to Remake Oneself." *Jiefang Ribao*, Shanghai, January 16, 1951

When Shanghai authorities carried out their first wave of mass set of arrests on April 27, 1951, slightly more than half of the 9,010 rounded up were classified as *tewu* or "backbones" for the GMD Party or the Sun Yat-sen Youth Corps (4887).[7] (The other half of those caught up in this first wave of arrests consisted of other sorts of social undesirables: "evil bullies," bandits, and the leaders of counterrevolutionary sects who would not have been called upon to register). There are no figures available that

[7] *SGZ*, p. 105.

detail how many of the 26,896 *tewu* counterrevolutionaries counted at the end of July 1951 had taken at face value the government's promises of lenience and registered in January 1951, how many were already on the police radar as suspect, and how many were informed on by those arrested in late April. But Shanghai's establishment of four new offices and special sections in local police stations to process the self-registration of *tewu* suggests that many must have trusted the government's assurances of lenience. There must have been thousands who then found themselves at the sharp end of a sudden and vicious police action only three months later. There were likely thousands more who had responded to the call to register and remake themselves without being singled out in the first sweeps in April and May of 1951. And they and their families must have noticed that many others in similar positions had been subjected to merciless and rapid dispatch.

Coming as it did so soon after this registration drive, the suddenness and viciousness of this active and public phase of Campaign to Suppress Counterrevolutionaries established a clear precedent and salutary warning. Promises made by the CCP could be revoked at will. The party arrogated to itself the right to abruptly change its line with neither apology nor scruple. Those who came forward when promised lenient treatment in the end might, and then again might not, be so treated, depending on such changeable and opaque criteria as the stage of a given campaign, degrees of direct pressure from cadres higher up in the hierarchy, quotas already filled or unfilled, and how local cadres interpreted the putative "hatred of the masses" as they made their choices of who should be singled out. Campaigns that heralded changes in party line could and did abruptly revoke whatever the CCP's previous assurances might have been.

The sharp strikes in the late spring of 1951 also established another chilling precedent in Sunan: the accused had no escape from the changeable criteria decided on and amended by the state itself. Assurances of lenience to the contrary, an honest surrender to the new government was no guarantee of clemency. Those implicated by others were treated harshly for neglecting to come forward and register. The best and perhaps only hope for mercy was cooperation, but security services reserved the right to determine how much cooperation was enough, and the way cooperation was best demonstrated was often by implicating others. In addition, the penitent was expected to bare himself as a heuristic example of the evils of the old society. This was accomplished by writing confessional autobiographies (*zizhuan* – 自传), and willingness to be displayed as a negative example. Whether clemency was or was not extended was all too often a function of the stage of the campaign, the temperament of the local cadre charged with implementing the campaign, and whether the locality's target quotas had already been met. Even those who were released or sentenced to the lightest form of punishment – *guanzhi* (管制 – ongoing supervision by the masses), had a large black mark entered in their personal dossiers (*geren dang'an* – 個人檔案), now greatly enlarged by a mass of damning documentation unearthed by the campaign.

In a remarkably similar way and using nearly identical language, the Guomindang also held out promises of light treatment and pardon for those who voluntarily surrendered (*zishou* – 自首) in order to remake themselves (自新 – *zixin*). The main difference between Sunan and Taiwan was that in Sunan decisions about lenience or prosecution were handled at local levels of government, typically comprised of a committee of the local party secretary, the top echelon of public security officers, and occasionally an outside cadre dispatched to guide the proceedings. In the ROC/Taiwan, the process of surrender and requesting a formal pardon was significantly more centralized and bureaucratic. In Taiwan, coming forward to surrender was but the first step in a formal review by a special central committee empowered to approve or decline the application of the individual in question. For those whose *zishou* was successful, a formal amnesty was issued that accepted the individual's application to *zixin* (turning over a new leaf/ "remaking the self"). Like the CCP, the GMD focused a great deal of its attention on combing through individual prior histories and checking on documentation, required individuals to write extensive personal autobiographies and full confessions, and participate in intensive (re) training for political indoctrination, complete with small group study sessions and criticism.[8]

These dynamics were in evidence in the most important Communist network broken by GMD security authorities in early 1950: the Taiwan Provincial Work Committee (Taiwan Sheng Gongzuo Weiyuanhui – 臺灣省工作委員會), the formal name of the Chinese Communist Party organization in Taiwan. In the autumn of 1949, the Ministry of Defence Security Bureau successfully conducted its first concerted drives against Communist networks (or "work committees" *gongzuo weiyuanhui* – 工作委員會) in Jilong, Gaoxiong, and at the leftist newspaper *Guangming Bao* ("Bright News"). Interrogations produced leads to the top leaders of the Taiwan Provincial [Communist] Work Committee itself. And the Guomindang's actions in managing this top echelon of Communist Party leaders in Taiwan illustrate in microcosm how it exercised the principle of lenience.

---

[8] Tsai Teh-pen, pp. 377–389.

The party secretary of the Taiwan Provincial Work Committee in the early 1950s was Cai Xiaoqian (蔡孝乾) (1908–1982). Cai was seconded by Zhang Zhizhong (張志忠) (1910–1954). Cai and Zhang were among the very few Taiwanese who had unimpeachable bona fides as committed revolutionaries in the Chinese Communist Party, with careers pursued mostly in China rather than in Taiwan or Japan.[9] By the late 1940s, Cai was an experienced revolutionary with experiences that paralleled the rise of the CCP itself: after finding his way to Shanghai in the revolutionary ferment of the mid-1920s, he joined the Chinese Communists, escaped to the Jiangxi Base Soviet after the GMD terror wreaked against the Left in April 1927, survived the purges of the early 1930s, came through the Long March (with a leg injury to prove it), and was the highest ranking Taiwanese in the CCP in Yan'an during the Sino-Japanese War. At the time of the Japanese surrender in August 1945, Cai was confirmed as party secretary for the Taiwan Provincial Work Committee.[10]

Zhang Zhizhong had spent considerable time as a young leftist and activist in socialist study societies in Taiwan and Xiamen before arriving in Yan'an for military and political training at Kangda ("Resist Japan University") in early 1939. The rest of Zhang's war years were spent in the Eighth Route Army engaging in propaganda work, and in August 1945 he was given the portfolio for the Taiwan Provincial Work Committee's military wing. After a month of training in Shanghai in January 1946, Zhang was infiltrated into Taiwan, and Cai followed some six months later.[11]

By any reasonable standard, Cai was a remarkably effective leader for the Communist Party in Taiwan in the nearly four-year period between his arrival in Taiwan in July 1946 and final capture at the end of April 1950. Until Chiang Kai-shek retreated to Taiwan with his government and military in 1949, the island was at best an afterthought for both the CCP and the GMD. Cai and Zhang were very much on their own in the late 1940s. They engaged in months of frenetic activity, managing to expand the membership of the Taiwan Work Committee from just a handful in early 1946 to between 900 and 2,000 party members by early 1950. Nor was Taiwan an easy environment in which to work: the February 28, 1947, uprising and harsh subsequent crackdown fell

---

[9] Most of the "old Taiwanese Communists" active in Taiwan prior to retrocession in 1945 had been crushed by the Japanese colonial government in the early 1930s.

[10] NCA, 0036=0410.9/4490442/001–001 through 001–016, "Cai Xiaoqian Zibaishu Gongci" (Supplements to the Confession of Cai Xiaoqian).

[11] This chronology draws from Lan Bozhou, *Taigong Dangren de Beige: Zhang Zhizhong, Ji Yun yu Yang Yang*, pp. 384–401; see also "Taiwan Gongzuo Weiyuan hui dengren an" (The Case of the Taiwan Work Committee) in NZASH, Vol. 2, p. 56.

disproportionately on Taiwanese intellectuals and the Left. Making matters worse, the initial collapse of GMD authority immediately after February 28 emboldened an ultra-left faction within the Communist party on Taiwan to declare the establishment of a People's Government in Taizhong. Cai, who believed such action was needlessly risky, argued vociferously against it. When the People's Government was crushed several days later by GMD army reinforcements, the leaders of the uprising fled to the mountains to continue armed resistance but were unable to win sufficient support from local aborigines.[12] The short-lived Taizhong seizure of power prompted the unwelcome attention of repressive authorities, and was a major setback for the Taiwan Provincial Work Committee when ongoing mass anger with the ineffectiveness and brutality of the GMD might have provided otherwise promising conditions for organizing intellectuals, workers, and peasants. After mid-1949, the leaders of the Taiwan Provincial Work Committee turned their attention to preparing for the "liberation" of Taiwan. Identifying activists, and, in the face of intensified suppression from the GMD on Taiwan, scouting out remote areas to establish small mountain base areas from which to continue the struggle were its most important activities. One of the sites identified for a small base area was in Luku (鲁窟) to the immediate east of Taibei; another, less well studied, was established in Wutu ku (乌涂窟) far into the mountains of Miaoli, west of Taibei.[13]

Despite its collapse in the rest of China, by late 1949 the GMD's internal security organizations in Taiwan were brutally effective. Between the end of October 1949 and the middle of February 1950, GMD security services had succeeded in arresting almost all the leaders in the Taiwan Provincial Work Committee, including Cai Xiaoqian (蔡孝乾), Chen Zemin (陳澤民), Zhang Zhizhong (張志忠), and Hong Youqiao (洪幼 瞧). The details surrounding these arrests, and particularly that of Cai Xiaoqian, the top man and party secretary, remain unclear. Chen Zemin was the first in the top echelon to be arrested, in Gaoxiong on October 31, 1949. After GMD security services secretly and "resourcefully" enlisted the help of watchful

---

[12] The leader of the Taizhong uprising was a female revolutionary by the name of Xie Xuehong. Xie and her close companion Yang Kehuang managed to escape Taiwan for Hong Kong, and eventually made their way to Beijing via Korea, where they spent the rest of their lives. Chen Fangming, *Xie Xuehong Pinzhuan*, pp. 224–246.

[13] The mass suppression and military storming of the Luku Base area continues to be mired in ambiguity: Feuchtwang's interviews of participants and their families suggests that most locals were not aware that Luku was a Communist base area at all. See Stephan Feuchtwang, *After the Event*, pp. 116–119, but at the same time, those who might have sympathized with leftist ideals had every incentive to stay silent on this matter, because compensation for past victimhood during the White Terror was explicitly denied to those who actually had been Communists (p. 62).

neighbors and conducted ten days of surveillance, Cai Xiaoqian was arrested in downtown Taibei three months later, on January 29, 1950. Official sources are reticent about subsequent events, but somehow Cai escaped from detention and then managed to evade capture on two further occasions, remaining at large for another three months. While Cai was in hiding, his wife and nephew managed to flee to the mainland, leaving behind Cai's youngest sister in law, Ma Wenjuan (馬雯鵑), who was then a sixteen-year-old student in the Taibei Girls' First Middle School. Upon Cai's first arrest and the flight of her near family to the mainland, Ma went into hiding with a series of sympathetic friends and relatives in preparation for her own attempted escape from Taiwan.

While still eluding capture, in mid-April 1950 Cai managed to arrange a clandestine meeting with the highest ranking Communist leader in the Tainan area, Li Madou (李媽兜). Through Li, Cai issued the "April 1950 Declaration," which called on the Communist underground in Taiwan to "develop work, consolidate, preserve military organization by fleeing to the mountains, and hold out until the PLA's invasion of Taiwan, which was [expected] to come no later than late June [1950]."[14] Unfortunately for Cai, he was himself unable to hold out that long. Very shortly after he passed the April 1950 Declaration on to Li Madou and only some two months before the outbreak of the Korean War, Cai was re-arrested for the second and final time in Jiayi, south-central Taiwan. Teenager Ma Wenjuan was picked up almost immediately afterwards in Tainan, where she was hoping to get to a plane bound for the island of Hainan.[15]

Cai's escape in January 1950 must have at a minimum been a huge embarrassment to the GMD security establishment and a huge loss of face for its leadership. The official records on Cai's case tactfully reveal nothing of his successful prison break, or that he managed to elude the GMD security establishment for three months thereafter. His permanent capture was, however, a much-welcomed propaganda coup. Cai was the highest ranking Communist on the island, the party secretary of the entire underground, and the linchpin for CCP underground operation and its preparation for the then widely anticipated PLA invasion of Taiwan.

The currently available evidence, though, suggests that for the CCP, Taiwan was a relatively minor sideshow. There was, for example, no direct link between the CCP Party central and the Taiwan Provincial Work Committee; all communication was filtered through the Fujian

---

[14] LMDA, "Li Maodou An Da Shiji" (Chronology of the Li Madou Case), p. 563.
[15] "Taiwan sheng gongzuo weiyuanhui dengren an." Guojia Anquan Ju (National Security Agency), Original file number 44901/444048, in NZASH, Vol. 2, pp. 55–61. NCAT (National Central Archive on Taiwan) 0036=0410.9=4490442=.

subsection of the East China Military Region. Almost all contact was by occasional courier rather than by the much quicker telegraph. Financial support was nearly non-existent: party leaders were expected to be self-reliant and work with exclusively local materials. Between 1946 and 1950, Cai appears have operated with minimal aid, support, and direction from the parent CCP. On only one occasion in these four years were the leaders of the Taiwan Provincial Work Committee called to meet with their superiors and plan for the future, when an extraordinary meeting was held in the relative safety of Hong Kong in June, 1948. Thereafter the East China Military Region headquarters decided that preparation for the eventual invasion of Taiwan was important enough to send Cai additional help, and they duly dispatched Chen Zemin to Taiwan to be the new second in command. The Chen appointment did Cai no favors, as Chen Zemin proved to be spectacularly ill suited for work in Taiwan. Lacking either experience in Taiwanese affairs or the ability to speak the local dialect, he was unsurprisingly ineffective in organizing the Communist underground in south Taiwan, and was the first arrested of the top leadership, having lasted for only fifteen months of underground work.[16]

While official sources do not directly reveal which of these leaders was the first to crack under questioning by the GMD security services, the timeline revealed in interrogation transcripts hint strongly that Chen Zemin was the first to be turned. Chen was captured in Gaoxiong in late October 1949. Even before he was transferred to the central HQ of the Taiwan Garrison Command in Taibei for full questioning, Chen indicated his desire to *zishou*. He formally surrendered to the GMD and renounced the CCP and any form of political activity on November 1, 1949, weeks before any of the others in the top echelon of the Taiwan Work Committee were apprehended.[17] This formal application to *zixin* (turn over a new leaf) almost certainly came at a high price. *Zixin* individuals were expected to make a full individual confession and demonstrate their sincerity through cooperation with the regime. Cooperation in turn was invariably measured by willingness to expose networks and name names.

With the exceptions of Zhang Zhizhong and his young wife Ji Yun, the entirety of the leadership of the Taiwan Work Committee formally defected to the GMD within a few weeks of Cai's re-capture in late April 1950. On the symbolically important date of May 4, the GMD

---

[16] NCA 0036=0410.9=44904440=2=026=003, "Chen Zemin Gongci" (Supplementary materials on Chen Zemin), August 15, 1950.

[17] NCA 0036=0410.9=4490440=1=020=0010 (fix). "Chen Zemin xianmu ya'e zhengzhi shenghuo jueding tuoli gongchandang" (Chen Zemin decision to leave the CCP), dated November 1, 1949.

Zhongyang Ribao (Central Daily News) published a front-page open announcement to the membership of the Communist Party in the names of Cai, Chen, and Hong. This proclamation ordered the Communists in Taiwan to cease operations immediately, disband their organizations, come forward to surrender and request amnesty, and speedily conclude their cases with the Guomindang government. Less than a week after this stunning publication, in a manner that was reminiscent of the way in which the CCP demanded that the accused publicly "acknowledge" (*chengzui* – 承罪) his errors, Cai renounced the Chinese Communist Party and openly acknowledged his "[prior] delusion that the CCP would liberate Taiwan" in a publicly aired radio broadcast – only some two weeks after he had passed a communication to Li Madou assuring the Party faithful that the liberation of Taiwan was imminent and urging them to flee to the mountainous interior. Eighteen months later, on October 9, 1951, in *Taiwan Xinsheng Bao*, Cai again repeated his plea to those still active in the Communist underground to come forward and surrender under the terms of the amnesty offered by the GMD. Here Cai's written words almost perfectly mirrored the CCP's cartoon visual of January 1951 with an enjoinder to transgressors to "go down the bright road" (*zouxiang guangming daolu* – 走向光明道路). This, however, was communicated quite differently from the humorous cartoons in Sunan publications. In Taiwan, the GMD reiterated rules and regulations, and presented its just dispatch of spies and subversives as part of political and legal order. As one example of this, on May 14, 1950, the news of Cai Xiaoqian's capture and his open exhortation to the CCP's remaining holdouts in Taiwan to give up, turn themselves in, and accept the amnesty offered by the GMD through applying to *zishou* (自首) was splashed all over the main news outlets. This was accompanied by neither humorous cartoon nor snappy editorial, but rather through a combination of terse factual report, a blurred photograph, and a reposting of the regulations.[18]

One can only imagine the pressure that Cai must have been under to become so visible a defector a mere few weeks after he had sent a secret directive to the Communist underground to keep the faith, withdraw to the mountains, and await the arrival of the PLA. It must have been excruciating to publicly renounce all that his career had stood for over the previous quarter century, when the "Liberation" of Taiwan was apparently only a matter of weeks away. Behind closed doors, Cai also gave up one underground network after another to his interrogators. By one, likely exaggerated, account he was directly responsible for the arrest

---

[18] LMDA "Li Madou An Da shiji," p. 564; and NZASH, Vol. 2, "Fabiao fei zhenggao dieshu," *Xinsheng Bao* October 9, 1951, p. 64.

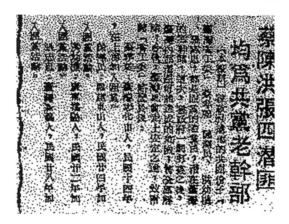

Image 3.3. "Hidden Bandits Cai, Chen, Hong, and Zhang are all Chinese Communist Party Old Cadres." *Taiwan Xinsheng Bao*, May 14, 1950

and imprisonment of over 1,800 individuals, and the execution of a substantial number of these.[19]

Cai and most of the rest of the top leadership formally petitioned to "turn over a new leaf" (*zixin*) and spent an unsettled period undergoing thought reform (*sixiang gaizao* – 思想改造) on Green Island, awaiting the official verdict on their petitions for a pardon. Whether by accident or design, this process took several months. There is no evidence that Cai and this top echelon of the Taiwan Provincial Work Committee were personally subjected to torture, and indeed when he was ill with a high fever, Cai was given medical attention, albeit with informers working in four-hour shifts who recorded everything he said in his delirious state. During these interim weeks of limbo, Cai and the others in the top leadership of the Taiwan Provincial Work Committee also had ample opportunities to witness the kinds of abuses visited upon less privileged political prisoners. Many years later, Ma Wenjuan recalled with horror the daily "vitamin injections" given to prisoners, after which some took ill, and others went insane.[20]

After their collective petition to "turn over a new leaf" was officially accepted, most of the group (Cai, Chen, Hong, and several others) were

---

[19] Weiji Baike entry Cai Xiaoqian. www.zh.wikipedia.org/wiki/Cai Xiaoqian. Accessed October 23, 2013.
[20] "Dang renshi Cai Xiaoqian jia shu Ma Wenjuan ji Cai Yian fangtan jilü" (Interview record of Cai Xiaoqian family members Ma Wenjuan and Cai Yian, April 10, 1998. NZASH, Vol. 2, pp. 62–63.

removed *en bloc* to the mountains north of Taibei in Shilin district, where they were given work in a research unit on Communist activities that had been established especially for them. Although the sources do not explicitly so state, they must have been held under some form of house arrest for quite some time. The conditions under which confessions were accepted normally required a lengthy stay under a *guanxun* (administration and training – 管訓) regime that was a halfway house between prison and release. Those undergoing *guanxun* lived in dormitories isolated from the rest of society, and were subjected to frequent political study sessions. In addition to indicating the correct answers, manifesting the right kind of behavior (*pinde* –品德), and showing the right kind of "spirit" (*jingshen* – 精神), participants in *guanxun* wrote daily diaries that recorded their "progress." Only after monitors approved were they permitted to re-join regular society.[21]

Cai's later career suggests that he was given a desk job and closely monitored for the rest of his life. He eventually married his much younger sister in law, Ma Wenjuan, who remembered in an oral history interview many years later that "on the whole they were treated well by the GMD." He spent the remainder of his career with high positions in a variety of Guomindang's military intelligence units, refrained from giving interviews about his post-1950 career, and passed away from old age and illness in 1982. Given his post-pardon reticence, we will never know for sure why, after a lifetime of service to the Chinese Communist Party, Cai so quickly chose to defect to an enemy he had fought against for the previous quarter century, and then, once having so chosen, to cooperate so fully. In the several months prior to the outbreak of the war in Korea, Cai and most of the others in the leadership group of the CCP in Taiwan gave GMD security organizations enough information to wipe out nearly the entirety of the Communist underground at a time when there was every reason to believe that the People's Liberation Army would resolve things in favor of the Communist Party in Taiwan in a matter of weeks.[22]

---

[21] Tehpen Tsai, pp. 362–363.

[22] Cai never publicly discussed either the reasons for his defection to the GMD or his activities as an expert researcher in the Anti-Communist Research Division of the Taiwan Garrison Command at Shilin. However, his third wife, Ma Wenjuan did give a brief interview to oral historian Li Xuanfeng, in April 1998. In this interview she stated that Cai's second wife and her younger brother managed to return to the mainland after Cai's arrest, leaving herself, the younger sister of Cai's second wife, behind. There is some uncertainty as to when Ma and Cai became romantically involved, raising the possibility that Cai may have chosen to throw in his lot with the Guomindang in part for family reasons and/or, or out of a sense of obligation to try to protect his young sister-in-law, whose capture slightly predated his second arrest in April 1950. See "Dangshi ren Cai Xiaoqian jia shu Ma Wenjuan ji Cai yian fantang jilü," in NZASH, Vol. 2, pp. 62–63.

As in Sunan, GMD lenience to those who voluntarily turned them-selves in was patchy. Nor was the promise to extend *zixin* status to those who requested it always honored. When the Party secretary of the Tainan municipal branch, Li Madou, was arrested with his common-law wife, Chen Shuduan (陳叔端) while trying to escape to the mainland by boat in February 1952, he had every reason to believe that cooperation would result in a period of *ganxun* and eventual pardon. The GMD policy of lenience for those who surrendered and requested amnesty had been well publicized: in the last four months of 1951 alone, GMD security organi-zations received 643 applications for *zishou*. Slightly less than half were regular CCP Party members (305 or 43.3 percent), followed by fellow travellers (153/23.29 percent), and those who knew Communists but had refrained from reporting this knowledge to authorities (130/20.21 per-cent). At the time the report was written, slightly more than half of these applications had been accepted (351/54.59 percent). Another 160 (24.88 percent) applications had been accepted in principle, with the paperwork still in process. When the annual report was compiled at the end of 1951, 113 individuals were still under investigation, and only 19 of 643 (2.95 percent) had been refused as non-compliant with regulations.[23]

Whether from pique, vindictiveness, or some other reason lost in the mists of time, GMD lenience of the sort that had been extended to the higher-ranking Cai Xiaoqian, Chen Zemin, and Hong Youqiao only two years previously was withheld from Li Madou. Admittedly, Li had been caught while trying to escape from Taiwan by boat, but it is hard to credit this as being somehow more culpable than Cai Xiaoqian's escape from detention and transmitting a formal declaration to the rank and file to run for the hills and await the liberation of the PLA. Li was also extremely cooperative after his arrest. After he was transferred from the Tainan municipal police station to the custody of the TGC in Taibei, he was extremely open with his interrogators. Li named names, explained his reasons for having joined the CCP in a forthright way, detailed on whom he relied while in hiding, wrote a full personal history as an underground leader, offered an astonishing level of detail in party organization and activity in the Tainan area over the previous several years, and gave up the names of a number of unbroken networks in south-central Taiwan.[24] Despite this post-arrest level of cooperation, when Li made a formal submission to "turn over a new leaf" (*zixin*) July 1952, his request was curtly denied on the grounds that "it was of no

[23] "Jiansu feidie yundong banjing zishou anjian fenlei tongji biao" (The cleaning out spies campaign management of surrender statistical form). NZASH, Vol. 1, p. 47.
[24] LMDA, "Li Madou Zibaishu" (Li Madou statement) February 16, 1952, pp. 121–132, and "Da shiji," pp. 565–566.

value" (*wu jiazhi* – 無價值), even though his rank in the Taiwan Provincial Work Committee and his actions fulfilled the relevant regulations for a formal pardon. Li's case was returned to the workings of the martial law court with a recommendation for "most severe punishment," and Li and Chen Shuduan were both executed in July 1953.

The Taiwan Garrison Command was even more severe, and seemingly even more arbitrary, in the way that it put down the putative Communist base area of Luku, in the mountains immediately east of Taibei in 1952, where GMD security organizations claimed that two non-local Taiwanese, Lü Heru and Chen Dachuan, had established a Communist base area. Luku natives remembered things quite differently, claiming that apart from one local by the name of Wu Chengming, no one knew the real identity of these two individuals other than that they were "outsiders" (*waidi ren* – 外地人). In this narrative, since no one knew who these outsiders really were, Luku villagers could have been neither leftist sympathizers, nor Communists. Nevertheless, when the base area was surrounded by thousands of soldiers and declared a military zone at the end of December, 1952, virtually the entire adult population were imprisoned in a small local temple, kept in a humiliating squatting position for days on end, and beaten and intimidated into confessing that they were participants in an armed Communist base.[25] The upshot of this police action was that, incredibly, Wu Chengming was never imprisoned. Even the supposed leader of this putatively Communist base, Chen Dachuan, was sentenced to only three years in a fairly comfortable prison, while forty-eight men, likely around half of the young to middle-aged male population of the area, were either executed or sentenced to long spells of imprisonment.[26] Many years later, the military commander who ran the Luku military operation, General Gu Zhengwen, came close to publicly admitting on camera for a 2001 documentary that there had in fact been no armed base area at Luku; neither had there been any Communists there who were posing any kind of threat to the state.[27]

---

[25] Feuchtwang, pp. 116–117. In fact, the final numbers of the imprisoned and executed may be higher than those remembered in oral histories. The official case summary and *panjue* of the Luku Base area incident are included in NZASH, Vol. 3, pp. 233–256. The summary of the case submitted for the permanent file on January 3, 1955, lists 70 arrested and still in prison. This list excludes the lightly punished Chen Dachuan as well as the names of the 16 scheduled for execution later in 1955. Adding these brings the recorded total of those imprisoned or executed up to 87. Feuchtwang, p. 44, states slightly different totals: 35 executed, 97 imprisoned, and another 32 either went into hiding or were sentenced to "supervision" (*guanzhi*) but not imprisoned.

[26] Feuchtwang, p. 135, fn. 3.   [27] Ibid., p. 62.

The Importance of the How in Policy Implementation: Clarion Call for a Mass Movement Versus Procedurally Determined Martial Law

After its first deliberately inclusive first year in power, the young People's Republic of China placed great emphasis on extending to the rest of China the kind of mobilizational campaign that had become part of its signature repertoire during the long years of base area struggle in North China. Through study of key documents and with little direct involvement from higher levels of the state, regional and local cadres were expected to rely on local resources to replicate desirable processes and outcomes. When well executed, the campaign fulfilled multiple requirements: it mobilized the state's organizations to take a policy seriously, signaled to local state organizations how they ought to go about implementation, and drew on the support and participation of society in the state's new projects. If in practice things didn't always go as planned, this kind of mobilizational campaign trusted the revolutionary power of the masses, seeking to merge mass emotion with the policy desiderata of the state in a highly public push to make a rapid breakthrough. When it worked, the CCP's campaign mobilization was appropriately harnessed to the CCP's core notions of class struggle, overcame the natural caution of its cadre administrators and quashed social resistance.

In contrast, Guomindang rhetoric and self-definition reified law (法律), rather than collectively displayed emotion, and stressed the individual's sober internalization of regime norms of law and rectitude. At every turn, the GMD damped down every hint of social mobilization or form of social organization that it did not directly penetrate and control. The ROC/Taiwan exemplified order, procedure, and regularity through the promulgation of laws, regulations, and openly published directives. The didacticism of the consolidating party-state in Sunan and Taiwan was constant: the individual was expected to engage in continuous self-cultivation into norms established by the state. But the *way* in which individual self-cultivation was to be expressed could not have been more different: enthusiastic embrace of class struggle and ongoing demonstration of revolutionary enthusiasm by active and public participation in Sunan, versus the self-cultivation of discipline, procedure, conformity to rules, and sobriety for the ROC/Taiwan.

If we turn to the most important document disseminated throughout officialdom for the Campaign to Suppress Counterrevolutionaries, the Double Ten Directive (October 10, 1950), it is clear that the campaign was, in the first instance, geared primarily to *abandoning* the precedents and practices of the CCP in its first year in power – precedents and

practices that had stressed moderation, inclusion, and patient education for all but the most die-hard supporters of the old regime. At the
same time the Double Ten Directive contained a significant degree of
ambiguity about how those precedents and practices of the regime's
first year ought to be reversed. After restating the reasons for the
campaign (to vanquish the sabotage of imperialist spies, exterminate
the remainder of the Chiang Kai-shek clique, guarantee the success
of land reform, and smooth the progress of economic construction),
the document reiterated the necessity of "resolutely cleaning out all
the bandits, *tewu*, evil bullies, and other counterrevolutionaries who
harm the people" and "raising the consciousness of the Party, the
state, and the people about the activity of counterrevolutionary
spies." After these preliminaries, the bulk of the "Double Ten
Directive" was aimed squarely at getting compliance and stiffening
the resolve of the local cadres who were responsible for the actual
implementation of the campaign. The state's prosecution of counterrevolutionaries was, in principle, designed to have maximum educational impact for the wider [urban] population: the document makes
it clear that the prosecution of individual counterrevolutionaries
required public sentencing and widespread dissemination through
newspapers and radio broadcasts.

At the same time, despite the Double Ten Directive's proscription of
"excessive lenience," and its order to "combine suppression and lenience"
(*zhenya kuanda jiehe* – 鎮壓寬大結合), other provisions allowed room for
cautious and rule-bound forms of implementation. Torture was forbidden
and death sentences had to be approved by higher levels before they could
be implemented. Cadres deciding cases were advised to refrain from relying on hearsay, and to require written proof of counterrevolutionary status
or counterrevolutionary activity.[28] These provisions suggested that the
campaign be, if not limited, then relatively rule bound and procedurally
("bureaucratically") oriented. Adherence to rules and procedure necessarily resulted in slow movement. Thorough investigations took time.
Confirming paper trails that provided incontrovertible evidence of counterrevolutionary status or activity required lengthy archival investigation.
Report writing and waiting for approvals from superiors for death sentences
created delay. Written proof was in short supply for those whose counterrevolutionary status was predicated on activity rather than prior office
holding. How were *e'ba* to be determined, and on what basis were they to

---

[28] "Zhonggong Zhongyang guanyu zhenya fangeming huodong zhishi" (Double Ten
Directive), JZWX Vol. 1, pp. 420–423. Yang Kuisong's work shows, however, that in
many areas of China hearsay, rumor, false charges, wild accusations, and concealed
killings were exactly what transpired over the course of the campaign.

be separated out from the merely disliked? How was evidence of "blood debt" to be obtained other than by hearsay? How, in practice, was suppression to be combined with lenience, or sharp and quick strikes with lengthy waits for written documents that confirmed guilt, or sharp and decisive strikes against the worst and most hated of counterrevolutionaries with the rule that stated that all executions be approved by superiors? On these questions of practical implementation, the Double Ten Directive was hopelessly ambiguous.

Subsequent guiding documents released later in 1950 and into 1951, much harsher in tone, gave broad hints as to how the CCP wished for these ambiguities to be resolved in practice. Shortly after the release of the Double Ten Directive, Luo Ruiqing, Minister of Public Security addressed the All China Conference on Public Security with a report that was widely disseminated to cadres throughout the country. Luo insisted on a policy that "executed some, jailed some, and subjected some to local supervision and control" (*sha yipi, guan yipi, guan yipi* – 殺一批関一批管 一批).[29] In the middle of December 1950, Mao cabled his approval of a tough line regarding counterrevolutionaries when he accepted a report by cadres in West Hunan, with the enjoinder to "hit according to policy, hit correctly, and hit with hatred" (*dade wen, dade zhun, dade hen* – 打得文打得准打得狠).[30] And, as we saw in the previous chapter, when Luo Ruiqing launched an investigation tour of south and central China that included the lower Yangzi valley cities of Nanjing, Wuxi, and Shanghai in February 1951, he was shocked into open criticism by the "gentle and refined" way in which the campaign was being conducted.[31]

In contrast with the PRC's loosely worded "Double Ten Directive," with its sharp break with moderation, and its invigorating call to stamp out counterrevolutionaries and educate the masses, the key documents of reference for the early years of the White Terror in Taiwan were explicit in their claims to continuity with the immediate and more distant past. Law in the post-1949 period in Taiwan built on precedent by extending and adding extraordinary regulations to earlier versions of martial law from 1947 and the Encirclement Campaigns of the mid-1930s. The martial

---

[29] Luo Ruiqing, "Zhongyang gong'an bu guanyu quanguo gong'an huiyi de baogao" (Central Ministry of Public Security report on All China Public Security Meeting), October 26, 1950. JZWX, Vol. 1, p. 443.

[30] "Mao Zedong guanyu zhenya fangeming fenzi de celue wenti de dianbao" (Mao Zedong's cable on problems of strategy in suppressing counterrevolutionaries). JZWX, December 19, 1950, Vol. 1, p. 509.

[31] "Guanyu Wuhan, Shanghai deng chengshi zhenfan gongzuo de kaocha baogao" (Investigation report on the suppression of counterrevolutionaries in Wuhan, Shanghai and other cities), LRGZ, March 20, 1951, pp. 55–58.

law (*jieyanfa* – 戒嚴法) declaration of May 1949 was buttressed by the government's "temporary" Special Articles (*dongyuan kanluan shiqi linshi tiaokuan* – 動員戡亂時期的條款), promulgated by the GMD-dominated National Assembly before the retreat to Taiwan. These "Temporary Articles" suspended the Constitution of 1946, cancelled further elections to the National Government's representative bodies, and concentrated further power in the hands of the Executive. They also abrogated nearly all civil liberties including the right to organize and the right to strike, and were extended indefinitely in 1954 by the ROC National Assembly, the rubber stamp legislative body in charge of constitutional amendments. After the crackdown on the student demonstrations of April 1949, the Executive Yuan and the Taiwan Garrison Command issued a barrage of further presidential orders and regulations laying out the punishments for subversion.[32]

Of this flurry of laws, regulations, and guidelines, there are three that merit special attention: the Taiwan Garrison Command's announcement of martial law for the province (May 19, 1949), the Presidential Order laying out the regulations for punishment of sedition (June 21, 1949), and the Presidential Regulations on Suppressing and Cleaning out Bandit Spies (*zongtong ling gongbu kanluan shiqi jiansu feidie tiaoli* – 總統令公佈 戡亂時期 檢 蕭飛碟條列).[33] These documents, like the other rules, regulations, revised regulations, and executive orders issued by the ROC government at this time were dry, legalistic, and formal. Even a cursory glance at their provisions suggests that they were at best general guidelines for action. For example, the Presidential Order of June 21, 1949, is excruciating in its listing of harsh punishments. Disseminating secrets to the enemy (regulation 4:2), hiding rebels or aiding them financially (regulations 4:4 and 4:6), acts of sabotage, arson, or water poisoning (regulations 4:7–8), inciting strikes (regulation 4:10), inciting the military or civil servants not to fulfil their duties according to law (regulation 5) were all offences punishable from ten years' imprisonment up to the death penalty. Anyone belonging to an organization deemed seditious – irrespective of whether the individual in question engaged in seditious activity – was also given an immediate sentence of ten years' imprisonment to life (regulation 6). The Presidential Order assumed that rural Taiwan had

---

[32] "Zongtong ling gongbu chengzhi panluan tiaolie" (Presidential Office promulgation of regulations for punishment of sedition) June 21, 1949, pp. 25–28; "Taiwan sheng zhengfu Taiwan sheng jingbei silingbu chugao quansheng jieyan" (Taiwan Provincial Government Taiwan Provincial Security Command Province martial [law]), May 19, 1949, CJDJ, pp. 44–45, and "Zongtong ling gongbu kanluan shiqi jiansu feidie tiaoli" (Presidential Office promulgation of regulations for cleaning out spies during the period of rebellion), June 13, 1950, CJDJ, pp. 32–34.

[33] Issued by the Executive Yuan on June 13, 1950.

a functioning *baojia* system of mutual security in which a family head would be directly responsible for the security infringements of nine other families. No such assumptions were made for urban areas, where mutual surveillance and reporting to security organizations in factories, government offices, schools, and occupational associations were to be conducted by every *two* individuals (Regulation 5).[34] Security organizations were also enjoined to quickly apprehend suspects, monitor their mail, and search for hidden weapons and seditious reading material (Regulation 6). Once arrested, individuals for whom there was no proof of sedition were to be freed; those with relatively light transgressions were to be sent for educational training (*ganxun*), and those with proof of guilt were to be sentenced "according to law" (Regulation 7).

These publicly articulated rules, however, revealed little as to how burden of proof was determined or standards of evidence established. Despite the ROC government's fetishization of law and procedure, these were rules that were in practice as loose and flexible as the campaign pronouncements for the suppression of counterrevolutionaries in the PRC. At the height of any given wave of arrests, almost anyone was fair game. In periods in which there was pressure from above to crack or bring a complex case to swift conclusion, a very loose view of seditious publications and reading material could be taken. Anyone who had *ever* been handed a periodical mentioning Marxism or the PRC's land reform law could be taken in and deemed a Communist, even if the activity in question had taken place before such activities were proscribed. More chillingly, anyone who had any knowledge of subversive activity without reporting it (*zhiqing bu bao* – 知情不報) was also liable for punishment "according to law."[35] This rule later hardened into the principle that anyone with knowledge of Communists was as bad as a Communist himself, and would be punished accordingly.

While they were undoubtedly harsh, the regulations also allowed for very wide latitude in interpretation. Abuses, the admission of questionable evidence, *post hoc* application of severe new rules, and the systemic encouragement of informing and snitching, backed up by formal rules that materially rewarded those in the security services whose cases secured conviction were all rife in the early 1950s. One set of regulations in operation between June 1950 and November 1953 offered clear financial incentives for individuals to inform on each other, with a regulation

---

[34] See Greitens, *Dictators and Their Secret Police*, which suggests that the level of surveillance and its degree of penetration in the ROC/Taiwan was matched by very few contemporary regimes, among them the Stasi in the DDR and North Korea, pp. 107–108.

[35] Regulation 5, "Zongtong ling gongbu kanluan shiqi jiansu tiaoli," CJDJ p. 32. Chen Yingtai, *Huiyi Jianzheng Baise Kongbu*, Vol. 1, p. 119.

that promised that 30 percent of the confiscated property of a "spy" that resulted in conviction would go to the informer and another 35 percent to the agency that successfully charged and convicted the offender.[36] Many of the severely sentenced were guilty of nothing more than belonging to suddenly proscribed study societies, mountain-climbing groups, sister-hood groups, or mutual financial aid groups. Those who had been seen reading socialist or left-leaning newspapers like the *Guangming Ribao* at a time when to do so had been completely legal could be charged retro-spectively with subversion. Even those who had been fully pardoned in the late 1940s could be thrown in jail (and worse) on hearsay in the early 1950s.

The case of Lin Rigao, while extreme, illustrates just how vicious *post hoc* punishment could be. Lin had been an early member of the Taiwan Communist Party in the Japanese colonial years. After he resigned from the party in 1930, he was arrested by the Japanese colonial authorities and served a five-year sentence. Upon his release from prison in 1936, he set up a business that traded in camphor, and over the course of the next decade became enough of a local notable that after the island's retro-cession to China in 1945, he was tapped for a series of local political positions, starting with head of propaganda for the local Sun Yat-sen Youth Corps. This position was followed by a succession of more power-ful and prestigious local appointments: town representative, advisor to the Taibei county government, and member of the local irrigation asso-ciation committee. After Lin fled into the mountains for months to escape government reprisal as a suspected "Taiwan independence" activist after the February 28 uprising in 1947, Li Youbang (李 友邦), who had long been associated with the left-wing of the Guomindang, served as Lin's guarantor.[37] With Li's support, Lin's formal application to "turn over a

---

[36] See Article 14 of regulations for "Zongtong li gongbu kanluan shiqi jiansu feidie tiaoli," June 13, 1950. Not surprisingly, this regulation led to an explosion of false arrests on very dubious grounds. In November 1953, Article 14 was amended to a more innocuous rule that provided that the proceeds of confiscated property be remitted to the Treasury and the payment to the informer and prosecuting agency would be much less. See also Greitens, *Dictators and Their Secret Police*, pp. 178–180, for the ways in which this incentive led to spying and informing on the flimsiest of evidence within the ROC/ Taiwan's fragmented security and military organizations themselves.

[37] Li Youbang was himself caught up in the murky world of accusation and counter accusation in the late 1940s and early 1950s, and his career was no less full of twists and tragic turns than was Lin Rigao's. Li was a Taiwanese who had served the GMD since his training in the second class at Whampoa military academy in the early 1920s; he had also written favorably about bringing the [GMD] revolutionary alliance to Taiwan. During the February 28 uprising, he was felt by his superiors to be divided enough in his loyalties that he was removed to Nanjing and incarcerated there for several months. He was released and permitted to return to Taiwan after his wife Yan Xiufeng travelled to Nanjing to make a direct plea to Chiang Ching-kuo for Li's release. In the five years from

new leaf" (*zixin*) was duly approved in 1948. In 1948–1949, he moved on to a successful career in local politics: first elected as mayor of Banqiao, when he was awarded a commendation for effective promotion of the rent-reduction program, then as head of the Taibei county Farmer's Association, one of the largest and most important in Taiwan, at which point Lin formally joined the GMD. Once a GMD Party member, Lin made the transition from local to provincial level notable. After the Executive Yuan Reform Commission appointed KC Wu (Wu Guozhen – 吳國楨), a relative liberal, governor of Taiwan in December 1949, KC Wu in turn appointed Lin as a high-level member (*gaoji weiyuan* – 高級委員) for the Taiwan provincial government. In the period of the most vicious crackdown on suspected Communists and fellow travelers between late 1949 and early 1953, Lin Rigao not only managed to have his past as an ex-Communist and suspected supporter of Taiwan independence officially forgiven, but he also began a promising political career as a local and provincial political player.

In the late winter of 1953, external events intervened to derail Lin's career, and ultimately to take his life. In 1952, Li Youbang was arrested, implicated by others as a secret Communist, and executed. Worse, KC Wu's more liberal ideas about self-government for Taiwan and his opposition to the growth of the police state fell afoul of Chiang Kai-shek, Chiang Ching-kuo, and conservatives in the GMD. Amid accusations against him as the engineer of a plot to topple the two Chiangs, Wu fled to the United States. Shortly thereafter, Chen Tonghe (陳通和), a member of the Taibei branch of the Communist Party, was arrested. Under questioning in prison Chen implicated Lin as still having contact with the Communist Party. At this point, Lin's entire history was again called into question. He was charged with a variety of crimes, notably "being acquainted with Communists," which under the martial law rules of 1953–1954 was "as bad as being a Communist oneself." Forty years later, Lin's son, who was at the time an eight-year-old, was still unsure as to why Lin had been so singled out for such harsh punishment, as his previous Communist activity had been openly acknowledged, officially renounced, and formally pardoned. Lin *fils* guessed that his father's strong

1947 to 1952, Li was the Vice-Chair of the Guomindang Taiwan Provincial Party Committee, and served on the all important Central Reform Committee as well. Two intersecting currents of circumstantial evidence led to Li's downfall in 1952: (1) his name occurred in secret Communist documents that surfaced during the prosecution of other Communist *anjian*; and (2) when he served as the head of the Taiwan branch of the Sun Yat-sen Youth Corps, one of his recruits later turned out to be a Communist. For a capsule summary of Li's career, see http://baike.baidu.com/item/%E6%9D%8E%E5%8F%8B%E9%82%A6/75374 and https://zh.wikipedia.org/wiki/%E6%9D%8E%E5%8F%8B%E9%82%A6, accessed June 11, 2017.

anti-corruption stance and fearless willingness to speak out against his fellow members on the Taiwan provincial committee might have made enemies. As was typical of the White Terror years, once Lin was arrested, previous friends and neighbors were too fearful to come to his defense, speak on his behalf, or even be seen having social contact with his family. They were "only able to shake their heads" in sorrow and mourn his ill fortune.[38]

The formally different modalities of quashing state enemies in Sunan and Taiwan – the mobilizational campaign versus impartially applied (martial) law rules – were mirror images of one another. The Campaign to Suppress Counterrevolutionaries was launched, at least in part, to *overcome* the slow, procedurally correct, and politically inconvenient processing of individual cases in favour of a quickly moving campaign juggernaut of state and mass action that identified and speedily dispatched counterrevolutionary subversives. In contrast, the ROC on Taiwan based its entire legitimacy and manner of policy implementation on a legal-bureaucratic modality that claimed to expand and regularize impartially applied rules and laws. But even if neither so realized, each covertly utilized the dominant modality of the other across the Strait. Campaign implementation in Sunan required that the state engage in a large number of bureaucratically determined processes: registering counterrevolutionaries, collecting and filing supporting materials, booking public accusation session venues and organizing crowd control, disposing of the executed, and inventory taking prior to reassigning counterrevolutionary property. In Taiwan, the putatively legal, procedural, and impartial application of martial law was in practice subject to campaign hysteria about subversion and heavily influenced by competition between rival security agencies and political interference from above.

Theaters of Terror (I): The Micro-hows

The differences between the two Chinas, and their approaches to policy implementation, were most stark in the realm of rhetoric, performance, and the ways in which state power was dramatized. Both regimes staged important shows in how they defined and treated internal enemies. The purpose of these shows was identical: not just to rid the polity of enemies and subversives, but also to demonstrate the state's unchallengeable authority and moral basis in so doing. Although different in content and tone, these shows were important heuristic devices, communicating to the citizenry at large what the new rules of the game were, the kinds of

---

[38] "Lin Shi xiansheng fangtan lü" (Mr. Lin Shi interview transcription), Interviewed by Zhang Yanxian and Hu Huiling, August 15, 1994. LRGZ, pp. 508–516.

words that were or were not safe to use, what would and would not be tolerated, and how the individual was expected to behave in the new order. And here these two consolidating regimes could not have chosen more different specifics of the staging, process, content, denouement, and audience management. The CCP's rhetoric of struggle, in combination with the extraordinary self-confidence, displayed through its insistence on educating and including the aroused masses, reflected the young state's vision of itself as the leader of mass popular revolution. It presumed that once properly educated and mobilized, the masses would be its willing and enthusiastic supporters. In contrast, the Guomindang betrayed no such confidence in either itself or its citizenry. GMD rhetorics and performance of martial law reified an authoritarian demand for submission and obedience and reflected the ideal of the state itself as the exemplification of continuity and legally constituted order, procedure, and regularity. Through laws, regulations, and openly published directives and orders, it asserted its legitimacy through its links to earlier versions of rules and laws that had been issued prior to the government's retreat to Taiwan. In Sunan, the young PRC put on a show of mass revolutionary enthusiasm, while in Taiwan the ROC countered with one of sober legality and terse correct procedure. To put it slightly differently, the PRC's theater of terror in Sunan played out a campaign modality of policy implementation while the ROC/Taiwan performance was one of strict bureaucracy, precedent, and procedure.

Both regimes resorted to publicity (propaganda) to set the tone for the suppression of state-defined enemies, and here there were large differences between the two regimes. By almost any measure – volume, coverage, humorous representation, and wide appeal – authorities in Sunan far outclassed their counterparts in Taiwan. The propaganda developed in the PRC to launch campaigns in 1950–1951 was explicitly proactive and full of motion, while in the months after its retreat to Taiwan, ROC government propaganda was, like the government itself, reactive, and defensive. The PRC's main central and regional newspapers gave wide coverage to a self-consciously and openly defined campaign. They published short articles, texts, summaries of the relevant regulations, and brief announcements of the numbers of counterrevolutionaries accused and put to death. They also included visual material that sought to educate through exhortation, humor, and emotional appeals to patriotism and righteous indignation. From the outset, the campaign stressed that the majority of "the people" were good, and that only a small minority were "bad." Therefore "the masses" had a job to do: to act collectively to first isolate, and then "hit against" the "bad" designated minority target. In Sunan the preparatory sub-campaign that encouraged counter revolutionaries to register and "remake themselves" in the winter of 1950–1951 even employed social groups that would under normal circumstances be highly suspect themselves. As can be seen in the depiction of registration in image 3.4, the friends and relatives of the counterrevolutionary were often represented as bringing collective familial pressure to bear on the individual as part of coming clean and reforming.

Image 3.4. "Family members and friends of bandit special agents must supervise and convince the guilty to register and turn over a new leaf!" (ca. 1950). Landsberger Collection. International Institute for Social History (Amsterdam). https://chineseposters.net/posters/e15-512.php

Stock stereotypes of hunched counterrevolutionary *tewu* cringing before the combined power of the masses and/or the public security arm of the state made for easy targets readily distinguished from the upright and righteous. The invariably foreign clothing worn by counter-revolutionary enemies in juxtaposition to the plain workers' clothing or quasi-military uniforms of the public security authorities served to underline counterrevolutionary associations with the alien and non-Chinese.

Anti-counterrevolutionary cartoons also sharply contrasted progressive and proper motion with improper motion and/or stasis. Those engaged in the "right" kind of motion invariably dominate the frame. The enlarged worker shines his light on the *tewu* agent trying to sneak away. The woman with the baby angrily points her finger and curses the counterrevolutionary while the soldier prevents the counterrevolutionary's attempt to make himself small. We only see the arm of the counterrevolutionary being pushed out of the frame as he cringes before the power of the people and the army; here the army enables the woman to have voice and berate the baddie. The worker and the PLA soldier are heaving with effort together to pull out the root of American imperialism and counterrevolution which is clinging on for dear life.

Image 3.5. "Special Agent, where are you running to?" (1951). Private Collection. International Institute for Social History (Amsterdam). https://chineseposters.net/posters/pc-195a-s-002.php

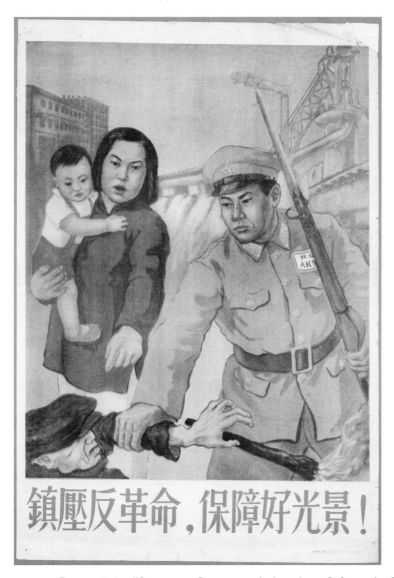

Image 3.6. "Suppress Counterrevolutionaries: Safeguard Good Circumstances!" IISH Collection. International Institute for Social History (Amsterdam). https://chineseposters.net/posters/e16-351.php

Image 3.7. Pulling out counterrevolutionaries by the roots, *Jiefang Ribao*, Shanghai, May 10, 1951

Propaganda created for the Campaign to Suppress Counterrevolutionaries was designed to appeal to the widest possible range of "good people," enlist their sympathies, warn them about the hard work involved with rooting out counterrevolutionaries (often visually represented as literal roots being dug out), and mobilize them to support representatives of state coercive power. This mobilizational propaganda was aimed at a new collective imaginary of "the good," who were visually represented by the young, the old, and workers, often working in harmony with public security or the People's Liberation Army. This was accomplished by publicity in newspapers, posters, and in special exhibitions that detailed the evils of counterrevolutionary special agents, sabotage, and spies in visible public venues.

Nanjing put on a well-attended public exhibition on counterrevolutionaries in one of the symbolically most resonant locations in the city: the old Presidential Palace of the vanquished Guomindang. Authorities in Sunan did not just imagine their public; different layers of government organization went directly to society to actively *create* a new kind of public. Government work units, educational establishments, and factories already nationalized by the Guomindang all held intensive political study amid mass propaganda sessions to educate the rank and file in the norms and goals of the campaign, but at this early stage in regime consolidation, this kind of intensive political study was limited because most workplaces were not yet nationalized. Most was implemented at the interface of state and urban society in the neighborhood district (*qu* – 區). In Nanjing, municipal district administrations conducted 25,558 mass education meetings over the course of the spring of 1951, ultimately "bringing education" about the campaign to 2,130,000, more than triple the entire population of the city at the time.[39]

On occasion, authorities in Sunan even disseminated news that hinted at some of the internal processes by which counterrevolutionary cases were reviewed. In mid-May 1951, the daily *Xin Suzhou Bao* gave extended coverage to the authorities' actions to suppress counterrevolutionaries and to educate the masses. It even included handy tips on how to hold a proper accusation meeting. On May 16, it published condensed vignettes from each of the seventeen individuals who were then serving on the Suzhou municipal committee that reviewed counterrevolutionary cases. Most were lay members of the public who detailed how their service in reviewing these cases had been transformative in their understanding of the government's deserved harshness towards counterrevolutionaries. On the same page, *Xin Suzhou Bao* ran another article by a Protestant organization called the China Protestant Aid Korea/Resist America Three New Campaign Preparatory Committee entitled "How to Run a Good Worship Meeting as an Accusation Meeting." In it the patriotic Protestant leadership pointed out the importance of church leaders in reminding the laity about the West's 100-plus years of imperialism and extraterritoriality, and that holding accusation meetings was an important "way to educate everyone" (*suoyi women yao kai kongsu dahui lai jiaoyu dajia* – 所以我們要開控訴大會來教育大家).[40]

Although the lay leaders of a Protestant church were clearly different from the CCP's own cadres, the instructional content in how to run a "good" accusation meeting was almost identical. Like local cadres in Shanghai, Protestant leaders in Suzhou were urged to encourage their believers to participate in other citywide mass accusation meetings and

[39] This figure was, of course, quite misleading. There were many ways in which "participation" (*canjia* – 參加) could be counted in the official statistics. It could mean anything from active participation as an accuser or informant, or simply being present for a particular meeting or briefing, *NGZ* pp. 193–194.

[40] "Bixu dazhangqi gu zhenya fangeming" (It is necessary to wave a big banner against counterrevolutionaries"), May 16, 1951, XSB, p. 3.

overcome their natural reluctance to engage in public accusation. They were also enjoined to prepare extensively to decide on whom to accuse, whom to invite to make the accusation, and to learn the motivations and mentality of each of the potential accusers. Each church was to establish a working accusation meeting group to identify a few "backbone elements" to be called on to participate during the actual accusation session, and to rectify shortcomings through advance dress rehearsals. Overly long accusations needed to be shortened and made punchier, unclear accusations required clarification, and thin accusations had to be elaborated. An accusation was deemed successful insofar as it was based on fact (*genju shishi* – 根據事實), with "every word being spoken from the heart" (*yao meiju shi cong xinli er jiangchulai de* – 要每句是從心裏而講出來的), thorough and straightforward, placing [the accuser] firmly on the side of the people." Finally, the China Protestant Aid Korea/Resist America Three New Campaign Preparatory Committee in Suzhou directly invited accusations from the public to be mailed in, complete with return address, with the promise that these materials might see eventual use in a national exhibition on the Three Great Movements.[41]

In contrast to the bright colors, rousing slogans, resolute motion, and imagined reservoir of popular mass support so prominent in PRC propaganda, most of the propaganda against subversion generated by the ROC/Taiwan was flat, dry, and usually represented in the monochrome black and white of legal text and terse public announcement. In Taiwan, there was no resort to the public as an imagined collective to support the government's goals. The government's strategy was quite the opposite: to break apart extant bonds of social solidarity and atomize individuals. While plenty of anti-Communist and pro-"freedom" propaganda was disseminated by official organizations such as the Oppose Communism/ Resist Russia (*fangong kang'e* – 反共抗餓) Committee and the Oppose Communism/Save the Country Youth Corps (*fangong jiuguo qingniantuan* – 反共救國青年團), these organizations were geared to whipping up patriotic sentiment in general rather than combating internal subversion. The government did not invite mass participation in outing sedition and neither was the public given any advance publicity about the government's anti-Communist activities. Since the government's job was to keep the public atomized and quiescent, cartoons, posters, and

---

[41] Liu Liangmo, "Zenyang kaihai jiaohui kongsu hui" (How ought the [protestant] church hold a good accusation meeting?"), May 26, 1951, XSB, p. 3.

even photographs pertaining to putative networks and cases of subversion were almost completely absent.

The information that did exist about the government's anti-Communist actions came in two print forms. Black and white text announcements that were publicly disseminated in official newspapers included republication of martial law rules and regulations, and occasional brief announcements that particular networks of sedition had been crushed, sometimes with a statement of the sentence levied. Only rarely were these announcements accompanied by photographs, or significant detail. The names of those who had been executed were also posted in prominent public places like the Taibei main rail station. In many cases the first that families knew of what had happened to their loved ones was when these lists were put up, and it was not unusual for families to learn from friends who had reached the Taibei train station first that their fathers and husbands had been executed or sentenced to lengthy periods of imprisonment.

For the CCP in Sunan, the public was imagined as a collective that was inherently sociable, mostly good, and ready to be collectively enlisted in the state's charge against enemies of the state. The GMD in Taiwan imagined nothing of the sort. Rather, for the GMD, urban society was composed of atomized individuals readily frightened into obedience by clearly articulated and prominently posted laws and rules, while rural society was organized through families subordinated to the state under the *baojia* system of collective responsibility. At best, individuals could be expected to internalize these new rules and laws. The CCP in Sunan engaged its public in open, collective space, bringing immense group pressure to bear on targeted individuals: in Taiwan suspects were targeted by unaccountable security organizations who often acquired their information about suspects from other, equally unaccountable, individuals.

The new rule that "knowing a Communist and not reporting it was as serious as being a Communist oneself" further cowed individuals and created incentives for reporting and informing. This strategy was a very effective way to further isolate individuals, as: (1) many could not be sure whether they did or did not know Communists (the Taiwan Provincial Work Committee was, of course, an underground organization, so who knew who might and might not be a Communist?); and (2) one could never tell who the informers were. While there were occasional newspaper articles that announced the smashing of individual Communist networks or the sentences doled out to particularly important "seditious" individuals, these accounts were irregular and did not give much away. More common was a *lack* of information: people were taken away by shadowy security organizations of one sort or another in the middle of the night (around midnight seems to have been a favoured time for security agencies to strike), while little news, from either newspapers or other official channels, was released even to the families of those taken away. Rumors there must have been aplenty, but except on rare occasions, there was little that was concrete, other than short daily articles in the government's official mouthpiece, the *Zhongyang Ribao*, on the need to be vigilant against Communists.

Apart from Cai Xiaoqian's May 1950 shocking public recantation and broadcast urging remaining members of the Taiwan Work Committee to lay down their arms and surrender, dramatic publicly disseminated news regarding the suppression of rebellion in the ROC was very unusual. Even Cai's public *mea culpa* was heard rather than seen – a disembodied voice uttering a script almost certainly given to him by the security establishment. There was no newsreel footage and certainly no live audience. The publicity given to even this most important of cases was minimal and factually terse: a heavily edited account with many of the relevant names redacted, followed by a small, blurred photograph of the four leaders at the top of the Taiwan Provincial Work Committee and Ma Wenjuan.

Very rarely, a more detailed profile of a particular case emerged, as was for the case of Wang Shenghe (汪聲和) and Li Peng (李朋) in early September of 1950. On September 3, 1950, *Taiwan Xinsheng Bao* ran an extensive ten-page spread of Wang and Li. The former was revealed as a spy for the Soviet Union, and the latter in charge of news and communication for the Taiwan Provincial Work Committee. Unusually, the newspaper also printed a partial copy of Li Peng's autobiography, photographs of telegraphs and bottles of secret ink, orders from the GPU in the Soviet Union, a time line of subversive activity, handwritten plans for secret activity in Taiwan, and examples of sheets of coded transmissions and their transcriptions into clear text. The next day, *Taiwan Xinsheng Bao*, followed up with a more succinct summary of the case, with a photograph of the accused in military court.[42] But typically, news about cases broken was confined to flat, usually short items which condensed the cases of putative Communists into two or three lines.

If the purpose of propaganda and the dissemination of news about counterrevolutionaries in the PRC was to educate the public by arousing moral indignation as first steps in creating an imaginary collective of "the masses" to aid the state in its prosecution of counterrevolutionary enemies, in Taiwan the purpose of propaganda was just the opposite: to

---

[42] TXB September 3, 1950, pp. 2–12; September 4, 1950 pp. 2–4.

Image 3.8. Announcement of the smashing of the Taiwan Provincial Work Committee. *Taiwan Xinsheng Bao*, May 14, 1950

discredit the top leadership of the Communist Party in Taiwan, and to keep an imagined public of both Taiwanese and mainlanders inert, fearful and atomized. Given these very different conceptions about what the state and its relations with society ought to be, the ways in which the PRC in Sunan and the ROC in Taiwan implemented and performed their respective campaigns against internal subversion were markedly different in staging, content, and audience, even though the denouement of state power ended in the same way, with the imprisonment or execution of the accused. The performances staged by the PRC were calculated for maximum public effect, while those put on by the ROC in Taiwan were shrouded in silence and secrecy. In form, the PRC put on highly public collective shows through the specific genre of mass accusation meetings (*kongsu hui* – 控訴會)/struggle meetings (*douzheng hui* – 鬥爭會). These in turn deployed a repertoire of techniques honed in the years of struggle and revolution during the Sino-Japanese war and the civil war: enjoining individuals to come forward and "speak bitterness" (*suku* – 訴苦) about their personal sufferings in the not-so-distant past. The public performance of a successful *suku* resulted in three desirable outcomes: (1) it generated the emotion and sympathy of the audience; so rousing them to action; (2) it gave voice to the hitherto marginalized and oppressed; and (3) it demonstrated the sharp break between the bright present and future from the sufferings of the past. The ROC/Taiwan state put on shows as well, but these were the shows of the military trial, primarily for the internal consumption of the state itself, rather than for wider publics.

Theaters of Terror (II): Staging and Processes

In the People's Republic, as soon as counterrevolutionaries were determined and incarcerated, they were put to another, equally important heuristic use. The state "hit hard" at such enemies, through the spectacle of mass public accusation (often followed immediately by execution). The public nature of *kongsu hui* garnered the emotional compliance and complicity of citizens in support for state-sponsored violence against targeted enemies and enabled the regime to collectively reaffirm its popular legitimacy while implicitly dirtying the hands of the masses who were roused to support such measures.[43] In contrast, the ROC/Taiwan performed its crackdown on domestic subversion by making arrests in secret, usually in the dead of night. It held prisoners incommunicado in prisons for months on end. Even as it insisted on its adherence to the forms of regular legal process, it continued to make administrative decisions about punishment of the accused in secret. After the formality of sentencing, security organizations immediately carried out execution in secret at a location that was never formally identified, only whispered about by those who feared for their families and friends.

Performances require a stage of some sort – from a stadium seating thousands to a very small enclosed space, such as a school room or a private house. Here there was a strong contrast between the PRC and the ROC. Accusation meetings in the PRC were of two types: the large and public accusation meetings attended by as much of the local public as could possibly fit into the venue, and smaller workplace accusation meetings that were held within the confines of the factory or enterprise. In the early 1950s, most public accusation meetings in Sunan were held out "in society" (*zai shehui* – 在社會). Local cadres chose venues for *kongsuhui* that were in large public spaces, preferably (but not always) outdoors. Usually, the locations chosen were the most communal of spots that

---

[43] Parts of the following section are drawn from my article, "Paternalist Terror: The Campaign to Suppress Counterrevolutionaries and Regime Consolidation in the People's Republic of China, 1950–1953," *Comparative Studies in Society and History*, January 2002, pp. 95–98.

could be found for a given location: in Shanghai, large *kongsuhui* were held at the old racetrack (now renamed the People's Park), which could accommodate thousands of spectators. In Nanjing, a mass rally was convened at the municipal Great Hall of the People. (In this case, the symbolic importance of the location likely outweighed its disadvantageous indoor location, as the Great Hall of the People had only two years before been the GMD National Government's Presidential Office.) In compensation for this relatively smaller inside space in which to witness the live action, the proceedings were broadcast over the radio to "400,000 people."[44] In smaller towns and villages, typical venues included public marketplaces and schoolyards.[45]

In contrast, in ROC/Taiwan the state's ultimate power of coercion and punishment was almost always exercised out of public sight, in the enclosed and indoor spaces of the prison, the interrogation room, and closed courtrooms where sentence was passed. Judgment, when it came, was typically via a judge who read out a pre-decided sentence in a small room that was part of the prison complex. No representatives from the public, including family members, were permitted to attend. There was seldom any counsel for the defendant. Guards often outnumbered prisoners by two to one. Tehpen Tsai's memoir describes these courtrooms within the prison complex as a row of cramped spaces, each smaller than a classroom, with three desks side by side on a platform, a portrait of Sun Yat-sen on the front wall and above that the flag of the ROC, and Chiang Kai-shek's portrait on the back wall above the judges' desks. He also notes the existence of benches crowding the room, and wonders why the authorities bothered with the benches, as the public was not permitted to attend the proceedings in any case.[46]

Photographs of these "trials" (which were in effect sentencing hearings) are rarely available, as the government was secretive about its judicial processes, and photos of actual sentencing were not included in the TGC archives.[47] But the one photo of a final hearing before execution that is

---

[44] *NGZ*, p. 193.

[45] For Sunan I have thus far been unable to locate records that specify the location of accusation meetings outside of Shanghai and Nanjing, but where we have information for other regions of the country for which we have materials they were held in highly public places. An enormous mass accusation session of "five major tyrants" before 30,000 was held at the Temple of Heaven on May 17, 1951, in Beijing: See Tao Siju, p. 46. At the opposite end of the scale, Wu Yunfei's oral history of rural Mulan county, Heilongjiang, specified the schoolyard of the county seat primary school as the site of an important accusation meeting. See Wu Yunfei, "Yi yici gong shenhui: Riwei tongzhi de Mulan" (Remembering a public trial, Mulan under Japanese puppet rule).

[46] Tsai Teh-pen, pp. 242–243.

[47] As a matter of administrative procedure, photographs *were* taken of the accused immediately before and immediately after execution. When I was working in the National

currently in the public domain, reproduced below, confirms the details in Tsai's memoirs. This photograph was taken at the time of the sentencing hearing of a four-person case against Wu Shi (吳 石) along with his courier, Zhu Shenzhi (朱 諶之), and two other close associates. The Wu Shi case was a particularly sensitive one, as Wu Shi was himself at the very apex of the GMD military (his final position was Deputy Chief of Staff at the Ministry of Defense).[48] Wu had been a high-ranking Fujianese military official whose military experience went back to the Xinhai Revolution of 1911, and his support for the GMD dated back to the mid-1920s. His trial occurred at a particularly intense stage of the White Terror, in the nervy weeks just before the outbreak of the Korean War in June 1950.

In this photograph, only three of the defendants are visible, but one can count eight security guards (the eighth is largely obscured by one of the defendants). The defendants are lined up and are standing against a rail that is perhaps a foot below a raised wooden platform for the judges. The judges are also off camera, but the slightly raised dais described by Tsai and one desk are well within the photographer's frame. In addition, there are two guards at the back of the room near the door and what appears to be a black curtain to the right and back of the room, suggesting that the room is not particularly large, and might well have been a makeshift

Archive Administration between 2008 and 2010 and just beginning to get access to White Terror cases from the early 1950s, it was possible to see full files, many of which included before and after photos execution photos, but reproduction of these photographs was not permitted. By 2012, administrative rules on declassification had come in to black out all such photographic evidence of execution on grounds of the protection of privacy.

[48] Trained at a military academy in Japan, Wu Shi had both the military credentials and support for China's revolution that went back to the 1911 Xinhai revolution. A classmate of Bai Chongxi, Wu decided to stand with the GMD under Chiang Kai-shek against the CCP amid the ferment of the 1920s. Like many others, he became increasingly disillusioned with Chiang Kai-shek's increasingly dictatorial powers during the war against Japan and the subsequent civil war. Before Wu was ordered to leave Hong Kong for Taiwan in August, 1949, he managed to make contact with the East China Military Region Headquarters, and offered to send intelligence to help prepare for the liberation of Taiwan. The Headquarters sent him a female courier by the name of Zhu Shenzhi (朱諶之) who, under her cover as a businesswoman, was to smuggle out of Taiwan a set of microfilms containing extremely sensitive military information about the GMD military capacities in Zhoushan and Little Jinmen, maps of Taiwan's defensive installations, the positioning of the GMD's naval fleet, its logistics and supply reserves, and the numbers and types of planes in its active air force. Because of Wu's senior position in the GMD military, he became the CCP's "Secret Agent Number One." Wu managed some six or seven clandestine meetings with Zhu before hints of her identity were picked up by GMD counterintelligence from Cai Xiaoqian's papers that were acquired by GMD security after his first arrest at the end of January 1950. Zhu was eventually discovered in Zhoushan in mid-February 1950, while attempting to return to Shanghai. Wu Shi was picked up shortly afterwards. Both were tried and executed on June 10, 1950. For details on Wu Shi, see http://baike.baidu.com/item/%E5%90%B4%E7%9F%B3/3771447#1 accessed June 11, 2017.

Image 3.9. Wu Shi sentencing hearing, 1950. (www.northnews.cn/2010/
1227/269949.shtml)

division of a larger space. Two figures in enlisted soldier military uniform
are present, and one appears to be overseeing the defendant as he wields a
brush to sign a thick document: another military figure in the uniform of
an officer sits to the left of the accused. Apart from the defendants, who
are in their prison clothes, everyone in this photograph is wearing a
military uniform of some sort. There are no spectators, no family, and
no lawyers for the defense. Clearly, the official rendering of judgments in
the ROC/Taiwan was a performance put on by the state that brought
down the entirety of its coercive power onto the isolated and exposed
individual; this was a performance that was held by the state, for the state,
as its demonstration of power and correct procedure.

In revolutionary Sunan, the staging of the state's struggle against counterrevolution through *kongsu hui* was quite the opposite of the closed court
appearances for reading out official legal judgment *panjue* in Taiwan.
Rather than being held in an indoor, closed-off space to which the public
had no access, *kongsu hui* typically took place in an outdoor, open space. The
judges did not sit on a raised platform that indicated their superior standing in
the proceedings. Instead it was the *accused* who was the focal point of action

on the raised stage to provide the best view for the mass audience. The local party secretary was a key player in the performance: he either strode or sat at a desk onstage. Guarded by armed police, the accused (sometimes as an individual, sometimes more than one) was led out. As the charges were read out, the accused was expected to drop to his knees in a show of penitence and submission to the power of the masses and the state.

The photo reproduced below does not indicate where this accusation meeting was held, but we do know that it was not in Shanghai. It was featured on the front page of Shanghai's *Jiefang Ribao* on April 11 as part of preparatory propaganda for the "high tide" of the campaign, but Shanghai's large-scale round ups and accusation meetings did not occur until the end of the month. Nevertheless, as this shot was disseminated for the Shanghai reading public and captioned in bold, the stock imagery is well worth considering. The cursive script above the first photograph reads "Suppress Counterrevolutionary Elements; Carry Forward the Peoples' Righteousness" (*zhenya fangeming fenzi; fayang renmin zhengqi* – 鎮壓反革命分子發揚人民正氣). The accusation meeting is held outside. The accuser, the accused, and the soldiers securing the prisoner are the main *dramatis personae* on the stage. What is most visible from the vantage point of the photographer on the stage is an enormous sea of faces in the crowd. So vast is the crowd that a microphone for the accuser is necessary. The accused has his head slightly bowed and the soldiers on either side are gripping his arms and pulling them back. He is fixed to one place by the guards while the accuser, a woman, is in contrast free of constraint and full of motion: her forearm is moving at the very moment that the photograph was taken.

While revealing a great deal about the contrast between the PRC and ROC/Taiwan, staging was but the first necessary component of the kind of performance put on by the state. More important was the primary audience for whom the show was mounted, and that the trajectory of the show be intelligible and moving. In revolutionary Sunan, the openly public nature of the performance, and the frequency with which cadres reported the very large numbers who "participated" (meaning those who were in the audience and watched or listened to the radio broadcasts of the proceedings) suggest that for the party-state the most important audience was the still inert, but potentially revolutionary mass public itself. Raising the consciousness of the masses, engaging their emotions, whipping up sympathy for victims, and unleashing righteous hatred against counterrevolutionary targets chosen by the state isolated accused counterrevolutionaries as surely as the sentencing sessions conducted by martial court judges isolated accused subversives in the ROC/Taiwan. On stage, he was the visible subject of a tidal wave of mass anger and derision.

Image 3.10. "Suppress Counterrevolutionary Elements: Carry Forward the People's Righteousness." *Jiefang Ribao*, Shanghai April 11, 1951

The entire point of this isolation was to provide a focus by which an otherwise large group of heterogenous individuals could become fused into a collective mass. When the public accusation session went well, individuals in the crowd merged both with each other and the state in its call for violence against these exemplars of evil. In Sunan "the masses" were mobilized not only to passively view the spectacle of the wicked getting their just desserts, but also to collectively receive instruction in the regime's core norms: for the individual to voluntarily participate in politics as an affirming chorus – in this case as an enthusiastic endorsement of the state's violence against its chosen enemies.

At this early stage in regime consolidation, it is not clear that the publics who attended accusation meetings in Sunan understood that they were part of a dramatic show put on by the state. (The masses learned quickly; a mere four years later, when another *sufan* campaign to clean out hidden counterrevolutionaries was launched, the old tactic of "patiently stirring up of the masses" no longer worked; the majority remained lukewarm or middling in their enthusiasm, and the backward continued to be "irritatingly asleep.")[49] As Elizabeth Perry relates, the ideal *kongsu hui* was well prepared for, was limited to no more than seventy-five minutes so as to

---

[49] SMA B123/2/1306. "Shanghai shi di'yi shangye ju zhuanmen xiaozu guanyu paidui gongzuo de zongjie (chugao)" ("Lining up" [individuals for checking materials] Work

avoid boredom, had activists sprinkled throughout the audience to shout slogans at key junctures when things began to flag, and was choreographed to whip up the emotions and righteous indignation of the crowd. Success was gauged by how enthusiastically the masses shouted slogans and supported the inevitable executions immediately following the proceedings.[50] Cadres were directed to identify and coach particularly sympathetic individuals: the very old, the very young, the infirm or disabled, and women. When the show went well, the masses were properly aroused, class consciousness was raised, and the event concluded with a roaring reaffirmation of the state's moral right in dispatching irredeemable evildoers. And, as might be expected, most of the accounts that we have of *kongsu hui* stress these very elements.

There were, nevertheless, risks that were inherent in putting on such a public show that to be deemed successful required such active support of the audience. There was always the potential for the show to veer off script. The prepared parts of the show could fall flat. Pre-coached accusers could be unconvincing. The accused targets could be ill chosen and not arouse the "right" kinds of hatred and indignation. The proceedings could drag. There were also occasions, albeit rare ones, when the accused refused to recognize his guilt and a very few even remained defiant to the end.

If the audience was either bored by the show or was not sufficiently aroused to play its chorus like part on cue, then the *kongsu hui* was deemed a failure. Because the state put such emphasis on arousing the masses' hatred through these displays of state power, there is scant direct evidence of failed or underwhelming mass accusation sessions in the written record. Cadres who wrote the final reports for their superiors would have had a powerful set of incentives to conceal, or at least minimize, details suggesting that things did not go to plan. Occasionally, though, hints of less than successful mass accusation sessions come through in the written record. For example, cadres at enterprises and factories under the Shanghai Workers' Federation were frequently criticized for their failure to prepare adequately for *kongsu hui*: the masses could be confused as to what the goals of the public accusation were, the choices of public targets were often insufficiently clear, and the masses were often puzzled as to why one individual was singled out for accusation when there were others, presumably as guilty, who were not.[51]

Preliminary Report, Shanghai First Commerce Bureau special small group), December 6, 1955.

[50] Perry, p. 116, original reference SMA B168-1-804, p. 43.

[51] SMA C1/1/28 (July or August 1951). "Shanghai gongren canjia zhenya fangeming yundong zongjie baogao" (Summary report on Shanghai workers' participation in the Campaign to Suppress Counterrevolutionaries).

More dangerously, there were other ways in which local authorities could lose control of the *kongsu hui* once the passions of the crowd were whipped up. The state actively sought the crowd's righteous indignation and hatred for identified counterrevolutionaries, and it tacitly indulged spontaneous crowd violence against the accused. In one instance in Shanghai, a crowd became so riled up over counterrevolutionary criminals that they rushed forward to stomp on the heads of counterrevolutionaries after they had been taken to a nearby park and shot.[52] There was, however, no such tolerance when individuals in a "stirred up" crowd brought forward new charges against the accused or worse, began to shout out spontaneous new charges against individuals not onstage. One sternly worded set of guidelines from Shanghai reiterated that public accusation meetings were *solely* for counterrevolutionaries who had already been investigated, arrested, and had lengthy cases prepared against them. Cadres were warned not to permit new accusations against other potential evildoers at *kongsu hui*. Tellingly, public accusation could only come *after* arrest, compilation of evidence, and "preparation" (i.e. establishing conclusive guilt coaching sympathetic individuals to make accusations, and conducting dress rehearsals). While public accusation before the masses was deemed a necessary component of the "high tide" of the campaign, it was made possible only after a sequence of bureaucratic backstage preparations had readied the key players, the script, and the stage for the performance. Combing through files to determine individuals' previous positions under the Guomindang, interviewing corroborating witnesses, establishing proof of bullying behavior, readying the platform, and identifying/coaching sympathetic accusers were all relatively routine, "rule of thumb" processes. These more bureaucratic, non-spontaneous, sequential measures necessary for a good show needed to be concealed from the mass audience. Few things could be more disruptive to the show put on by the state than for individuals in the audience to confuse the seeming spontaneity of the public accusation session with genuinely spontaneous accusations against untried, unvetted individuals whose guilt had not already been concluded by the state.[53]

The way in which the ROC/Taiwan ensured the isolation of accused individuals was diametrically opposed to that of revolutionary Sunan. In Taiwan the accused was removed abruptly from society, confined in a

---

[52] Elizabeth J. Perry, "Moving the Masses: Emotion Work in the Chinese Revolution."

[53] SMA C21/1/98, Zhang Benqian, "Wuyue siri zai shiyu qingnian ganbu jinian wusi qingnian jieji zhongguo xin minzhu zhuyi qingniantuan chengli erzhou nian dahui shangde baogao" (Report to the Shanghai city and suburban conference to commemorate May Fourth Youth and the two years' anniversary establishment of New China's Youth Corps), May 4, 1951.

prison, and then whisked to a small room where the immediate audience (judges, military police) consisted of the same people who were the key players who would pass (and carry out) sentence. In Taiwan the bureaucratic modality of law was itself the legitimating show. These were staged by the state for itself: at the sentencing hearing the individual's role was to accept his guilt and submit to the authority of the state's judicial process within the closed confines of the prison, rather than to recognize his guilt in a public display before a mass audience. The performance reiterated the legitimacy of the ROC state's legal procedures of martial law, now entered in perpetuity on the correct forms. This process broke the individual down into constituent categories, labeled him according to clearly stated bureaucratic rules, rendered a sentence in accordance with those criteria, and filed him away with the appropriate official stamps. The public was not engaged; indeed the regime's very silence about process and outcome was in its own way a form of communication. Citizens were left to draw their own conclusions over what was neither justified, nor explained. There was no information about process, and publicity about outcome was minimal. In many cases, accused individuals and their families received copies of their official judgments months after sentencing and punishment, or not at all. In this way, publics were atomized and individualized, rather than fused with each other and the state: families, friends, and co-workers of the accused were left to speculate as to how martial law was applied in practice. Once an individual had been arrested, spirited away to prison, or worse, family members faced further social ostracization and isolation at just the time when they were most in need of social support. Usually, the imprisoned were men who often left behind wives and children to fend for themselves in a society without either social insurance or adequate employment opportunities. Few were willing to risk being seen to help the families of defined enemies of the state.

Conclusion: Campaign Aftermaths and Chronic Tensions

For both the new revolutionary government in Sunan and the ROC/ Taiwan, the principles, staging, and processes that dramatized the state's prosecution of domestic enemies drew from both campaign and bureaucratic modalities of implementation. The PRC in Sunan proudly proclaimed its commitment to the campaign by deploying its campaign repertoire of stirring up the people, emotional mobilization, and public solidarity with the masses in its implementation of the Campaign to Suppress Counterrevolutionaries. Due to the slippage inherent in a campaign modality in designating targets, and the ever-present danger that campaign mass mobilization against those targets could go off script, bureaucratic modalities of hierarchy, preparation, and control were present throughout the campaign, but were largely concealed from the public eye. Public security bureaus arrested; suspected counterrevolutionaries had cases against them investigated; and those determined guilty were then, quite literally, put on a stage before a large crowd. The open and public drama of the public accusation/struggle meeting was integral to the revolutionary state's conception of itself and what it expected from its citizenry. Its key *dramatis personae* served as a personification of old regime evil and New China's righteous triumph. The drama and script were a key focal point for mobilizing and educating mass publics as to regime norms and vocabularies. If the public face of mass accusation sessions was a campaign modality repertoire taken to its logical extreme, it concealed a bureaucratic modality reality of careful, bureaucratic planning. Behind the scenes, it took weeks to organize the legal case and evidence, arrange for the venue, identify and coach activists and sympathetic victims, and run dress rehearsals.

In its prosecution of domestic enemies, the ROC/Taiwan presented exactly the opposite of the PRC in Sunan. It claimed that its prosecution of traitors was logical, sober, bound by precedent, and above all *legal*. The public justification for suppressing Communists and cleaning out spies was explicitly rule driven and handed down by fiat. The intensive bursts of police actions against the suspected were never called campaigns. The way in which the ROC/Taiwan represented itself to the accused, to domestic society, and to its key external patron (the United States) required a show of formal procedure through military courts; closed courtrooms handed down sentences. These shows were produced to provide a sheen of bureaucratic and legal legitimacy to what was often a deeply flawed and arbitrary process. The rules were written in such a way that they could be stretched to accommodate almost any action against any reasonable, or not so reasonable, target. Although clothed in a language of law and precedent, and formally implemented in a show of judicial process, the reality of the White Terror was one of politically driven quasi-secret campaigns, which in extreme cases like the suppression of the Luku Base Area shaded into outright military campaigns that were launched against whole districts for no obvious reason other than regime paranoia.

These campaigns to suppress subversion – one openly acknowledged and the other not – were blunt and clumsy instruments of policy implementation, but in both cases, they were crudely successful. In Sunan, the party-state did succeed in identifying and crushing very large numbers of potential political competitors and other social undesirables. The ROC/Taiwan equally succeeded at breaking the Communist Party, along with many more who might eventually have put some sort of brake on the government's intentions in both cities and the countryside. Both dramatized terror, but the type of show, the script, and the audiences invited to watch were very different. In Sunan the state put counterrevolutionaries on stage to generate emotional identification between itself and the "masses," and begin what would prove to be a lengthy process of educating those masses in a new set of revolutionary norms of language and political participation. In contrast, the ROC's show was very circumscribed, where the director, the producer, and the main audience was the state itself. In Taiwan, the show was a procedural and legal one that legitimated the state's police actions, and shielded from scrutiny the campaign(s) of police intensification that brought the accused into the state's prison system in the first place.

The evidence we have at present suggests that after the initial and very severe crackdown of the early 1950s, the sheer viciousness in the implementation of martial law declined over time. It is difficult to tell whether this reduction in active campaigns of terror was because all the likely Communists and their supporters had been extirpated, because the regime was more secure and discriminating in its deployment of domestic violence, because people in Taiwan had learned to speak the regime's language and be very careful about expressing themselves, or because reforms within the security services transformed an organizationally fragmented and competitive set of security organizations into a system of domestic security that was better integrated and more socially embedded. Whatever the mix of reasons, the number of political cases under martial law dropped dramatically after 1954 from 301 in 1954 to 78 in 1955, and from then down to almost none in the late 1950s.[54] After the mid-1950s the Taiwan Garrison Command could, and did, launch periodic reminders about what would and would not be tolerated for the remainder of the martial law period. There was an especially vicious military-cum political witch hunt to suppress democratically minded reformers in the prosecution of Lei Zhen in 1960. But these later crackdowns tended to impose lengthy prison sentences rather than executions on those found guilty, and neither the GMD elites, nor most among the Taiwanese needed many of these types of reminder after the mid-1950s. Those formally designated "Communist bandits" or "the seditious" and their

---

[54] Lin Zhenghui "1950 niandai xingong huo zuoyi zhengzhi anjian" (Political cases of communists or left sympathizers in the 1950s), in Zhang Yanxian and Chen Meirong, *Jieyan Shiqi baise kongbu yu zhuanzhin zhengyi lunwen ji*), table No. 3, "Shenggong wei xiangguan anjian panjue renshu bianhua tu" (Comparative table of legal judgments on the Taiwan Provincial [CCP] Committee," p. 155. See also Greitens, *Dictators and Their Secret Police*, pp. 180–182.

families, remained shamed and socially isolated. Those imprisoned and executed could not be discussed. Hatred of the Guomindang and disgust with the regime went underground. And the ruling authorities remained for the most part content with the external form of acquiescence.

None of this obtained in revolutionary Sunan, where the Campaign to Suppress Counterrevolutionaries was followed immediately by other campaigns deploying similar techniques (minus the killing) to cow, isolate, and remake other suspect social, economic, and status groups: the *sanfan* (Three Antis) against "corrupt and wasteful" bureaucrats, the *wufan* (Five Antis) of 1952–1953 against "corrupt" private businessmen, and thought reform in 1953 against intellectuals. Once the party line shifted to the abrupt nationalization of enterprises in 1955, the CCP launched another anti-counterrevolutionary campaign, the *sufan* (肅反), that now turned inward to ferret out counterrevolutionaries who had "wormed their way" into socialist China's work units. The 1955 *sufan* campaign was plagued by unclear targets and ultra-leftism from the outset. The campaign repertoires introduced by the Campaign to Suppress Counterrevolutionaries in 1951 – political study, secret accusation, checking on materials, and mass accusation sessions – were by now well understood. And in 1955 those targeted were within (*neibu*) the confines of the nationalized work unit rather than "outside" in open public space. Accusers, compilers of documents, and convenors of mass accusation sessions and activists with the most to gain from making accusations were all workplace associates.

While the *sufan* campaign executed very few people in comparison with the Campaign to Suppress Counterrevolutionaries, the numbers who initially fell into the *sufan* net were many times larger. The sub-categories of those to be counted as counterrevolutionaries were substantially expanded and the burden of proof for counterrevolution was dramatically lowered. In the Sunan of 1951, counterrevolutionaries were so designated by engaging in activity that was explicitly proscribed by the regime, being particularly hated by the masses, or until very recently having been in high formal position in a counterrevolutionary GMD organization. Four years later, as little as a continued association with a family member or friend deemed counterrevolutionary, or an accusation of thinking counterrevolutionary thoughts was enough to merit an investigation.[55]

---

[55] SMA B122/2/1192. Shanghai di'san shangye ju shipin zhan (grain stations) "Cancun wulei fangeming, xinshi zhanzui ji fangeming shehui jichu diaocha tongjibiao" (Shanghai Third Commerce Bureai grain station statistical form on the social basis for the remaining five types of counterrevolutionaries and criminal counterrevolutionaries), September 20, 1955.

In the *sufan* campaign, cadres, activists, and the rank and file of the work unit, were all unclear as to how to delineate the majority "good" from the minority "bad." In Sunan, where so many had supported the Guomindang or had friends and relatives who had, the issue of how to distinguish between those who had mere "general historical questions" (*yiban lishi wenti* – 一般歷史問題) and those who were "real counterrevolutionaries" was critical. Other important distinctions were made in principle between: (1) those with "ideological questions" (*sixiang wenti* – 思想問題) and those with more serious "political questions" (*zhengzhi wenti* – 政治問題); (2) those with "complex social relations" (*shehui guanxi fuza* – 社會關係複雜) and those with more problematic "individual questions" (*geren wenti* – 各人問題); and (3) those who had been historical counterrevolutionaries (i.e. counterrevolutionaries in the past) (*lishi fangeming* – 歷史反革命) and those who were actively counterrevolutionary in the present (*xianxing fan geming* – 現行反革命). Little guidance was given to cadres as to how to make these determinations in practice.[56]

With so many different types of undesirables, different degrees of undesirability, and different categories of counterrevolutionary to consider, the *sufan* campaign predictably tacked to the hard left. Although guidelines stipulated a distinction between "backward elements" (*luohou fenzi* – 落後分子) and real counterrevolutionaries, those with "bad work attitudes" were often subjected to struggle meetings despite proscriptions against so doing. While official documents for the campaign suggested that "only a minority of around 5 percent of people" were counterrevolutionaries," summary reports on *sufan* from Shanghai's First Commerce Bureau reveal that over 15 percent of the workforce was designated counterrevolutionary in the initial "high tide" of the campaign, and many more were slated to be put in that category.[57] At this point the campaign was reined in, and most put on the list of counterrevolutionaries were then reclassified as part of the non-counterrevolutionary majority.

Despite this backtracking, the kinds of excesses on display in the *sufan* campaign of 1955 pointed the way to the future. The CCP was deeply attached to the elements of its campaign repertoire that valorized struggle,

---

[56] SMA, B123/2/1036. "Shanghai shi di'yi shangye ju zhuanmen xiaozu guanyu paidui gongzuo de zongjie (chugao)" ("Lining up" [individuals for checking materials] Work Preliminary Report, Shanghai First Commerce Bureau special small group), December 1955.

[57] SMA B123/2/1036. "Yishang ju zhuanmen xiaozu guanyu paidui gongzuo de zongjie" (The Shanghai First Commerce Bureau Special Small Group on "Lining Up"). December 1955.

the remaking of the self, the mobilization of the masses, and the merging of the masses with the will of the CCP through mass accusation sessions that isolated the individual while solidifying mass group support for the state. It continued to deploy these repertoires well after the CCP's policies had extirpated all potential opposition and fundamentally transformed society through collectivization in the countryside and the mass nationalization of enterprises in urban areas. Once people were ensconced in their work units, mass accusation ceased to be an outdoor spectacle that educated the public into the norms and language of the state. Once transferred to the much smaller and confined indoor spaces of work units, they strengthened extant internal hierarchies and afforded defined activists an opportunity to burnish their revolutionary credentials.

These trends towards a lower burden of proof and increasingly vague guidelines for how to distinguish the counterrevolutionary from the merely "politically backward" would intensify in subsequent campaigns in the 1950s and beyond into the 1960s. In the mid-1950s, no one could reasonably have anticipated either the Anti-Rightist Campaign or the Cultural Revolution. But the underlying repertoire that future mass campaigns drew upon was acted out in full public view as early as 1951. They did not weaken once obvious potential social competitors of the state (college professors, private businessmen, and holdover GMD officials) were either destroyed or intimidated into silence. The CCP's deep attachment to a campaign modality remained strong. It continued to insist on the tried and trusted campaign repertoire that had served it so well in winning the civil war and consolidating its hegemony: political study, small group discussion, criticism and self-criticism, targeting an ill-defined but minority "enemy," inviting the popular involvement of the "good" majority, requiring the masses to be "stirred up," and disdaining regular, precedent-based rule application as "formalism." After the early 1950s, when the ROC/Taiwan state had bared its teeth and demonstrated through its vicious anti-Communist campaigns that it would tolerate no opposition or organization that it did not at least oversee, it was in practice willing to be satisfied with the external forms of individual compliance. In Sunan, by contrast, it was clearly not enough to simply submit to the new order. Even after all the usual suspects had been removed or incorporated into the state on fundamentally different terms by the campaigns of the early 1950s, the PRC continued to launch campaigns that demanded the increasingly enthusiastic participation of the masses, and were never fully concluded, because there was always more to be done in terms of revolutionary fervor, revolutionary commitment, and revolutionary results.

4   Repertoires of Land Reform Campaigns in Sunan and Taiwan, 1950–1954

From Removing Enemies to Generating Support: Land Reform Campaigns in Sunan and Taiwan

The previous two chapters on the Campaign to Suppress Counterrevolutionaries and the White Terror have traced how these two regimes sought to ensure their domestic security through radical and vicious campaigns to, quite literally, "cleanse" the regime of political, military, and socio-economic opposition, thus simultaneously expanding the coercive apparatus of the state, establishing new rules of the game, and prompting the population to internalize a new set of norms about what was and was not permissible in terms of public political discourse and political participation. Given that the protracted nature of China's civil war between Communists and Nationalists had made it exceptionally difficult to distinguish friend from foe, deepening Cold War and the outbreak of regional hot war in Korea led both the CCP and the GMD to become extraordinarily focused on internal security.

Coercive measures to crack down on presumptive subversives, however, were limited in their usefulness. They were brutally effective in removing an often vaguely defined "bad" from the polity, but were unable to generate positive social or economic "good." Land reform programs offered just such social and economic goods by: (1) redressing inequality in the countryside; and (2) giving impoverished farmers incentives to work hard and increase agricultural production, thus providing a stronger base for national economic development. Like the Campaign to Suppress Counterrevolutionaries and the White Terror, land reform initiatives in Sunan and Taiwan were conducted as political campaigns, and they often overlapped with ongoing campaigns against enemies of the state. This was particularly so in Sunan, where land reform and the Campaign to Suppress Counterrevolutionaries were implemented at the same time in the spring of 1951, drew from the same campaign repertoire, were carried out by the same local cadres, and often focused on the same targets. In practice, particularly in the peri-urban countryside around Shanghai, the two campaigns merged with each other to such an extent that it was impossible to

168

separate one from the other. In Taiwan, these linkages were much less obvious because the two campaigns were implemented by quite different state organizations, answered to different superiors, did not communicate with each other, and presented very different faces to the public. Antisubversive internal security measures were kept well hidden from society, while land reform campaigns were given maximal publicity. But even in Taiwan there were surprising, if seldom remarked on, crossovers between internal police actions and land reform.

While land reform in Sunan and Taiwan contained elements of coercion, its coercive core was softened substantially with material and moral incentives. Land reform held out the establishment of new, presumptively fairer and more rational platforms for national development, promised the fundamental transformation of deeply unequal social and economic relations in the countryside, and publicly displayed the regime's positive moral worth and capacity to govern through the ways in which each pursued its version of land reform. As land reform was so heavily freighted by these regimes' morally based claims to rule, land reform campaigns were pushed through with maximum publicity and instruction for the population. Because of this openness, the methods by which land reform campaigns were made intelligible and implemented were nearly as important as the actual results. Unlike the suppression of subversion, which could continue indefinitely against the government's shifting definitions of domestic enemies, land reform lent itself to a clear, morally based narrative with an obvious beginning, middle, and conclusion that could be mapped against a larger aspirational story of progress, social fairness, and economic development.

Both the PRC in Sunan and the ROC on Taiwan launched significant, and ultimately successful, land reform campaigns in the early 1950s. Two generations later one might well ask why two such mutually hostile regimes felt it so necessary to invest so much of their political capital, go to so much effort, and exhibit so much mimesis, in their respective pursuits of land reform programs at this time. I suggest that the PRC in Sunan and the ROC in Taiwan looked to land reform initiatives for identical reasons. They both subscribed to the notions that successful land reform was: (1) an economically essential precondition for national development; and (2) required for regime legitimacy.

State elites on both sides of the Taiwan Strait drew on very similar pre-1949 rhetorics in their diagnosis of the "problem" of rural land tenure and used land reform campaigns instrumentally in very similar ways to impose new forms of party-state hegemony on the countryside. Land reform campaigns made it possible for outsiders – whether as part of the PLA drive south from Shandong or technocrats based in Taibei – to mobilize local officials, attract the energy and commitment of large numbers of the young, bring the countryside to heel, recast rural society by wiping out old elites, and establish the conditions for the emergence a loyal new order in the countryside. There were, of course, important differences between the CCP's variant of land reform in Sunan and the GMD's in Taiwan. The former used the land reform campaign to assign to rural families what would become permanent class-status categories based on Marxist-Leninist-Maoist notions of "exploitative" class relations, and insisted on a highly public form of collective violence against class enemies that not only extirpated landlords as a class, but also eliminated landlords as individuals. The latter made every effort to transform landlords as a class by accelerating their involvement as individuals into state capital enterprises through compensation in state factory bonds. These two land reform campaigns also differed fundamentally on questions of violence and inclusion in the new polity. The CCP in Sunan required public violence and mass participation in the decimation of "exploiters" as a category. The GMD in Taiwan concealed land reform's latent violence, and explicitly integrated ex-landlords, now occupying new roles as small freeholders and aspiring state capitalists, into the new GMD-dominated economic and political order. Through the pursuit of land reform campaigns, these two regimes were able to imagine, perform, and dramatize themselves and their agendas, establishing templates and norms for the future.

These two chapters also explore how these regimes used land reform to establish ideational and power-based forms of hegemony in the countryside that updated, extended, and imposed repertoires of campaign implementation. These repertoires were drawn from the immediately preceding republican period, political elite perceptions of success and failure in the immediate past, and regional and international influences. For both the "revolutionary" and "conservative" types of land reform, these elements combined to frame the rhetorics, narratives, and practices surrounding the conceptualization and implementation of land reform, often with leaders that were either in ignorance of conditions in the countryside, or willing to disregard local conditions that might have suggested different approaches. For regimes so diametrically opposed in ideology, land reform campaigns in Sunan and Taiwan had an enormous amount in common during their early to middling stages. They diverged sharply only in the middle to final stages, when their differences became most visible in the way in which each created a foundational narrative of land reform that was performed in rural public space. In Sunan, the young People's Republic of China insisted on land reform as a real-life action drama that culminated in the triumph of good over evil: a morality play with a moment of resolution in the public and violent expulsion of evil landlords and bullies immediately prior to the integration of the "good" rural public with the morally righteous state. In Taiwan, the ROC engineered a very different kind of happy ending in which rural society was set to rights by the precise and careful removal of excess property from those who had too much, before all rural classes were then reintegrated with each other on the basis of a new, fairer rural order, and then ultimately with the state.

Land Reform in Sunan and Taiwan at Mid-Century: Pre-1949 Repertoires and "Lessons Learned"

Although there are two separate and substantial literatures on land reform for both China and Taiwan,[1] there are only a few works that systematically attempt to compare the two programs, and the most recent of these was published over thirty years ago. Fortunately, the present combination of increasing, if uneven, archival openness and the decreasing political salience of the land reforms of the early 1950s makes it possible to begin to reconsider land reform on the two sides of the Taiwan Straits with a degree of critical distance. Scholars in China and Taiwan are now beginning to do so for both the 1940s and 1950s, although to the best of my knowledge none of this more recent scholarship does so in an explicitly comparative fashion.[2] A fresh look at the "revolutionary" and the

---

[1] There are substantial bodies of literature in English and much larger ones in Chinese on land reform for both the People's Republic of China and Taiwan. For China, the core texts are William Hinton, *Fanshen: A Documentary of Land Reform in a Chinese Village* (1966), Isabel and David Crook, *Revolution in a Chinese Village: Ten Mile Inn* (1959 and later editions), and Ezra Vogel, *Canton Under Communism: Programs and Politics in a Provincial Capital, 1949–1968* (1969). Later generations of scholarship include John Wong, *Land Reform in the People's Republic of China: Institutional Transformation in Agriculture* (1973) and Ben Stavis "China and the Comparative Analysis of Land Reform" (1978). For Taiwan, the primary works in English are Chen Cheng, *Land Reform in Taiwan* (1954), Tang Hui-sun, *Land Reform in Free China* (1954), and T. H. Shen, *The Sino-American Commission on Joint Rural Reconstruction: Twenty Years of Cooperation for Agricultural Development* (1970), pp. 56–69.

[2] Chao Kang's *Economic Effects of Land Reforms in Taiwan, Japan, and Mainland China: A Comparative Study* made exactly this attempt for comparative political economy; Stavis suggested that it was important to engage comparison of land reform in China and Taiwan with other countries. But since the early 1980s, scholars have tended to focus on land reform in either the People's Republic of China or in Taiwan. For ongoing revisionist approaches to land reform in Taiwan, see Xu Shirong (Hsu Shih-jung), "In Fact, Landlords were not Landlords." Liu Shiwei and He Zhiming, "Zhanhou chuqi Taiwan yedian guanxi zhi tantao jian lun gengzhe you qitian zhengce" (A discussion of landlord and tenant relations and the land to the tiller program in early post-war Taiwan). For the People's Republic of China, see Gao Wangling, "Tudi gaige: 'gaitian huandi' de shehui yundong" (Land Reform: a world turned upside down social movement) Man Yong, "Shenfen de konghuang: Anhui sheng Fuyang diqu tugaizhong de zisha xianxiang" (The terror of status: suicide during land reform in Fuyang district, Anhui), and Cao Shuji, "Liangzhong 'tianmiantian' yu sunan tudi gaige" (Two types of land and land reform in southern Jiangsu).

"conservative" variants of the Chinese state at mid-century suggests that both considered landholding and rural immiseration to be central issues of governance. Between the historical legacy of late imperial China, an agrarian empire that had long prioritized the right to subsistence as the cornerstone of social stability, and contemporary questions of national development, it would have been extraordinary for an underdeveloped state with a substantial rural population not to be preoccupied with questions of rural livelihood and land tenure.

By 1949, a remarkable consensus had emerged on both sides of the Taiwan Strait: that land reform was necessary, desirable, and popular. Rural immiseration had been made visible by the appalling famines in North China in 1920–1921, and in northwest China in 1928–1930. Progressive elites and intellectuals had been pressing for the state to play a role in the alleviation of peasant distress for a generation. China had the world's largest absolute number of peasants and one of the worst population to arable land ratios. These grim figures were compounded by land parcelization, and half a century of militarization, foreign invasion, and weak governments incapable of providing relief when markets broke down. The Chinese state's long-standing concern with rural conditions was reinforced by global processes of rapid decolonization after 1945, when states of very different ideological hues – from Marxist-Leninist China to nationalist India to the ex-colonial Philippines – were attempting to implement land reform. The postwar international development community and academia were similarly involved in land reform programs and policy analysis, resulting in a policy discourse on the economic and political necessity of land reform that cut across Cold War ideological alignments and cohered for roughly a generation after World War II. Questions of land tenure, the peasantry, national economic development, and on what basis the state would engage with the countryside stood at the very heart of building new states and transforming old ones from the 1940s until well into the 1970s.[3]

In Sunan and Taiwan, commitment to land reform also had another, more instrumental function. It was *the* key program through which the People's Republic of China and the ROC/Taiwan penetrated and reordered state–society relations with their respective rural areas in the early 1950s. The truly significant differences between the two hinged not on whether land reform was important or would be implemented, but on *how* it should be implemented. The CCP insisted that by definition,

---

[3] Virtually every piece written on land tenure and agricultural economy on republican-era China from the 1920s to the present points to the twin problems of land parcelization and pressure on arable land. See R. H. Tawney, *Land and Labour in China*, pp.41–46, pp. 54–77 for an early and still compelling description.

meaningful land reform had to be carried out through a popular mass movement that involved violent class overthrow: the GMD shied away from violence and towards integration of all social groups. The CCP claimed that land reform was a necessarily violent and rapid overthrow of exploiting classes supported by properly organized and "stirred up" peasant masses. The Guomindang party-state equally explicitly gravitated towards gradualist incorporation of all to secure rural stability "through a peaceful and bloodless reform."[4] That the CCP and GMD lined up on opposite sides of the issue of rapid, violent and divisive class struggle versus gradualist "peaceful" incorporation and unity should come as no surprise, as these different preferences were at the philosophical heart of the political divisions that had led to nearly a quarter century of bitter civil war. Rather the surprise is how much land reform programs on both sides of the Taiwan Strait in the early 1950s had in common *despite* these sharp ideological disagreements on questions of violence and class struggle.

By the middle of the twentieth century, several different streams fed into a broad political discourse on land and rural poverty in China. As a specifically modern issue of underdevelopment and economic stagnation, how to manage China's enormous rural hinterland became a major issue among the modernizing urban elites in the May Fourth period (1919), accelerating during the revolutionary 1920s when the nascent Sunist party-state made a formal commitment to relative equalization of land holdings through a land to the tiller policy.[5] Efforts to reform land tenure began in the mid-1920s, as moderate groups promoted reformist rent-reduction experiments from "above," while other more radical groups attempted violent expropriation of landlords from "below," notably captured in Mao's famous "Report on the Peasant Movement in Hunan" in 1927. In the quarter century between the mass movements-cum-militarization that brought the GMD to power in 1927 and the CCP's final victory in 1949, both gradualist/reformist and radical/revolutionary approaches to land reform were inconclusive and subject to reverses; the former petered out in the face of invasion and disruption, and the latter was subject to reversal, cancellation, and landlord reprisals until well into the civil war period (1945–1949).[6]

---

[4] Both rhetorics occur repeatedly throughout the contemporary documents on land reform. For typical examples of each, see Cheng Tan, "Zenma yang xuexi tudi gaige caofa?" (How to study the draft land reform law), *Tudi Wenti Caokao Ziliao* (Reference Materials on Land Problems), Vol. 2, Guangzhou: Xinhua, 1950, p. 1; GSG FY53, 313/1285–4, "Land Reform on Formosa: Information for Dr. J.B. Grant of UNMHO Office at Ceylon."

[5] Tang Hui-sun, forward, n.p., and p. 14.

[6] Tang Hui-sun, pp. 29–30; Stephen Averill, *Revolution in the Highlands: China's Jinggangshan Base Area*, pp. 239–249

Although the CCP's own policies regarding land reform shifted over time, the long years of revolutionary struggle in the rural hinterland resulted in a constellation of ideas and a repertoire of practices that we now call the Maoist version of rural revolution. One part of this repertoire stressed an intensive practical investigation of social and economic problems articulated in a distinctively Marxist-Leninist idiom. Another insisted on the assignment of what would come to be fixed class categories based on occupation and the degree to which the individual household's living was made by "exploitation" of others' labor, rather than relying on its own. A third perennially oscillated between insistence on mass mobilization, genuine participation, and the necessity for local leaders to ensure that mass mobilization would result in the ends pre-determined by higher levels of the CCP. A fourth extended an inner-Party tradition of criticism and self-criticism to outside targets, which resulted in the dramatic public mass criticism and denunciation of assigned targets under the direction of the CCP.

Most scholars agree that the CCP's years in Yan'an (1936–1949) were critical to the coalescence of the CCP's distinctive repertoires for rural campaigns. Despite repeated bombing by the Japanese during the Sino-Japanese War and a brief invasion by the Guomindang military in 1947, Yan'an was relatively well protected militarily. This was also a period in which the CCP faced multiple challenges from administering and attracting popular support in such a large and impoverished territory under wartime conditions, to socializing large numbers of patriotic young intellectuals who knew little of Marxist theory and less of Leninist discipline, and to engaging in an unceasing propaganda battle with the GMD for the hearts and minds of the Chinese population and the sympathy of outsiders. It was at Yan'an that a distinctly Maoist set of practices were added to the CCP's revolutionary repertoire: lengthy periods of study of key revolutionary texts, criticism and self-criticism, the Party's insistence on the mass line "from the people to the people" with heavy doses of popular participation, and the dramatic spectacles of public accusation and struggle against defined enemies and internal miscreants, leavened by a compelling narrative.[7]

As these repertoires were developing, the specifics of the CCP's land-reform campaigns shifted from the moderate (e.g. rent reduction) during the Kangzhan period (1937–1945) to the radical (e.g. violent expropriation and mass struggle sessions to draw hard lines between the "them" and the "us") during the latter stages of the civil war (1945–1949). By the late 1930s there was little reason to doubt the CCP's commitment to the

---

[7] Apter and Saich, pp. 74–81, 130–133, 181–183.

peasantry, its willingness to implement a range of programs to promote both more production and more social justice for the peasantry, and its systematic preference for the poorest within the peasantry. And through the long years of struggle in the countryside, trial and error, and reversals along with successes, the CCP under Mao forged an identity and legitimacy that was wrapped up in a repertoire that not only relied on the poor peasantry, it virtually *required* the poor peasantry to be appropriately "stirred up," mobilized, and participate in the revolution to make it their own.[8]

In contrast, the National Government was perpetually hamstrung in its efforts to alleviate rural distress and land reform three ways. First, its base of support in urbanized and highly commodified Sunan limited its experience and reach into the parts of China that were truly impoverished. Second, while it claimed monocratic authority over all of China, the government's real projective power was severely limited, and thus it had to cut deals with a constantly changing kaleidoscope of local militarists and elites. And finally, its inflexible hostility to the CCP's methods of violent rural revolution made it necessary for the GMD to distinguish itself from the "chaos" of the Other's commitment to "stirring up" by promoting local social order. This imperative, in combination with its weak projective power, resulted in the government's reliance on established local elites for whom the best kind of land reform was no land reform. Such was its distaste for the violent removal of local elites that even when the GMD military took over Communist base areas that had undergone land reform, it returned the land to pre-land reform local notables whose commitment to the GMD was at best highly problematic.[9]

Before 1949, the GMD did accommodate individual projects geared to alleviating rural poverty. It permitted the rural reconstruction experiments of Liang Shuming and James Yen in Zouping and Ding counties.[10] It trialled its own experimental rural reconstruction projects in Jiangning and Pinghu counties.[11] But the central government had nowhere near enough

---

[8] Keating lays out clearly how even contiguous areas within the same region in the impoverished northwest had very different experiences in terms of who was willing and able to support the first stages of tenancy reform, see particularly pp. 170–175.

[9] Averill, 2006, pp. 283–284.

[10] See Guy Alitto, *The Last Confucian: Liang Shu-ming and the Chinese Dilemma of Modernity* and Charles Hayford, *To the People: James Yen and Village China* for seminal studies on Liang Shuming and James Y. C. Yen; for a more recent evaluation of the rural reconstruction movement, see Kate Merkel-Hess, *The Rural Modern: Reconstructing the Self and State in Republican China.*

[11] I am indebted to Robert Cole for directing me to this example. See *Dizheng Yuekan* (Land Government Monthly), Special Issue on Adjusting the Pinghu County Cadastre, 14: 10 October, 1936. See especially Wang Jie, "Pinghu xian zhi hangkong celiang" (Pinghu County Aerial Survey), pp. 1667–1678.

trained and loyal personnel to implement such reforms itself on a national basis. This meant that rural reconstruction in the pre-war Sino-Japanese War period remained confined to specially designated experimental areas that were not, and could not be, scaled up. The Ding and Zouping experiments were overrun early in the Sino-Japanese War. After a painful year of retreat to the interior in 1937–1938, the Guomindang government was of necessity almost exclusively focused on extracting sufficient grain from the countryside, continuing to field its armies, and desperately trying to ensure the basic political loyalty of its own vastly expanded bureaucracy. In the early stages of the civil war (1945–1949), plans to address rural distress were widely discussed in agricultural economics circles. But in such heavily militarized circumstances little coordinated central government support was forthcoming.

When it came, the National Government's response to the problems of the countryside was the product of a coalition between Chinese progressives and agriculturalists such as James Yen (Yan Yanchu), Chiang Monlin (Jiang Menglin), and T. H. Shen (Shen Zonghan) with Americans deeply worried about the CCP's increasing appeal in the countryside. The first tangible product of this coalition was the Economic Cooperation Act (ECA) that stipulated that 10 percent of the economic aid given to China was to be earmarked for rural reconstruction specifically to combat Communism. These ECA funds made possible the initial establishment of a hybrid development organization called the Joint Commission of Rural Reconstruction (JCRR) which consisted of Chinese and American technocrats to draw up projects for rural development aid. The JCRR was formally established in late 1948, just as the GMD was definitively losing the civil war.[12] By this juncture, land reform as part and parcel of revolution in the countryside had become central to the CCP's identity, mass base, and perceptions of its own success. Land reform for the GMD was belatedly conceived as so necessary and overdue a response to the Communist success in the countryside that it was handed over to a technocratic organization nominally part of, but in practice independent of, the regular institutions of the Republican Chinese state. The JCRR's brief was to make recommendations, draw up programs, and generally strengthen the regular institutional capacity of the GMD regional and local state in actual program delivery for rural modernization.

Despite the unbridgeable political gap between the CCP and GMD, there continued to be a broadly convergent diagnosis about land reform, its place in the Chinese revolution, its role in the outcome of the civil war, and its importance for regime consolidation. Both subscribed to different

---

[12] Joint Commission on Rural Reconstruction, *General Report* I, 1950 pp. 2–3.

interpretations of the same morality tale. For the CCP, surprisingly quick military victory further ensconced the importance of land reform in its repertoire of making rural revolution. The convergence between the CCP's repertoires of social investigation, political study, and stirring up the masses in making rural revolution and its unexpectedly rapid, even miraculous, victory in the civil war in 1949 suggested that it was only logical to extend to the rest of the country a version of land reform that deployed the same successful pre-1949 repertoires. For the GMD, its inability to implement any kind of effective land reform on the mainland of China became an equally compelling, but negative story of failure: how its own moral and practical failings led to disaster and traumatic loss. The GMD leaders in charge of reviving the party, consolidating the state, and promoting rural development in the early 1950s did not quite come out and admit that they deserved to lose the mainland because of their failure to implement meaningful land reform, but they certainly came very close to doing so.[13]

The CCP's fusion of radical land reform and military success in the civil war of the late 1940s also made for a compelling political argument in favor of land reform. The CCP's claims to be concerned with, and more importantly, its ability to do something about the most serious problems of China's vast poor peasantry – shortage of land and lack of secure subsistence – were in fact temporally correlated with the active support of the poor peasantry and the CCP's overwhelming political and military victory in the civil war. Conversely, the GMD's hesitant, piecemeal, and ineffective measures in dealing with the ills of the rural peasantry were inextricably part of the larger military and economic failures of the GMD in losing the mainland. They were burned into the consciousness of the GMD political elite that fled to Taiwan in 1949–1950 as a critical factor in the GMD's collapse. These "lessons" of success and failure were also reinforced by deepening Cold War in East Asia. By the early 1950s, China's closest neighbors in Northeast Asia (what would emerge as the two Koreas and a conservative Japan firmly locked into alliance with the United States) were undergoing different versions of land reform. Land reform in what would become North Korea was being planned by the Soviets and enthusiastically taken up by the DRPK, was partially implemented in what would become South Korea at the behest of the US military, and perhaps most importantly of all, had already been imposed by a reformist SCAP in occupied Japan in the late 1940s.[14]

---

[13] *JCRR*, pp. 1–4.
[14] Ki Hyuk Park, "Outcome of Land Reform in the Republic of Korea"; see also Ronald Dore's great classic, *Land Reform in Japan*.

For all these reasons, the Chinese states on either side of the Taiwan Strait stand out as instances for which land reform programs were unusually politically salient, deeply embrocated with Cold War rivalry, justified in the name of social justice and economic development, and practically linked with a wider set of imperatives in regime consolidation and state building in the countryside. Indeed, the PRC and the ROC/ Taiwan stand as perhaps our most important and accessible test case for comparing "successful" versions of revolutionary and reformist approaches to land reform.[15] Authorities in the PRC and the ROC/ Taiwan fixated on resolving what each conceived of as the key "problem" of the countryside: overconcentration of land in the hands of too few, inheritance patterns that so increased parcelization that land holdings were unable reliably to feed the households that worked them, unfavorable terms of tenancy, entrenched rural poverty, and insufficient agricultural surplus to fuel industrialization.

Land reform campaigns occupied two simultaneous yet distinct niches for regime legitimation. For those concerned with questions of fairness, equality, and social welfare land reform was an important social good in itself, because low concentrations of land holdings and favorable conditions for tenants were critical indicators of social justice. Economic planners understood that the positive incentives that accompanied relative equality of landholding were a precondition for economic growth, because in economies dominated by agriculture, the base of any program of industrialization had to be predicated on consistent agricultural surplus. State makers on both sides of the Taiwan Strait also favored land reform because of its importance for regime consolidation. For the "conservative" ROC/ Taiwan as well as for the "revolutionary" PRC, the extraordinary mobilization of state institutions to implement campaigns for social justice and economic development made it possible for the state to augment its presence in the countryside, which was critical to a larger process of remaking the agricultural hinterland in a manner to the regime's liking.

Land reform required the state to concentrate political, human, organizational, and material resources. Collecting information about the countryside down to the level of the farming household meant that the state had to be

---

[15] The two Koreas and North and South Vietnam are the two other cases that would appear to lend themselves readily to this comparison. However, in the ROK, conservative political elites never committed to land reform as a priority in the way that the Guomindang in Taiwan did. With the aid of the Russian occupation, the nascent DRPK implemented full expropriation of landlords, but in what became South Korea, only a partial land reform was pushed through by the US military occupation. See Inhan Kim, "Land Reform in South Korea under U.S. Military Occupation, 1945–1948." In the case of Vietnam, the Republic of (South) Vietnam implemented so little land reform so late in its existence that it cannot qualify as an instance of success.

able to generate sufficient capacity to penetrate down to the grass roots. Successful implementation of land reform presumed the ability to radically restructure the countryside, and to link new constellations of rural economic and social organization to the state. For the young PRC, successful implementation of land reform in Shanghai and Sunan was particularly important because "New China" needed to demonstrate its active implementation of signature programs beyond its original base in north China. Successful land reform in Taiwan was even more crucial for the GMD; without it the government had no way to claim Taiwan as a positive example and model province demonstrating its righteous rule for the rest of China.

In addition there were secondary, external audiences and sources of support for land reform: the Soviet Union, the non-aligned developing world, and the United States. Although the details of the Soviet Union's direct involvement in land reform in China need to await the further opening of archives in Moscow, Mao himself hinted at the importance of the Soviet Union in his reference to the "great help" given by the Comintern in the CCP's pre-1949 land revolution, when he placed land reform on a par with such important events as the Northern Expedition and the war of resistance against Japan.[16] Meanwhile, for the ROC/Taiwan, the United States was critical in establishing, staffing, and funding the JCRR, which in turn funneled aid, organized training programs, developed rural development projects large and small, and was among the most important actors in augmenting the vision and practical capacity of the government organization most responsible for delivering land reform initiatives – the Taiwan Provincial Land Bureau (Taiwan Sheng Dizheng Ju – 臺灣省地政局) and its subsidiary units at the level of the district station.[17]

Overlapping Claims and Reality Disconnects

Symbol, rhetoric, and practice came together in the land reform campaigns of Sunan and Taiwan in ways that consolidated new forms of hegemony and demonstrated the state's moral virtue. For the young People's Republic of China, the seriousness with which it took land reform demonstrated its continuing commitment to social justice, its symbolic moral correctness in pursuing class struggle in the countryside in the pre- and post-1949 period, and its claims to offer a model for revolutionary movements in Asia. In Taiwan, a land reform program distinctly its own and differentiated from that of the revolutionary PRC

---

[16] Mao Zedong, "Comrade Mao Tse-tung [Zedong] Delivers Detailed Report on the Dissolution of the Comintern," 26 May 1943, www.prisoncensorship.info/archive/etext/classics/mao/cwcia/cwm9_1.pdf. Accessed November 30, 2011.

[17] Yager, pp. 105–106: Chen Cheng, p. 21.

signaled the government's admission of its previous failures in the countryside, its current commitment to rectify itself, and its provision of a different model of gradualist, incentive-based land reform to counter that of the CCP. For both, land reform was also integral to asserting *de facto* control of the countryside, offering new carrots and sticks, and penetrating to the grass roots of rural society. And ideationally, land reform programs were among the most important ways in which these regimes communicated their ethos and preferences to mass rural publics.

The PRC in Sunan and the ROC in Taiwan both claimed that their version of land reform was successful. At the time, these claims were largely accepted by sympathetic outsiders. Subsequent generations of analysts have been less rosy in their assessments, pointing out that land reform never resulted in the huge bursts of sustained agricultural productivity that were promised; nor did it resolve the problem of land parcelization.[18] At the same time, scholars concur that as a redistributive and political policy, land reform in Sunan and Taiwan was extremely successful, creating substantially more equality between farming families and removing entrenched rural elites likely to block the government's attempts to reorder the countryside. By one estimate, land reform in Sunan succeeded in redistributing about 33 percent of the region's agricultural land to about two-thirds of its agricultural households. By another, the five districts of Zhenjiang, Changzhou, Suzhou, Songjiang, and Wuxi redistributed 43.06 percent of Sunan's arable land, while the Shanghai Outer Districts redistributed a smaller proportion (30.83 percent) of its arable land.[19] The ROC/Taiwan's signature Land to the Tiller program of 1953 eventually redistributed 23.4 percent of all Taiwan's farmland to 39.5 percent of Taiwan's farming households, and, in combination with other rural reforms (the revival of Farmer's Associations, Irrigation Associations, and permitting competitive elections for local offices) tied rural Taiwan firmly to the ruling Party.[20]

Cadres in Sunan and the greater Shanghai area also linked land reform to a "new mood" (*xin qifen* – 新 氣氛) in rural villages. This "new mood" encompassed: (1) the consolidation of the people's

---

[18] For the ways in which land reform was an economic disappointment but a great political success, see Stavis, pp. 63–77; Schurmann, p. 437 and Meisner, p. 99.

[19] Robert Ash, "Economic Aspects of Land Reform in Kiangsu, 1949–1952." See also SSTH, "Shanghai shi jiaoqi tudi gaige chengguo tongji" (Land reform statistical results for Shanghai's Outer Districts) and "Sunan qu tudi gaige chengguo tongji" (Land reform statistical results for Sunan districts).

[20] Yager, p. 118. For land reform in Taiwan, the analysis that links land reform (particularly the Land to the Tiller program) to state development is more sanguine: Kuo and Myers, pp. 53–60, and Koo, "Economic Consequences of Land Reform in Taiwan," pp. 150–157.

democratic government dictatorship; (2) village production movements; and (3) (improvement in) peasant life. Consolidation of the people's democratic dictatorship in practice meant mobilizing rural support for the Aid Korea/Resist America movement, the Campaign to Suppress Counterrevolutionaries, and establishment of the People's Government. The "new mood" was also made apparent by rural production campaigns, which included "patriotic production increase competitions" (*aiguo zengchan jingsai* – 愛國增產競賽), the establishment of mutual aid teams, nursery child care for the peak agricultural seasons when peasants were at their busiest, and rural cooperative retail outlets. Direct improvement in peasant life included classes for basic literacy through "blackboard education," village hygiene, and village cultural activities.[21] In Sunan, authorities also claimed that the energy released by land reform campaigns resulted in a substantial expansion of rural associational life. Peasant associations expanded in size from 2,946,825 (or 25.67 percent) of the rural population to 4,417,131 (or 38.47 percent). In the Shanghai outer districts, the percentage was even higher: with an increase of 62.3 percent (from 96,966 to 157,395) of the agricultural population now participating in a peasant association.[22] Youth associations and people's militias also had sharp upturns in membership: youth associations in Shanghai's outer districts saw increases of 52.87 percent, and throughout Sunan peoples' militias grew from 2.7 percent of the population (277,260) to 4.7 percent of the population (485,163).[23] While we have no way of knowing how enthusiastically rural people participated in this wave of CCP organized associational activity, it is quite clear that the young People's Republic intended that the mobilization for the land reform campaign be linked directly to other targets for progressive and revolutionary action, from establishing key units of rural association to the kinds of "modern" activities in rural life that earlier generations of progressives had also attempted (literacy drives, village hygiene), to immediate production drives, and to other ongoing national campaigns. By design, the enthusiasm unleashed by the land reform campaign was meant to carry over into many other rural, regional, and national activities the regime wished to promote.

[21] SSTH. "Tudi gaige hou nongcun xin qifen" (The new mood in villages after land reform).
[22] SSTH. "Sunan qu tudi gaige qianhou nongmin xiehui huiyuan tongji biao" (Statistical form on peasant association numbers before and after land reform) and "Shanghai shi jiaoqu tudi gaige quanhou nonghui huiyuan yezhan qingkuang tongji" (Statistics on numbers of members in peasant associations in the Shanghai outer districts before and after land reform).
[23] SSTH. "Shanghai shi jiaoqu tudi gaige hou qingniantuan zuzhi de fazhan qingkuang tongji" (Statistics on Shanghai outer districts membership in youth associations after land reform).

For its part, the ROC/Taiwan also claimed that its land reform initiative resulted in successful spillovers into other arenas of rural life. Like Sunan, these included increased agricultural yields, and augmented labor and capital investment in land. But unlike the PRC, the ROC/Taiwan also made much of the effects of land reform in increasing rural incomes through better incentives and greater application of the principles of "scientific farming." Guomindang officials also explicitly linked the Land to the Tiller program to a measurable spike in a higher standard of living for rural families, increased enrolment of children in school, and increased numbers of farmers in public office. This bump upwards in rural living standards was indicated by such measures as the square footage of newly built houses (an annual average increase of 374,455 square feet in the three years before the Land to the Tiller program to 1,139,143 square feet in the three years after the Land to the Tiller program), a doubling in the number of new bicycles bought (from 10,795 to 21,543 per annum), and a dramatic increase in the number of radios bought (151 per annum in the pre-1953 and 1,103 per annum post 1953).[24]

Despite the different repertoires each adopted in pushing through land reform campaigns, many of the rhetorical framings and relevant diagnoses of rural problems that undergirded land reform programs in Sunan and Taiwan were nearly identical, and converged with the global developmental norms of the time. Both shared a distaste for the "inefficiency" of small freeholder-based, "fragmented" agriculture and an affinity for the big, visible, and noticeable projects emblematic of mid-twentieth century modernity: concrete, dams, infrastructure, and factories.[25] The

[24] Chen Cheng, Table 4, "Improvement of Farmer's Living Conditions Before and After the Implementation of the Land to the Tiller Program in Taiwan Province," p. 88. In this classic text, written by the reformist GMD governor of Taiwan in 1960 to justify both the GMD's land reform programs and their sharp (and better) differences with the land reform (and collectivization) in the People's Republic of China, Chen Cheng also includes several tables to "prove" the efficacy of Taiwan's land reform that are at best spurious. For example, Table 13, "Number of School Age Children and School-Going Children Before and After the Land Reform in Taiwan Province," p. 314, gives figures for the entire ten-year period between 1948 and 1959 (which was presumably the last year that statistics were available before the book's publication). By 1948, the percentage of school-going children in Taiwan was already high by the standards of developing countries at 77.10 percent. In every single year between 1948 and 1959, the percentage of school-going children increased, and in the early years of the 1950s it increased by between 0.90 percent (1949) and 3.8 percent (1953). By 1955 the percentage stood at 92.30 percent. Although the pattern was one of steady, incremental increase, it is notable that the ex-governor of Taiwan felt it important to link a rural social good (increased school attendance) with land reform.

[25] The literature here is vast. James Scott's seminal overview *Seeing Like a State: How Certain Schemes to Improve the Human Condition Have Failed* relies on examples that apply the core principles of Taylorism and scientific management to other sectors. For

long years of struggle in the countryside for the CCP led to a more ambivalent stance on big industry and cities as emblematic of dissoluteness and corruption as well as modernity, but this squeamishness was temporarily suspended when the young PRC adopted the Soviet model of urban privilege and crash state-led industrialization in the early 1950s.[26] The place agriculture had in the developmental profiles of China and Taiwan also converged. The CCP and GMD both held that land reform was economically desirable (to lay the groundwork for further consolidation and efficiency in agriculture), socially necessary, desired (if not actively demanded) from "below," and politically paramount. Indeed, the very legitimacy of the regime in the countryside was presumed to depend on the successful implementation of land reform.

Given this substantial convergence of opinion from such bitter political rivals, it is startling to read contemporary materials from Sunan and Taiwan that make clear that in neither was land reform in the early 1950s obviously economically necessary, populist, or particularly demanded from below. Official publications and reports on land reform contain data indicating that in both Sunan and Taiwan, tenancy was already in sharp decline in the years immediately prior to the 1950s, and the economic position of most landlords was already quite weak.[27] In both, significant numbers in the rural population had already diversified their income streams by engaging in agriculture only part time or had moved out of agriculture altogether for more lucrative and prestigious jobs. For example, the JCRR's report on land reform in 1954 stated that in 1950, before rent-reduction programs were implemented with some vigor, only slightly more than half of Taiwan's total population was classified as agricultural (3,745,803 of 7,555,558). Of this, almost half of the population (a total of 682,467 farming households) only 35.8 percent were classified as tenants (in contrast to the 57.7 percent classified as owner cultivators or part-owner cultivators). This was an already significant drop from just before Taiwan's retrocession to China in 1945, when 60 percent of the population was engaged in agriculture.[28] More significantly, the relative proportion of tenant-cultivated land in Taiwan had been dropping precipitously for some time. In 1939, tenants cultivated 56.3 percent of Taiwan's agricultural land, but by 1950 tenanted land

---

more China-centered representative examples, see David Pietz, *Engineering the State: The Huai River and Reconstruction in Nationalist China* (Routledge, 2002).

[26] Schurmann, pp. 239–271: Deborah Kaple, *Dream of a Red Factory* pp. 55–71.

[27] Kathleen Bernhardt, *Rents, Taxes, and Peasant Resistance: The Lower Yangzi Region 1840–1950*, pp. 220–224.

[28] Tseng Hsiao (Zeng Xiao), *The Theory and Practice of Land Reform*, p. 82, which in turn cites the *Taiwan Agricultural Year Book*, compiled by the Taiwan Provincial Department of Agriculture and Forestry.

accounted for only 40.6 percent, and over the next two years the proportion would plummet to 34.5 percent, although there is almost universal
agreement that the reduction of tenanted land in the early 1950s was an
entirely sensible reaction to the widespread anticipation of the kind of
compulsory land sales that the Land to the Tiller Act did in fact implement in 1953–1954.[29]

Reports written by frustrated CCP officials in the outer districts and
nearer counties around Shanghai in 1950 and 1951 paint a similar picture. Time and again, they wrote that most landlords were smallholders
who only rented out a portion of their holdings. In the far outer districts of
the municipality of Shanghai that were rural and otherwise indistinguishable from the nearer Sunan counties, much of the male working population only worked in agriculture part time. Most aspired to becoming
factory workers and many migrated, at least part time, to where the
factories were. Absentee landlords were extremely common, and economic and social relations were "very complicated." Some cadres went
as far as to warn against imposing methods of "pure class struggle"
(*danchun douzheng* – 單純鬥爭) that were inapplicable at best and coun-
terproductive at worst. In the outlaw-riven marshes just east of Shanghai
proper, landlords were "of many types, simultaneously engaged with
industry or other kinds of work."[30] The tactic of drawing hard "objective"
lines between exploiters and exploited that had served the Chinese
Communist Party so well as a means of "stirring up" the rural population
in favor of the land reform campaign in North China simply did not play
well in Sunan, where conditions were so utterly different. Across Sunan,
the percentage of the rural population classified as agricultural ranged
widely from a low of just under half in Shanghai's inner suburb of
Yangjing (38,835 of a total population of 80,280 or 48.38 percent) to
Shanghai county's more typical nearly 90 percent (146,955 of 164,457,
or 89.35 percent).[31] In Sunan in general, but in Shanghai's ex-urban
districts in particular, even smallholders of modest means frequently
rented out their land while "laboring" in other sectors, and it was equally

[29] See Hui-sun Tang, "Table Showing the Total Population and Agricultural Population of
Taiwan Province, 1940–1952" (p. 12), "Table Showing Different Kinds of Farming
Families in Taiwan Province, 1940–1952" (p. 13), and "Table Showing the areas of
Owner-Cultivated and Non-Owner Cultivated Land in Taiwan Province, 1939–1952"
(p. 14).

[30] SMA A71/2/82. "Yangjing qu tugai gongzuo zongjie baogao (1)"(Yangqing land reform
summary district report), November 16, 1951.

[31] These figures are drawn from SMA A71/2/1599, "Yangjing qu tugai qianhou qingkuang
tongji biao" (Yangwing district statistics for before and after land reform) and MHA
13/1/37 "Shanghai xian quxiang xingzheng jianzhi ji hukou tongji biao" (Shanghai
county district and village administrative establishment and household registration statistical form), 1951.

commonplace for those whose primary occupations were in other sectors either to buy or to keep some land that would be rented out. Under these circumstances superiors found "some [local] cadres [to be] muddle headed" in their footdragging and inability to rouse the masses to a "high tide" of public vitriol against landlords at mass accusation sessions. Meanwhile, "some" cadres grumbled loudly enough about their misfortune (*daomei* – 倒霉) in being tasked to implement what they considered to be impossible, only to be to be heard and reported to higher levels.[32]

Social investigation work under the Guomindang in Taiwan was not nearly as prominent a feature of regime consolidation as it was in the People's Republic. The reports that were commissioned and the statistics that were deemed important in preparation for land reform in the early 1950s included little to no data on the sources of farm income, patterns of migration, and rates of urbanization that feature so prominently in the local reports in preparation for land reform in Sunan. However, it stands to reason that if nearly half of Taiwan's population was not engaged in agriculture by 1950, then that half must have been engaged in other kinds of economic activity. And if the share of the Taiwanese population engaged in agriculture dropped from 60 percent on retrocession to 50 percent in 1950, then some 10 percent of Taiwan's working population had made the move into other sectors in the very recent past. As was the case in Sunan, most Taiwanese landlords were medium or smallholders, roughly half of whom were also engaged in agricultural labor, even if they did rent out a portion of their land.[33]

More problematically, there appeared to be embarrassingly little *a priori* enthusiasm for overturning the class order as stipulated by the CCP in Sunan or in actively participating in land reform in Taiwan, despite regime insistence that land reform was necessary and popular. Preliminary investigations of the outlying districts of Shanghai suggested that land ownership patterns and types of "exploitation" were both "very complicated." Particularly in the districts close to the city proper, definable landlords of any description only owned a fraction of the land, handicraft workshops and small factories were already ubiquitous, land renting was subcontracted to people outside the local area, and petty rentiers with multiple sources of income comprised the largest group of

---

[32] MDA 13/1/35. "Shanghai xian "Diyi leixing xiang dashu zongjie" (Shanghai county, No. 1 type village: Dashu village summary report), February 1, 1951.

[33] SMA A71/1/71. "Shanghai shi jiaoqu tudi gaige zongjie" (Shanghai municipal outer district land reform summary report), November 25, 1952, and Guoshiguan (GSG) 313/1285–3, FY 52, Hui-sun Tang, "A Proposed Plan for Private Land Purchase in Taiwan," March 11, 1952.

landholders.[34] What little class hatred existed was expressed as grumbling against the rent collectors for the occasional larger absentee landlord, but even in these circumstances there did not seem to be a great deal of underlying resentment for the regime to tap. Reports from the *jiaoqu* make it clear that the most severe local tensions in rural and semi-rural areas around Shanghai were neither between landlord and tenant, nor even between tenant and rent collector, but between long-established residents and impoverished incoming migrants, often those deemed "squatters" by those already in residence.[35] Indeed the early stages of the land reform campaign in Sunan from early July to mid November 1950 almost ran aground in the face of the profound lack of enthusiasm for stirring up class consciousness by either cadres or the rural population.

Formulaic reports of cadres engaged in "actively enthusiastic work" (*jiji reqing gongzuo* – 積極熱情工作), raising class consciousness (*tigao jieji juewu* – 提高階級覺悟), and "obtaining definite work experience" (*gongzuo shang qude yiding de jingyan* – 工作上取得一定的經驗) concealed a great deal of cadre confusion. At the outset of the campaign many cadres were bewildered by the precepts of the campaign. Its insistence on land reform juxtaposed Marxist notions that "scientifically" justified the campaign by insisting on the imposition of new class categories (i.e. landlords as exploiters) with demands for mass participation through the tried and trusted technique of "stirring up the masses" (*fadong qunzhong* – 發動群眾). In Sunan these categories flew in the face of what was "scientifically" verifiable through investigation into land holding, land rental, rural occupation and local income streams. Many local cadres must have experienced a severe disconnect between the categories they were expected to work with, and the realities of the rural social and economic circumstances in which they were exercising state authority.

For example, in the inner suburban district of semi-industrial Wusong, the population was dutifully classified as 1.1 percent landlord, 1.2 percent landlord mixed with other occupations, 1.1 percent rich peasant, 22.3 middle peasant, 25.9 percent poor peasant, 1.9 percent "in commerce," 32.6 percent workers, 9.7 percent petty rentiers, and 1.8 percent either unclassified or other. But the text of the report makes clear that the very few of those classified as peasants were in fact engaged in agriculture full time, and of those that were, the majority were either recent incomers to the area and/or were female. Land tenure was "extremely complicated,"

---

[34] SMA B14/1/21. "Shanghai shi jiaoqu tugai gongzuo baogao" (Work Report on Land Reform in Shanghai's outer districts), February 21, 1951.

[35] SMA A71/2/81. "Wusong qu tudi gaige baogao 1951" (Wusong district land reform report 1951), November 18, 1951, p. 105 of file.

with no fewer than five quite complex different kinds of "exploitative" land rental arrangements in place, and the report admitted that even a full year after the beginning of the land reform campaign that the masses had really never come to be sufficiently "stirred up."[36] In a situation in which petty rentiers outnumbered identifiable landlords by a factor of almost ten to one and almost all those designated "peasants" relied on multiple sources of income, it is little wonder that "the class line was unclear" (*jieji luxian bu mingque* – 階級路綫不 明確). "Some" cadres thought that after a month of training it was possible to go out and implement "pure study" (*danchun xuexi* – 單純學習), but on encountering reality in the field, they came to the unacceptable conclusion that "there were few landlords . . . [which led to] doubt that land reform could actually stir up the masses." Such honest cadre reports on actual rural conditions in Sunan cut no ice with superiors, who responded somewhat testily that the remedy for such shortcomings was further study of appropriate models, notably from the land reform experiences of cadres in Zhejiang, who had "unified theory and practice" in an exemplary fashion.[37]

It was the *political* imposition of will from above, rather than anything that was immediately economically necessary or popularly demanded from below that broke through the dissimulation, bewilderment, and foot dragging of local state officials in Sunan. A major work conference on the implementation of land reform in Sunan was held in Shanghai in November 1950, at which local cadres were put on notice that their repeated excuses ("*my* village doesn't have any exploiters") would no longer be accepted. After the Shanghai work conference, the land reform campaign in Sunan abruptly moved into a much more radical stage. The conference's insistence on stringent implementation of guidelines from above concentrated the minds of the state's local agents and overcame delay and obfuscation, but also led to predictable problems. As local cadres scrambled to be seen to be more vigorous in their prosecution of the land reform and meet their targets, campaign implementation lurched uncontrollably leftward, culminating in uncounted instances of "indiscriminate struggle and indiscriminate beating" (*luandou luanda* – 亂鬥亂打) that in turn alienated some peasants, puzzled many more, and even dismayed the compilers of a report on the subject for the Investigation Department of the Sunan District Land Reform Committee. After the Land Reform Conference, cadres throughout Sunan started routinely to disregard earlier regulations and guidelines.

[36] SMA A71/2/81. "Wusong qu tugai gongzuo baogao," pp. 100–105 of file.
[37] Ibid. pp. 117–118 of file.

For example, rules that required "uniting with" middle peasants and absolutely forbade targeting them collided head on with the principle that the subjects of struggle sessions had to be those who were "hated most" by the masses. In Sunan those who were most hated by the masses were often neither landlords, nor even absentee landlords, but were those who stayed local and had actively collaborated with a succession of Japanese-dominated regimes during the War of Resistance between 1937 and 1945. These ex-collaborators were frequently middle peasants. In Sunan at least, those who aroused the most hatred were those whom their neighbors considered to be *political* traitors, not those the regime defined as *economic* exploiters. Joining with middle peasants and insisting on "stirred up" masses whose targets were those most hated with the most blood debts were in clear contradiction, but campaign guidelines gave no hints as to how to resolve this problem. In addition, while the campaign forbade cadres from conducting struggle sessions against the relatives of "exploiters," local authorities frequently did substitute the mothers, wives or adolescent sons of landlords as objects of struggle to replace absentees, and this practice was also disapproved of by the masses.[38]

One of the chronic headaches for cadres in Sunan was that the region's economic and social structure simply did not produce sufficient numbers of exploitative landlords who were sufficiently hated by the masses to meet the bureaucratic demand from above to put on public accusation sessions. In Shanghai county's rural Dashu xiang, there were a mere four landlord households from a total of 789, and of these, two were "commercial landlords" (*gongshangye dizhu*), one had fled, and the sole remaining landlord worked his own fields, had no major discernible crimes or failings, and was well liked by the local villagers. Ultimately, the best that the local authorities could do by way of struggle targets in Dashu was to produce two individuals, neither of whom was a landlord. Although the archives do not reveal exactly what crimes against the people he had committed, the first target was a "bandit" (*tufei* – 土匪) by the name of Zhu Jiejun. Zhu was so reviled that it was very straightforward for the local cadres to mobilize the local community against him. In fact, people came to be so "stirred up" that even after Zhu committed suicide while in custody, the crowd that was gathered for the scheduled public accusation session against him demanded that his corpse be displayed to receive continued public accusations. The second target was a "village bully" by the name of Tang Luoxiong, who was handed over to the district

---

[38] SMA B14/1/21. "Shanghai shi jiaoqu tugai gongzuo baogao" (Work Report on Land Reform in Shanghai's outer districts), February 21, 1951; JPA 3006/3/271, "Guanyu fadong qunzhong douzheng de cailiao zhailü" (Notes on materials relating to stirring up the masses' struggle), April 1951.

center authorities in Beiqiao to be the object of an enlarged, district wide "united struggle session" attended by thousands in May, 1951. Tang disappears from the public record after he was handed over to the district, and we have no further information about what happened to him, but it is likely that one whose "crimes" were serious enough to merit being the subject of a district-wide enlarged accusation meeting was executed immediately after the conclusion of the meeting.[39]

Although the bureaucratic incentives from above to foment class struggle, stir up the masses, and make a proper example of exploitative landlords were intense after November 1950, Sunan's deficit in the "right" kinds of landlords ripe for struggle resulted in local cadres making rough approximations in their choice of targets: typically by targeting those deemed counterrevolutionary, or "evil bullies" as either credible dangers to the regime, or genuinely hated by the masses, or both. In this way, local cadres could fill out the forms indicating their compliance with the repertoire dictated from above of convening mass accusation sessions to "stir up the masses." But these rough guesses could and did lead to other issues. As we saw in Chapter 2, the category of "evil bully" was much more subjectively determined than those of *tewu* counterrevolutionary, for which there was a definable standard confirmed by paperwork. Similarly, landlords were defined by objective and measurable criteria of landholding and income derived from "exploitation." In many cases the category of "evil bully"/"exploiter hated by the masses" opened the door to local grudges and/or targeting whichever local elites had previously collaborated with the Japanese. It was an easy enough matter to round up the usual suspects. It was infinitely more difficult to find suspects who fulfilled the necessary criteria in a location such as Sunan, where there were numerous opportunities to move out of agriculture and/or migrate.

Even when authorities singled out a likely "exploiter," the "masses" might not fall into line. The "exploited" had agency, and could well not self-identify as particularly exploited and downtrodden by landlords, even after the educative measures of the early part of the campaign. In some locations in Sunan, notably the sub-district of Hufeng in Wujin county, and the Chendu subdistrict of Jinsong county, the masses continued to hold embarrassingly positive opinions of their own local landlords insisting "that our landlords are all pretty good people." In Hufeng, even after the local landlord was hauled off to jail, the masses continued to refer to him by the honorific "Mr." (*xiansheng* – 先生), while in Fengguan's

---

[39] MDA 13/1/35. "Shanghai xian, di'yi lei xiang dashu xiang zongjie" (Shanghai county, No. 1 type village: dashu village summary report), February 1, 1951.

Piaoyang District, villagers insisted that "[their] landlords were honest and true, and were 'laboring landlords' (*laodong dizhu* – 勞動地主) [rather than exploiters]." In this case, the masses even suggested that such good landlords ought to be eligible for participation in the local peasant association, and did not understand why local cadres did not permit this. Some of these details suggest implicitly that on the eve of land reform, in at least parts of the Sunan countryside, many landlords continued to be seen by their poorer neighbors to be a source of protection, literacy, support in a time of need, or simply as extensions of local family networks. In the aforementioned case of Chendu, Jinsong, villagers continued to insist that their landlord was a good person, literate, reasonable, deft at smoothing over day-to-day problems, and even willing to help out the less fortunate as a go-between for matchmaking. In Xibing, such was the local feeling towards one local landlord that the masses sent food to him while he was incarcerated pending his struggle session. Even those the regime labeled as bandits or local bullies were not necessarily hated. In Yangjiawan a captured "bandit" (*tufei* – 土匪) was so popular that two hundred people gathered outside the local public security bureau to protest his arrest. In yet another documented case in Jiangxi village, Lianxu district, Jinsong county, poor peasants were moved to take up a collection to help tide over the accused landlord's mother.[40]

The kinds of richly textured reports from Sunan that decried the lamentable state of peasant consciousness during the early stages of the land reform campaign were never generated in Taiwan. But careful reading of otherwise bland official reports reveals hints that the early stages of land reform in Taiwan were also met with significant lack of interest, stonewalling, and occasional quiet resistance. In a paper given to a general conference on world land tenure issues in Madison, Wisconsin in November 1951, Tang Hui-sun, then head of the JCRR Land Division, wrote about the problems of the first stages of the rent reduction program in Taiwan with a frankness that is elusive in his later, glowing summary report on the land to the tiller program in 1954. In 1951, he cited figures of over 10,000 cases of "voluntary" lease termination between landlord and tenant, widespread collusion between landlord and tenant in which

---

[40] JPA 3006/3/271. "Guanyu fadong qunzhong douzheng de cailiao zhailü" (Notes on materials relating to stirring up the masses' struggle), Sunan Tugai Jiancha chu, April, 1951. Since the compiler of these investigation notes clearly had a bias towards illustrating how poorly the peasantry of Sunan was responding to the call to be "stirred up," there is no way to ascertain how frequent or typical these responses were. However, that these limp and noncompliant responses were recorded at all marks a significant departure from the more typical formulaic insistence on enthusiastic and stirred-up masses, and suggests that these kinds of reactions were much more widespread than the occasional allusion to bored or "not stirred up" masses in most official reports might otherwise suggest.

the latter pretended to be a hired laborer rather than a tenant, and false sales whereby the tenant would formally purchase the rented land and then resell to the original landlord at a higher price.[41] Official accounts invariably framed the collusion, false sales, and "voluntary" lease terminations as evidence of the economic weakness and lack of education of tenants vis-à-vis landlords that required even stronger action on the part of the state to ensure a fairer playing field. But even official JCRR materials admit that "there were cases wherein the [lease] termination was made actually with the consent of the tenant because the latter was a relative of the landlord and wanted to help him out of his economic difficulties."[42] This kind of activity can equally be understood as low level, widespread resistance to the state's new intrusiveness in rural relations, and a probable reflection of the power of longstanding customary obligations between landlord and tenant in the face of outsider interference.

Campaign "Bleed" in Labeling and Dispatching Landlords

Although they did so in characteristically different ways, land reform campaigns in Sunan and Taiwan converged with campaigns to suppress real and imagined internal enemies in the Campaign to Suppress Counterrevolutionaries (for Sunan) and the White Terror (for Taiwan) in the early 1950s. This was particularly the case in the peri-urban areas around Shanghai and other cities in Sunan in the spring of 1951, when the land reform campaign's "high tide" was in practice indistinguishable from the "high tide" of the Campaign to Suppress Counterrevolutionaries. We have already seen that in Sunan many of the individuals singled out for prosecution and struggle in the land reform campaign were not even landlords, and were often assigned other, less objectively determinable labels within the broad category of counterrevolutionary, such as such as traitor (*hanjian* – 漢奸) or evil bully (*e'ba* – 惡霸). For example, in Shanghai County, then a rural county administratively separate from the "far outer districts" (*yuan jiaoqu* – 遠郊區) of Shanghai proper, of the 493 individuals arrested and processed in the land reform campaign, only

---

[41] GSG 313/1285–3, FY 52, Hui-sun Tang, "Rent Reduction and Land Purchase Program in Formosa," unpublished paper given to the Conference on World Land Tenure Problems, University of Wisconsin, Madison, November 2, 1951. Official accounts cite this amount of collusion, false sales, and "voluntary" lease terminations as evidence of the weakness of tenants vis-à-vis landlords, and the unfair advantage that landlords held over their tenants; another way to read this is as evidence of massive, low-level resistance on the part of landlords and tenants to the intrusion of the state into rural relations.

[42] *JCRR*, p. 29.

roughly half (243, or 49.3 percent) were deemed to have any kind of landlord status at all. Of the remaining 250, 87 (17.65 percent) were labeled "evil bullies" (e'ba – 惡霸), 44 (8.92 percent) counterrevolutionaries (fangeming –反革命), 7 (1.42 percent) the leaders of counterrevolutionary sects (fandong huimen tou – 反動會門頭), and a suspiciously large catch-all category of "other" (qita – 其他) at 110 (22.31 percent). From this overall figure of 493, only 121 – roughly a quarter of the total (24.54 percent) – were identified with an objectively determinable negative political status such as the GMD Three People's Principles Corps, tewu (GMD "special affairs"), or leadership of a proscribed religious sect.[43] In the Shanghai jiaoqu, the picture was similarly complicated. Not surprisingly, given the frequent influx of newcomers and the paucity of inhabitants engaged in full-time agriculture, in inner districts like Yangjing, significant numbers of those targeted were not landlords, either. In Yangjing, thirty out of seventy-eight (38.46 percent) were either rich peasants, the peculiar hybrid category of "half businessman-half landlord" (banshang bandizhu – 半商半 地主), or "other."

Although it is impossible to gauge how typical Shanghai county was, there is a good deal of evidence that suggests that throughout Sunan there were substantial departures in practice from the ostensible targets of the land reform campaign. As of May 1951, in three combined villages in the Zhenjiang Special District's Gaowan district, only half of those struggled against (74 out of 145) were landlords, while in Dantu's Zhundao Xiejiao, less than half were landlords (22 of 48 or 45.83 percent), with the other "targets" middle peasants (17 out of 48 or 35.41 percent), poor peasants (3 out of 48), and businessmen (6 out of 48/ 6.25 percent). In other areas of Sunan the percentages of landlords were even lower: in Linnan, Wujin County only 9 out of 32 (28.15 percent) were landlords, with the rest "rich peasants, middle peasants, and petty rentiers." Where they exist, the early and incomplete statistics on the numbers of the "targets" who committed suicide under the pressure of the land reform campaign also point to a campaign environment in which surprisingly large numbers of those targeted in what was ostensibly a campaign against landlord exploitation and overconcentration of land were not landlords at all; in Changshu county, only 10 out of 25 (40 percent) who committed suicide in custody were landlords.[44]

---

[43] MDA 13/1/37 "Shanghai xian jiesu tugai gongzuo douzheng qingkuang tongji biao (2)" (Shanghai county final statistics on struggle work), November 18, 1951. The statistician who filled was off by two in his account. The form indicates a total of 493, but the sub-categories add up to only 491.

[44] JPA 3006/3/271. These numbers are all drawn from the text of the Sunan Tugai Jiancha Chu, "Guanyu fadong qunzhong de cailiao zhailü," April 1951.

Since the authorities in Taiwan did not record numbers in a way that incorporated class status and occupation around questions of land reform, and had every incentive to put land reform in the most positive possible light, the statistical evidence from Taiwan does not reveal which households (if any) actually suffered as a result of land reform. But as was the case in Sunan, there was a real, if unacknowledged, overlap between the contemporaneous security crackdown and land reform in Taiwan. Beyond occasional oblique references to effective land reform being the best way to contain unrest and disorder in the countryside, as "by 1948, the villages in Taiwan … were also showing signs of unrest and instability," the relentlessly civilian documents of the JCRR betray little hint of the White Terror round-ups that were raging in the early 1950s.[45] The records of Taiwan Garrison Command, on the other hand, display no such reticence and make clear that those who resisted land reform measures were prosecuted under the official category of "lawless landlords" (*feifa dizhu* – 非法地主). "Lawless landlords" in turn fell into one category in a wider set of martial law classifications, which also singled out actors (counterfeiters, smugglers) who under other circumstances might have simply been categorized as petty criminals rather than "rebels" (*panluan zhe* – 叛亂者).

The "lawless landlords" who resisted land reform were not the only rural people to fall afoul of the state's crackdown against putative subversion. As detailed in Chapter 3, local magistrates who, like Lin Rigao, were seen to be overly zealous in implementing the 375 Rent Reduction policy could be accused of being Communist (because presumably it would only be a true Communist who would take government directives for social justice quite that seriously). On the other hand, anyone whose actions smacked of resistance to either rent reduction (in 1950 and 1951) or to the Land to the Tiller program (in 1953–1954), was also fair game for suppression. Individuals who were even seen to be in the possession of reading material that discussed alternative visions of land reform were singled out for scrutiny, included in larger "cases" (*anjian* – 案件), and harshly punished for "sedition " under the strictures of martial law.[46] The closer campaigns

---

[45] T. H. Shen, p. 57; see also Cheng Chen, pp. 47–48.

[46] For examples of statistical forms that include landlords as a subversive category see "Taiwan sheng bao'an silingbu junfachu 41 niandu shenjie anjian gao shenfen tongji-biao" (Taiwan provincial security command, Martial law section: 1952 statistical review of high status cases), in NZASH Vol. 1, p. 85. Examples of including recalcitrant land-lords and local notables in larger networks of "subversion" can be found in "Liang Yunhan An" (the case of Liang Yunhan), NCA document # 0042/1571//33901034/ 105/001, and "Xie Ruiren an" (the case of Xie Ruiren, NCA, document # 0039/ 3132023/23/1/001).

of suppression and "cleansing" got to rural grass roots in Taiwan, the more likely they were to run up against these kinds of alternative visions.

In 2008, the Taiwan Foundation for Compensating Improper Verdicts on Sedition (FCIV) in the Martial Law Era very kindly aided me by searching its database for cases whose official judgments (*panjue* – 判決) that included key words referring to land reform (*tudi gaige* – 土地改革) and 375 rent reduction　(*sanqiwu* – 三七五). This search resulted in a list of 159 individuals who were punished, sometimes very severely, for participating in, or even being aware of, a different version of land reform than that being promoted by the regime in the early 1950s. The highest concentrations of opposition to the regime were clustered in the country-side of three counties of Taoyuan (57 or 35.84 percent of 159), Tainan (24 or 15.09 percent), and Miaoli (18 or 11.32 percent). Other counties only accounted for between one and seven individuals charged and pun-ished on these grounds.[47] The sentences handed down for these charges ranged from the relatively light (a year of re-education) to the incredibly severe (death penalty).

To see how these dynamics played out in practice, consider the case of the Madou Branch of the Tainan District Taiwan Work Committee. At the height of the White Terror in 1950, the Taiwan Garrison Command prosecuted some thirty-five individuals it associated with this case. Along with the usual charges of providing the leadership for an underground branch of the Communist Party in traitorous preparation for the arrival of the Communists in Taiwan, one of the most serious accusations levied upon the presumptive leaders of this group was that they "had organized a small group to take over the governing of the [local] 375 (Rent Reduction Committee) and had encouraged [land] tenants to engage in struggle, destruction, and spread disorder."[48] In another case prosecuted in 1953 that eventually expanded to encompass upwards of seventy-five indivi-duals, the mere accusation of possessing a copy of the Communist Land Reform Law was more than enough to warrant prosecution as a Communist rebel.[49] In the Taiwan of the early 1950s, it was evidently only those government officials in charge of deliberating the form that land reform would take who were at liberty to read anything as subversive as the Communist Land Reform Law. Those on the receiving end of land reform

---

[47] FCIV printout, "Quyu tongji biao" (District Statistics [on individual cases of those charged with sedition on grounds of land reform and rent reduction activity]). August 26, 2010.

[48] "Xie Ruiren An" (The Case of Xie Ruiren), National Central Archive [NCA], document ~0039/3132023/23/1/001.

[49] "Liang Yunhan An" (The Case of Liang Yunhan), NCA ~0042/1571/33901034/105/001.

policies were not even to be permitted to be seen in close proximity to such potentially dangerous material. Anyone who stood out during the land reform campaigns of the early 1950s ran the risk of serious trouble because there were so many ways to attract the suspicion of the authorities. One could be accused for obstructing the GMD's version of land reform, for discussing an alternative vision of land reform, or even for promoting the GMD's own land reform policies with too much vigor and enthusiasm.

Even when it did not directly accuse peasants of being Communist due to supporting the "wrong" kind of land reform, the "White Terror" also hit hard at very local level rural associations if the organization in question was neither established, nor penetrated by the state. This particularly seems to have been the case in Tainan county, which in the estimation of the Nationalist security apparatus was especially stroppy and restive.[50] One of these, named the Ox Plowing Society (Niuli hui – 牛犁會) was charged with having set up a local branch of a Communist network at the behest of proven Communist agent Li Madou (李媽兜), whom we met a chapter ago. Li Madou's junior co-conspirators were named in the documents as Huang X, Zhou X (Laotong), and Feng X (Jin), who were charged in absentia with continued rural agitation against the 375 Rent Reduction measures. After Huang, Zhou, and Feng fled the area after Li Madou's arrest, local security swooped into the village of Zhongying in Tainan county, claiming that an active branch of the Ox Plowing Society had been set up in the village with the express intention of agitating against the 375 Rent Reduction Program.

This charge rang especially hollow. None of the presumed leaders of the Ox Plowing Society were young, educated, had any history of leftist agitation, had any demonstrated involvement with Communists, or had any known connection to the Li Madou network other than the misfortune of general geographical proximity. All but one of the accused (of sixteen) were local farmers aged between thirty-three and fifty-seven. Most were illiterate tenants. When brought in for interrogation, one tenant by the name of Zhou Zhuling, who was eventually freed without further charge, insisted under torture that he could not even read or write his own name, much less know anything about seditious secret organizations. After the police beat Zhou several times, drenched him with water, and extracted a promise that he would tell all honestly, they asked him whether he ever engaged in labor pooling with other tenants. Zhou responded that "yes – in order to do the plowing in preparation for the

---

[50] Nearly half of the disputes over leases between tenant and landlord for the entire island (4,190 of 9,098) in the first half of 1951 were in the Tainan agricultural region. *JCRR* "Number of Lease Termination Disputes Raised and Settled in Taiwan," p. 166.

release of (irrigation) water,[51] [we do] help each other out without officially hiring [each other]" after which he released from custody.[52] Zhou
was one of the luckier ones. Others accused of being in the Niuli Hui were
much less fortunate, with jail terms of between two and fifteen years'
imprisonment.

More research needs to be done into the formation of the Niuli Hui and
similar rural mutual help arrangements to ascertain whether in fact any of
these were actual left-leaning associations (*hui*) that existed outside the
imagination of overly exercised security agents, and if so, whether they
had any links to speak of with Communists. Communists certainly would
dearly have loved to penetrate these kinds of pre-existing rural associations, and it is within the realm of possibility that they sometimes managed to so do. But if the Niuli Hui was typical of the kinds of informal self-
help associations that existed all over rural Taiwan, there is scant evidence
that they were under Communist influence. Between Zhou's responses of
stupefied disbelief to be accused of being a Communist, the meaning of
the Niuli Hui (Ox Plowing Society), the Guomindang's known lack
of tolerance for any form of organization that was not directly penetrated
by the GMD, and its extraordinary paranoia in the early 1950s, it is likely
that the Niuli Hui was nothing more than an informal local association
formed during the Japanese colonial period for pooling labor and sharing
draft animals at peak agricultural seasons. Such arrangements were common in rural Taiwan (and China, where they became the basis for mutual
aid teams shortly after land reform was completed). Rice paddy cultivation is notorious for its heavy inputs of labor, particularly when irrigation
water is set to be released downstream, because plowing and transplant-
ing seedlings need to be done quickly, lest the precious water be wasted.
The harsh treatment of the Niuli hui suggests that even an informal and
innocuous seasonal association that remained outside the direct oversight
and control of the Guomindang was suspect and ripe for suppression,
particularly if it was in any way suspected of articulating a vision for land
reform outside the officially designated one.

Establishing Hegemonies and Telling Stories

Land reform in the countryside of Sunan and Taiwan proved to be as
much a reflection of regime hegemony as it was a set of techniques to

---

[51] In the heavily irrigated Taiwan plain, labor short seasons were timed around the release of
water from irrigation associations upstream.
[52] Shan Tianlu, *Nanying Baise Kongbu zhi* (Nanying White Terror Gazeteer), pp. 114–121.
The details of Zhou's interrogation are from an interview Shan Tianlu conducted with
Zhou in Zhongying village, Xiaying town, Tainan County, on April 3, 2000.

impose regime hegemony. Both had to convince large numbers of their relevant publics that not only was land reform critically important, but also that the way in which each implemented its variant of land reform was uniquely valid and legitimate. In North China, where the CCP's repertoires of land reform had been refined and carried out, there was enough convergence between the party's cardinal tenet of the desirability/necessity of land reform and the "objective" rural conditions of land tenure and immiseration that these were credible claims. Eyewitness accounts by sympathetic outsiders like Hinton and the Crooks present enough vignettes to confirm the population's genuine enthusiasm for the method and the outcome of land reform.[53] But the CCP's campaign repertoires for land reform did not travel well to central and south China, where rural conditions were very different. Nor were the circumstances in which the government found itself in 1950–1951 like those in the late 1940s, when the CCP needed to fire up support to stiffen resolve for the civil war. After an initial year in power in which inclusiveness and moderation ruled, the government needed to convince its own cadres and larger publics that violent, abrupt land reform was necessary to smash feudalism. Gradualist and inclusive methods applied to land reform as "peaceful division of the land" (*heping fentian* – 和平分田) were suddenly singled out as unacceptably "fake." Local cadres charged with implementing the land reform campaign needed to be converted not only to the completion of land reform, but to activating the CCP's specifically mandated repertoires of campaign implementation: "stirring up the masses" (*fadong qunzhong*), and cathartic "face to face struggle" (*mian dui mian douzheng* – 面對面鬥爭) in front of the masses.[54]

Local cadres were inculcated into this repertoire in several ways. They intensively studied official land reform regulations, learned about the wicked and exploitative nature of landlords, attended meetings and conferences that clarified what higher levels of the party-state expected of local levels in how they went about implementing the land reform campaign, and occasionally received outside teams that further guided the process. After the Sunan government chose sixty-one experimental villages for their representativeness in the late summer of 1950,[55] they

---

[53] The sympathetic eyewitness accounts of Hinton and the Crooks present a good deal of evidence to confirm that the methods and outcomes of land reform were popular; later works by Wou and Goodman corroborate the view of the masses as receptive, active participants in the land reform campaigns of Shanxi and Henan.

[54] JPA 3006/3/271, "Guanyu fadong qunzhong douzheng de cailiao zhailü." April, 1951: MDA 3–2-33, Sunan tudi gaige gongzuo de zongjie cao'an" (Draft summary report on Sunan land reform work), December, 28, 1951.

[55] MDA 3/2/33, ibid.

learned from the experiences of those villages that had already undergone land reform.

Local cadres were the first, but by no means the only, subjects who needed to be won over by the campaign. The CCP was insistent that the experience of land reform in "New Liberated Areas" like Sunan be publicized to wider regional and national audiences, and they chose a specific vehicle for this kind of dissemination: the investigative "study tour" (*canguan yu xuexi* – 參觀與 學習). The study tour had two components: heuristic personal testimonial and reiteration of CCP's class-based analysis of the countryside, supported by detailed descriptions of the results of "objective" social investigation into rural economic life. The CCP's educative propaganda buttressed the findings of the study tour, asserted that the crisis of feudalism in the countryside was real, reiterated the GMD's failures, and restated the CCP's necessarily violent policy of smashing feudalism by breaking the economic and social power of the landlord class.

Between the autumn of 1950 and the summer of 1951, there were at least three groups of urbanites that were organized into "visit and access" teams (*canguan fangwentuan* – 參觀訪問團) to go to the Sunan countryside to investigate land reform. The first was organized at the highest levels of the Central People's Government Political Division in Beijing and the East China Military District. This delegation included individuals from non-CCP, non-GMD democratic parties who knew little of rural conditions. Nineteen individuals traveled down from Beijing and another nine were already resident in Sunan. The group underwent intensive study of land reform before being assigned to shadow land reform work teams for a period of two to two and a half weeks. The CCP's assessment of this group's experiences was generally positive. Their summary reports pointed out the "definite increase in level of knowledge" (*renshi shang yiding chengdu de tigao* – 認識 上 一定程度提高) that the land reform study tour had fostered. Members of the team were convinced of the feudal nature of the Sunan countryside, and were on several occasions moved to tears by the suffering of the poor peasants. Two of the Beijing-based members the team even requested to stay on to continue land reform work. The report also admitted to some bumps along the way. Several of the Beijing members of the group continued to have very limited understanding of the importance of stirring up the masses, and were recalcitrant in small group discussion sessions, retorting "We're from Beijing, how much further away could we get [from that position of understanding]?" Old habits of intellectual arrogance and urban privilege also died hard: one of the intellectuals on the study tour caused resentment by his demands for peasants to carry his belongings, and another dismissed group discussion with the locals over the Aid Korea/Resist America campaign, asserting that "since he had been to university and studied the revolution, he [already] understood a lot about these things."[56]

The second group was a more modest detachment of around twenty from Suzhou who went to "visit and access" land reform in Wu county's Guangfu township, about which little else is known.[57] The third group, which was by far the most important of the three, was a special delegation of professors and high-level academics from Beijing's most elite universities who went to Sunan at the height of the campaign in the spring of 1951 for a month of visit and access. Pan Guangdan of Qinghua University was the ranking academic in attendance and leader of the team. At this time, Pan was perhaps China's premier sociologist and socio-linguist, and his involvement gave the team instant intellectual credibility. The essays and testimonials produced by this team reasserted the correctness of the CCP's class-based diagnosis of rural problems in locales far removed from those in North China, and fully acquiesced in the CCP's assertions that its methods of study, stirring up the masses, and cathartic accusation prior to the actual division of the land were essential. The writings of this elite group of scholars also described their own *personal* transformations over the course of the investigation tour as powerful awakening experiences to the plight of the peasantry. Some of the essays written at the end of the study tour were published in national newspapers: *Remin Ribao, Xin Guancha*, and *Guangming Ribao* – thus making their narratives of eye-witness testimony and personal awakening a potent source of propaganda for the entirety of the nation. These essays were also collected in a special publication brought out by the Sunan People's Administrative Office Land Reform Commission later in 1951.

The visit and access study team's essays directly tackled sensitive subjects: why Sunan must be considered feudal and the reasons why land could not be peacefully divided despite its commercialization and high level of economic specialization (Shi Wenqi), why "simple division of land" would not do to redress the myriad ways in which "feudalism" and exploitation was perpetuated through landholdings (Pan Guangdan and Quan Weitian), and how

---

[56] JPA 3006/2/224. Sunan qu dangwei tongyi zhanxian shang zuobu, "Guanyu canjia sunan tudi de gezhong minzhu pai qingkuang" (The situation on democratic parties' participation in Sunan land reform), May 16, 1951.

[57] Unfortunately little information about the activities of the Suzhou group is available, beyond a tantalizing photograph of the members of the team with the header "Suzhou shi gejie renshi zuzhi de tudi gaige fangwentuan daoda Wuxian guangfu zhen" (Suzhou personnel organizations' land reform investigating team arrives in Guangfu town, Wu county), in SSTH n.p.

land reform prompted dramatic changes in peasants' consciousness. These pieces also reaffirmed the CCP's vision and techniques for land reform to be transformative and liberating for both the peasants and for those privileged to have participated in the special investigation.[58]

The Pan Guangdan-led Sunan study tour was critically important for national propaganda about land reform. Marxist-Leninist-Maoist categories and repertoires that had been incubated in the different circumstances of land tenure and rural revolution in north China were declared to be identically useful in diagnosis and treatment of rural poverty in the very different conditions of the south. Now refracted through the writings of elite Beijing academics, the CCP's position that "peaceful" land reform through simple division of land was insufficient to resolve the problems of exploitation and rural underdevelopment sent a strong signal to the rest of the country to expect violent, class-based land reform. The personal transformations of high-status individuals to the CCP's campaign repertoires implicitly suggested that other "unawakened" urbanites could undergo similar kinds of conversions in the future. The study tour of the Beijing academics accomplished several goals in one fell swoop: it educated a tranche of top academics and professionals in Beijing into the new norms and vocabularies of the regime. It swatted aside all the reasonable objections that could be made against the implementation of the CCP's version of land reform outside of North China. It demonstrated through "objective" facts that exploitation was just as rife, and the CCP's methods for overcoming the problems of the countryside just as applicable, in central and south China as they had been in North China. And it disseminated these findings and personal experiences on a national scale.

What we do not know is how genuine these writings were. Since seasoned Communist revolutionary cadres accompanied the study tour at every stage of its investigations in Sunan, it is likely that intensive study and small group discussion sessions made clear what was expected in these final summaries. It is probable that the propaganda bureau was at least lurking in the background when these memoir-essays were written. With two generations' remove, it is impossible to know whether these senior academics truly believed what they were writing in their accounts of having participated in investigation and study of land reform in Sunan,

---

[58] See "Beijing gedaxue jiaoshou huadongqu tudi gaige canguantuan zongjie" (General summary of Beijing universities' professorial group visiting tour of the Eastern China region land reform), p. 198, Pan Guangdan and Quan Weitian, "Sunan nongcun fengjian shili de jige tedian" (Several special characteristics of feudal power in Sunan villages), pp. 5–8, and Shi Wenqi, "Wo suo jiandaode sunan tudi gaige yundong" (The land reform movement in sunan that I saw), pp. 88–89, all in Sunan renmin xingzhengshu tudi gaige weiyuanhui, *Wo suo Jiandao de Sunan Tudi Gaige Yundong*, 1951.

or whether they acceded to the pragmatic position that compliance with the state's desires was necessary if not also desirable. Perhaps the personal beliefs of individuals matters less than the praxis of accommodation to the state's new forms of hegemony in New China. Whether or not individuals truly believed what they were writing, the content of these essays illustrates the degree to which senior intellectuals were, as early as mid-1951, already acting "as if" they had internalized both the new Marxian categories of class analysis, acknowledged the suffering of the rural masses and the CCP's unique role in alleviating that suffering, and conformed to the CCP's new script that insisted on their own individual "awakening."[59]

On Taiwan, the JCRR and its progressive supporters of land reform initiatives did not engage in study tours for high-ranking intellectuals or insist on public adoption of unfamiliar Marxist categories of feudalism and class struggle. However, the JCRR, the governor of Taiwan, Chen Cheng, and progressives in the Taiwan provincial and National government constructed a parallel narrative that staked GMD legitimacy on an equivalent counter morality tale. They admitted that the Communists had engaged land reform to the immediate detriment of the GMD, but insisted that everything about the *manner* in which the Communists pursued land reform was immoral and/or disastrous. This insistence on the core evil of class struggle implied that Guomindang land reform on Taiwan needed to be as distinct in manner and outcome as possible from land reform in China. For the GMD, a successful land reform in Taiwan that was sharply distinguished from the violence on the mainland was politically necessary above and beyond helping unfortunate and exploited tenants. If Taiwan were to become an external manifestation of the government's revived legitimacy, then a visibly moderate, inclusive, and well-executed land reform was necessary to demonstrate the government's inner virtue and right to rule. Only by explicitly linking its land reform in Taiwan to its prior efforts in China would anyone take seriously GMD claims that its actions in Taiwan were a credible demonstration of what it could do, given the chance, in China itself.

---

[59] In the different authoritarian context of Syria, see Lisa Wedeen, "Acting 'As if' Symbolic Politics and Social Control in Syria." Pan Guangdan would go on to co-write another more academic treatise on land reform in Sunan with Quan Weitian that would elaborate on the importance and necessity of land reform in Sunan. While ostensibly more academic, with lengthy discussions of different types of land rents, there is little question that this longer piece was equally important in establishing the validity of the categories already pre-decided by the CCP: the opening section is subtitled "Who Says that Jiangnan isn't feudal" (*Shei shuo jiangnan wu fengjian*). See Pan and Quan, *Sunan Tudi Gaige Fangwen*.

Given these high rhetorical stakes, the GMD, with help from the JCRR, needed to distinguish the promising present from the mistakes of the immediate past without repudiating that past in entirety. This was done by linking the immediate present to the GMD's last efforts in the countryside before the final retreat to Taiwan. JCRR officers wrote critically of the 1920s through the 1940s as a period of disappointment and lost opportunities. They decried the GMD's earlier failures to redress land issues and its "production first, land reform later" mentality. They drew a sharp distinction between the failures of the 1920s and 1930s and the JCRR's last-ditch efforts to implement rent reduction in the few experimental counties in Fujian that the GMD still held in 1949. Although this pilot program in Fujian had to be abandoned when the GMD military retreated, the JCRR claimed it as the starting point for the progressive present, when the multiple programs for land reform begun in 1949 were being brought to full fruition in Taiwan.[60]

The government's virtue and competence in promoting land reform on Taiwan could only resonate beyond the special circumstances and small size of Taiwan if the government could also claim that its experiences in Taiwan could be replicated in other locales across China. This in turn required that the land tenure conditions for Taiwan's peasants be rhetorically posited as analogous to those in the rest of China. The JCRR, Chen Cheng (the GMD governor of Taiwan), and Shen Zonghan (TH Shen, Head of the Land Division and later Commissioner for the JCRR) all explicitly linked the GMD's recent land reform efforts in China and Taiwan. Shen Zonghan stressed that "the inhabitants of Taiwan . . . have all retained the cultural background and ways of life of their motherland and are no whit different from their brothers and sisters on the other side of the Taiwan Straits." This reasoning implied that the principles and procedures that the JCRR had formulated and tried out in the mainland provinces proved equally workable in Taiwan and required only slight readjustments or modifications to suit local conditions.[61] By this sleight of hand, policies that were inherently easier to implement on a relatively small island with a completely different twentieth-century political experience and complete (if out of date) cadastral surveys left over from Japanese colonial rule were now reimagined, with Taiwan as the recipient of successful policies worked out on the mainland, in preparation for eventual export back to the mainland.

In 1960, when land reform in full had been completed only six years previously and the People's Republic was in the grip of a severe famine, Chen Cheng wrote at length about the ways in which the Guomindang

---

[60] *JCRR*, p. 1.   [61] T. H. Shen, p. 53.

version of virtuous, gradualist, and "scientific" land reform was far superior to the Communist version of land reform. "We" had "implementation" of soberly constructed programs that retained private property, increased production and laid a foundation for self government; while "they" had a reign of terror, unceasing, intensified class struggle, and a nationalization that resulted in all land becoming the property of the Chinese Communist Party, turning all farmers into slaves.[62] While these pronouncements were shrill polemics at the height of the Cold War and must be seen in this light, the GMD's linkage of its "good" version of land reform – accomplished without loss of life, and with landlords compensated for the loss of their land – may well have burnished the image of the ROC/Taiwan in its overall diplomatic competition with the PRC, and in the hearts and minds of many business interests within overseas Chinese communities at the time.

In the early 1950s, the excesses of super-collectivization during the Great Leap Forward and the ensuing famine were far in the future. When putting together a meaningful and credible land reform was under discussion in the early 1950s in Taiwan, political elites put tremendous emphasis on distinguishing the Nationalist vision of land reform in Taiwan from its counterpart in China. One fortuitously preserved Executive Yuan discussion on the specifics of the signature Land to the Tiller (*gengzhe you qitian* – 耕者有其田) even laid out the parameters of the debate as follows. The purpose of Land to the Tiller program was "to abolish an irrational system of tenancy, to establish an open and fair system of private land ownership, and to return land ownership to the tiller," but there was considerable uncertainty as to how to accomplish these goals. A chart was made up on an oversized piece of paper that was folded in on itself several times. With a nice, if perhaps unintended, touch, the key tenets of the Communist version of land reform were laid out on the left side of the chart, which enumerated what was known about the goals and methods of the Communists. The right side of the chart laid out three or four possibilities that the Nationalists could choose by way of response. Each of these possible options was (negatively) framed by the (presumed) goals and methods of the Communists: *if* those awful "*gong-fei*" (Communist bandits) over there had engaged in class struggle and public humiliation of landlords, then as a matter of definition we good people *over here* could only consider approaches to land reform that explicitly ruled out class struggle and public humiliation of landlords. If the Communists had done x and y, then we could only countenance engaging with what was demonstrably non-x and non-y. For the

---

[62] Chen Cheng, pp. 125–129.

Guomindang, the range of the possible in land reform was defined largely by what the CCP had *not* done. Fortunately, there were normally two or three credible options that the CCP had not obviously engaged in their pursuit of land reform for the GMD to consider.[63] It was crucial to distinguish "our" good and pure form of land reform from "their" evil and depraved version. For both the CCP and GMD, land reform was a critical litmus test of regime legitimacy. The critical elements of land reform implementation revolved around not only *what* the outcome of land reform ought to be, but *how* the policy itself was to be implemented.

[63] GSG 071.204, Xingzheng Yuan, Mishu chu, "Taiwan gengzhe you qitian yu gongfei 'tugai'" (Taiwan's land to the tiller and Communist bandit 'land reform'), August 2, 1953.

5   Theaters of Land Reform
Bureaucracy, Campaign, and the Show, 1950–1954

Common Agendas, Common Methods: Campaigns as Heroic Mobilization for Remaking the Countryside

In the early Cold War, regime legitimacy required that the PRC and the ROC/Taiwan demonstrate effectiveness in addressing the needs of the people. Despite their mutual hostility, these two regimes converged in their assessment of land reform as a signature policy to so do. Land reform promised immediate social justice for those at the bottom of rural society, the release of more agricultural productivity, and a sounder rural platform upon which to base rapid economic development. It was broadly supported by both superpowers. Land reform also offered a way for each, particularly the ROC/Taiwan, to differentiate itself from its rival across the Taiwan Strait. The PRC in Sunan and the ROC in Taiwan both implemented land reform as campaigns, with extraordinary mobilizations of people and resources to accomplish an announced set of goals. The repertoires deployed in the early to middle stages of the campaign, when propaganda was disseminated and the size of the state temporarily enlarged, were strikingly similar for such ideologically hostile regimes. But core differences in the content and style of campaign delivery were even more important than these early-stage similarities because it was through the public performances of these differences that each demonstrated its virtue, its *modus operandi*, and its claims on the rural population. Whether landlords were isolated and destroyed (as was the case in Sunan) or transformed and incorporated (as was true in Taiwan), a powerful message was sent to rural populations about what to expect from the new regime. Both regimes solicited popular participation, and although they used starkly different ways to invite and channel this, the PRC in Sunan and the ROC in Taiwan engaged in a didactic process of instructing the rural public at large about new regime norms, institutions, and acceptable political language. This was accomplished through very different forms of public theater, whereby each staged its own preferred version of land reform: the roused public that merged with the state in Sunan, versus the careful procedures of limited local elections in Taiwan.

Land reform campaigns in Sunan and Taiwan were heroic and extraordinary, rather than routine and workaday. The language of administrative mobilization and training for land reform reflected this, even for the GMD regime that had every conceivable ideological reason to avoid vocabulary that might be readily associated with the Communist "Other" across the Taiwan Strait. Both shared a necessary first step: the mobilization of the bureaucracy and the intensification of its focus on the implementation of the program. Despite their significant differences in ethos (violence versus inclusion), ideology of implementing organization (Marxist-Leninist revolutionary party versus technocratic administration), and rates of implementation (relative speed in Sunan and deliberately slow and careful sequencing in Taiwan), land reform campaigns in Sunan and Taiwan were implemented in a roughly similar arc: (1) lengthy preparation to mobilize and intensify focus within the relevant part of the state bureaucracy itself; (2) training and socialization of extraordinary numbers of temporary staff to implement the campaign; (3) intensive propaganda aimed at rural society to educate the population as to the necessity, desirability, and mechanics of the program; (4) creation of local representative organizations (peasant, women, and youth associations) in the PRC and Rent Reduction Committees (later transformed into Farm Tenancy Commitees in Taiwan) to mobilize popular rural support to back up the campaign; (5) the state's actual transfer of excess land to those in land deficit; and (6) a period of consolidation, summing up, report writing, and recording the final results. The first three and the final stages of this process in Sunan and Taiwan (mobilization of state organizations, dramatic and temporary expansions in numbers of state agents sent down to the countryside to oversee or implement some part of land reform, intensive propaganda blitzes, and final checking and assessment of results) were not only roughly equivalent: the actions taken were also often identical. However, the fourth and fifth stages that invited in mass participation and redistributed excess land were starkly different.

Mobilizing and Expanding the Bureaucracy: Propaganda and Training

Land reform campaigns were among the most important measures taken by the PRC in Sunan and ROC in Taiwan in the early 1950s to reorder state–society relations in the countryside. Their successful implementation required the presence of a cohort of committed state agents willing and able to go to the countryside and penetrate to the level of the village.

This was no easy or straightforward set of tasks, even in relatively small Taiwan. Pushing through a major program to fundamentally recast the countryside required accurate knowledge of the entire cadastre of land holdings. This alone was an enormous undertaking – one that had run aground more than once in the 1930s and 1940s in the face of the GMD's limited administrative capacity and local resistance. Extraordinary political will from above to push through accurate surveying was a necessary but insufficient pre-condition for implementation. Land reform also required an extraordinary expansion in the capacity of the state, which in turn required: (a) stiffening the resolve of existing state agents; and (b) recruiting and dispatching newly deputized state agents to the countryside to carry out such necessary tasks as preliminary investigations, data entry, and record rectification. Nor was simply expanding the size of the state on an extraordinary basis to implement land reform policy enough by itself. The newly recruited and the state agents already *in situ* needed to know not only what had to be done in the countryside, but how it needed to be done.

For these reasons, the initial stages of land reform campaigns in Sunan and Taiwan put a good deal of time and effort into propaganda for the now mobilized and expanded instruments of the state itself. Implementing such a large-scale campaign to reach so deeply into rural society meant that in Sunan and Taiwan, the preparations for land reform necessitated the training of very large numbers of people, often young, to go down to the most grassroots level of the countryside to augment the administrative capacity local cadres (for Sunan) and a combination of hamlet/village chiefs and local offices of the Provincial Land Bureau (for Taiwan). Training extra personnel to oversee land reform was integral to the state's extension of direct power, now directed to reordering economic and social relations in the countryside and vertically integrating the administrative offices of the state bureaucracy. In Sunan land reform went hand in hand with a substantial expansion in the ranks of basic-level cadres. In the Shanghai suburbs alone, some 460 lecturers and teachers from local universities and middle schools were trained and sent to the countryside to implement land reform. There they were accompanied by 4,616 activists who were largely from poor peasant backgrounds. Once in the countryside, a substantial minority of these activists never left. Over one-fifth (1,042 of 4,616, or 20.57 percent) were eventually regularized as permanent cadres. In late 1950, the Sunan Party Village Work Committee also planned to train an eventual further 11,333 cadres to provide guidance and support for the three land reform districts of Suzhou, Changshu, and

Songjiang.[1] Those in charge of land reform in Sunan may not have thought of the campaign in quite this way, but one of the most important by-products of the land reform campaign was to identify and train large groups of committed loyalists, some of whom would remain in the villages to which they had been dispatched to implement land reform, thereby establishing a stronger rural core of CCP cadres to guide later rural campaigns.[2]

Similar training exercises took place in Taiwan under the auspices of the Joint Commission on Rural Reconstruction, as the technocratic bureaucracy mobilized to extend its reach down to every village and hamlet. Between 1949 and 1952, when land reform was articulated through rent reduction, the JCRR oversaw the training of over 4,000 staff workers to implement the "375" (*sanqiwu* – 三七五) program to limit the rents that a landlord could levy to 0.375 of the harvest. In the 1952 run up to the Land to the Tiller program of 1953[3] (*gengzhe you qitian* – 耕者有其田), the JCRR then trained an additional 2,000 clerks to carry out the massive project of checking and re-entering of land-ownership record cards for the entire cadastre of land under cultivation on the island. The Land to the Tiller program of 1953 required the greatest mobilization of training resources of all: first training the entirety of the Taiwan Provincial Land Bureau; then training at county and district station land offices. Provision was also made for supplementary technical training for an additional 2,400 field workers, and top-up training of the 3,000-odd members of local farm tenancy committees and 6,537 hamlet and section chiefs.[4] When all this was completed in June 1953, an astonishingly large number – 33,110 – had been prepared to carry out the Land to the Tiller program in Taiwan. Most, but not all, of these trainees were already in positions at very local levels of rural organization. In addition to 6,537 hamlet chiefs and clerks, there were 19,611 rank and file hamlet representatives for landlords, freeholders, and tenants who received training on the Land to the Tiller program.[5] The ROC government in Taiwan also set out administrative measures to encourage the revival of two other

---

[1] JPA 3006/3/360. "Benhui (zhonggong sunanzu dangwei nongcun gongzuoweiyuanhui) Sunan ganbu xunlian tongjibiao" (Chinese Communist Sunan group party village work committee Sunan cadre training statistics). N.d., 1950.

[2] SMA B14/1/80, "Shanghai shi jiaoqu xunlian ganbu shu peiyang jiji fenzi qingkuang" (The situation for Shanghai municipal outer district cadre training and the cultivation of activists), and "Sheng tudi gaige qianhou xiangcun jiceng ganbu bianhua qingkuang tongjibiao" (Statistical form on changes in village level local cadres before and after land reform), both p. 13 of internally numbered file, dated December 31, 1951. SMA B14/1/6/ "Jiaoshi canjia tudi gaige di'yi xiaozu mingdan ji duiyuan tongjibiao" (Instructors participating in land reform: the first small group name list and statistics), 1951.

[3] Hui-sun Tang, pp. 50–51.   [4] Hui-sun Tang, p. 116.   [5] *JCRR*, p. 66.

rural organizations that had atrophied in the late 1940s: farmers' associations (*nonghui* – 農會) and irrigation associations (*shuili hui* – 水利會).[6] The leaders of these reconstituted organizations were also enlisted to help implement the Land to the Tiller Program.

In both Sunan and Taiwan, successful land reform relied on committed and knowledgeable state agents, and required general support from urban and rural populations. Publicity about land reform programs was disseminated widely in national, regional, and local press and in the reproduction of pamphlets that laid out basic questions and answers to illustrate the gravity of rural land tenure problems and the government's measures for resolving these injustices. Effective propaganda was also needed to convince much larger numbers of farming families in the countryside that these new policies were reasonable, comprehensible, and necessary. It was here that propaganda work came into its own, resulting in a range of different kinds of public "shows" that blurred the boundaries between propaganda, education, and entertainment.[7]

The local state in Shanghai and throughout Sunan organized public exhibitions on land reform that instructed, entertained, and appealed to the emotions of a wide spectrum of city people. For example, the Suzhou administrative district, which comprised the counties of Changshu, Kunshan, Taiqiang, Wujiang, and Wuxian, convened a special committee in early 1951 to put on a travelling public exhibition at the height of land reform in April. Each county sent in its own materials to a specially convened committee in Suzhou, which organized the show. After the exhibition was curated, it was briefly hosted in the county seat of each of the participants. The largest and most prominent site for the land reform exhibition was in downtown Suzhou itself, on the second floor of the People's Department Store. It was arranged in three color-coded sections, each of which displayed a mix of material artifacts, photographs, cartoons, and maps. The organizers paid particular attention to displaying cartoon caricatures that illustrated structural injustice, including one prominently depicting a landlord brandishing two knives over a cringing peasant.[8]

The first section of the exhibition was captioned in somber black to underscore the crimes and evils (*zui'e* – 罪惡) of the feudal and

[6] Mick Moore, "The Fruits and Fallacies of Neo-Liberalism: The Case of Irrigation Policy"; on Farmers Associations see Chun-chieh Huang, *Taiwan in Transformation: Retrospect and Prospect*, pp. 35–36 and Axel de Lasson, *A Restudy of the Taiwan Farmers' Associations*.

[7] See Tao Dayong et al., *Tudi gaige yu xin minzhu zhuyi geming* (Land Reform and the New Democracy Revolution).

[8] SuMA B2/2/12. "Suzhou Tugai Zhanlanhui Zhanlanpin Ximulu" (Detailed Catalogue of the Exhibition Objects of the Suzhou Land Reform Exhibition Committee), April 1951.

exploitative immediate past. It featured photographs of landlord extra-vagance, examples of unfair contracts between landlord and tenant, and the tools of torture that landlords resorted to as a means of keeping tenants in their place. These artifacts all underscored the deep structural injustice of landlord exploitation, and the ways in which landlords and the system they propagated incubated the more general evils of bad govern-ments, national traitors, and sectarianism. The second section, also cap-tioned in black, focused on the process of land reform and the government's progressive humaneness in making land reform possible. After a quick reminder of the exploitative nature of rent contracts, this middle segment of the exhibition charted how, under land reform poli-cies, landlords resisted and were struggled against by the roused masses, how with the government's assistance, poor peasants wrested the fruits of struggle from landlords, and the ways in which the common people poured forth with enormous support for the campaign. The organizers were quite specific about the layout of the third, concluding part of the exhibition, which was captioned in celebratory bright red. This final section concentrated on the positive effects of the campaign. Here the new and positive atmosphere (*qifen* – 氣氛) in villages that had undergone land reform was on display. Villagers were depicted as victorious masters. There were photographs of abundant crops, smiling peasants, much improved access to education through still shots of children and women learning in small groups, and copies of patriotic compacts for grain production to support the Aid Korea/Resist America war. All of these positive developmental and patriotic depictions came together in a col-lective joyous affirmation of having "turned the body" (*fanshen* – 翻身).[9]

Since these travelling exhibitions were held in urban locations (Shanghai, Suzhou, Wuxi) and county seats (Kunshan), they were geared to educating a primarily urban, or at least quasi-urban, set of publics into the righteousness of the government's actions in the countryside. But, ultimately, the most important audience that required education was the rural public itself. Propaganda was taken straight to villages with simpli-fied narratives disseminated through the CCP's preferred repertoire of small group meetings. Educative propaganda was deliberately blurred with good old-fashioned entertainment: new plays and operas updated older performative genres to emphasize the drama and righteousness of land reform. These productions typically featured a full complement of new revolutionary archetypes to engage the emotions: the abused peasant

---

[9] SuMA B2/2/12. "Suzhou Tugai Zhanlanhui Zongjie" (Summary report on the Suzhou land reform exhibition), May, 1952.

girl, the emasculated young peasant male, the helpless peasant elders, the evil landlord, and the revolutionary (now enlightened) woman.[10]

Many of the forms displayed in propaganda dissemination for the land reform campaigns in Taiwan by the JCRR were astonishingly similar. Although its English language publications referred to "publicity" rather than "propaganda," like the CCP, the JCRR prioritized didactic dissemination. The JCRR's seriousness in combining education with publicity was demonstrated in its preparation for the Land to the Tiller program, which had a project publicity budget that was even larger than its budget for training nearly 2,000 extra personnel. The forms of land reform propaganda in Taiwan were also virtually identical to those the CCP employed in Sunan: cartoons were commissioned; informational newsreels were made; land reform plays were written and staged; and a new ditty glorifying the JCRR's developmentalist approach to rural agriculture by extolling the wonders of raising happy pigs was set to an older folk tune, almost perfectly replicating the CCP's success in adapting *yangge* dances from the far northwest of China for performances in Sunan and elsewhere.[11] Intensive deployment of propaganda followed. Once written and rehearsed, these dramatic performances were slated to be performed at the rate of one per every three villages throughout Taiwan. In addition, the JCRR subsidized the projection of a reel of educational slides about the Land to the Tiller program to be run in over 120 cinemas. The JCRR disseminated huge quantities of printed material that explained, exhorted, and entertained. Fully half of the JCRR's already large printing budget was devoted to publicity materials, many of which entertained as much as they informed. Cartoons, movie synopses, posters, pictures, and the texts of locally performed plays along with more mundane copies of program regulations were all printed and widely circulated.[12] Land reform in Sunan and Taiwan was tied explicitly to a larger narrative that explained why China had been so chronically poor and underdeveloped for so long, and how the party-state was going to lead China into a glorious future embracing strength and modernity. The early phases of land reform campaigns in Sunan and Taiwan drew on substantially overlapping core agendas and repertoires – in the ways in which they

---

[10] Xiao Mu, Tugai Xuanchuan ju (Land Reform Propaganda Plays). See also Brian DeMare, *Mao's Cultural Army: Drama Troupe in China's Rural Revolution*, pp. 125–135 on the new standard archetypes in land reform operas.

[11] Chen Kaige's film *Huang Tudi* (Yellow Earth) is probably the best-known depiction of this genre, but scholarly treatments of the subject include David Holm, *Art and Ideology in Revolutionary China*. See also GSG313 FY 53; "The hog raising song," September 11, 1953.

[12] GSG 313/1285-3 FY 52, "A preliminary budget estimate for the private land purchase project in Taiwan," prepared by Taiwan Land Bureau, April 1952.

mobilized the bureaucracy, temporarily expanded the number of state agents through intensive short-term training courses, and disseminated educative propaganda to both new state agents and their populations at large.

Campaign Differences: Classificatory Schemes and State Violence

Despite their commonalities, it was critical for each of these party-states to distinguish, and to be seen to distinguish, its version of land reform from that of the "Other," as for each one of the most politically sensitive forms of competition in the countryside was the presence of an alternative version of land reform propagated by its ideological rival. When the JCRR was desperately attempting to implement a rent-reduction program in the counties of Fujian that the Nationalists still held militarily in 1949, the CCP issued dire warnings that "whoever tries to carry out land reform outside our ranks will be killed."[13] In Taiwan, anyone suspected of promoting methods or slogans for land reform that the government deemed "communist" was a prime target for the severe state repression of the White Terror. While the general sequencing of land reform campaigns in Sunan and Taiwan ran in parallel – mobilizing the bureaucracy, training extra personnel, dispatching outsiders to the countryside, backing up on ground action with external supervision and checking, creating local representative organizations, assessing who owned what land, and final tidying up, rechecking and entering new records – these similarities in campaign trajectory were outweighed by the ways in each regime insisted on the uniqueness, moral validity, and separation of its version of land reform from its rival. This was particularly the case for the ROC/Taiwan, which was by far the weaker and more reactive, with more to prove at this still early stage in regime consolidation.

Land reform campaigns in Sunan and Taiwan in the early 1950s diverged in three significant and interrelated ways: (1) the degree to which questions of class, struggle, and public state violence were an integral component of the campaign; (2) how the campaign was implemented; and (3) the way in which rural participation was invited in. In Sunan, redistribution of land could not take place if local cadres did not know where the wealth was, who owned what, and who counted as an exploiter or the exploited as stipulated by the government's guidelines. Therefore, cadres were expected to launch intensive preparatory investigations in the countryside according to the model first developed in North

---

[13] *JCRR*, p. 7.

China. This process provided an entry point to a larger state project of classification and registration of the entire rural population based on the way in which local cadres fit rural households into the *a priori* economic status categories of landlord, rich peasant, middle peasant, poor peasant, and poor and hired (landless) laborers in which the primary distinction was between those who were "exploiters" who profited by the labor of others or "non-exploiters" who relied solely on their own labor. These new bureaucratic status labels deliberately inverted older rural ones. In this way, the CCP's new classification scheme simplified and fixed its results in new moral binaries that stressed the unbridgeable difference between "exploiters" and "non-exploiters."

As described in the last chapter, this new system of Marxist-inspired class statuses fit the realities of rural life in Sunan so poorly that in the late summer and early autumn of 1950 many local cadres either protested to their superiors that these categories simply did not apply, or dragged their feet in implementing a scheme that they felt made no sense. In the end, remonstration, footdragging, or the actual social and economic conditions of Sunan did not matter.[14] After the November 1950 land reform cadre conference in Shanghai made it clear that local cadres not only had to implement land reform, but also had to do so in a way that conformed to the CCP's script of stirring up mass hatred of exploiters, cadres all over Sunan rushed to comply. This campaign-driven turn from "patient education" towards intensified enforcement and mass mobilization made it possible to sweep away resistance and accomplish a bureaucratic set of tasks much more quickly than would normally have been the case. The revolutionary state's insistence on investigation and classification of every rural household as part and parcel of land reform may not have made objective sense in the light of rural Sunan's actual conditions, but it definitely enabled the party-state's full penetration of the countryside on the terms that it deemed appropriate.

While the Guomindang had no great love for Taiwanese landlords, its approach was quite different. Unlike the PRC in Sunan, the ROC/ Taiwan premised its entire land reform program on the principles of gradualism, peaceful deployment of material incentives to compensate those who had "excess land," and transformation of loosely defined rural groups (tenants and landlords) into new statuses of small freeholders and state capitalists. Land reform in Taiwan was characterized as a sober, carefully phased, peaceable, technocratic exercise that explicitly rejected

---

[14] See also Eddy U, "Rise of Marxist Classes: Bureaucratic Classification and Class Formation in Early Socialist China," on the ways in which the government also rushed to classify the urban population with fixed class labels.

notions of even corporate class consciousness, much less class struggle in its relentless focus on the individual farming family.[15] Rather than divide classes and affix class labels to the advantage of the majority and the detriment of a labeled minority, land reform in Taiwan was designed to create only winners: for the individual rural family, for the state, and for the public good of development.

The GMD offered landlords two different forms of compensation for the state's compulsory purchase of their "excess" land: 70 percent of the compensation was remitted in bonds for rice and sweet potatoes, and 30 percent was issued in shares in four of the largest state industrial enterprises, the Taiwan Cement Corporation, the Paper and Pulp Corporation, the Agriculture and Forestry Development Corporation, and the Industrial and Mining Corporation.[16] In Taiwan, the explicit goal was to *transform* rural economic relations to give as many people as possible a stake in the newly congealing political and economic system. Impoverished and disadvantaged tenants were lifted up to become small holders; and landlords were forced to sell their "excess" holdings to the state, which then contracted with individual tenants to sell the land at preferentially low rates to be repaid slowly over the course of the next ten years. The state expected landlords to become state capitalists, and tenants to become smallholders. The GMD sought to blur rather than accentuate class distinctions by accelerating the movement of landlords out of agriculture altogether, while binding them closer to the state.

The transformation of rural landlords into state capitalists was neither as rational, nor as smooth a process as had been anticipated. While the Land to the Tiller program of 1953–1954 professed to make every effort to be fair to both landlords and tenants by leaving 2.5 *mou* to landlords and recompensing landlords over ten years in agricultural bonds and shares in state-owned industry, in practice these compensatory schemes often did not work out as planned. "Landlords" were designated as such when they had a larger than average land holding, but in reality, landholdings that appeared to be large were often paper fictions. Many Taiwanese rural families informally designated one individual to register the land of all the families to cut down on paperwork and reduce administrative intrusion

---

[15] Chen Cheng, *Land Reform in Taiwan*, pp. 71–73. These notions were directly reflected in Chen Cheng's memoir and analysis of land reform in Taiwan in the early 1950s; Chen reiterated the principles of land reform in Taiwan as: (1) abolition of tenancy through peaceful and gradual means; (2) compulsory purchase and resale through the government to avoid direct contact between landlord and tenant; (3) orderly procedures; (4) equal protection of other enterprises; and (5) continued protection of owner-farmers. See also *Land Reform in Free China*, pp. 164–169. That this seldom worked out as intended and that many landlords were economically ruined by such "largesse" is another matter.

[16] Ibid., pp. 75–78.

from the state. When it became clear that some sort of compulsory land redistribution was in the offing, those who had done so went to adjust the official paperwork to reflect realities on the ground. They were immediately suspected of attempting to subvert the intention of the land reform by artificially reducing their holdings. There may well have been landlords who tried to limit the impact of the Land to the Tiller Program by registering the land they genuinely controlled in the name of relatives, but it never seems to have occurred to the planners in the government that the converse could also be true: that the rush to formally divide the land might reflect artificially inflated holdings. In addition, the government bonds for shares in state enterprises distributed to landlords were frequently worth significantly less than their face value. Many landlords were not adept at negotiating the new world of state-sponsored capitalism. Some became impoverished and reliant on the charity of their previous tenants.[17] But these unfortunate results were never intended by the Land to the Tiller program, which sought simultaneously to create a more level playing field in the countryside, even out rural inequality, and promote the transformation of individual rural households from tenant to small freeholder, and landlord to state capitalist. These strategies enabled the GMD to link itself to both longstanding norms of China's agrarian past about hard work and upward mobility and contemporary ideas about meritocracy. In contrast, the CCP's core strategies of sharp demarcation between exploiters, the exploited, and the neutral marked a sharp break with the past and contained the core elements of a new, quasi-caste system of social differentiation in the countryside.

Land Reform Campaigns as Dramatization of Power (I): The Nature of the Show

Closely linked to these differences in content were the substantively different ways in which land reform was communicated to and performed for a multiplicity of publics: domestic urbanites, peasants in the countryside, and external audiences in an emerging bipolar order. The CCP and GMD used the land reform campaigns in the early 1950s to differentiate themselves from one another and communicate essential values about themselves to their populations. In Sunan and Taiwan, state legitimacy was imagined, regime norms were conveyed to the population, and the rural population was invited in to participate in the implementation of

---

[17] Xu Shirong (Hsu Shih-jung), "In Fact, Landlords Were Not Landlords."

land reform through the dramatization of state power. These dramas of land reform differed in almost every respect: the types of shows that were put on, their staging, scripts, narratives, and pace.

Land reform in Sunan drew on the same campaign repertoires as the Campaign to Suppress Counterrevolutionaries. The campaign organized highly public mobilization against state-defined enemies simultaneously to mobilize support for the regime and instruct the population into the new regime's normative expectations. In Sunan, the Campaign to Suppress Counterrevolutionaries and land reform *required* the anger of cathartic mass emotion to accompany the graphically corporeal destruction of the "old" (feudal, corrupt) as a form of cleansing and public identification with the "new" (modern, clean and bright). Not only were the repertoires and techniques of the Campaign to Suppress Counterrevolutionaries and land reform identical, the two campaigns merged so indistinguishably in parts of rural Sunan that it was quite impossible to tell which one the local cadre was implementing.

In Taiwan, land reform was equally heuristic, but the content and the norms that were being conveyed to the population were quite different. Like the police actions that were unleashed in the name of suppressing sedition, land reform campaigns in Taiwan publicized adherence to bureaucratically determined rules, procedures, and "law." But in Taiwan there were important differences between repertoires of suppression, which relied on secrecy and those of land reform, which required openness. Land reform programs could be propagandized, made public and visible in ways that the White Terror crackdowns could not. Land reform sub-programs (375 Rent Reduction, the sale of public lands, and most of all the Land to the Tiller program of 1953–1954) were among the few ROC initiatives of the early 1950s that could credibly present the state as a benevolent but determined guarantor of social justice and economic development to a subject population that considered the government to be alien, incompetent, and repressive. This led to performances that prioritized the public display of legal procedure and due process, but also invited a degree of support through a highly controlled, but still public theater of voting and elections.

In order to make clear these two different conceptions of what the state-enlightened subject was supposed to do, land reform campaigns in Sunan and Taiwan were implemented in very different ways that demonstrated the core values of each regime. First was a profound difference in campaign pacing. In Sunan, land reform was meant to be sharp, focused, and above all rapid. The peak of the land reform campaign "high tide" reached by the "stirring up" (*fadong* – 發動) of the masses at an open public accusation session was designed to be particularly quick: public accusation was followed by swift dispatch of the landlord/evil bully, after which the landlord holdings and property were to be immediately divided, followed straightaway by a final joyous coming together in a final public blaze of the old land deeds.

Throughout 1950, the party-state sent out investigating teams to survey actual rural conditions in Sunan. Land reform was trialled in a number of experimental villages (*shidian cun* – 試點村) in the late summer and early autumn. Some counties conducted land reform in the late autumn and winter of 1950–1951. Others waited until the spring of 1951. The Shanghai outer districts and Shanghai county delayed until April and May 1951, when the land reform "high tide" converged with that of the Campaign to Suppress Counterrevolutionaries. But when the public and dramatic face of the campaign swung into "high tide" gear through mass meetings, public accusation, and assignment of the "fruits of struggle," things moved very quickly indeed, typically in a matter of a week or two. Above all, the "high tide" required that the masses directly participate in land reform by being present at public accusation/struggle meetings.

The description below of land reform in Qingpu county is instructive in its depiction of how the campaign was pushed through in Sunan:

The investigation of eight administrative villages, 44 villages and 5 unified towns began in the spring of 1950 ... by the end of August, each district had seven experimental areas that had implemented land reform; in the first half of September the second group of 27 villages and one town began, in the second half of September a third group of 23 villages and 5 towns, and by the end of November, the entire county had finished up.

Land reform work went through the training of backbone (cadres), propaganda mobilization, and division of classes. The county party committee convened three land reform cadre training sessions that 451 cadres attended, of whom 96 were land reform work team members who were sent to help with land reform work in villages after participation in the district experimental villages.

The county Peasant Association convened four peasants' representative meetings with 3,117 participants; and 10,500 people participated in district-level peasant representative meetings, which disseminated propaganda about the significance and purpose of land reform. At the beginning of September 1950, the District Land Reform Committee formally established a thirteen-member land reform committee, in order to pursue the line of "relying on poor peasants and hired laborers, uniting with middle peasants, neutralizing rich peasants and isolating landlords," in succession dividing classes, collecting land and distributing the "fruits of victory."

In the middle of land reform, the districts held a total of 1,072 public accusation meetings; 137,000 participated, and [of these] 3,855 individual peasants uncovered and accused landlords and evil bullies of criminal behavior. According to law, the entire county collected 437,227 mou of land, including

6,017 mou of "black earth" (land concealed by landlords). Of this total, 332,069 mou was taken from landlords, and the remaining 105,158 mou from half land-lord half rich peasants, rich peasants engaging in trade while renting land, petty rentiers, and other kinds of public land. According to policy, this land was distributed to poor peasants and hired laborers, middle peasants, and others engaged in labor. In order to transform landlords into self-supporting laborers, they were given a parcel of equivalent land. Undergoing the process of land reform has realized "land to the tiller" (*gengzhe you qitian*). Land reform ... through public meetings also redistributed landlords' excess property of 426 carts, 371 boats, 370 head of water buffalo, 2,156 pieces of furniture, 4,786 dwellings, and 540,000 kg of grain to poor peasants and hired laborers. On May 15, 1951, the county government promulgated "land reform house ownership certificates" (also called "land reform certificates"). These were distributed in three batches, concluding at the end of July, with the issuing of more than 61,000 certificates" (italics indicate emphases added).[18]

The Qingpu county gazeteer makes clear that once the necessary preparations and background investigations had been made, local authorities put a premium on speedy resolution: mobilization, mass accusation meetings, and redistribution in the second and third tranche of villages was condensed into one intensively charged period of approximately two weeks in September 1950. Even laggard villages in Qingpu had completed the process by the end of November.

In other areas, particularly the Shanghai *jiaoqu* and in Shanghai county immediately to the south of the city, land reform was delayed until roughly the time at which the Campaign to Suppress Counterrevolutionaries had ratcheted up, in late April and May of 1951. But when it came, the implementation phase of land reform in the greater Shanghai area was equally rapid. Records for Shanghai county show that virtually all the villages in the county had completed land reform by late June 1951. The majority of these pushed through their "high tides" in a matter of one to two weeks. There were even some cases in which the "high tide" condensed the final classification of the rural population, the obligatory mass accusation session, the immediate dispatch of landlord/bully baddies, the division of the land, and the burning of the old title deeds into one supercharged four- to five-day period.[19] Final registration of the results, record keeping and the hearing of appeals, resolution of difficult cases, and border

---

[18] QXZ, pp. 199–200.

[19] MDA 13/1/37. "Shanghai xian guqu" (Shanghai county districts). This map shows forty-eight districts in the county, with the dates of their first (preparatory), second ("high tide"), and third ("concluding") phases of land reform. Of these, twenty-three completed the second stage in a week or under, twenty-three in between one and two weeks, none in more than two weeks, and two for which there is no information.

adjudication dragged on through 1952, but these were relatively straight-forward bureaucratic exercises of entering data into the files.

The difference between land reform in Sunan and that in Taiwan is stark. In contrast to the emphasis on a swiftly moving "high tide" in Sunan, those in charge of land reform in Taiwan went out of their way to differentiate their version of land reform with the one on the mainland at every stage of the proceedings. This held true for both content and manner of implementation. If the Communists insisted on rapid, public and emotionally charged "high tides" to implement land reform, then as a matter of principle the Nationalists had to demonstrate that their version of land reform was sober, gradualist, carefully planned, and technocratic. If the Chinese Communists were violent, dramatic, and sweeping, then the Nationalists needed to be peaceful, incentive oriented, and careful in process. And indeed everything written in the official *ex post facto* narratives of land reform in Taiwan suggests that land reform was accomplished by three carefully planned and executed projects that progressed in natural sequence between 1949 and 1953–1954, with a process "starting from 1949 and [was] brought to a successful inclusion in 1953."[20] In these official descriptions, the JCRR and the Nationalist government jointly developed land reform out of four quite separately initiated and deliberately gradualist administrative initiatives that built on each other between 1949 and 1954: the "375" rent reduction (1949, but accelerating in 1951–1952), the sale of public land (1951–1952 at various points), the re-checking and re-registration of the entire cadastre (1952) and only then the signature program for land reform in Taiwan, the Land to the Tiller program (1953, but comprehensively assessed and declared to be an overwhelming success in 1954).

The JCRR-GMD narrative of land reform in Taiwan offered to contemporaries and commemorated for posterity stressed its gradualism, inclusiveness, and its ability to re-establish rural social order by giving everyone a stake in the system as tenants became freeholders, and landlords became directly invested in state industries. In principle, no one was to be harmed and all were to become better off as the state returned all to a roughly level playing field by curbing landlord excesses and unfair extractions. The culmination of land reform – the "Land to the Tiller" program – was presented at the time as orderly, rational, and the crowning glory of the regime's lengthy commitment to planned, carefully phased land reform initiatives. With the benefit of hindsight, it is clear that the Land to the Tiller program was nothing of the kind. Rather, Land to the Tiller

---

[20] Hsiao Cheng, *The Theory and Practice of Land Reform*, p. 96 and Joint Commission on Rural Reconstruction *Land Reform Annual Reports*, p. 20.

was a dramatic campaign of regime mobilization in response to the problems engendered by the sudden enforcement of the longstanding but ineffective "375" Rent Reduction program in 1951–1952, when the regime began a campaign to intensify implementation of the 375 Rent Reduction measures. Unfortunately, this sudden burst of enforcement triggered unanticipated problems. The "375" Rent reduction program was by itself uncontroversial. It had featured in the GMD's commitment to rural China from the days of Sun Yat-sen, and was, at least on paper, an essential plank of GMD rural policy after 1949 in Taiwan.

Between 1949 and 1951, the "375" Rent Reduction was implemented in a top-down, controlled way. Rules were drawn up and publicized, "375" Rent Reduction Committees were formed locally, and centrally trained inspectors were sent down to the countryside to check on results. To read the reports of the JCRR, which only rarely and obliquely refer to "unrest" in the countryside, one would never know that naked coercion underpinned the entirety of the land reform policies – policies that were simultaneously an effort to "stabilize" the countryside and a reflection of stability in the countryside.[21] Even now there is substantial agreement in the literature that land reform in Taiwan was both uniquely progressive and devoid of violence: in the words of one scholar, "throughout the reform period of 1949 to 1953, there was not a single known instance of violence."[22]

Propaganda to the contrary, this presumptive lack of violence was more a reflection of JCRR and Taiwan *dizheng* lack of involvement in repression than a product of the GMD's uniquely peaceful approach to land reform. As we saw in the last chapter, the Taiwan Garrison Command's security operations in the Taiwanese countryside between 1949 and 1953 included those who did not acquiesce in the JCRR-GMD version of gradualist rent reduction. The nervous, reactive GMD government did not tolerate any activity, speech, or publication that so much as hinted at dissent on the regime's official vision of land reform and rural order. Even progressive officials like Lin Rigao could be accused (and sentenced to death) for having prosecuted the government's own programs for rent reduction too vigorously. Equally, those who participated in anything other than the now tamed GMD-supported farmers' associations, openly criticized the 375 rent reduction program, or showed evidence of awareness that the CCP had a very different vision of land reform could be prosecuted and held incommunicado (or worse) until a confession was

[21] Chen Cheng, *Land Reform in Taiwan*, p. x, xii, T. H. Shen, *The Sino-American Commission on Joint Rural Reconstruction*, p. 57.
[22] Hung-chao Tai, *Land Reform and Politics: A Comparative Analysis*, p. 285.

exacted. The coercive arm of the GMD state in Taiwan wasted no time in vigorously suppressing those who were not quiescent in the state's version of "375" rent reduction, even as it also prosecuted those who were overly committed to its implementation. Thus, the state's signals in how seriously rent reduction should be taken were unclear, and in 1949–1950, very little actual rent reduction was in evidence.

To overcome this stalling out of the government's key land reform program, in 1951 the JCRR launched two ambitious projects: (1) the reclassification and re-registration of all of Taiwan's arable land; and (2) training a cadre of inspectors to go to the countryside and check on the implementation of the 375 Rent Reduction. Dispatching inspectors to check on the progress of the rent-reduction policy demonstrated the regime's seriousness about continuing land reform, but it neither ensured robust implementation of the 375 Reduction, nor resulted in the kinds of anticipatory acquiescence that the presence of inspectors presumed. To the utter dismay of the planners in the JCRR and the Taiwan provincial Land Bureau, rather than lessening social conflict in the countryside, the regime's new seriousness in implementing rent reduction triggered widespread evasion, unilateral lease cancellations, and waves of disputes between landlords and tenants. More vigorous enforcement of rent reduction prompted landlords to claw back losses by shifting their customary responsibility for hefty irrigation association fees onto tenants. As farmers downstream were dependent on the timely release of water from irrigation associations, bitter contention over lease terms escalated dramatically over 1951–1952. The sudden uncertainties over land tenure meant that land prices dropped. And just when conciliatory mechanisms for adjudicating disputes between landlords and tenant were most necessary, investigations revealed that the local 375 Rent Reduction Committees that had been established in the late 1940s to resolve disputes between landlord and tenant proved mostly to be either landlord dominated, or to exist only on paper.[23]

Ironically, the government's sudden enforcement of its long-standing 375 Rent Reduction policy accelerated exactly the rural unrest that it was trying to ameliorate. In turn, this led to the government's abrupt abandonment of rent reduction in favour of the much less gradualist and more stringent Land to the Tiller Program (*gengzhe you qitian* – 耕者有其田). Although never officially so labelled, the Land to the Tiller program bore all the hallmarks of a campaign: the rapid expansion of state capacity, intensive propaganda, and a big push for visible and defined results, even as their planners were occupied at every turn by the imperative to

[23] *JCRR*, pp. 8–11, 20–30.

distinguish their rationale, their methods, and their outcomes from the land reform campaign in the People's Republic of China.

Land Reform Campaigns as Dramatization of Power (II): Different Registers of Rural Representation

Violence, either overt or implied, was at the heart of land reform in Sunan and Taiwan. What differed was how direct or implicit the violence was, and how the violence was entangled with or clearly separated from the dramatization of land reform. Campaign planners in Sunan and Taiwan both presumed that regular, organized representation from "below" was necessary for the successful implementation of such a game-changing program in the countryside. They made efforts to organize the grass roots into Peasant Associations in Sunan and Rent Reduction Committees/Farm Tenancy Committees in Taiwan. The role that these representative bodies played in land reform was, however, very different. Throughout 1950, local cadres throughout rural Sunan had organized and held elections for local peasant, women, and youth associations. But in practice these new associations seemed to have had surprisingly little direct input into the campaign.

The review of land reform in Qingpu cited earlier suggests that in Sunan the campaign was dominated by three different parties: (1) the local land reform committee (a small group of leading cadres, sometimes supplemented by outsiders appointed by the county government); (2) regular local cadres sent up to the county for special training sessions; and (3) pre-identified local activists. Occasionally, the county or district would send in work teams to "guide" the process of land reform, but normally it was up to local cadres to interpret signals and directives from above. Cadres ordered to establish peasant associations did so, but frequently distrusted them because they could easily come to be dominated by rich peasants (and possibly even landlords through the backdoor). This worry was not completely irrational: in at least one documented case in Miaoyang, Changshu, the "masses" openly wondered why landlords were not permitted to join peasant associations, and questions were even asked about why landlords could not stand for election as small group representatives.[24]

In Sunan, popular participation in land reform was not, as might have been expected, articulated through elections and regularized expression of interests via local peasant associations. Rather, the CCP conceived of rural participation in land reform campaigns in terms of collective public

[24] JPA 3006/3/271.

performance. Insofar as Peasant Associations contributed to Sunan's land reform, they seem to have been confined to propaganda dissemination and, on occasion, helping to get everyone out to public accusation meetings. The real mass participation occurred at public accusation/struggle meetings (*kongsu hui* – 控訴會 or *douzheng hui* – 鬥爭會).

The form of the mass accusation session aimed to gather nearly the entirety of the rural population into a single participant-spectator audience in one place, where the specific theatrical device of "speaking bitterness" (*suku* – 訴苦) was acted out by pre-coached activists and victims, selected well in advance of the proceedings for their capacity to stir up the sympathy of the crowd. Like the public accusation meetings of counterrevolutionaries, the events themselves needed to *appear* to be spontaneous, directly participatory, and unmediated by intermediate organizations and visible procedures, even though there was an enormous amount of behind-the-scenes preparation to stage the event. The show had many functions: to educate the public, to stiffen the resolve of cadres, to give activists a chance to establish their credentials, and to graphically expunge the impure and unreconstructed from the body politic. The show required that the individual merge with the collective audience. It further demanded that this newly imagined public be (literally) given voice with a culminating roar of collective catharsis that erased the boundaries between state, society, and individual. Despite the very different society and economy of rural Sunan, the CCP continued to insist on applying a form (public gathering), process (emotional high of the "stirred up" masses), and content (hatred towards defined class enemies) that had served it so well in making rural revolution in North China. The party-state in Sunan remained deeply attached to not only the results of land reform, but also to the specific revolutionary ethos it embodied, the way in which it instructed the wider population in the Party's normative values, and the momentary, but nonetheless real merging of popular and state will.

The instructions handed down to local cadres insisted that the process of accusation had to be dramatically embodied as a confrontation of archetypes: the now chastened evildoer, the righteous victim, the loud exhortation of an indignant crowd, merged into a collective whole, and, just offstage, the state that was putting on the production. The public drama of mass struggle sessions provided a stage upon which newly privileged local voices were articulated through direct participatory action unconstrained by clear rules and procedures. Indeed, clarity about rules and procedures was seen to be the antithesis of a proper "high tide." The Chinese Communist Party's notion of the land reform campaign actively required that after preparation, organization, propaganda, and investigation of who owned what property, the peak of the campaign's "high tide" should result in appropriately mobilized masses stirred to action. The masses could only raise their revolutionary consciousness if they vented their rightful hatred of the landlord exploiter. This public expression of anger by definition supported the new government's bloody violence against defined enemies.

Like the high tide accusation meetings of the Campaign to Suppress Counterrevolutionaries, public accusation sessions in land reform were far from the spontaneous events that they may have seemed to the participant audiences of the time. Local cadres planned carefully for these public spectacles. They chose and prepared the sites of the accusation meeting. They identified and coached activists and sympathetic accusers. They rehearsed in advance when a given accuser was to come forward onto the stage of the mass struggle session. They decided on which accusers would come forward in what order, and provided accusers with rough scripts to ensure that the crowd was first warmed up by less serious accusations before the most graphic cases of blood debt released the highest level of sympathetic emotion towards the end of the show. In the Shanghai outer district village of Meituo, such was the emphasis on preparation for the big public struggle meeting that there were *three* preparatory meetings of the relevant rural cadres to "unify understanding, move forward mobilization, and strengthen policy education." Cadres were also expected to form a full plan for the accusation meeting, organize the logistics, and "fully grasp and review" the materials pertaining to their targets. They were counseled to commence accusation meetings no earlier than 4:00 pm, but to end them before 6:00 pm to avoid hunger, boredom, and wandering attention from the masses. They were also instructed on the seating order for the audience: those from the district were seated first and closest to the stage, and observers from outside the district were to be allowed in somewhat later, further from the proceedings. Such was the obsession with planning and control that local cadres in Meituo even went so far as to run full dress rehearsals several days before the main event, complete with selected individuals from "the masses" to sit in the audience. Since the two accused – a landlord by the name of Cai Heng, and an "evil bully" by the name of Sun Jize, were in detention, local cadres reckoned that this early run-through was a good way to smooth out organizational issues, pre-educate the public, and stiffen the resolve of activists. Local cadres in Meituo admitted that the masses who attended this rehearsal did wonder aloud why the later accusation meeting attended by thousands was necessary. What Cai Heng and Sun Jize thought of having to play the part of accused villain more than once in a real-life drama with deadly consequences at the denouement of the final performance can only be imagined.[25]

While cadres were expected to prepare obsessively for mass accusation meetings ahead of the proceedings, the actual "high tide" (*gaochao*) of the event was supposed to be in the hands of the masses. Cadres were admonished to avoid making decisions themselves, but to leave key dramatic moments to the now "stirred up" masses. Instruction booklets issued to local cadres insisted that formulaic slogans be avoided, and reiterated that the sight of the targets on stage was expected to result in appropriate slogans of "sound and color" (*yousheng youse* – 有聲 有色). In the mass accusation meeting in Meituo, this formula was followed quite closely when the stirred-up crowd directly incited the public beating of "evil bully" Sun Jize. Instructions stipulated that the collective voice of the masses was, in theory, to be heeded. When the crowd shouted "bow your head" to the accused, he was supposed to bow his head; when it followed up with "drop to your knees," he was supposed to drop to his knees. If the crowd agitated for the accused to be beaten, the leading cadres in charge were supposed to encourage the accuser to acquiesce to the demands of the masses. At the peak of the "high tide," when the crowd was called on to decide the fate of the accused, if the masses called for immediate public revenge to be taken, the authorities were to permit the accused to be beaten to death *in situ*, or to lead the accused off the stage to be publicly executed forthwith. In instances when the crowd wished to show mercy after the accuser spoke bitterness and the accused recognized his guilt, the target could then be turned over to the regular processes of the people's courts.[26]

Cadres from higher up also insisted that the public accusation sessions had to include the wronged engaging in direct "face to face" (*mian dui mian* – 面對面) accusation with the target. The evildoer was required to "publicly acknowledge" his previous crimes (*chengzui* – 承罪) before the masses *[as] without this kind of public acknowledgement of crimes the entire [process] is fake* [italics added].[27] Individual contrition, and by extension the recognition of the state's new categories of pure and depraved, good classes and bad classes, even by representatives from the depraved bad classes themselves was felt to be a necessary component of proper

---

[25] SMA A71/2/76/30. "Zhonggong Shanghai shi Meituoxiang zongzhi weiyuanhui, guanyu erci douzheng hui de jieshao cailiao" (CCP Shanghai Municipality Meituo village combined committee, introductory materials on two struggle meetings), 1951.

[26] SMA A71/2/76/30. "Zhonggong Shanghai shi Meituoxiang zongzhi weiyuanhui guanyu erci douzheng hui de jieshao cailiao," ibid.

[27] JPA 3006/3/271. Sunan Tugai Weiyuanhui Mishuchu, "Guanyu fadong qunzhong wenti de baogao," 1951.

resolution to the onstage drama. If the accused did not express penitence, ask for forgiveness, and symbolically accede to the state's new order, then the mass accusation session was judged unsatisfying and incomplete. Not coincidentally, in the rare instances in which there are detailed accounts of those who refused to acknowledge their crimes (and by extension the authority of the state), such as the abovementioned Sun Jize, the cadre who wrote up the final report was palpably indignant that Sun "died without recognizing his mistakes," thus denying the validity and legitimacy of New China.[28]

Records from Qingpu county, Shanghai county, and the Shanghai *jiaoqu* confirm that large numbers of mass struggle sessions were convened and that those "targets" predetermined to be most evil and hated were promptly led off to the execution ground. The degree to which "the masses" happily played their part in this drama is, however, uncertain. One set of figures from Shanghai county suggests that crowds were often enthusiastic in their condemnation of state enemies: nearly a third (224 of 779) of recorded "accusation targets" (*douzheng duixiang* – 鬥爭對象) "were strung up and beaten as they were struggled against" (*douzheng zhong bei diaoda* – 鬥爭中被 吊打). What are we to make of these numbers that suggest that in this one rural county to the south of Shanghai, audiences were easily roused to participate in excessive state-sanctioned violence against designated enemies when the state called for violence to be done? Was Shanghai county typical? Were these crowds either given free rein or actively encouraged by local cadres? Were those who rushed to "string up and beat" the accused a minority, and if so, what was the reaction of the majority who witnessed these events? Was this staged, ostensibly popular and spontaneous violence instigated by activists and tolerated by local cadres, or were local cadres themselves the instigators? Were most of the people who witnessed the spectacle genuinely "stirred up," or did they have sneaking sympathy for the accused? And, how do we square this evidence with qualitative reports that detail repeated examples of the sympathy of the "masses" for their own landlords?[29]

Given the bureaucratic incentives for local cadres to report dutifully that the public accusation meeting had been a success, that the crowd's consciousness had been raised, and that the accused had admitted his mistakes amid a resounding "high tide" of collective emotional hatred for state enemies and support for the state's righteousness, it is not surprising

---

[28] SMA A71/2/76/30.
[29] QDA 1/1/38. "Douzheng cishu tongjibiao" (Statistics on numbers of struggles). 2–3. 1951; MDA 13/1/37 "Shanghai xian jiesu tugai gongzuo douzheng qingkuang tongjibiao" (Statistics on Shanghai county struggle sessions at the conclusion of land reform), November 18, 1951.

Image 5.1. Landlord undergoing public accusation, Zhenjiang. (http://
daminhvn.net/suy-tu-nghien-cuu/nhin-lai-hau-qua-tai-hai-cua-cuoc-cai-
cach-ruong-dat-tai-trung-quoc-13183.html)

that there are only hints of anything else in the archival record. There are,
however, scattered accounts that suggest that while some were often eager
to participate in violence, others were either simple spectators or were even
quietly disapproving of the proceedings. Mass public audiences could and
did adopt a "plague on both your houses" attitude. In one struggle meeting
in Taicang county, Liangbei village, two people from the crowd rushed the
stage, taking over the proceedings.[30] After the struggle meeting was over
many in the audience could be heard grumbling that "those conducting the
struggle were all bad people." In Gaodu's Qiqiao village, things did not go
to plan at all. Rather than coming off with contrition on the part of landlords and a convincing reaffirmation of public support for the regime, the
proceedings against three landlords resulted in the audience washing their
hands of the entire business, opining that "both the recipients and the
actors [of the struggle session] were all bad – [this is just a show of] bad
people beating up other bad people."[31]

---

[30] This instance of rushing the stage would have been more than enough for the cadre in
charge to have been smacked down with a stern reprimand from superiors, who cautioned against allowing new, unproven accusations to be brought forth spontaneously
from the crowd.

[31] JPA 3006/3/271. "Guanyu fadong qunzhong douzheng cailiao zhailü," April 1951.

At present, many of the available qualitative reports on land reform *kongsu hui* in Sunan are either so formulaic ("the crowd was stirred up"), or so heavily focused on negative anecdote in order to make a point ("the masses were *not* stirred up [and cadres need to prepare more thoroughly and do better]") that it is impossible to gauge how typical or atypical the anecdote in question might be. The record in Sunan is thus far lacking in the kind of detailed and lengthy eyewitness accounts that convey whether the violence unleashed in public accusation meetings was genuinely popular, whether it brought about the free-flowing tears and spontaneous accusations that were typical of the land reform campaign described by Hinton and the Crooks for North China, whether it was the product of a small minority, or whether in fact it only took place with the active connivance of local cadres and activists.

In the Shanghai outer district of Zhenru, the poor and hired peasants in Luchangqiao and Changtou villages who ought to have been the campaign's main reservoir of support remained frustratingly "unstirred": even the poorest held throughout the entire campaign that the house arrest and public struggle session against landlords had nothing to do with them personally. Meanwhile, most middle peasants remained "asleep" and refused to be stirred up at all.[32] In another small (non) event in Luqiangqiao, authorities identified a poor peasant named Qian Ahyou as having been particularly wronged by landlords. For whatever reason, Qian remained (in the view of the local cadres who wrote the eventual report) incomprehensibly reluctant to appear at struggle sessions and play his part in the proceedings. Qian preferred to lie low and avoid the entire business for some three to four days, and finally had to be (directly) "accompanied to the meeting by the village cadre," whereupon Qian was presumably prevailed upon to conform and make the requisite public accusation.[33] The regular reports from Shanghai county, the *jiaoqu*, and Sunan in general are replete with stock complaints about the "backward political consciousness of the masses." When specific examples of this sort of mass "backwardness" are cited, they include the cynical view that Chiang Kai-shek's return was right around the corner, and that the process of land reform had nothing to do with *them*.

A critical report on the difficulties of stirring up the masses compiled by the Sunan Land Reform Investigation Unit is full of detailed if anecdotal evidence confirming that, in many locales, cadres had to overcome a great deal of natural hesitation by the "masses" to be "stirred" to physical

---

[32] SMA A71/2/84. "Zhenru qu Diantai xiang Luchangqiao cun Changtou cun tugai jianchazhong de qingkuang baogao" (Investigative report on land reform in Zhenru district, diantai village, Luchangqiao and Changtou hamlets), August 11, 1951.

[33] Ibid.

violence. In one case in Jiading county, Mawei district, Beiguan village, cadres were clearly inciting the audience to demand physical violence when the performance on stage apparently went off script. A local cadre placed in the crowd shouted out (for the accuser on stage to) "go ahead and hit him!" (the accused). At this juncture, "From the stage [where the accused and a peasant who was 'speaking bitterness' were standing], the district cadre who was directing the proceedings instructed the accuser 'if the masses say "hit him" then you have to go ahead and hit him.'" But the accuser demurred with the repeated insistence that: "I've never hit any-one before, and I will not hit him." As the crowd continued to call for him to use physical force, the man on the stage eventually hit the accused twice. The crowd continued to bay for more violence, and in the end the accuser landed some seven or eight blows. In this case there were three elements that incited a clearly reluctant performer: the triggering call of the local cadre from the audience, the formal authority of the district cadre on the stage, and mass hysteria from the assembled crowd.[34]

In other localities, things played out differently. Local cadres could and sometimes did dampen down the physical violence of accusatory theater by keeping tight control over the proceedings, or even discreetly postpon-ing the show until tempers had cooled. In Kunshan's Yebi district, Yebi village, the local cadre opened the public accusation session with a warn-ing to the crowd that "*he* was the one passing judgment, and that anyone who went ahead and 'strung up and beat' an accused target would have to take responsibility for so doing." In another instance involving a particu-larly despised "little tiger" (*xiaohu* – 小虎), a local cadre by the name of Zhang Zhihua refused to let the prisoner go to his appointed struggle session, fearing that if the prisoner had to face the public, he would surely be beaten to death.[35]

The presently available qualitative evidence is profoundly ambiguous on the most important question at all: how public accusation meetings were received and understood by the crowds that were called to partici-pate in this publicly performed drama as spectators, witnesses, and choruses. Some accounts suggest that the show of mass accusation ses-sions followed the script and the outcomes desired by higher levels in the CCP: representing popular will and whipping the crowd into a frenzy of popular support for the regime's dispatch of now isolated class enemies. Numerous local reports present statistics to suggest that the majority of the rural population "participated" (*canjia*) in accusation sessions as the audience. Formulaic reports conclude that "the masses were stirred up"

[34] JPA 3006/3/271. "Guanyu fadong qunzhong douzheng de cailiao zhailü," April 1951.
[35] Ibid.

and that justice was done, with resounding affirmation in support of the state's violence. In some cases, it is clear that after the leftward move of the land reform campaign in November 1950, some cadres and activists incited the masses to publicly denounce and commit violence against those deemed hateful exploiters. Other accounts point to the limits that local cadres could (and did) put on the degree of uncontrolled violence that they would permit on their watches. The script handed down from on high required a dramatic culmination of "stirred up" masses accusing evil landlords and reaffirming collective unity with the state and its violence against defined enemies. Sometimes the show went well. But occasionally it seems it did not. Sunan was, after all, a region in which the dividing line between exploited and exploiters was blurred, landlords were weak, social and economic mobility was high, and in many places local people appeared to have thought that their own local landlords were not such bad sorts at all. We cannot know for sure about something so variable and subjective, but it does stand to reason that perhaps the "masses" were less enthusiastic than the large numbers of those in attendance at these public struggle sessions would otherwise suggest. In 1950–1951, the CCP demanded that the drama of the mass accusation meetings developed under wartime conditions in North China be fractally replicated through-out central and southern China. But this script of spontaneous violence, stirred-up masses, and copious tears was one that seems not to have transferred all that well to postwar, militarily secure, and commercially dynamic Sunan.

These partial and ambiguous narratives on the "high tide" of Sunan's land reform suggest that in some cases the state did put on a convincing show; in others the majority felt fear and pity for the accused; and in still others, most felt that the entire undertaking had nothing to do with them. Given the demands placed on local cadres that public accusation meet-ings be put on in a certain way and demonstrate key markers of success (an aroused crowd that shouted the right slogans, face-to-face accusa-tions, and the penitent accused acknowledging prior crimes and errors on stage), it is not particularly surprising that cadre reports on the struggle meeting invoke the formula decreed from on high: the masses were stirred up and raised their revolutionary consciousness, the evil received their just punishment, and everyone supported the righteousness of the revolu-tionary's state's actions. Occasional hints of other reactions do come through in these cadre reports: sometimes the masses were "asleep," felt that the accusation of prior evildoers had nothing to do with them, or were unaccountably reluctant to participate in direct personal violence against the state's chosen embodiments of evil. Ethnography in other regions of China suggests that some of those who witnessed the executions of landlords exhibited unease with the state's violence in the land reform campaign of the late 1940s and early 1950s. And the abrupt 2017 ban of the novel *Soft Burial* that explores the aftermath of human suffering and disconnection in families whose members committed suicide when they were prosecuted as landlords indicates that land reform still stands as a pillar, if an increasingly ambiguous one, in the CCP's master narrative of its own success.[36]

The CCP remained deeply attached to the form of mass accusation meetings, which demanded that the individual in the crowd, the crowd itself, and the regime come together in (temporary) revolutionary unity. The large venues for the stage, the simplified emotional narratives of prior suffering to appeal to a public sense of justice, and the now-shackled representatives of evil personified were all integral components of a performance designed to generate a unified sense of heightened emotion in the assembled crowd. The collective fury unleashed in this very public fusion of state power and popular support against the clearly defined internal enemy/Other, was the very reverse of a bureaucratic modality of implementation based on the principles of hierarchy, precedent, proce- dure, and process. Indeed, the very *point* of the mass accusation meeting "high tide" was to steamroller normal procedures and processes with raw emotional power that fused the state and the "stirred up" public.

The mass struggle meeting was as much a heuristic device for educating the participants in the audience about the new regime's norms and rhetoric as it was a means for dispatching individuals deemed to be enemies of the state. (Speedy and secret execution or imprisonment would have done the job just as well if the objective was simply to rid the body politic of internal saboteurs and enemies as quickly and effi- ciently as possible.) The state claimed to represent, reproduce, and make public the legitimate position and opinions of "the masses"; the masses in turn learned what was expected of them through new forms of political participation unmediated by organizations or procedures. Further, the public and staged nature and form of the mass struggle session provided a visible point of rupture with the "old" – it not only rid society of enemies,

[36] Gregory Ruf, *Cadres and Kin: Making a Socialist Village in West China, 1921–1991*, p. 71, and pp. 86–87; Hinton, *Fanshen*, pp. 133–138. Fang Fang's *Ruan Mai* (軟埋 – Soft Burial) was published by Renmin Wenxue Chubanshe in 2016. Although it won the 2016 Luyao Literature Award, it prompted a torrent of sharp criticism for its "nihilism," "its attempt to vindicate the landlord class," and its "reflection of ideological class struggle in the current terrain." The novel itself is available online at www.bannedbook.org/resour ces/file/5871 (accessed June 16, 2017). See also Oiwan Lam, "China bans 'Soft Burial', a novel about deadly consequences of land reform," www.hongkongfp.com/2017/06/12/ china-bans-soft-burial-award-winning-novel-deadly-consequences-land-reform/, accessed June 17, 2017.

it did so in such a way as to communicate to the largest possible number of ordinary people that the new government was deadly serious in its commitment to transforming the old society. Public accusation sessions also implicitly bloodied the hands of all of those who shouted in support of the regime's violence against enemies. When the show went well, local participation and representation was articulated through a publicly affirmed emotional union of crowd and state. Mass representation was not channeled through regular procedures or formal organizations. Rather it was fused to the state in a dramatic, but temporary, emotional high that provided a widely understood moment of no return – after which nothing would ever be quite the same again.

State violence and local participation in land reform were also very significant in the ROC/Taiwan, but could not have been more differently imagined, acted upon, or played out in public. The GMD/JCRR account of land reform in Taiwan is one of a carefully thought out, gradualist, peaceful, orderly, and inclusive process that in principle benefited everyone, landlords included. It drew on a lineage stretching back to the Sun Yat-sen, the National Father, who proposed rent reduction for tenants in 1924. The JCRR and the Taiwan provincial Land Bureau understood that the best land reform would be one that was fully taken on board with the participation of those affected, but rural participation in land reform would have to be of a very different kind than that practiced in the PRC. Rather than the emotional "stirring up" of crowd emotions, with its free-flowing tears and spontaneous violence to overcome regular procedures and institutional hierarchies, the ROC/Taiwan and the JCRR made provision from the outset to channel local representation into formal organizations that took on adjudication on behalf of the state. Over the course of the early 1950s these took two forms: Rent Reduction Committees (*sanqiwu weiyuanhui* – 三七五 委員會) which were in operation between 1949 and 1952, and Farm Tenancy Committees (*gengdi zudian weiyuanhui* – 耕地租佃委員會 or *zudian weiyuanhui* – 租佃委員會), which replaced the ineffective Rent Reduction Committees in 1952–1953. Since Rent Reduction Committees proved utterly unable to contain the "social instability" that ensued from the suddenly vigorous implementation of rent reduction in 1951–1952, it was important for the regime to reconfigure local land reform institutions if land reform was to fulfil its primary function – to build support for the regime rather than accelerate violent contention in the countryside.

The JCRR's first step in resolving this problem was to invite an external expert in rural development, Wolf Ladejinsky, to return to Taiwan to investigate rural conditions. By 1951, Ladejinsky was a known and trusted figure in agricultural development circles in East Asia. He had already served for five years as agricultural attaché to General MacArthur for SCAP in Tokyo, and was recognized as the chief figure behind a successful land reform program in Occupation-era Japan. In the autumn of 1949, he had been given leave from SCAP to investigate rent-reduction programs in the parts of Sichuan then still under Guomindang control, and after Sichuan was no longer safe for JCRR operations, he continued his work in Taiwan. As early as 1949, Ladejinsky made clear his doubts about the usefulness of the 375 Rent Reduction Committees in rural Taiwan, and recommended in the strongest of terms that they be reorganized along the lines of their counterparts in Japan, which ensured a majority of tenant representation.[37] It was not, however, until after Ladejinsky made a second investigation tour to Taiwan in the spring of 1951, that he produced an even stronger report recommending the establishment of islandwide Farm Tenancy Committees to replace the defunct and/or discredited Rent Reduction Committees. This time, the JCRR and the government accepted his plan. New Farm Tenancy Committees were to be constituted for townships, counties, and municipalities (as municipalities frequently included rural areas within their administrations). They would include the heads of the township/county/municipality Taiwan Land bureaus as *ex officio*, but the representatives of these committees were to be chosen from a mix of different rural occupational statuses, with fixed numbers of landlords, owner cultivators, and tenants. Crucially, by design, these committees were to have slightly more tenant representatives than landlord representatives.[38]

The creation of these new rural institutions was accomplished through a campaign within a campaign: an islandwide set of indirect elections to return delegates to these newly established Farm Tenancy Committees. In this way, representative bodies were brought into existence through a process that was controlled, but nonetheless open, public, and moderately theatrical. After elections were held, Farm Tenancy Committees met regularly (usually once monthly) behind closed doors for a three-year term. The creation of Farm Tenancy Committees through local elections required the regime to put on a public show to which the public was indeed invited to participate. These shows, however, were very far removed from those put on by the People's Republic of China.

---

[37] *JCRR Annual Report on Land Reform*, p. 30. See also T. H. Shen's later insistence that this provision was at the heart of the successful land reform effort on Taiwan in Joseph Yager, p. 106, and Louis Walinsky, *The Selected Papers of Wolf Ladejinsky*, p. 95.

[38] GSG 315/4486. "Final Report: Reorganization of 343 Land Commissions in Taiwan," February 15, 1952.

Competitive elections generally lend themselves to circumscribed dramatic performances. In the course of an election, public speeches and campaigning for votes and support are at least permitted if not actively encouraged, and election campaigns are perhaps the best-known way in which politicians in representative democracies attempt to engage the emotions and garner the support of some cross-section of the voting public. At the same time, elections are also rule bound, delimited in time with a clear beginning, middle, and end, and at least in theory result in clear winners who hold office for a fixed period, after which another round of elections is held. It is through this interplay of bureaucratically delimited rules for process and open-ended results that the GMD state on Taiwan permitted some dramatization of politics from "below." The actual elections to Farm Tenancy Committees were open and competitive, but as was the case for *kongsu hui* in Sunan, convening elections required a fair amount of preparation that was bureaucratic and procedural. In Sunan the extensive preparation and stage management (organizing the public space and stage, getting the masses to attend, coaching the accusers) was hidden from view. The mass audience was simply called to view the final spectacle, and cheer and applaud at the right moments. In the ROC/Taiwan the open and visible and the closed off and concealed were precisely the opposite. Information about the new committees and their functions, new electoral rules and processes, and postings about each stage of the election were all publicly disseminated. The relevant rules and procedures for elections to Farm Tenancy Committees were publicized on posters and leaflets. Localities were expected to hold elections to Farm Tenancy Committees according to fixed rules with set plans and rigid timetables. These plans built in the time to allow limited campaigning and speech making before a concluding general meeting at which delegates were elected. Indeed, the state's new rules and procedures were the main thing that was performed for the rural public as part of the state's legitimating claims. It was *after* the public performance of rule-based elections that the workings of the new Farm Tenancy Committees were closed off to the public and concealed within the offices of the local Land Bureau.

A work plan from Yongkang town in Tainan county for the second round of elections to Farm Tenancy Committees in late 1955 reveals how rule-driven the election process was, and how much coordination was required throughout the island. The leaders of municipalities, counties, towns, and villages were told to offer between one and two days of lectures and instruction on how to convene elections. County chiefs took instruction from the province, townships from counties, and villages from townships. The active electoral season began in villages, with fifteen days of investigation and checking the credentials of candidates who put themselves forward, five allowed for advertising the candidates, one to announce the time and place of the actual election, two to make final checks with superiors on how many members would be elected to a given committee, and another twelve of registering, checking on, and advertising the names of those on the reserve list. The actual elections were to be held in an open meeting (*da hui* – 大會) and the results of the elections disseminated within a ten-day period thereafter. After the results of the election were entered and checked, the entire process was repeated, with the newly elected members of the Farm Tenancy committees at the village level electing those for the township Farm Tenancy Committees, and those at the level of the township electing those on the county or municipality Farm Tenancy Committees.[39]

Electees were returned to Farm Tenancy Committees according to their occupational status (landlords, freeholders, and tenants) and tenants held a reserved quota that equalled or exceeded the seats of freeholders and landlords combined. The first step in the electoral process was to compile of a list of eligible voters according to whether the individual was a landlord, tenant, or freeholder. Regular village and township offices screened the applications of prospective candidates and drew up a list of those who were eligible that was then posted in a public location. From this list each hamlet and section elected two tenant farmer representatives, one owner-farmer representative, and one landlord representative. This process was then repeated for larger territorial units: the township, the county, and the prefecture or municipality (which in this context meant the ex-urban rural areas surrounding major cities), which elected larger committees of two representatives from local government, five tenants, two owner farmers, and two landlords.[40]

JCRR records suggest that most localities managed to hold the first round of these elections (5,655 of 6,459 villages, 319 of 372 townships) on schedule between April and mid-June of 1952, and the voting participation rate in the elections was gratifyingly high at 98 percent.[41] At the same time, there is much that is opaque about how these elections worked in practice. Like elections to Peasant Associations in Sunan, these elections were held in open group meetings rather than at a ballot box, quite possibly through a show of hands. There is little information that hints at how

---

[39] YTA 0044/132/1/1/044. "Gexian shi zhengfu ji ge xiangzhen gong suo gengdi zudian weiyuanhui gaixuan gongzuo jindu biao," October 13, 1955 (Work Progress chart on county, city, and township government elections to Land Reform Committees).

[40] This information is drawn from Tang Hui-sun. pp. 56–58. See also Hung-chao Tai, p. 284.

[41] *JCRR*, p. 52.

individuals campaigned for these committees, and it appears that in many locations ordinary farmers were reluctant to take on the additional burden of public office. One JCRR report suggests that Land Bureaux found it extremely difficult to encourage qualified farmers to put themselves forward for these new offices and that it was "only after the utmost cajolery that they (farmers of good reputation) finally showed up, registered themselves as candidates and entered the election.[42] Even less is known about what kinds of public theatrical "shows" might have accompanied these elections. What is clear is that the highest echelons of the JCRR believed that the Farm Tenancy Committees that resulted from these elections were critical to the later success of the Land to the Tiller program.

On paper, Farm Tenancy Committees were given substantial powers: supplying aid and guidance for the proper implementation of rent reduction, appraising annual yields, making recommendations for rent reduction or exemption on the grounds of poor harvests, adjudicating disputes over tenancy, and ultimately deciding on what land ought to be compulsorily purchased by the state for resale to tenants or retained by landlords.[43] Farm Tenancy Committees were animated by the same principles as the other associational bodies re-established by the government in the early 1950s: farmers' associations, irrigation associations, and merchants' associations were all intertwined with the state in ways that allowed the state to devolve some of its routine work to intermediary organizations. Unlike farmers' associations, which were granted hefty economic subsidies in return for collecting the rice tax and managing a rice-for-fertilizer barter scheme on behalf of the provincial Grain Bureau,[44] Farm Tenancy Committee members were unsalaried volunteers. The boundaries between elected Farm Tenancy Committees and the Taiwan provincial government Land Administration bureaus (*dizheng ju/chu* 地政局/地政處) were blurred at best. As already noted, the local head of the *dizheng chu* or *ju* was invariably present on the Farm Tenancy Committee as an *ex officio* member and well may have exercised a great deal of informal influence. The state also had significant direct and indirect oversight over the workings of these elected committees. The Taiwan Provincial Land Bureau (*dizheng ju*) gave compulsory two-week training courses to recent electees "to acquaint them with their functions and responsibilities and the relevant laws and regulations."[45] The minutes of the Farm Tenancy Committees were routinely reported to the

---

[42] Ibid.
[43] Tai Hung-chao, *Land Reform and Politics: A Comparative Analysis*, 284–285.
[44] Strauss, "From Feeding the Army to Nourishing the People: The Impact of Wartime Mobilization and Institutions on Grain Supply in Post-1949 Sunan and Taiwan."
[45] Tang Hui-sun, p. 59.

relevant *dizheng ju* or *dizheng chu* for review. Difficult cases were passed up to higher level Farm Tenancy committees, the district-level *dizheng chu* and, more rarely, turned over to the regular court system for adjudication. It is entirely possible that the *dizheng ju* government officials did more than simply review the work of the Farm Tenancy Committee and enter its decisions for the formal record.

Whatever the Farm Tenancy Committee's actual degree of independence from, or enmeshment with the state might have been, the government took the establishment of these bodies very seriously. Over the course of 1952, no fewer than 3,032 committee representatives were elected to serve on Farm Tenancy Committees in every village, township, county, and municipality in Taiwan. These committees also possessed significant local powers of adjudication.[46] One set of figures states that between January 1952 and July 1956 township-level committees conciliated 31,759 disputes and referred 16,462 to prefectural or municipal level committees, of which 9,418 were conciliated and only 5,321 were referred to courts. While there is little information about how these committees worked in villages, township Farm Tenancy Committees had a substantial presence. They met regularly from late 1952 onward, and in many locations their work continued well into the 1960s. They also appear to have possessed substantial quasi-judicial authority: reviewing documents, hearing evidence, and directly questioning disputing parties.

To give a sense of the powers of these Farm Tenancy Committees, consider the workload of the Farm Tenancy Committee in Hunei township, Gaoxiong county. In its monthly session of January 1953, it met to resolve four cases. The substance of these cases ranged from: (1) a claim of incorrect borders for a plot (and therefore the amount of rent owed in the second quarter of 1952); (2) a landlord who refused to dissolve a rental contract with a tenant; (3) a tenant by the name of Jiang Chunfang who petitioned the committee to force his landlord Lin Zengyue to sell land to him rather than to a third party; and (4) the landlord Bi Chuifu, who flatly refused to sell his land to his two tenants, Tao Jinzong and Ye Baishi, on the grounds that Bi was dividing the land to give his younger brother his rightful share.[47] Each of these disputes brought the two

---

[46] GSG 313/1285-8. FY 56. A particularly detailed example of farm tenancy committees questioning plaintiffs and respondents can be found in GCA, 0042/155.1.56/01/08/017, in a dispute in Hunei district between a landlord named Du Chaozong and five tenant respondents who had failed to pay the agreed rent due to a claimed "natural disaster" in the first growing season of the year.

[47] GCA 0042/155.1.56/01/03/014. Gaoxiong xian Hunei xiang gongsuo, "Chengsong benxiang zudian weiyuanhuyi zhaokailinshi huiyi bing diao jieye dian zhengyi anjian" (Hunei township farm tenancy committee meeting to resolve tenant disputes). Dated January 6, 1953; hearing held on December 29, 1952.

contending parties before the committee, which had the power to ask questions, note responses, make judgments, and then pass the decision up to the county-level government for ratification and entry into the formal record. In the fullness of time, the Gaoxiong county government issued a certificate of resolution of each of these disputes without change to the decision of the committee.[48]

In addition to these bread and butter disputes about plot borders, lease cancellation, and the rights (or lack thereof) of landlords to divide their land with relatives, in fairly short order Farm Tenancy Committees began to consider other sorts of claims. Landlords brought disputes for non-payment of rent in the few quarters prior to the implementation of the Land to the Tiller program; tenants pleaded economic hardship, illness, or recent injury.[49] In some locations, Farm Tenancy committees were even called upon to take on larger roles in types of local land disputes never envisioned by the JCRR or the Taiwan Provincial Land Bureau. For example, in 1955, in Yongkang town, Tainan county, a land dispute between two government bodies, the local branch of the Taiwan Sugar Factory and the local agricultural school was brought before the Yongkang Municipal Farm Tenancy Committee to adjudicate.[50]

As it sought to remake and stabilize rural Taiwan, the GMD's preferred option was to blur the boundaries of state and society by creating a committee of local stake holders and call on them to take over some portion of the state's work. The Guomindang party-state went out of its way to provide for a regularized form of participatory representation for local interest articulation (and get help with resolving some of the local conflicts brought about by the government's new policies). In Taiwan, local representation in land reform was regularized, formally organized, procedurally oriented, and designed to be deliberately inclusive of different economic status groups in rural society. After the openness and procedurally delimited theater of the initial elections, this work seems to have done behind closed doors.

---

[48] GCA 0042/155.1.56/01/10/021. "Gaoxiong xian zhengfu gengdi zudian weiyuanhui zudian zhengyi tiaojie chengli zhengmingshu" (Gaoxiong county government land to the tiller committee certificate of adjustment for tenant disputes), November 2, 1953.

[49] GCA 0042/155.1.56/01/09/017. Taiwan sheng, Gaoxiong xian Zudian weiyuanhui an, "Hunei xiang gongsuo gengdi weiyuanhui zhaokai liu yuefen linshi huiyi bilü" (Minutes of Hunei township land to the tiller committee meeting of June 10 [1953]). In this case the tenant Chen Fu owed his landlord Wang Wanquan NT1,710 rent for the second quarter of 1952, but claimed to be unable to pay due to injury; he was excused after indicating his willingness to pay at a later date.

[50] YTA 0044/132/1/1/007. Unfortunately, the records only reveal that the case was brought, not what the eventual decision was.

In Sunan and Taiwan, the state organized local forms of popular representation to support its unique vision of land reform. For both it was not only important to publicize and implement land reform campaigns, but to implement them in ways that made the state's land reform programs visible, and to draw in "the people's" participation in the process of land reform. This was critical to the legitimating claims made by each that land reform was necessary for social justice, for economic development, and was demanded (or at least roundly welcomed) from below. Land reform campaigns served as one of the key vehicles by which the ruling party-state in Sunan and Taiwan penetrated and recast the countryside. This penetration and rejigging necessarily led to systematically favoring some groups while marginalizing, transforming or simply exterminating others. Publicity regarding land reform, and the ways in which public participation in the process was solicited also served as a heuristic means of instruction and early socialization as to what the core norms of the state were to be. While the legitimacy claims and instrumental uses of land reform campaigns for state-building ends were identical for the PRC in Sunan and the ROC in Taiwan, the ways in which these two party-states "brought in" local participation were diametrically opposed. In Taiwan, carefully planned, procedural, and electoral forms of local representation were explicitly designed to dampen down emotion and become permanent institutions of rural deliberation and adjudication linked to and penetrated by the local state. This variant of public participation was confined to segmented, procedurally oriented elections, after which rules and procedures were delegated to an elected committee, whose deliberations and application of rules took place in enclosed official or semi-official space. In Sunan public, violent, emotional collective will was deliberately whipped up to merge with that of the state in an intensive, but short dramatic burst. Here the public and participatory theater of land reform collapsed representation into a show of emotion, underpinned by public unity with regime goals; a dramatic moment of fusion between the crowd and the state backed up by the shocking reality of state violence and public summary execution against those demarcated as the irretrievably bad, evil, and exploitative.

Legacies of Success Compared

Land reform in revolutionary Sunan and "conservative" Taiwan carried an emotional and legitimating valence far beyond the objective importance of the presumptive overconcentration of too much land in the hands of too few. Land reform also served to make visible each regime's core values: the mass line and participatory rural revolution in Sunan and the sober technocratic exercise of gradualism and inclusion in Taiwan. Land reform campaigns in Sunan and Taiwan exhibited a surprising number of commonalities and points of real convergence. The ways in which land reform was used instrumentally were identical: to clear the countryside of all meaningful social organizations, institutions, and individuals who could act as a brake on the expansion of state power; to penetrate to the grass roots of rural society; and to fundamentally re-cast rural political and economic institutions in the dominant party-state's preferred image. Land reform campaigns also went through similar stages of bureaucratic mobilization and intensification: training of activists, expansion in the projective capacity of the state, propaganda dissemination, inviting in rural representation, and issuing of new official documents of land ownership.

What differed in these land reform campaigns was equally significant. While land reform campaigns required substantial investigation into landholding and classifying the entire agricultural population (either in the simple ROC formula of landlord, freeholder, tenant or the more complex PRC formula of landlord, upper, middle, and poor peasants, and hired laborer) what was done with the classifications that resulted from these investigations diverged enormously. In Sunan, perhaps the most important long-term result of land reform was how these newly assigned class statuses in the countryside became attached permanently to individual families, even when the categories in question were a poor fit with the realities of rural life. Land reform in the ROC/Taiwan had precisely the opposite intention, which was to accelerate the transition of tenants to freeholders and landlord families out of agriculture and into state industrial capitalism.

The state in Sunan and Taiwan both put on heuristic performances to communicate its core values and what kinds of public participation the state encouraged. These shows conveyed starkly different norms and expectations. In Sunan land reform campaigns demonstrated the state's continued attachment to a kind of mass mobilization that sought to side-step, override, or conceal bureaucratic modalities of policy implementation in favor of a public drama of direct revolutionary populism that fused individuals into a public demonstration of collective will with each other and the state. The ROC/Taiwan also held public performances in its solicitation of citizen participation, but their content was categorically different: to encourage regular if also limited and indirect voting to create an intermediary body, the Farm Tenancy Committee, that was neither state nor society, but rather an intertwined hybrid of the two.

While land reform's economic outcomes continue to be contested, there has long been consensus that land-reform campaigns in China and Taiwan were outstandingly effective as part of a wider *political* process to break the power of old rural elites and penetrate the countryside.[51] But perhaps land reform's other main contribution – hiding in plain sight for over two generations – has been its performative and legitimating functions. In both Sunan and Taiwan, these two variants of land reform became so integral to the legitimizing narratives for both regimes that it is hard to imagine a world in which these land reform campaigns in China and Taiwan could have been anything other than wildly successful.

Land reform in China demonstrated the regime's commitment to rural revolution, made public its ideal to pursue social justice by relying on its close links with the masses (and indeed creating a narrative of close links with the masses even where none had previously existed), and prepared the way for greater consolidation and "efficiency" in agriculture as the base of a larger developmental project. In Sunan, as in the People's Republic of China more generally, these larger goals were followed almost immediately after the conclusion of land reform with a new party-state initiative to promote mutual aid teams. From mutual aid teams, it was a relatively short logical step to collectivization a few years later. In Taiwan, the "successful" prosecution of gradualist and technocratic land reform was geared to (and was on its own terms, successful in) redeeming the Guomindang's earlier failures in the countryside on the mainland, demonstrating its differences with the CCP, and even providing the raw materials for a set of claims to regional if not international leadership in promoting technocratic programs for land reform elsewhere in non-Communist Asia.[52] Also in Taiwan, the levelling of the playing field through Land to the Tiller was conceived of as a preliminary first step towards the greater concentration and rationalization of land holding, in this instance to be carried out through administrative reorganizations by the state's Land Bureaus in the 1960s and 1970s.[53]

A new generation of historians in China and Taiwan, temporally removed from the highly politicized and rhetorical claims that tied successful implementation of land reform campaigns to regime legitimacy and consolidation, will almost certainly accelerate their questioning of

---

[51] Stavis, "China and the Comparative Analysis of Land Reform": Vivienne Shue, *Peasant China in Transition: The Dynamics of Development Toward Socialism, 1949–1956*, pp. 42, 91.

[52] This was in evidence in the participation of JCRR and Land Bureau top personnel in international conferences on land reform in the 1950s and 1960s, close links to the UN, and the eventual internationalization of the Land Reform Training Institute (*tugai xunliansuo*) to accommodate trainees from other less developed countries who had not yet implemented land reform in the 1960s. See Sein Lin, *Land Reform Training Institution: An Historical Perspective*, pp. 1–8.

[53] Bain, *Agricultural Reform in Taiwan: From Here to Modernity*, pp. 128–129, 237–259.

these assumptions of success.[54] But the fact that these these assumptions of successful land reform have stood largely unchallenged for over fifty years is itself indicative of success of the most important kind: the ways in which the state's rhetoric, campaigns for land reform, and subsequent results became fused in a logic of state expansion and rightful regime consolidation in the rural areas of Sunan and Taiwan; a logic that is only now beginning to be disaggregated and rethought.

---

[54] For the PRC, see Zhang Yiping, *Diquan biandong yu shehui zhonggou: Sunan tudi gaige yanjiu, 1949–1952*, Mo Hongwei, *Sunan Tudi Gaige Yanjiu*, and most recently and controversially, Fang Fang, *Ruan Mai*, on Taiwan see Xu Shirong, 2014.

Conclusion

In the introduction to this volume, I suggested that in the current literature on state building and state formation there is a gap between Weberian and Gramscian approaches that might be usefully bridged. Weberians assume that, with the right kinds of institutional design, good choices on the part of political leaders, and sufficient resources, effective state institutions with necessary state capacity will follow. Gramscians tend to sidestep questions of capacity to concentrate on the realm of ideas, cultural practices, and the ways in which individuals negotiate the "everyday state."[1] I posit that by linking "softer" concerns about culture and practices with "harder" questions of state formation, we might better understand the processes by which the state's administrative institutions come to function under the challenging circumstances in which most states in the developing world find themselves. Under conditions of material scarcity and regional insecurity, and indifferent to hostile local populations, *how* do states elicit the commitments of the staff in their administrative organizations, generate sufficient capacity to make it possible to implement core or new state projects, and go about explaining, justifying, and rendering these projects comprehensible and legitimate to wider public audiences?

Strong Institutions in Weak Polities, my first scholarly foray into questions of state building, focused on the strategies deployed by the weak state in Republican-era China in the 1930s to elicit commitments and generate capacity. Especially important state organizations in tax (the Salt Inspectorate) and diplomacy (the Ministry of Foreign Affairs) implemented a two-pronged approach that insulated state administrators through impersonal civil service systems, thus dampening down political interference from above. These were unusually successful organizations that were recognized as such in their own time and even

---

[1] See Adam White, ed., *The Everyday Life of the State: A State-in-Society Approach*, Benedict J. Tria Kerkvliet, *The Power of Everyday Politics : How Vietnamese Peasants Transformed National Policy*, and Salwa Ismail, *Political Life in Cairo's New Quarters: Encountering the Everyday State* as exemplars of this approach.

imitated: new divisions set up by the Ministry of Finance explicitly adopted a Salt Inspectorate model. But these strategies were not easily replicated elsewhere because tax and foreign affairs were such outliers. They: (1) provided expertise and services without which the state could not function, giving them unusual standing with political leaders; (2) benefited from unanimity and consistency in what political leaders expected of them; (3) had core activities that required minimal changes in citizen behavior; (4) engaged in the kinds of activities that had little need to justify themselves or seek public legitimacy; and (5) were costly in both the salaries and resources necessary for training. From education to rural development to social welfare to forestry to public hygiene, most state organizations had core goals that were either contested or required significant change in citizen behavior, had minimal support from political leaders, and/or became sites of factional intrigue themselves. The successes achieved by tax and foreign affairs were genuine and significant, but they only applied to a relatively narrow if unusually important and well-protected band of the state's activities.

In order to generate: (1) the active commitments of those who staff the state; (2) the successful implementation of core programs; and (3) plausible bids for legitimacy with the public, most aspiring states need to develop strategies for capacity building that go beyond the bureaucratic insulation of administrators. While analytically separable, in practice these three fronts of capacity building are inextricably linked. Without firm commitments on the part of its agents, the state cannot hope either to implement policy or to make itself intelligible and legitimate. Without effective policy implementation that can be conveyed to citizens, there will be more social resistance and less legitimacy. In turn increased social resistance and reduced legitimacy make it infinitely more difficult for state administrators to do their jobs and maintain their commitments, particularly for those that come from the locales in which they serve. These are, of course, exactly the kinds of circumstances in which many developing states find themselves. So *how* do new regimes simultaneously engage all three of these fronts of capacity generation, often when the extant capacity for so doing is at best unproven, and/or when recent experience points to significant failure? Are there attributes that successful cases of regime consolidation share? If so, are there more general principles that might be extended to other, less successful cases, or is the realm of culture and practices in state building inextricably wrapped up in the particularities from which they arise?

To shed light on these questions, this book engages a direct comparison between two successful variants of the Chinese party-state in the middle of the twentieth century: the young People's Republic of China and its efforts to consolidate its state in the Sunan/greater Shanghai region, and the older but decisively defeated Republic of China and its efforts to consolidate its state on the island of Taiwan. Although we are now used to thinking of the People's Republic of China and the Republic of China/ Taiwan as especially effective exemplars of the revolutionary and conservative types of state in the Cold War era that were utterly dissimilar in every important way, in 1949 these consolidating party-states had a great deal in common, and there was little reason to predict particularly rosy outcomes for either. Despite their obvious political differences over issues such as the primacy of class struggle, alignment on different sides of a deepening Cold War, and bitter enmity after over two decades of civil war, these were regimes with similar party-state structures, a mutually entangled history, primacy given to the military, tendencies towards a cult of personality of the Supreme Leader, shallow to non-existent roots in the societies to which they had come as armies of occupation, comparable agendas about what state projects needed to be undertaken, and even partially overlapping repertoires about how state projects ought to be implemented. The challenges each was tasked with negotiating were substantial and ran in parallel: establishing internal security, restoring war-ravaged economies, issuing viable currencies after devastating periods of hyperinflation, and feeding hungry cities were just a few of the most pressing issues. In Sunan, the revolutionary People's Republic needed to find a way to restore social order and industrial production while strengthening its revolutionary commitments to transform state and society. For its part, the ROC/Taiwan was so shaky and contingent in 1949 that the expectation was widespread that it would not survive to the end of 1950. Both regimes were also hampered by lack of embeddedness in local society, which saw in their new rulers outsiders who sometimes quite literally spoke a different language. Despite these objective challenges and unpromising local environments, each became very successful in achieving the core tasks it set itself. This monograph lays out not only what these core tasks were and the structural conditions for why they were successful, but the mechanics, strategies, and the performatives inherent to *how* this *became* so.

Agendas for Regime Consolidation and State Legitimacy

The necessary but insufficient precondition for regime consolidation was to establish the coercive institutions of the state and to, *viz* Weber, to ensure that the state had a monopoly on the legitimate means of force. This necessary first step for regime consolidation was only partially met by the Guomindang between 1927 and 1949 and the continued existence of military competitors remained a negative instructional example that was lost on no one after 1949. Compared to either the ROC before 1949, or the many developing states contending with insurgencies since then, both the young PRC in Sunan and the ROC in Taiwan were very fortunate. In Sunan, the enemy's military had been utterly vanquished and scattered by the summer of 1949; in Taiwan, the removal of the GMD central government and central military units to the island established a coercive presence that was inordinately large relative to an unarmed society. As we saw in Chapters 2 and 3, armed challengers and active subversives were quickly apprehended and dispatched in both Sunan and Taiwan. This overwhelming preponderance of force meant that it was relatively straightforward for both to quickly institute the bare minimum for successful regime consolidation – the establishment of state coercive organizations able to ensure internal security and social order, their active deployment of the means of state coercion to wipe out all politico-military competitors – and, through state-to-state diplomacy, the conclusion of foreign alliances to guard against direct foreign invasion.

Decades of civil war, mutual betrayal and infiltration, and an armed enemy dead set on overthrow, now juxtaposed with regional hot war and ever-deepening global Cold War tensions made it imperative for each to draw sharp boundaries against the enemy "Other." This was partially a matter of government assertion of simple geographical control over its territory. Throughout late 1949 and 1950, both increasingly demarcated themselves spatially by patrolling borders, monitoring ports, intensely surveiling boat traffic, closing air and sea links, and choking off exit options for those who previously passed through these spaces without incident. But at least as important for a later trajectory of state building were the state actions that sharpened and insisted on the *internal* demarcation between friend and enemy, the loyal and disloyal, the supporter and subversive, and the revolutionary, waverer and counterrevolutionary. Because supporters, enemies, and waverers looked so alike, may well have worked for or sympathized with the other side in the recent past, and indeed were often to be found in the same families, it was often difficult to ascertain who fell into what category. The criteria for assessment varied over time, often reflecting leaders' paranoia and fears about regional security. The outbreak of war in Korea and the run-up to China's direct involvement in the conflict created an environment in which state invective against presumptive domestic enemies became highly charged, police actions against suspected enemies vicious, the sentencing of those in custody unpredictable, the social shunning and economic precariousness of the accused's families normal, and fear of internal fifth columns deliberately whipped up to steamroller potential sources of opposition and reduce social resistance to the expanding state.

Beyond these necessary minimums in establishing physical control over territory, hardening borders, insisting on the violent expulsion of the disloyal and suspect, and securing international alliances, the PRC in Sunan and the ROC in Taiwan were committed, muscular regimes that set themselves other ambitious tasks: extending the reach of the state to very local levels of urban and rural society, generating sufficient capacity to implement signature state programs ranging from land reform to the registration of the entire population to completely remaking the content of the educational curriculum for school-age children, and managing to secure at least forms of acceptance if not the active support of most of society. Both succeeded in implementing these self-imposed agendas with astonishing speed. After both regimes had sorted out real or *de facto* diplomatic alliances to guarantee their external security in the early 1950s, it only took several years beyond that to implement their most important programs. In 1949, the future of the PRC in Sunan seemed uncertain and that of the ROC in Taiwan was downright precarious. At the end of 1954, both were well-consolidated regimes. They had vanquished internal enemies (real and imagined), brought urban civil society to heel, penetrated the countryside, established the instruments of educational orthodoxy and ideological control, and had either directly or indirectly provided core goods and services to the population such as employment assignments, inexpensive food, and land reform. They could do so because they were able effectively, if often brutally, to remove opportunities for individuals to leave, communicate to citizens regime norms about what was and was not acceptable, provide goods and services of value such as internal security, employment, cheap and readily available supplies of grain to urban areas to populations with recent experiences of none of these, and gain the active commitments of enough sectors of society to secure the acquiescence of enough others to become, on their own terms relatively stable and well consolidated. By the mid-1950s, each was on a trajectory that was accelerating in a different direction: the PRC in Sunan towards more a mobilizational and radical form of revolution and the ROC in Taiwan towards its own interpretation of revolution as modernizing party-state led developmentalism.

Modalities of Implementation: Bureaucracy, Campaign, and Performance

This monograph argues that to understand the successful outcomes of these two party-states, it is important to look beyond either the successes themselves or the state institutions immediately responsible for them, and to focus on the workings of *how* the state's signature policies were communicated, justified, and implemented. Since nothing could be done, in terms of communication or implementation, without state administrators, the first substantive chapter focuses on state personnel as embodiments of and agents for the state. The party-states in Sunan and in Taiwan differed in the ways they sought to manage state personnel. The authorities in Sunan were deeply ambivalent about the prospect of institutionalizing personnel systems. After a few abortive experiments that used material incentives to encourage work efficiency, party leaders fell back on general notions of heroic cadres who maintained close links with the masses, relied on revolutionary consciousness, and did more with less. The limited information we have about evaluation and promotion suggests that, in Sunan, cadre evaluation and promotion were irregular occurrences that tended to take place after the conclusion of large campaigns, when cadres had ample opportunities to demonstrate their commitments and leadership skills in implementing a distinctively Maoist set of campaign repertoires. In contrast, the GMD in Taiwan was eager to formalize and institutionalize personnel policy through recruitment into state organizations by open civil service examination and systems of annual evaluation.

These differences over systems and institutionalization were essential points of demarcation between the revolutionary People's Republic of China in Sunan and the reformist Republic of China in Taiwan. The former remained suspicious of systems and institutionalization even as it expanded the size and reach of its formal institutions, set personnel quotas through *bianzhi* systems, and developed complex rankings and salary scales. The latter based much of its legitimacy on the principle of its own "legality" and was enamored of regular systems, rules and guidelines in its prosecution of subversives. This divergence over questions of systems and institutions should not obscure the substantive overlaps in how these two party-states thought about their administrators and what was expected of them. In both Sunan and Taiwan, state administrators were expected continuously to display attributes of inner virtue/commitment and external skill/ability in doing work well. Both insisted on state administrators who accepted orders, quickly absorbed necessary technical and practical skills, conducted themselves with proper demeanor and conscientiousness, and demonstrated the ability to *chi ku* ("eat bitterness"/work hard under difficult circumstances). The paths to realize "virtue and talent" were indeed different. The CCP stressed intensive training courses to make up deficits in either revolutionary loyalty or technical know-how, and the GMD assumed that systems of open civil service examinations and annual evaluation would select for and ensure appropriate commitment and work competence. At the same time both the CCP and the GMD drew on a much older rhetoric of "virtue and talent" that assumed that inner virtue was manifested in outer work accomplishment, that greater cultivation of the former would result in visible increases in the latter, and greater application of individual commitment would inevitably lead to more positive outcomes despite difficult objective work environments. This view of state administrators, as human agents possessing both moral commitments for service to be activated as well as technical skills to accomplish specific tasks, directly supported the two main ways in which state policies were implemented.

In terms of what state administrators *do,* I suggest that there are two basic modalities of policy implementation – the bureaucratic and the campaign – both of which are communicated, justified, and legitimated through different kinds of performances. Predicated on organizational hierarchy in which decisions made at higher levels of the organization are incumbent and binding for lower levels, bureaucracy is rule based and precedent driven. In principle, in a bureaucratic organization, the individual is replaceable while the authority/discretion that is attached to a given role is not. The bureaucratic modality reiterates *regularity* and predictability. In contrast, whether it is openly called "campaign" or not, the campaign modality stands outside the ordinary, regular, and rule based to mobilize human and material resources on an *extraordinary* basis to focus attention on the rapid achievement of a goal or cluster of goals. The bureaucratic and campaign modalities alike simplify complex social realities. The bureaucratic does so through a process of *division* – breaking down wholes (people, diseases, forests, economic productivity, oceans, air) into constituent parts that are standard, measurable, and interchangeable. This process of standardization makes it possible for the blunt administrative organizations of the state to record and store information about society and the environment, achieve internal coherence, act on decisions made at higher levels and inform those higher up about what has been accomplished – the complex of activities that James Scott calls "seeing like a state." Campaigns simplify as well, but they do so by collapsing often complex social and economic phenomena into narratives – often simple narratives of moral good and evil – that seek to mobilize the commitments of state administrators, engage the support of at least part of society, and reduce social resistance from other quarters of the public.

Performance permeates both bureaucratic and campaign modalities. This was visibly so in the early 1950s, when the PRC in Sunan and the ROC in Taiwan set about realizing two of their core objectives: (1) crushing internal opposition while stiffening internal loyalty; and (2) pushing through meaningful land reform. Chapters 3 and 5 detail many of the dramatic and participatory performances engaged over the course of the more open and social mobilizational variants of campaigns such as mass rallies, demonstrations, and *kongsu hui*. In revolutionary Sunan, the government explicitly conceived of its mass accusation sessions against defined target counter-revolutionaries and landlords as an important form of public performance – complete with stock characters, scripts, dress rehearsals, and instructions for staging. It had multiple objectives: to isolate political outcasts, provide a focal point for outrage, generate mass support, and begin a process of instructing the population in the categories and goals valued by the regime, not least of which was the requirement that the "masses" actively participate in the revolution on terms determined by the party-state. These performances, taking place in public, often at outside venues, were geared to generate publicly articulated legitimacy for the state as the crowd chorused its approval of state violence against enemies of the revolution. At the same time, these public performances were inherently risky ventures. Although the results were predetermined, the processes that led to these outcomes could not be fully controlled. Performers on stage could play their roles badly, as in the case of the accuser who was resistant to beating up his putative class enemy. Leaders could fail adequately to convey the reason for the state's violence against the accused. Audiences sometimes did not recognize that their job was to be an affirming chorus, and that bringing unprocessed accusations into public in the heat of the moment was strictly forbidden. Conversely, the majority in the audiences could and sometimes did realize all too clearly where the power in the performance resided, and tune out the entire show as having nothing to do with them.

More circumscribed and limited campaigns are also conveyed through performance, albeit performances with different content, players, staging, and messages. In Taiwan the elections to Farm Tenancy Committees as part of the larger Land to the Tiller Campaign were, like the public accusation sessions in Sunan, performed in public, but the content they conveyed – of limited public participation according to established rules – was integral to a wider message of sharp demarcation between the "good" and inclusive version of land reform practiced by the GMD and the "bad" and violent type of land reform implemented by the CCP. Performance also features in bureaucratic modalities of policy implementation. In Taiwan, a quintessentially rule bound and bureaucratic process – the military trial/sentencing hearing – in which the evidence had already been collected, statements transcribed, and rules for categorizing the severity of the crime established, still needed to be performed, as the suppression of traitors and subversives necessarily concluded with a show of judicial due process via the GMD military courts. The stage was internal to the prison and the state rather than outdoors in a public arena, and the main audience for these performances was the state itself rather than a mass public. The state's staging of a closed-door show, and its insistence that the accused recognize the authority of the court and formally recognize his guilt, suggest that its performance through the military court was as necessary a component of its self-legitimating understanding as the public mobilizational *kongsu hui* was for the CCP in Sunan. These shows were different in content, message, dramatic form, and audience. But the closed bureaucratic modality of the military court, the semi-open campaign to elect representatives to newly formed Farm Tenancy Committees, and the mass mobilizational accusation meeting all involved performances that engaged the emotions, mobilized or stiffened commitments, and asserted legitimacy.

The relationship between bureaucratic and campaign modalities of policy implementation resists easy categorization. In the light of what we know occurred later in Mao's China, when both Party and State were destroyed in the pursuit of ever more radical visions of revolutionary purity in the ultra-leftist campaigns of Great Leap Forward in the late 1950s and the Cultural Revolution between 1966 and 1976, it might seem that rule and precedent-based forms of policy implementation and the extraordinary intensifications of campaigns are in inevitable tension, if not outright contradiction with each other. Certainly, Mao's later uneasy formulation of "Red and Expert" suggested that the two were akin to oil and water. But at the outset of regime consolidation in 1949–1950, neither the CCP, nor the GMD conceived of these modalities as mutually exclusive any more than they imagined that "virtue and talent" (in the CCP formulation) or "work accomplishment and demeanor" (in the GMD's) could not happily coexist and generate better outcomes for individuals and the state they served.

Rather, bureaucratic and campaign modes of policy implementation are based on very different organizing principles and logics; the first to establish hierarchical and coherent state organizations and the second to fire up the commitments of people within those organizations in the enactment of non-routine policies. Often, even typically, the same individuals in state organizations are charged with implementing both bureaucratic and campaign modes of action. Depending on circumstances and requirements from above, they may be required to shift, sometimes quite rapidly, between one modality and the other. In this early period of regime consolidation, it was imperative for the state to generate greater institutional capacity. The CCP called this "strengthening organization" (*jiaqiang zuzhi*) and the GMD called it "[activity] according to law." In the first instance, organizational "strengthening" meant establishing discipline and rules, and ensuring that state administrators were apprised of directives and objectives further up the hierarchy. But, critically, "strengthening organization" was also as flexible as cadres needed to be themselves. During campaigns, *jiaqiang zuzhi* could be, and was, turned to classic campaign repertoires: mobilization, intensifying work, and stirring up the masses.

An extant and functioning bureaucratic modality of policy implementation is a precondition for the successful prosecution of a campaign. Different though convening a *kongsu hui*, a blitz to check and re-enter Taiwan's entire cadastre, and holding elections for Farm Tenancy Committees may have been from each other, all were campaigns predicated on the unseen but necessary regular bureaucratic workings of the state to investigate, collect, store, and retrieve information about suspects, land holdings, the wealth (hidden or otherwise) of individual households; reserve public spaces for public accusation meetings and manage large crowds within those spaces, administer prisons, feed and water prisoners: post announcements, organize meetings, prepare materials, coach activists and accusers, agree upon and then disseminate regulations to electees, and so on. Many, if not most, of these necessary back-office activities were ordered, rule oriented, and paperwork heavy.

Campaign and bureaucratic modalities can be mutually reinforcing in another way: a well-considered campaign might bring about a substantial expansion of regular state organizations. A focused campaign carries the potential to condense and accelerate normally gradual processes of preference formation, coalition creation, publicity, norm dissemination, bureaucratic mobilization, and implementation. When there is a clear and obvious target to achieve, a well-executed campaign can serve to dramatically (if often temporarily) expand state capacity. A campaign will often not only fire up the commitments of state agents already in service, but also recruit and train part-time staff (often students or recent graduates). Propaganda/publicity about the policy, the state's extraordinary deployment of human and material resources, and the educative measures that are part of the campaign aim to overcome social resistance by appealing to normative buy-in from key social actors.

The assumption that campaigns result in the strengthening of state organizations with the projection of state power deeper into society was very much part of the state-building repertoire of the CCP and the GMD in the early 1950s. The Campaign to Suppress Counterrevolutionaries rid society of "bad elements" and also launched a process whereby the party-state collected and stored an enormous amount of potentially damning information about thousands with questionable political or social backgrounds. Its coercive and monitoring reach was extended into big state factories. CCP propaganda about the importance of land reform in Sunan established a new hegemonic orthodoxy that structured all investigation into rural social and economic life. The land reform campaign identified sympathizers and activists, substantially expanded the scope of the state, and stiffened the commitments of state agents already *in situ*. Even before the drama of the public accusation meeting, these newly mobilized personnel were deployed intensively to assess the entire rural population by household and assign each household a permanent class label. In Taiwan, police actions against presumptive subversives were clothed in a rhetoric of legality and rules, but equally gave the military and coercive wing of the state license to operate almost unchecked, and to intrude into very local levels of society. Similarly, sub-campaigns associated with land reform in Taiwan – notably the push to re-register the entire cadastre and the organization of elections to Farm Tenancy Committees – required both knowledge of rules and procedures (the bureaucratic modality of policy implementation) and committed, focused, rapid implementation by the newly trained. Certainly, there was little in Sunan or Taiwan in the early 1950s to indicate that bureaucratic and campaign modalities of policy implementation undercut each other; rather, there seems to have been convergence around the notion that the extraordinary demands of regime consolidation amid significant regional insecurity required (or at least permitted) the state to advance a range of game-changing policies through the extraordinary vehicle of the campaign, and to "strengthen itself" in the process.

Campaigns and Trajectories of the State

While the campaign modality does not necessarily collide with the bureaucratic modality of state action, it is undeniable that the different logical underpinnings of campaign and bureaucracy create the potential for tension and conflict. If unchecked by political leaders or uncontained by the "normal" rules and procedures that buttress hierarchy and create coherence, campaigns can and do undercut precedent and predictability. They encroach on and override the remits of other arenas of state action, particularly those like the legal system, whose entire raison d'être is based on rules and precedent. And they can throw into chaos the regular, if unexciting, workings of the state by incentivizing the neglect of routine activities, sidelining regular rules of evidence and proof, and easing out or overriding those who counsel caution. Conversely, bureaucratic procedures and routines can and do routinize campaigns. Once those in state organizations know how to run campaigns and those in the audiences understand what to expect, the free-flowing emotions of the early campaigns are increasingly replaced with routinized rituals in which each party plays their appointed role.

It is here that perhaps the biggest difference emerged between the "revolutionary" CCP in Sunan and the "conservative" GMD in Taiwan. The Chinese Communist Party so identified its successes and legitimacy with the repertoires of the mobilizational campaign during the Sino-Japanese and civil war periods, when it attracted a substantial number of poor peasants that served to sweep it to a miraculously quick victory in 1949, that it simply could not abandon or even downgrade the campaign modality after it came to power. In Sunan, it was not enough simply to dispatch counter-revolutionaries and redistribute land. Counterrevolutionaries had to be exposed and land reform conducted in accordance with the mobilizational campaign repertoires that had become inseparable from the process of making a successful revolution: identifying classes, establishing close links with the (good) masses, stirring up and educating them into the principles and priorities of the party-state, and a culminating dramatic public confrontation between the representative of evil from the old society and the newly empowered raised up by New China. Only such a deep attachment to this repertoire of revolution can make sense of the CCP's castigation of "peaceful land reform" in Sunan or its insistence that the public accusation session conclude with "face to face" confrontation and acknowledgment of guilt by the accused. The campaign modality's heightened emotion, melodramatic confrontation between good and evil, and resounding public affirmation of the correctness of the CCP's violence in Sunan were not simply effective tactics to push through signature policies in the early 1950s, they were commensu-rate with the successes and vitality of the revolution itself.

This *de facto* equation of campaign mobilizational repertoires with the revolution itself made it very difficult, if not impossible, for the CCP to repudiate or even sidestep these practices after regime consolidation. Even after the revolution had accomplished goals beyond its wildest imagination by 1956 – successfully silencing or exterminating all social groups that could have resisted the CCP's policies, fighting the world's superpower to a standstill in Korea, pushing through collectivization in the countryside, achieving the socialization of enterprises in cities, and establishing the base of heavy industry and a planned economy – the leaders of the Chinese Communist Party were unable to resist the impetus to ever-more radical and utopian campaign mobilizations. Part of the reason for this was the unique position and ideological dominance of Mao, who strongly favored campaign over bureaucratic modalities and deeply mistrusted institutionalized inequality in any form, even (or most particularly) if it were expressed through the Chinese Communist Party itself. But Mao's preferences are not solely to blame for later, disastrous campaigns like the Great Leap Forward and the Cultural Revolution: the campaign modality itself was encoded into the DNA of the Chinese Communist Party after it came to power with a miraculous speed that no one had anticipated in the late 1940s. If Mao had been so right in the late 1940s about the revolutionary potential of the masses and the importance of close links with the people, then who was to say that he was in error now? And if counterrevolutionaries and revisionists had taken over the CCP by the mid-1960s, then surely expunging them and setting the CCP back on the right path to revolution via campaigns made sense if all was not to be lost. Once suspect classes had been crushed or cowed, the basic institutions of socialism established, and most of the population organized into work units that were sites of economic production and political control, much of the revolution turned inward to stem counter-revolutionary backsliding, using the same campaign repertoires that had been deployed to such positive effect in public space 1940s and early 1950s.

The GMD in Taiwan had no such attachment to mobilizational campaigns. In direct contrast to the CCP in Sunan, which always remained uneasy about permanent institutions and continued to be drawn to the campaign because re-enacting the mobilizational campaign reiterated the successful tactics of the revolution itself, the GMD in Taiwan was more limited in its deployment of campaigns of policy intensification, and it directed those campaigns to quite different ultimate goals: to penetrate, reorganize, and *re-institutionalize* society around Guomindang-controlled organizations and practices like functioning courts, farmer's associations, merchant associations, and local GMD party factions. Unlike the CCP, which continued to promote its revolution in ways that placed ever larger burdens of commitment and zeal on cadres and citizens, the GMD imagined itself as a regime devoted to social order, legality, and duly convened institutions that reorganized society in a congenial form; it assumed that once the right institutions were up and running and the right kinds of laws publicized, that people would fall into line and comply. Where the CCP remained ambivalent about regular procedures and institutionalization, the GMD reified both under the mantra of "law." Even in a reality in which the laws themselves were vague and unevenly implemented, GMD institutions and shows of (martial law) "legality" suggested that for the GMD the reiteration of legal procedure demonstrated core regime values in much the same way as the CCP's desire to "stir up the masses" did in mobilizational mass campaigns. Because the GMD had such faith in institutions and law, it was satisfied with much less demonstration of devotion and loyalty. After the obvious suspects had been dispatched, the police state up and running, and the fundamental institutions between state and society reconfigured, the GMD was normally satisfied with the forms of external compliance from the population. Rates of arrest and incarceration for political crimes dropped steeply after 1954, after which the occasional reminder/wave of arrests to counter too much free expression served as a salutary reminder of the limits of state's tolerance and its expectations. Ironically, the very practices that made the revolutionary variant of the Chinese state so successful in coming to power in the first place were those that led to enormous tensions and internal destruction after it had vanquished obvious enemies and accomplished its core goals in the early to mid-1950s, while it was the severity of the Guomindang's failures before 1949 that concentrated political will, enabling the kinds of policy campaigns that led to new, ultimately quite stable, institutions penetrated by the party-state in the early 1950s.

While the Chinese state is, by virtue of its scale and centuries-old tradition of statecraft, an important stand-alone case for regime consolidation and state building, it is worth asking how applicable to other histories and cultural contexts this story of performance is, with its oscillating mixes of bureaucratic and campaign modalities of policy implementation. Because state-making processes and the cultural registers in which actions are rendered comprehensible and legitimate vary so dramatically, any approach that seeks to integrate a Weberian focus on structure and institutions with a Gramscian sensitivity to culture and micro-processes must necessarily pay close attention to the specifics of both. This said, we might venture a few suggestions about how to think about similarities and differences in how bureaucratic and campaign modalities may contribute to state-building processes in general. First, some structural conditions make for objectively much greater difficulty than others. Civil wars, insurgencies, aggressive neighbors with large numbers of co-ethnics, and societies that are deeply polarized on ethnic or religious grounds all create environments that might well lead either to near-exclusive prioritization of establishing internal security, or to hesitation in implementing most policies for fear of upsetting fragile internal equilibria. In these kinds of situations, bureaucratic and campaign modalities are not likely to get off the ground. Second, state agendas about what is necessary and desirable vary. While ensuring internal and external security, establishing viable government institutions, extracting or otherwise ensuring adequate resources, and making claims to sovereignty are almost universal across different kinds of states, many other commitments (e.g. to education, social welfare, public health, infrastructural development, environmental protection) are frequently contested in terms of what should be done and how it should be done. If state agendas are themselves sufficiently contested by political elites to result in deadlock, then neither bureaucratic, nor campaign modalities are likely to be relevant because policies will be blocked from going beyond the planning stages.

But where there is the combination of agreement about goals and unproven/insufficient capacity to achieve those goals, states are likely to find themselves deploying variants on the bureaucratic and campaign modalities that featured so prominently in Sunan and Taiwan in the early 1950s. Although the cultural symbols, narratives, and performances that resonate with implementers and citizens will always be highly context specific, mixes of campaigns and bureaucracy are very common, particularly in developing countries that are seeking to increase state capacity in their realization of particular objectives. To cite a few, anti-malarial campaigns in sub-Saharan Africa in the 2000s, Brazil's extraordinary push to prepare for the World Cup in 2014, India's repeated ventures into dam building, Malaysia's efforts to educate school children about water conservation, and the dramatic operation to rescue a group of stranded boys from a cave in Thailand in July 2018 all speak to the ongoing importance of campaigns as extraordinary mobilizations of resources to accomplish particular focused goals. At the same time, all of these campaigns to accomplish extraordinary goals relied on, or were directly implemented by more regularized and routinized bureaucratic processes. Anti-malarial campaigns required large numbers of people to be trained for work in local communities, and mosquito nets to be ordered and delivered; rescuers for stranded boys needed to be mobilized, equipped, transported, and briefed (and local doctors needed to be mobilized and at the ready for when the boys were brought out); Brazil required "Billions [spent] ... on new stadiums, upgraded stadiums, improved transportation facilities, new hotel space," and broad security measures; before any ground could be broken on a dam in India, a multitude of state organizations needed to be brought into alignment, approval granted for projects, and disbursement of resources agreed, and the management of very complex projects planned; and educating school children in Malaysia about water conservation required training teachers, developing handouts, funding transport, and coordinating with schools over open slots for teachers to come in.[2] Each of these projects also engendered performances to appeal to moral commitments (and in some cases, counter-performances): local aides in Africa demonstrating that their community work in distributing mosquito nets was a critical measure in public health; sponsoring state organizations in India that large dams were required for regional development; teachers in Malaysia committed to disseminating new truths about water conservation and SEALS dramatically mobilized to mount the operation to save the boys in the cave. Campaign and bureaucratic modalities of policy implementation continue to be important organizing principles, and the specifics of how they are represented and played out in performances remain a source of ongoing scholarly interest.

---

[2] James Gerstenzang "Where malaria is a memory: A village in Africa reflects the success of the eradication effort, the kind of turnaround Bush touts on his trip," *Los Angeles Times,* February 19, 2008. See http://articles.latimes.com/2008/feb/19/world/fg-malaria19, accessed July 7, 2018; Alan Taylor, "Brazil prepares for the World Cup," *The Atlantic* June 10, 2014, www.theatlantic.com/photo/2014/06/brazil-prepares-for-the-world-cup/100755/, accessed July 10, 2018; "Parents of boys trapped in Thai cave tell coach: don't blame yourself," www.theguardian.com/news/2018/jul/07/parents-boys-trapped-thai-cave-tell-coach-dont-blame-yourself-rescuers-race-against-time. Accessed July 8, 2018; Sanjeev Khagram, *Dams and Development: Transnational Struggles for Water and Power* (Ithaca and London: Cornell University Press, 2004); Global Environment Centre," Water Conservation Programme for Schools in Malaysia" www.gec.org.my/index.cfm?&menuid=358&parentid=92, accessed July 8, 2018.

Appendix 1: List of Interviewees

Chen Yingtai. 陳英泰

Chen was staunchly Taiwanese and found himself on the receiving end of the White Terror of the 1950s at an early stage. After graduating from the Taibei branch of the Taiwan government Special Economics School, he was appointed to the Bank of Taiwan, and was arrested in 1951 as a Communist and participant in the Chong Guohui case. Chen insisted verbally that he had never been a Communist and was a socialist. Whether Communist or socialist, he never bent in the face of GMD threats and imprisonment, and he eventually served twelve years on Green Island and in labor camps. One of the earlier activists in the movement for redress for victims of the White Terror, at the time of the interview he was a vigorous and tough character in his late seventies who had just completed an excoriating two-volume memoir of his experiences that chronicled the lapses in GMD judicial procedure.

Interviewed at the Institute of Modern History, Academia Sinica. Taibei, Taiwan, August 4, 2005.

Luo Wanlei. 羅萬雷

After serving as a school principal in Hunan between 1932 and 1936, Luo took the fourth sitting of the national upper civil service exam in 1936, passed, and was assigned to the Ministry of Personnel as a section member with a *weiren* appointment. After a hiatus of three years, he returned to the Ministry of Personnel in 1939 with a *jianren* appointment to section chief. Luo spent the remainder of his career in the Ministry of Personnel, eventually rising to vice-ministerial rank.

Interviewed in Taibei, January 5, 1989.

Wang Hua-chung (Wang Huazhong). 王華中

Originally from Guizhou, Wang was a young man on his way up in the late 1940s. He was devoted to the GMD, which had made possible his rise

259

from an impoverished background. After graduating from Zhengzhi Daxue and passing the *gaokao,* he was appointed to the Examination Yuan. He was one of the fortunate few who managed to reach Taiwan in 1949. I was able to interview him on several occasions between January 1989 and August 1995. On the first of these occasions he had not yet retired and had reached one of the highest positions within the Examination Yuan as one of the Committee of Examiners. At the time of the interview in May 1995, he had retired and therefore had a lot of time on his hands to drink tea and chat about old times.

Interviewed Taibei, May 5, 1995.

Wang Wenqing. 王文清

Wang was a young man in his early twenties when he was recruited into the Subei (North Jiangsu) Administration in early 1949. Later that year he was transferred to the Sunan (South Jiangsu) Administration in Wuxi as a secretary based on a combination of his "clean" family background and his good calligraphic hand.

Interviewed in Nanjing, December 19, 1997.

Zhao Qiwen. 趙啓文

At the time of the interview, Zhao was a mid- to late-career official in the Ministry of Personnel with the solid, if unspectacular, rank of *kezhang* (section head), after several decades of service. Most unusually he was himself not a member of the Guomindang Party.

Interviewed in Muzha, Taibei, in the Examination Yuan offices, July 4, 1995

Zhou Weixun. 周維尋

As a high-school senior, Zhou fled Beijing ahead of advancing Japanese troops, eventually arrived in Yunnan, and graduated from the Department of Government, Yunnan University in 1943. After the war, he moved to Nanjing, where he was eventually appointed to the Ministry of Personnel as a section member. He did not take the Examination Yuan's *gaokao* despite his position in the Ministry of Personnel, where he worked throughout the civil war. He was among the 50 percent of the Ministry of Personnel staff that elected to remain in Nanjing in 1949.

Interviewed in Nanjing, March 25, 1989.

Appendix 2: List of Archives

CC:	Chen Cheng Collection. Microfilm. University of California, Berkeley.
DS:	Department of State, United States National Archives.
GCA:	Gaoxiong County Archives, Taiwan.
GSG:	Guoshiguan [Academia Historica], Taibei.
JPA:	Jiangsu Provincial Archive, Nanjing.
MDA:	Minhang District Archive [Minhang, Shanghai].
NCA:	National Central Archive, Taibei, Taiwan.
NMA:	Nanjing Municipal Archive.
QDA:	Qingpu District Archive [Qingpu, Shanghai].
SMA:	Shanghai Municipal Archive.
SuMA:	Suzhou Municipal Archive.
TPA:	Taiwan Provincial Archive Nantou, Taiwan.
YTA:	Yongkang Town Archives, Taiwan.

Documentary Collections, Reports, and Periodicals

CJDJ. Bi Yuexun, Zeng Pinqiang, and Xu Ruizhi, eds., *Cong Jieyan dao Jieyan 1945–1987* – 從戒嚴到 解嚴 (Documentary Collection on Democratization Movement in Postwar Taiwan: The Martial Law Era,1945–1987), Vol. 1. Taibei: Guoshiguan, 2000

HDZB. *Huadong Zheng Bao* – 華東政報 (East China Government Report)

JCRR. JCRR *Annual Reports on Land Reform in the Republic of China from October 1948 to June 1964*. Taipei, JCRR. October 1964

JTZRK. *Jieyan shiqi taibei diqu zhengzhi anjian xiangguan renshi koushi lishi baise kongbu shijian chafang* – 戒嚴時期臺北地區政治案件相關人士口述歷史 白色恐怖事件查訪 (Oral history on martial law era political cases in the Taibei area). Taibei: Taibei Wenxianhui 1999

JZWX. *Jianguo yilai zhongyao wenxian xuanji* – 建國以來重要文獻選集 (Selected Collection of Important Documents since the Establishment of the Country"). Beijing: Zhongyang Wenxian Chubanshe, 1992

KJY. Jia Jingde, ed. *Kaoshi Yuan Kaoshi Jishu Yanjiu Weiyuanhui Yanjiu Baogao* 考試院考試技術研究委員會研究報告 (Research report on the Examination Yuan Research Council on examination techniques): Kaoshi Yuan, 1952.

LMDA. Ou Suying, ed. *Zhanhou Taiwan Zhengzhi Anjian: Li Madou An Shiliao Huibian* – 戰後臺灣政治案件：李碼兜案史料匯編 (Postwar Taiwan Political Case: Collected Materials on the Li Madou Case). Xindian: Guoshiguan, 2008

LRGZ. Luo Ruiqing, *Lun Renmin Gong'an Gongzuo* – 論人民公安工作 (Discussions on People's Public Security Work). Beijing: Qunzhong Chubanshe, 1994

LRGA. Zhang Yanxian and Xu Fangting, eds., *Zhanhou Taiwan Zhengzhi Anjian: Lin Rigao An Shiliao Huibian* – 戰後臺灣政治

262

案件：林日高案史料彙編 (Postwar Taiwan Political Case: Collected Materials on the Lin Rigao Case). Xindian: Guoshiguan, 2008

MZX: *Mao Zedong Xuanji* – 毛澤東選集 (Collected Works of Mao Zedong). Beijing: Renmin Chubanshe, 1961

NGZ. *Nanjing Gong'an Zhi* – 南京公安志 (Nanjing Public Security Gazeteer). Shenzhen: Haitian Chuban she, 1994

NZASH. *Taiwan Diqu Jieyan Shiqi 50 niandai zhengzhi anjian* (Vols. 1–5) – 臺灣地區戒嚴時期五十 年代政治案件史料匯編 (Compilation of Historical Material of Political Cases in the Period of Martial Law in Taiwan). Nantou: Taiwan sheng wenxian weiyuanhui, 1998

QXZ. Ma Wen, ed. *Qingpu Xianzhi* – 青浦縣治 (Qingpu county gazetteer). Shanghai: Renmin Chubanshe, 1990

RXC. Niu Yongjian, ed. *Zhongguo Renshi Xingzhenghui Chengli Dahui Tekan* – 中國人事 行政會成立大會特刊 (Special publication on establishing China's Personnel Administration Committee). Kaoshi Yuan, May 1951

SSTH. *Shanghai shi Jiaoqu Sunan Xingzhengqu Tudi Gaige Huaji* – 上海市郊區蘇南行政區土地改革畫集 (A pictorial record of land reform in the Shanghai outer districts and in the Sunan administrative region). No publisher/pagination. December, 1952. http://book.duxiu.com/bookDetail .jsp?dxNumber=000007446550&d=D86EEA408284366E E66D162C5DCD9B0F&fenlei=040707&sw=%E5%9C% 9F%E5%9C%B0%E6%94%B9e%E9%9D%A9%E7%94 %BB%E9%9B%86), downloaded December 15, 2016

SGZ. Tang Qingyao, ed. *Shanghai Gong'an Zhi* – 上海公安志 (Shanghai Public Security Gazeteer). Shanghai: Shanghai Shehui Kexueyuan, 1997

SWM: *Selected Works of Mao Zedong*. London: Laurence and Wishart. 1954

TSSA. Wu Wenxing, ed. *Taiwan Sheng Shifan Xueyuan 'Si-liu' Anjian* – 臺灣省 師範學院四-六案件 (Taiwan Provincial Teacher's Institute April 6 Incident), Nantou: Taiwan Wenxian Weiyuanhui, 2001

TXB. *Taiwan Xinsheng Bao* – 臺灣新生報 (Taiwan Newborn News).

XKCJT. *Xing xianhou Kaoshi Yuan Chengli Sanzhounian Jiantao Huiyi Tekan* – 行憲後考試院 成立三周年檢討會議特刊 (Special publication on the Examination Yuan's self criticism conference to commemorate the third anniversary of the implementation of the constitution), Kaoshi Yuan, 1951

XGWA: Xu Jinfa, ed., *Xuesheng Gongzuo Weiyuanhui An* – 學生工作委員會案 (A Documentary Collection on the Case of the Student Affairs Committee). Taibei: Guoshiguan, 2008

XSB. *Xin Suzhou Bao* (New Suzhou News)

ZALFT. Cai Qingyan et al., eds., *Jieyan Shiqi Zhengzhi Anjian zhi Falü yu Lishi Taotan* – 戒嚴時期政治案件之法律與歷史討談 (Discussion and Investigation of the History and Law of Martial Law Era Political Cases). Taibei: Caituan Faren Jieyan Shiqi Budang Panluan ji Feidie Shenpan Anjian Buchong Jijin Hui, 2001

Bibliography

Works in Chinese

Cai Hui-yu (Huiyu Caroline Tsai), *Guangfu Taiwan yu Zhanhou Jingzheng: Taiwan Jingcha Ganbu Xunlian ban Koushu Fantan Jilü* [The Retrocession of Taiwan and Postwar Police Administration: An Oral History of the Taiwan Police Cadre Corps]. Nangang, Institute of Taiwan History, 2014

Cao, Shuji. "Liangzhong 'tianmiantian' yu sunan tudi gaige" [Two Types of Land and Land Reform in Southern Jiangsu], in Xie Guoxing, ed. *Gaige yu Gaizao: Lengzhan Chuqi Liang'an de Liangshi, Tudi yu Gongshang ye Biange* [Reform and Reconstruction: The Transformation of Rice Supplies, Land Reform, and Industry and Commerce in Early Cold War Mainland China and Taiwan]. Institute of Modern History, Academia Sinica Press, 2010, pp. 97–132

Chen, Cuilian. "Taiwan jieyan shiqi de tewu tongzhi yu baise kongbu fenwei" [Analysis of Martial Law Period Special Security Organizations and White Terror], in Zhang Yanxian and Chen Meirong, eds., *Jieyan Shiqi Baise Kongbu yu Zhuanxing Zhengyi Lunwen Ji.* [Collected Essays on Martial Law Era White Terror and Transitional Justice] Taibei: Taiwan Lishi Xuehui, 2009

Chen, Fangming. *Xie Xuehong Pingzhuan* [Commentary on Xie Xuehong]. Taibei: Maitai Chuban, 2009

Chen, Yingtai. *Huiyi Jianzheng Baise Kongbu* [Recollections of a Witness to the White Terror], Vols. 1–3. Taibei: Tangshan Chubanshe, 2005

Gao, Wangling. "Tudi gaige: 'gaitian huandi' de shehui yundong" [Land Reform: A Social Movement that Turned the World Upside Down]. www.aisixiang.com /data/16705.html, accessed April 10, 2018

Gong, Jianhua. *Xiandai Ganbu Xue* [Contemporary Cadre Studies]. Guangzhou: Guangdong wenhua chubanshe, 1988

Lan Bozhou. *Taigong Dangren de Beige: Zhang Zhizhong, Ji Yun yu Yang Yang* [The Tragic Song of Taiwan Communist Party Personnel: Zhang Zhizhong, Ji Yun and Yang Yang]. Xinbei: Taiwan Renmin Chubanshe, 2012

Lin, Zhenghui. "1950 nian dai qingong huo zuoyi zhengzhi anjian" [Political and Left-wing Political Cases in the 1950s], in Zhang Yanxian and Chen Meirong, eds., *Jie Yan Shiqi Baise Kongbu yu Zhuanxing Zhengyi Lunwen Ji* [Collected Essays on Martial Law Era White Terror and Transitional Justice]. Taibei: Taiwan Lishi Xuehui, 2009

Liu Shiwei and He Zhiming. "Zhanhou chuqi Taiwan yedian guanxi zhi tantao jian lun gengzhe you qitian zhengce" [A Discussion of Landlord and Tenant

Relations and the Land to the Tiller Program in Early Post-war Taiwan], *Taiwan Shi Yanjiu* (10:2)

"Mao Zedong yu sanfan yundong" [Mao Zedong and the Three Antis Campaign]. *Gangyi Lishi* [Internet History], June 29, 2009, http:history.news.163.com/09/0629/03/5CUQ5CP200013FM5.html. Accessed August 5, 2016

Man, Yong. "Shenfen de konghuang: Anhui sheng Fuyang diqu tugaizhong de zisha xianxiang" [The Terror of Status: Suicide during Land Reform in Fuyang District, Anhui], *Ershi Shiji* No. 159, February 2017, pp. 53–67

Mo, Hongwei. *Sunan Tudi Gaige Yanjiu* [Sunan Land Reform Research]. Hefei: Hefei Gongye Daxue Chubanshe, 2007

Pan, Guangdan and Quan Weitian. *Sunan Tudi Gaige Fangwen Ji* [Records of Interviews on Sunan Land Reform]. Beijing: Sanlian Shudian, 1952

Pan Zhenqiu. *Gongtong wei Fazhan Difang Jiaoyu er Nuli:* [Together Develop Local Education Industriousness]. Taibei: Zhongxing Shanzhuang, 1968

Shan, Tianlu. *Nanying Baise Kongbu Zhi* [Nanying White Terror Gazeteer]. Tainan: Tainan xian Wenhua Ju, 2001

Sunan Renmin Xingzhengshu Tudi Gaige Weiyuanhui, ed. *Wo suo Jiandao de Sunan Tugai Gaige Yundong* [The Land Reform Movement in Sunan that I Saw]. Shanghai, 1951

Tao, Daoyang, et al., *Tudi Gaige yu Xin Minzhu Zhuyi Geming* [Land Reform and the New Democracy Revolution]. Shanghai: Zhanwang Zhoukan, 1951

Tao, Siju, ed. *Xin Zhongguo Diyiren Gong'an Buzhang – Luo Ruiqing* [Luo Ruiqing – New China's first Minister of Public Security]. Beijing: Qunzhong Chubanshe, 1996

Wang Dongyuan. *Ganbu Xunlian Wenti* [Questions on Cadre Training]. Chongqing: Zhongyang Xunliantuan di Wuqi Jiangyan Lü, 1939

Wu, Yunfei. "Yi yici gong shenhui – Riwei tongzhi de Mulan" [Remembering a Public Trial – Mulan under Japanese Puppet Rule], *Mulan wenshi ziliao*, No. 4. Mulan: Heilongjiang, 1989

Xiao, Mu. *Tugai Xuanchuan jü* [Land Reform Propaganda Plays]. Hangzhou: Zhongguo Ertong Chuban, 1950

Xu Shirong. "Zhanhou liangzheng tizhi de jianli yu tudi zhidu zhuanxing guocheng zhong de guojia dizhu yu nongmin" [Postwar Grain Management Systems, and Landlords and Farmers in Land System Changes], *Taiwan shi Yanjiu*, 9:1, 2002

Yang, Kuisong. *Zhonghua Renmin Gongheguo Jianguo Lishi Yanjiu* [Historical Research on the Establishment of the People's Republic of China]. Nanchang: Jiangxi Renmin Chubanshe, 2009

Yang, Youwu and Wang Zhenchuan, eds., *Zhongguo Gongwuyuan Baike Cidian* [Encyclopedia on China's Public Servants]. Beijing: Guoji Wenhua Chubanshe Gongsi, 1988

Zhang Kaifeng and Man Yong. No title. *Ershi Shji* (*Twentieth Century*) 9:30, 2004

Zhang, Yanxian. "Daoyan: baise kongbu yu zhuanxing zhengyi" [Preface: White Terror and Transitional Justice] in Zhang Yanxian and Chen Meirong,

Jieyan Shiqi Baise Kongbu yu Zhuanxing Zhengyi Lunwen ji. [Collected Essays on Martial Law Era White Terror and Transitional Justice] Taibei: Taiwan Lishi Xuehui, 2009

Zhang Yanxian and Gao Shuyan. *Luku Shijian Yanjiu Diaocha* [The Luku Incident Research and Investigation]. Taibei: Taibei Xian Zhengfu Chubanshe, 1998

Zhang Yiping. *Diquan Biandong yu Shehui Zhonggou: Sunan Tudi Gaige Yanjiu, 1949–1952* [Land Power Change and Social Reconstruction: Research on Sunan Land Reform]. Shanghai: Renmin chubanshe, 2009

Zhongguo Guomindang Taiwan Sheng Dang Bu. *Sheng yixia geji Lingdao Ganbu Baoju Rencai Shouce* [Handbook to Preserve Talent for Leading Sub-provincial Cadres], Taibei: 1970

Works in English

Alexander, Jeffrey C. *The Performance of Politics: Obama's Victory and the Democratic Struggle for Power.* Oxford: Oxford University Press, 2010

"Performing Counter-Power: The Civil Rights Movement," in Jeffrey C. Alexander *Performance and Power.* Cambridge and Malden, MA: Polity Press, 2011, pp. 147–158

Alitto, Guy. *The Last Confucian: Liang Shu-ming and the Chinese Dilemma of Modernity,* 2nd ed. Berkeley and Los Angeles: University of California Press, 1986

Apter, David and Anthony Saich. *Revolutionary Discourse in Mao's Republic.* Cambridge: Harvard University Press, 1994

Ash, Robert. "Economic Aspects of Land Reform in Kiangsu, 1949–1952," *The China Quarterly* No. 67, September 1976, pp. 519–545

Averill, Stephen C. "The Origins of the Futian Incident," Tony Saich and Hans J. van de Ven, eds., *New Perspectives on the Chinese Communist Revolution.* Armonk: M.E. Sharpe, 1995, pp. 79–115

Revolution in the Highlands: China's Jinggangshan Base Area. New York: Rowan and Littlefields, 2006

Austin, John L. *How to Do Things with Words,* 2nd ed. Cambridge: Harvard University Press, 1975

Bain, Irene. *Agricultural Reform in Taiwan: From Here to Modernity.* Hong Kong: Chinese University Press, 1993

Beisner, Robert. *Dean Acheson, A Life in the Cold War.* Oxford: Oxford University Press. 2009

Bernhardt, Kathleen. *Rents, Taxes, and Peasant Resistance: The Lower Yangzi Region 1840–1950.* Stanford: Stanford University Press, 1992

Brown, Jeremy. "From Resisting Communists to Resisting America: Civil War and the Korean War in Southwest China, 1950–51," in Jeremy Brown and Paul G. Pickowicz, *Dilemmas of Victory: The Early Years of the People's Republic of China.* Cambridge: Harvard University Press, 2007, pp. 105–129

Burns, John. *The Chinese Communist Party's Nomenklatura System.* Abingdon and New York: Routledge Press, 1989

Capoccia, Giovanni. "Critical Junctures and Institutional Change," in James Mahoney and Kathleen Thelen, *Advances in Comparative Historical Analysis*. Cambridge: Cambridge University Press, 2015, pp. 147–179

Capoccia, Giovanni and Daniel Kemelen, "The Study of Critical Junctures: Theory, Narrative and Counterfactuals in Historical Institutionalism," *World Politics*, 59, April 2007, pp. 341–369

Chan, Gerald. "Taiwan as an Emerging Foreign Aid Donor: Developments, Problems, and Prospects," *Pacific Affairs* 70(1), 1997, pp. 37–56

Cheek, Timothy. *Propaganda and Culture in Mao's China: Deng Tuo and the Intelligentsia*. Oxford: Clarendon Press, 1997

Chen, Cheng. *Land Reform in Taiwan*. Taipei: China Cultural Press, 1954

Chen, Yung-fa. "Suspect History and the Mass Line: Another 'Yan'an Way'," in Gail Hershatter, Emily Honig, Jonathan N. Lipman, and Randall Stross, *Remapping China: Fissures in Historical Terrain*. Stanford: Stanford University Press, 1996, pp. 242–260

Cole, Catherine. *Performing South Africa's Truth and Reconciliation Commission*. Bloomington: Indiana University Press, 2009

Crook, Isabel and David Crook. *Revolution in a Chinese Village: Ten Mile Inn*. London: Routledge, 1959

De Lasson, Axel. *A Restudy of the Taiwan Farmers' Associations*. Aachen: Herodot/ Alano Verlag, 1989

De Mare, Brian. *Mao's Cultural Army: Drama Troupes in China's Rural Revolution* Cambridge: Cambridge University Press, 2015.

Diamant, Neil. *Embattled Glory: Veterans, Military Families, and the Politics of Patriotism in China, 1949–2007*. New York: Rowman and Littlefield, 2009

Dickson, Bruce. "The Lessons of Defeat: The Reorganization of the Kuomintang on Taiwan, 1950–52," *The China Quarterly*, No. 133, March 1993, pp. 56–84 *Democratization in China and Taiwan: The Adaptability of Leninist Parties*. Oxford: Oxford University Press, 1997

Dirlik, Arif. "The Ideological Foundations of the New Life Movement: A Study in Counterrevolution," *Journal of Asian Studies*, 34: 4, 1975, pp. 945–980

Domes, Jürgen. *The Internal Politics of China*. New York: Praeger, 1973

Dore, Ronald. *Land Reform in Japan*. Oxford: Oxford University Press, 1959

Dutton, Michael. *Policing Chinese Politics: A History*. Durham and London: Duke University Press, 2005

Elman, Benjamin A. *Civil Examinations and Meritocracy in Late Imperial China*. Cambridge: Harvard University Press, 2013

Ertman, Thomas. *Birth of the Leviathan: Building States and Regimes in Early Modern Europe*. Cambridge: Cambridge University Press, 1997

Falleti, Tulia. *Decentralization and Subnational Politics in Latin America*. Cambridge: Cambridge University Press, 2010

Ferlanti, Federica. "The New Life Movement in Jiangxi Province, 1934–1938," *Modern Asian Studies*, 44, 2010, pp. 961–1000

Feuchtwang, Stephan. *After the Event: The Transmission of Grievous Loss in Germany, China and Taiwan*. Oxford and New York: Berghan Books, 2011

Gamble, Jos. *Shanghai: in Transition: Changing Perspectives and Social Contours of a Chinese Metropolis*. London: Routledge, 2005

Gerth, H. H. and C. Wright Mills. *From Max Weber: Essays in Sociology*. New York: Oxford University Press, 1946

Goldman, Merle. "The Party and Intellectuals," *The Cambridge History of China*. Vol. 14, Part I, Cambridge and New York: Cambridge University Press, 1987, pp. 218–258

Goodman, David S. G. *Social and Political Change in Revolutionary China*. Lanham: Rowman and Littlefield, 2000

Goodman, Tanya, Ron Eyerman, and Jeffrey C. Alexander. *Staging Solidarity: Truth and Reconciliation in a New South Africa*. London: Routledge, 2011

Guo, Xuezhi. *China's Security State: Philosophy, Evolution, and Politics*. Cambridge: Cambridge University Press, 2012

Greitens, Sheena Chestnut. *Dictators and their Secret Police: Coercive Institutions and State Violence*. Cambridge: Cambridge University Press, 2016

Hayford, Charles W. *To the People: James Yen and Village China*. New York: Columbia University Press, 1990

Herbst, Jeffrey. *States and Power in Africa: Comparative Lessons in Authority and Control*. Princeton: Princeton University Press, 2002

Hinton, William. *Fanshen: A Documentary of Revolution in a Chinese Village*. New York: Vintage, 1966

Holm, David. *Art and Ideology in Revolutionary China*. Oxford: Oxford University Press, 1991

Hsiao, Cheng (Xiao Zheng). *The Theory and Practice of Land Reform*. Taipei: China Research Institute of Land Economics, 1953

Huang, Chun-chieh. *Taiwan in Transformation: Retrospect and Prospect*, 2nd ed. Piscawaty, NJ: Transaction Publishers, 2014

Huang, Xin. "In the Shadow of *Suku* (Speaking Bitterness): Master Scripts and Women's Life Stories," *Frontiers of History in China* 9:4, 2014, pp. 584–610

Hung, Chang-tai. *Mao's New World: Political Culture in the Early People's Republic*. Ithaca: Cornell University Press, 2011

Ismail, Salwa. *Political Life in Cairo's New Quarters: Encountering the Everyday State*, Minneapolis: University of Minnesota Press, 2006

Johnson, Chalmers. *MITI and the Japanese Miracle: The Growth of Industrial Policy, 1925–75*. Stanford: Stanford University Press, 1982

Joint Commission on Rural Reconstruction. *Land Reform Annual Reports, 1949–1960*. Taipei, 1964

Jowitt, Kenneth. *Revolutionary Breakthroughs and National Development: The Case of Romania*. Berkeley and Los Angeles: University of California Press, 1971

Kaple, Deborah A. *Dream of a Red Factory: The Legacy of High Stalinism in China*. Oxford: Oxford University Press, 1994

Kang, Chao. *Economic Effects of Land Reforms in Taiwan, Japan, and Mainland China: A Comparative Study*, Madison: University of Wisconsin Land Tenure Center, 1972

Kaviraj, Sudipta. "Gandhi's Trial Read as Theatre," in Julia C. Strauss and Donal D. C. Cruise O'Brien, *Staging Politics: Power and Performance in Asia and Africa*. London: IB Tauris, 2007, pp. 71–89

Keating, Pauline. *Two Revolutions: Village Reconstruction and the Cooperative Movement in Northeastern Shaanxi, 1934–1945*. Stanford: Stanford University Press, 1997

Kerkvliet, Benedict J. Tria. *The Power of Everyday Politics: How Vietnamese Peasants Transformed National Policy*. Ithaca and London: Cornell University Press, 2005

Kim, Inhan. "Land Reform in South Korea under U.S. Military Occupation, 1945–1948," *Journal of Cold War Studies*, Vol. 18:2, Spring 2016, pp. 97–129

Korolkov, Maxim. "Arguing about Law: Interrogation Procedure under the Qin and Former Han Dynasties," *Études chinoises*, 30 (2011) pp. 37–71

Koo, Anthony Y. C., "Economic Consequences of Land Reform in Taiwan," *Asian Survey* (6:3), March 1966

Kuhonta, Erik. *The Institutional Imperative: The Politics of Equitable Development in Southeast Asia*. Stanford: Stanford University Press, 2012

Kuo, Tai-chun and Ramon H. Myers. *Taiwan's Economic Transformation: Leadership, Property Rights and Institutional Change, 1949–1965*. London: Routledge, 2012

Kurtz, Marcus J. *Latin American State Building in Comparative Perspective: Social Foundations of Institutional Order*. Cambridge: Cambridge University Press, 2013

Lieberman, Evan. *Race and Regionalism in the Politics of Taxation in Brazil and South Africa*. Cambridge: Cambridge University Press, 2003

Lieberthal, Kenneth, *Revolution and Tradition in Tientsin. 1949–1952*. Stanford: Stanford University Press, 1980

Governing China: From Revolution Through Reform, 2nd ed. New York: Norton Press, 2004

Lin, Hsiao-ting. *Accidental State: Chiang Kai-shek, the United States, and the Making of Taiwan*. Cambridge, Harvard University Press, 2016

Lin, Sein. *Land Reform Training Institute: A Historical Perspective*. Taoyuan: Land Reform Training Institute, 1993

Liu, Shaoqi (Liu Shao-ch'i). *How to be a Good Communist*. Peking [Beijing]: Foreign Languages Press, 1951

Liu, Wennan. "Redefining the Legal and Moral Roles of the State in Everyday Life: The New Life Movement in China in the mid-1930s," *Cross-Currents: East Asian History and Culture Review*. 2:2, June 2013, pp. 335–365

MacFarquhar, Roderick. *The Origins of the Cultural Revolution*: (Vol. 1). *Contradictions Among the People 1956–57*. New York: Columbia University Press, 1974

Mann, Michael. "The Autonomous Power of the State: Its Origins, Mechanisms and Results," *Archives Européens de Sociologie*, Vol. 25, 1984, pp. 185–213

Manning, Kimberly Ens and Felix Wemheuer, eds., *Eating Bitterness New Perspectives on China's Great Leap Forward and Famine*. Vancouver: University of British Columbia Press, 2011

Marx, Karl and Frederick Engels. *The Communist Manifesto*. New York: International Publishers, 1948

Meisner, Maurice. *Mao's China and After: A History of the People's Republic*, 3rd edition. New York, Free Press, 1999

Mendel, Douglas. *The Politics of Formosan Nationalism*. Berkeley and Los Angeles: University of California Press, 1970

Merkel-Hess, Kate. *The Rural Modern: Reconstructing the Self and State in Republican China*. Chicago and London: The University of Chicago Press, 2016

Moore, Mick. "The Fruits and Fallacies of Neo-Liberalism: The Case of Irrigation Policy," *World Development*, 17:11, 1989

Munro, Donald. *The Concept of Man in Contemporary China*. Ann Arbor: University of Michigan Press, 1977

Myers, Ramon H. and Ting-lin Hsiao. "Breaking with the Past: The Kuomintang Central Reform Committee on Taiwan, 1950–1952," Stanford: Hoover Institution Press, 2007. www.hoover.org/sites/default/files/uploads/documents/KMT_LP3.pdf

Nakajima, Chieko. "Health and Hygiene in Mass Mobilization: Hygiene Campaigns in Shanghai, 1920–1945," *Twentieth Century China* 34:1, November 2008, pp. 42–72

Park, Ki Hyuk. "Outcome of Land Reform in the Republic of Korea," *Journal of Farm Economics*, 38:4, Nov. 1956, pp. 1015–1023

Pepper, Suzanne. *Civil War in China*, 2nd ed. New York: Rowman and Littlefield, 1999

Perry, Elizabeth J. "Moving the Masses: Emotion Work in the Chinese Revolution," *Mobilization: An International Quarterly* 7:2, 2002, pp. 111–128

Pietz, David. *Engineering the State: The Huai River and Reconstruction in Nationalist China*. London: Routledge, 2002

Pierson, Paul. "Power and Path Dependence," in James Mahoney and Kathleen Thelen, *Advances in Comparative Historical Analysis*. Cambridge, Cambridge University Press, 2015, pp. 123–146

Robespierre, Maxmilien. "Speech to the Convention," February 5, 1794, www.worldfuturefund.org/wffmaster/Reading/Communism/ROBESPIERRE'S%20SPEECH.htm, accessed September 24, 2012

Ruf, Gregory. *Cadres and Kin: Making a Socialist Village in West China, 1921–1991*. Stanford: Stanford University Press, 1998

Schechner, Richard. *The Future of Ritual: Writings on Culture and Performance*. London: Routledge, 1993

Performance Studies: An Introduction, 3rd ed. London: Routledge 2013

Schoenhals, Michael. *Spying for the People: Mao's Secret Agents, 1949–1967*. Cambridge: Cambridge University Press, 2013

Scott, James. *Seeing Like a State: How Certain Schemes to Improve the Human Condition Have Failed*. New Haven: Yale University Press, 1999

Schurmann, Franz. *Ideology and Organization in Communist China*. Berkeley and Los Angeles: University of California Press, 1966

Selden Mark. *China in Revolution: The Yen'an Way Revisited*. Armonk: M.E. Sharpe, 1995

Shen, T. H. *The Sino-American Commission on Joint Rural Reconstruction: Twenty Years of Cooperation for Agricultural Development*. Ithaca: Cornell University Press, 1970

Shue, Vivienne. *Peasant China in Transition: The Dynamics of Development Toward Socialism, 1949–1956*. Berkeley and Los Angeles, University of California Press, 1980

Skocpol, Theda. *Protecting Soldiers and Mothers: The Political Origins of Social Policy in the United States*. Cambridge: Harvard University Press, 1992

Skowronek, Stephen. *Building a New American State: The Expansion of National Administrative Capacities*. Cambridge: Cambridge University Press, 1982

Slater, Dan. *Ordering Power: Contentious Politics and Authoritarian Leviathans in Southeast Asia*. Cambridge: Cambridge University Press, 2010

and Nicholas Rush Smith. "The Power of Counterrevolution: Elitist Origins of Political Order in Asia and Africa," *American Journal of Sociology* 121:5, March 2016, pp. 1472–1516

Sochor, Zenovia A. "Soviet Taylorism Revisited," *Soviet Studies*, 33:2, April 1981, pp. 246–284

Soifer, Hillel David. "The Causal Logic of Critical Junctures," *Comparative Political Studies* 45:12, 2012, pp. 1572–1597

State Building in Latin America. Cambridge: Cambridge University Press, 2015

Stavis, Ben. "China and the Comparative Analysis of Land Reform," *Modern China* 4:1, January 1978

Steinmo, Sven. *The Evolution of Modern States: Sweden, Japan, and the United States*. Cambridge: Cambridge University Press, 2010

Strauss, Julia C. "From Feeding the Army to Nourishing the People: The Impact of Wartime Mobilization and Institutions on Grain Supply in Post-1949 Sunan and Taiwan," in Katarzyna Cwiertka, ed. *Food and War in Twentieth Century East Asia*. London: Routledge, 2006, pp. 73–92

"Strategies of Guomindang Institution Building: Rhetoric and Implementation in Wartime *Xunlian*," in Terry Bodenhorn, ed. *Defining Modernity: Guomindang Rhetorics of a New China, 1920–1970*. Ann Arbor: University of Michigan Press, 2002, pp. 195–221

Strong Institutions in Weak Polities: State Building in Republican China, 1927–1940. Oxford: Oxford University Press, 1998

"*Wenguan* (lettered official), *Gongwuyuan* (public servant), and *Ganbu* (cadre): The Politics of Labelling State Administrators in Republican China," Indiana East Asian Working Paper Series on Language and Politics in Modern China, No. 6, Summer, 1995. Available at www.indiana.edu/~eas c/publications/doc/working_papers/Issue%206%201995%20July%20IUEA WPS%20Cheung,%20Strauss.pdf

Tai, Hung-chao. *Land Reform and Politics: A Comparative Analysis*. Berkeley and Los Angeles: University of California Press, 1992

Tang, Hui-sun. *Land Reform in Free China*. Taipei: Joint Committee on Rural Reconstruction, 1954

Tanner, M. Scot. "Who Wields the Knife? An historical-institutional Analysis of Chinese Communist Police and Intelligence Organs (1927–1950)," unpublished manuscript

Tawney, R. H. *Land and Labour in China*. Boston: Beacon Press, 1932

Taylor, Frederick. *The Principles of Scientific Management*. New York: Harper and Brothers, 1911

Taylor, Jay. *The Generalissimo's Son: Chiang Ching-kuo and the Revolutions in China and Taiwan*. Cambridge: Harvard University Press, 2000

Teiwes, Frederick. *Politics and Purges in China*. Armonk: M.E. Sharpe, 1979

Tilly, Charles, ed. *The Formation of National States in Western Europe*. Princeton: Princeton University Press, 1975

Contentious Performances. Cambridge: Cambridge University Press, 2008

Regimes and Repertoires. Chicago and London: University of Chicago Press, 2006.

Tsai, Tehben, translator Grace Hatch. *Elegy of Sweet Potatoes: Stories of Taiwan's White Terror*. Upland, California, 2002

Tucker, Nancy B. *Taiwan, Hong Kong, and the United States, 1945–1992: Uncertain Friendship*. New York: Twayne Publishers, 1994

Tsai, Hui-yu Caroline. *Taiwan in Japan's Empire Building: An Institutional Approach to Colonial Engineering*. London: Routledge, 2009

Tudor, Maya. *The Promise of Power: The Origins of Democracy in India and Autocracy in Pakistan*. Cambridge University Press: Cambridge, 2013

U, Eddy. "The Making of Chinese Intellectuals: Representations and Organization in the Thought Reform Campaign," *The China Quarterly* No. 192, 2007, pp. 971–989

"Rise of Marxist Classes: Bureaucratic Classification and Class Formation in Early Socialist China," *European Journal of Sociology*, 2016, 57:1, pp. 1–29

Vogel, Ezra. *Canton Under Communism: Programs and Politics in a Provincial Capital, 1949–1968*. Cambridge: Harvard University Press, 1969

Vu, Tuong. *Paths to Development in Asia: South Korea, Vietnam, China, and Indonesia*. Cambridge: Cambridge University Press, 2010

Wakeman, Frederic Jr. "Cleanup: The New Order in Shanghai," in Jeremy Brown and Paul Pickowicz, *Dilemmas of Victory: The Early Years of the People's Republic of China*. Cambridge: Harvard University Press, 2007, pp. 21–58

"*Hanjian* (traitor)!: Collaboration and Retribution in Wartime Shanghai," in Wen-hsin Yeh, ed. *Becoming Chinese: Passages to Modernity and Beyond*. Berkeley and Los Angeles: University of California Press, 2000, pp. 298–341

Policing Shanghai, 1927–1937. Berkeley and Los Angeles: University of California Press, 1996

Walinsky, Louis, ed. *The Selected Papers of Wolf Ladejinsky*. Washington: World Bank Press, 1977

Wedeen, Lisa, "Acting 'As if' Symbolic Politics and Social Control in Syria," *Comparative Studies in Society and History* 40:3, July 1998, pp. 403–423

White, Adam, ed. *The Everyday Life of the State: A State-in-Society Approach*. Seattle: University of Washington Press, 2013

Wilson, Woodrow. "The Study of Administration," *Political Science Quarterly*. 2:2, pp. 197–222 [1888]

Wong, John. *Land Reform in the People's Republic of China: Institutional Transformation in Agriculture*. New York: Praeger, 1973

Wou, Odoric. *Mobilizing the Masses: Building Revolution in Henan*. Stanford: Stanford University Press, 1994

Wu, Guo. "Speaking Bitterness: Political Education in Land Reform and Military Training under the CCP, 1947–51," *The Chinese Historical Review*, 21:1, 2014. pp. 3–23

Wu, Naite, "Transition without Justice or Justice without History: Transitional Justice in Taiwan," *Taiwan Journal of Democracy* 1:1, July 2005. pp. 77–102

Xu, Shirong [Hsu, Shih-jung], "In Fact, Landlords were not Landlords," unpublished paper, "Cold Front: The Chinese Cold War Experience in Comparison," conference, Chinese University of Hong Kong, September 15–16, 2014

Yager, Joseph. *Transforming Agriculture in Taiwan: The Experience of the Joint Commission on Rural Reconstruction*. Ithaca: Cornell University Press, 1988

Yang, Kuisong. "Reconsidering the Campaign to Suppress Counterrevolutionaries," *The China Quarterly* No. 193, March, 2008, pp. 102–121

Yashar, Deborah. *Contesting Citizenship in Latin America: The Rise of Indigenous Movements and the Postliberal Challenge*. Cambridge: Cambridge University Press, 2005

Zarefsky, David. "What 'went wrong' with the first Obama-Romney Debate," Chapter 36 in Catherine Palczewicky, ed. *Disturbing Argument: Selected Works from the 18th NCA/AFA Alta Conference on Argumentation*. London: Routledge, 2015, pp. 244–249

Index